GW00363263

THE
WEX
FORD
BOOK

Michael Dy[...]

Wexford Bay from the Wexford Opera House – by Gerard Hore.

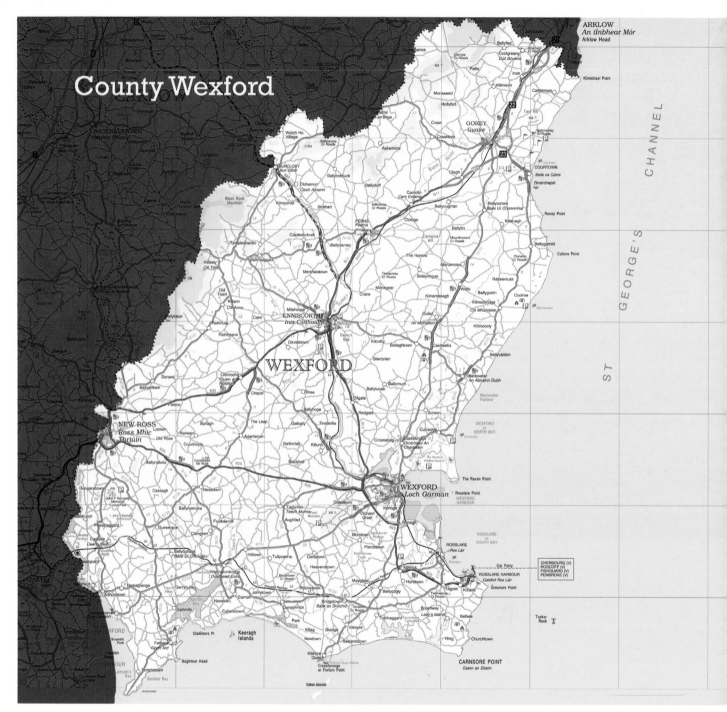

County Wexford

First edition 6-inch mapping series which shows the official spelling of the place names.
This map dates from c.1839 and is the basis for all mapping names.

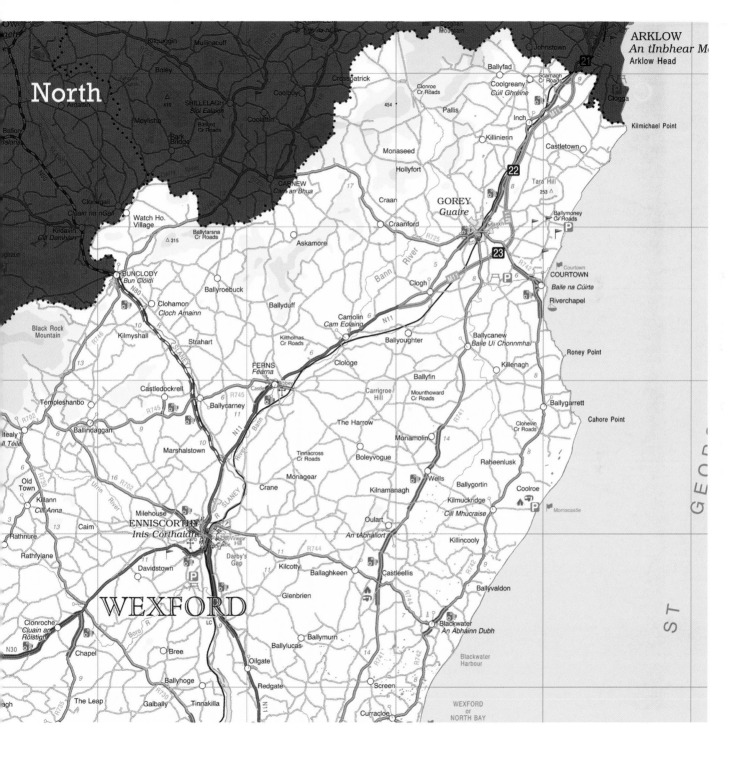

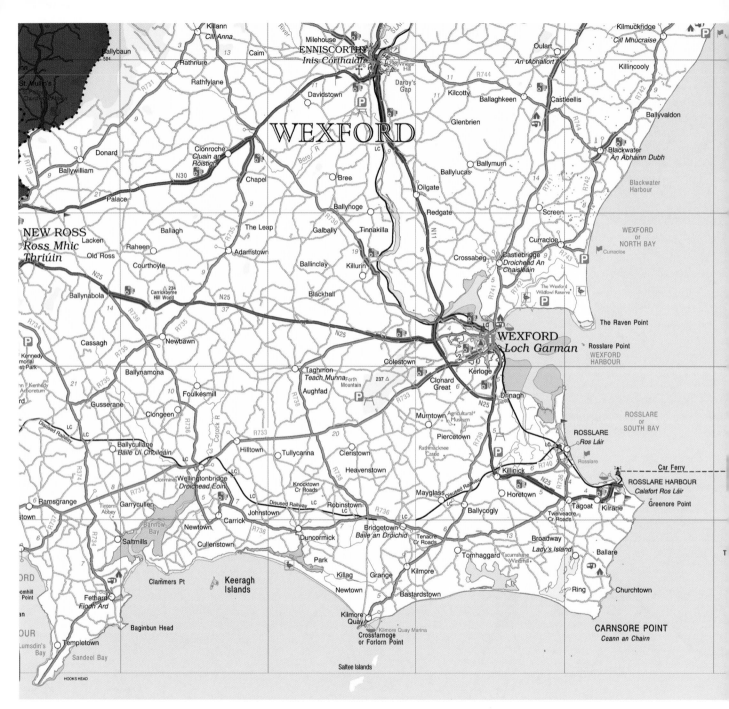

South

THE
WEX
FORD

WHO'S WHAT AND WHERE'S WHERE

BOOK

MICHAEL DOYLE MICHAEL FREEMAN PHIL MURPHY

This Project has been supported by
Tá tacaíocht ag an togra seo ón

wexford
local development
Forbairt Áitiúil Loch Garman

'The European Agricultural Fund for Rural Development: Europe investing in rural areas'

National Development Plan 2007 - 2013

The European Agricultural Fund for Rural Development: Europe Investing in Rural Areas.

Comhshaol, Pobal agus Rialtas Áitiúil
Environment, Community and Local Government

To those who dare

We're from Mighty, Mighty Wexford!

"It's very special for me to be here on the quay where I have walked so many times – in the shadow of the Twin Churches to one side and the Ballast Bank to the other. Flanked by two Wexford boys, Mayor George Lawlor and festival chairman Ger Lawlor, that I have known for 30 years. Look at us, kids – if you don't eat your vegetables, this is what happens.

"Especially nice to be here with Jackie, the Wexford girl I married during the 40th Wexford Festival Opera, and to be able to look down on Finn and Seán in the crowd.

In fact all three of us Wexford boys are married for some time to three of the happiest women in Wexford. Extensive surveys around the world have proven that it is every woman's dream to marry a Wexford man. Isn't that right?

"This is Wexford's day. For 62 years we have gathered here and turned our faces to the sky. The child in every one of us looks forward to this day and we are proud of it. The fireworks. We speak of them in the same breath as Christmas and St Patrick's day. That day when the shops run out of ice cream cones and there is a ninety seven per cent chance that it will rain.

"We see fireworks on the television at the Olympics or Times Square and we are not impressed. We've been doing fireworks much better than that for years.

Our fireworks fly so high that they can be seen in Enniscorthy. Which is the whole point.

"What is it about Wexford people that makes us so unique? Why does culture flourish here even in hard times – especially in hard times? What does it mean to be from Wexford?

This is what we are.

"We are storytellers. We are drama groups and arts centres. We are dance academies and seanchaís, playwrights and journalists with an integrity that is refreshing these days. We are novelists. We are gathered by the river and the sea watched over by the Blackwater lightship under a handful of stars from our perch on the Bower Wall.

"We hold our gatherings at meal time. We are Italian and Chinese. We are Greek and French. We are rissoles and chips. We love a nice cuppa tea and a Jaffa cake if you're opening them. And sports… we live for our hurling and football. The purple and gold are our favourite colours.

"And now we have pink too. In boxing we punch above our weight. In kettlebells we are the best swingers in the world... congrats to the Wexford contingent of the Irish Kettlebell Club who just returned from the world championships. Our camogie players are surely descended from the Fianna, so fierce and skilled are they on the field of play.

"We are music. We love it to our bones. We are the singing pubs and the swinging pubs and two people who know the difference. We are soirées and musicals and light operas and the best pantomimes in the country. We are the water and the wine, the sky and the ground, Little Miss sunshine, all 24 hours a day from South East Radio DJs, who we don't listen to just because they are local – it's because they are the best.

"We do the shamrock shuffle by Billy Roche and The Roach Band, we dance at the crossroads, we laugh before sunset and we cry before dawn. We are kids with guitars and drums in someone's garage all the way to the Jerome Hynes theatre and the Spiegeltent.

"We are the people. We are Menapians all, and our arms are welcoming. We are Mexico city, we are Bordighera, we are Warsaw and New York. We are London and even occasionally Kilkenny when we are feeling especially forgiving.

"We are the past. We remember the clash of 1996 ash. We walk Viking streets. We all have a bit of Norman in us. We are the sea and its bounty of mussel and lobster and we are the last stop before America. We are Hook Lighthouse and Selskar Abbey. We sit on Vinegar Hill with our ancestors watching the cannon below.

"Tonight we are the spaces in the crowd, the spaces where our loved ones were. I still feel my father's right hand on my shoulder and see the other pointing towards the sky. We are the memories of fizzy orange and ninety-nines. We are our parents and grandparents and even sons and daughters who once shared this Wexford night.

"But even though this is a night to remember those who have gone, it is not a night for grieving but a celebration, for the fireworks will light their faces and the music will surely be heard on high, for it is divine.

"We are unusual. No one talks like us. We fasten our lacens. We are howya huns. Everyone is writing a book or a play or in a group. There is not one ordinary person in the whole town or maybe we are all ordinary. But we are all individuals.

"We are the Festival Opera. It is ours and we are experts. We love to see the artists arrive every autumn. We discuss with great animation which is the best opera. Whether Verdi is Italy's greatest composer or was it in fact Puccini. These are not conversations heard in every town.

"But we are not every town. We are Wexford. Mighty mighty Wexford – and we lead the way in so many things. And I am delighted to be a Wexford man to be allowed to say:

'Everywhere I go people always ask me who we are, Where do we come from? And we tell them, We're from Wexford. Mighty, Mighty Wexford!'"

– From address by Eoin Colfer, internationally popular author and native of Slade, Co. Wexford, who performed the official opening of the 62nd Wexford Festival Opera. With him at the opening fireworks spectacular were his fellow students of Wexford CBS, Cllr. George Lawlor, Mayor of Wexford, and Ger Lawlor, chairman of the Wexford Festival.

"We are Menapians all, and our arms are welcoming. We are Mexico city, we are Bordighera, we are Warsaw and New York. We are London and even occasionally Kilkenny when we are feeling especially forgiving".

Our Native Place

County Wexford in the South East of Ireland, is about 50 miles from the capital Dublin city and 15 miles from Waterford city. The county is roughly 25 miles wide and 50 miles long, surrounded by the sea on the east and the south, a confluence of rivers on the west, a mountain range in the north west while in the north the county merges into Co Wicklow and Co Carlow through acres of some of the richest agricultural land in the world.

Wexford is unique in its history, its geography, its strategic positioning, its rural and urban features, its flora and fauna, its proximity to mainland Europe, its cultural diversity, its collections of microclimates and its people of Welsh, English, Norse, Norman, Viking, Celt, French and Spanish ancestry who have contributed so much as ordinary workers and as extraordinary leaders to national development and to the development of many other countries around the world.

This book grew from conversations between co-editors Michael Doyle, Michael Freeman and Phil Murphy. The concept was further developed by Sean McNulty of Dolmen and by Helen Ashdown and Paddy Whelan.

This book acknowledges ordinary people and extraordinary people, decision-makers, the Wexford diaspora, opinion leaders, icons, heroes, community and county leaders, old, elderly and young people who are going to be our future leaders and custodians of our land, homes, businesses, communities and culture.

It acknowledges the contribution of our ancestors, our deceased relatives and neighbours who have worked to preserve this place and those who emigrated and have made their own significant contribution to other countries and home.

It illustrates the resources of the county in 2013. It is a footprint in time.

The book further shows us the riches that we have – our land, our culture, our wise old people and our educated and talented young people. It shows that we can do it,- whatever it is.

We hope that this book will inspire you from reading the profiles and the accompanying features. We hope it will become a catalyst for people to talk and share, reach their potential while giving attention to their native place, their heritage and their rich resources of talent, environment and community.

Michael Doyle, Michael Freeman, Phil Murphy.

Walk in the forest at Tintern Abbey.

Time to be Roused

By Liam Griffin

Anthony Cronin, scholar, poet, writer and true son of Enniscorthy knows his own people. He said: 'The people who populate the land between the Blackstairs Mountains and the sea are slow to rouse, but when roused, are fearsome.'

When Wexford people are roused they are fearsome. We have proven it in hurling and otherwise on the field of play. We have proven it in business and we have proven it in our parishes and communities.

Ireland has been through a tough time. National statistics show that County Wexford has likewise. Now is the time to rouse ourselves once more and take the opportunity that the world offers us again.

This book, featuring more than two thousand of our people, shows we have talent and skills in abundance. Our people bring this talent to the development of small business, major corporations, communities and whole countries. We are amongst the leaders in academia, the leaders in entrepreneurship and the leaders in creativity.

In the past we rose together for all our successes. Unity is our strength as a people. Our history proves that to be true.

Agriculture and Tourism are the bedrock of the county's economy. Now we must build on this bedrock. We have embraced the world of technology. Many of our young and well-educated people are bringing this new technology and their skills and talents to other countries.

We hope they will return even more experienced to build a better Ireland.

Our new opportunities are in building our domestic economy based on people who 'make things'. Lessons from the past tell us that long-term sustainable jobs can be created through fostering apprenticeships. We must encourage entrepreneurship, risk and innovation, at every level. This is doing the things we actually enjoy, have enthusiasm for and feel fulfilled doing.

Show me someone who has done something worthwhile and I will show you someone who has overcome adversity. Thousands of County Wexford people have overcome adversity.

They are leaders in their families and their communities. We must now cultivate an atmosphere of celebrating those local champions who look ordinary but are anything but ordinary, in order to make County Wexford a better place with full-employment and good quality of life and living.

It is time to put our collective minds together and move forward with an identifiable plan to achieve this.

We are the Model County. We can do it. It is time to be roused again.

In the County Hurling Championship 2013 final.

Profiles A-Z 1

1 Arts 17

Writers, actors, singers, directors, musicians, entertainers, painters, sculptors. County Wexford is teeming with talent that is acknowledged across the world. The main venues are Wexford Opera House, Wexford Arts Centre, Gorey Little Theatre, St. Michael's Theatre, New Ross and The Athenaeum, Enniscorthy.

2 History 39

County Wexford's rich cultural tapestry is woven with threads of the cultures and traditions of Vikings, Normans, Celts, French, Spanish and English who invaded this strategically placed maritime county.

3 Diaspora 73

They are on every continent in the world. They are in the US, Canada, South America, Britain, mainland Europe, China. They have built whole communities and they occupy some of the most influential positions. They are the Wexford diaspora.

4 Business 96

County Wexford has a reputation throughout the world for its quality workforce and its culture of entrepreneurship. Ongoing indigenous investment and Foreign Direct Investment (FDI) are necessary for increased economic growth and jobs.

5 Agriculture 125

County Wexford earned the name the 'Model County' from its reputation in Europe as a producer of quality food. Today the county's leading farmers and agri-business are supplying food products across the world.

6 Religion 153

County Wexford's priests, brothers and nuns have influenced and inspired the lives of the people for centuries. Many of them in their capacity as teachers, nurses and evangelists, have changed whole communities and societies.

7 Civics 173

The people of County Wexford are served by excellent governance which oversees infrastructural development, library services, and other amenities.

8 Sport 201

County Wexford's sports heroes include local, national and international champions and Olympians.

9 Anthems 239

County Wexford songwriters and poets are noted everywhere for their celebration of love, the range of human emotions and battles, wars and sporting achievements. Their creations provide a context to the County's defining moments in history and in happiness.

The Enniscorthy Brooch

The Enniscorthy Brooch is as exquisite as it is intricate. A fine delicate piece of medieval jewellery, only 29mm in diameter, it is a ring brooch fashioned from gold, encrusted with garnets and emeralds. It bears a Lombardic inscription + AMES: AMIE: AVES M PAR CES PRESET – I love: friend: I am yours with this gift.

This type of brooch was a common gift between lovers in medieval times. The brooch now rests in the British Museum.

The first written record of the brooch is in Lewis' Topographical Dictionary of Ireland when he speaks of a 'curious brooch of gold, enriched with emeralds and garnets.' The story that it was found in the ruins of the last standing tower of the Franciscan Abbey in Enniscorthy after the night of the 'Big Wind' of October 1839, may very well be apocryphal. However, by some means it ended up in the possession of Counsellor Cookman Esq. of Monart, who exchanged the brooch with one Redmond Anthony of Piltown, Co. Kilkenny. He was a well-known collector of antiquities.

What it was exchanged for is unrecorded. In Mr Anthony's meticulously kept records of all his treasures, he catalogues it as a Bishop's Brooch which was found in the ruins of the 'old Abbey'.

In 1848, after the death of their father, and in fear of debtors' prison, his sons sold his collection, in several lots, to the British Museum, Great Russell Street, London.

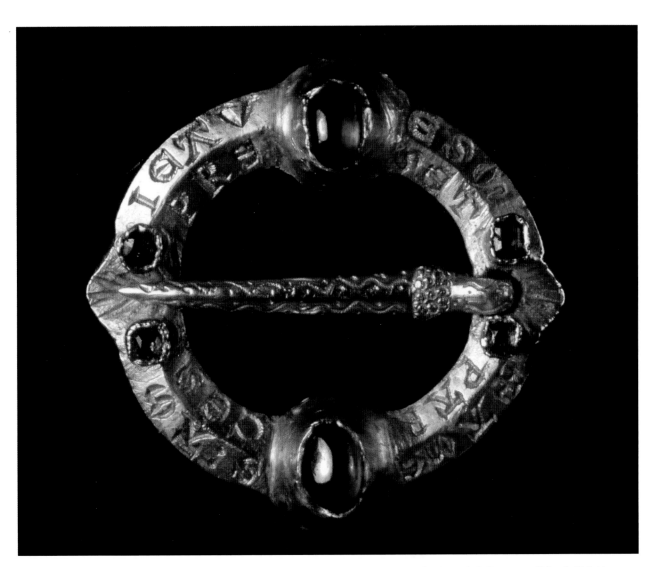

The Enniscorthy Brooch © Trustees of The British Museum.

> There are only two kinds of people in this world –
> Wexford people and all the rest who wish they were
> from Wexford – **Patrick Roche**

Profiles

Aherne, Alan, Group Sports Editor, *People Newspapers*, Wexford; a native of Wexford town, son of Tom and Mary, Pinewood Estate; educated at Wexford CBS and the College of Commerce, Rathmines, he has spent all his working life with *People Newspapers*, in various editorial roles, mainly to do with sport; served Wexford County GAA Board as Public Relations Officer and did much to improve match programmes; he has produced impressive GAA Yearbooks and histories for Sarsfields football club and St. Ibar's-Shelmalier camogie club. He was a member of Stellah Sinnott's management team that brought Wexford to a first All-Ireland senior camogie title for 32 years in 2007, and in 2013 managed St. Ibars-Shelmalier to a first County senior camogie title for eleven years, beating an Oulart-The Ballagh team that has dominated the game for the past decade.

Allen, Agnes, née Bernie, Munster Hill, Enniscorthy; antiques' dealer, daughter of James and May, Court St., Enniscorthy; married to Brigadier Douglas Allen MBE, RIP; they have one son, James; Doug had two sons from a previous marriage, Jeffery and Simon. Agnes worked for the Israeli Foreign Missions, run by the International Red Cross, micro-filming archives from Nazi concentration camps, the films later being sent from Germany to Yad Vashem World Holocaust Research Centre, Tel Aviv, who supplied the documentation for the Nuremburg Trials; manageress and then superintendent of Navy Army Air

Street Theatre from Buí Bolg at the Bullring, Wexford town.

1

force Institute in Malaysia and Singapore, controlling over 26 shopping outlets, also in Borneo, Hong Kong, Malaysia and Cyprus where her work covered the Middle East; returned to Germany in 1969 as superintendent in charge of Holland, Brussels and Southern Germany, before getting married to Brigadier Douglas Allen MBE and returning to England where Doug worked for the BBC.

There were 2,173 babies born in Wexford General Hospital in 2012.

Allen, Bertram, son of Bert of Slaney Meats' fame, at only 18 years of age is one of the most exciting prospects not just in Irish show jumping but on the world scene. He caused a sensation as the youngest Nation's Cup rider in the history of equestrian sport in Linz, Austria, in May 2013, with two clear rounds. He confirmed his arrival at the top level when he beat 66 of the world's best show jumpers in the opening competition of the Nations' Cup Final weekend at Barcelona at the end of September 2013, finishing with almost two seconds in hand on the Ballywalter Farms' mare, Molly Malone V. This topped off a remarkable season in which he was successful at major venues all over Europe. Since his father was a dedicated horse lover, Bertram had his first lessons as a child. He marked his 15th birthday on 1 August 2010 by winning individual gold and team silver in the pony class at the European Championships in England on Acapella Z. As a junior, he took team gold at the European Championships in Austria, and this year he won the European Youngster Cup in Paris. Bertram now lives in Hünxe in Germany and his parents travel over to watch him in the major competitions. It is important to him that he and his eight horses do not have to make the tiring trip to the mainland every time he wants to take part in top events. When not travelling to one of the world's show jumping arenas, he likes going shooting, rugby and football. However, when asked about himself, he says: "Well … horses are my life. They mean everything to me."

Allen, Bert and Maurice, owners of Ballywalter Farms, Gorey, made the *Sunday Times* business list of Ireland's Top 250 for 2013. They transferred ownership of their Wexford-based Slaney Meats Group from Lanber Group Unlimited to Lotan Holdings in the British Virgin Islands in 2010. They have a property and investment portfolio worth at least £248m stg, having netted £190m from the 2007 sale of the Bewley Hotel chain. Lanber Group also owns 18.7% of Irish electricity supplier, Gaelelectric, a German window manufacturer and a commercial building in Dusseldorf.

Allen, Dennis, born on 2nd January, 1896, was a Fianna Fáil politician. He failed to win a seat in the General Election held in June, 1927, but later that same year, in September, 1927, he was elected on the Fianna Fáil ticket for Wexford. He was re-elected in the 1932 General Election, but he lost his seat in the 1933 General Election. Following the death of the Fine Gael TD, Sir Osmond Esmonde, he won the consequent by-election on 17th August, 1936, and was returned to the Dáil. He was re-elected at each subsequent election, and when he retired from politics in 1961, his seat was won by his son, Lorcan. He was co-founder of the National Ploughing Association in 1931.

Allen, Lorcan, born on 27th March, 1940, is a farmer, auctioneer and Fianna Fáil politician. He has long been prominent in Gorey politics. He was elected to Dáil Éireann as a Fianna Fáil TD for the Wexford constituency in the 1961 General Election, winning the seat previously held by his father, Denis Allen. He was aged twenty-one years and six months at the time and is the third youngest ever TD. He was re-elected in six subsequent General Elections, but was defeated in the November, 1982, General Election. He contested the next three General Elections but was unsuccessful. When Charles Haughey appointed his first Government in December, 1979, he appointed Lorcan Allen to Minister of State in the Department of Agriculture, and the Wexford TD continued to hold this position in the 1982 Government.

Arthur, P.J., Ballyroebuck, born Co. Clare 1943; married to Rose, née Bailey, Ferns, they have five children; principal of Ballyroebuck NS 1964-2006; mentor of Kilrush Schoolboys' Rackard League winning team 1966 and '67, first County title for the parish; President of South Wicklow Drama Festival; founder of Ballyroebuck Marching Band and Kilrush Comhaltas Group; active member of Sliabh Buidhe Rovers Athletic Club from 1972-98; a keen gardener and camper-van enthusiast.

Asple, Denis, chartered and certified accountant and extensive Wexford town business owner; attended CBS, Enniscorthy and St. Peter's College, then studied accountancy and set up own accountancy practice, Asple and Co., in Wexford town in 1970s; member of successful Ballyhogue Football teams and team member with Nick Power, Nick Fortune and the famous Foley brothers, Joe, Mick and Willie;

Bailey, Anthony, born Co. Wexford, 1966, New Ross Town Clerk; married to Lorna, née Halpin, Carrigbyrne, they have one daughter and two sons; formerly worked in the Central Bank of Ireland in Dublin; coaches the Geraldine O'Hanrahans U14 hurling team.

Whiskey manufacturer John Power, Edermine House, needing workers for his Dublin distillery each autumn made an arrangement with 150 fishermen from Oylegate. They formed an alliance that continued for many years. He built houses known today as 'Power's Range', in the village for them.

Bailey, Nick, born 1972, percussionist drummer; son of Joe and Bridie, High Street, Wexford; married to Róisín Dempsey, Greenville, Enniscorthy; front man and composer of Extreme Rhythm, Europe's leading high-impact percussion ensemble; performed with Riverdance The Show, Kelly Clarkson, The X Factor, Celtic Woman, Celtic Tenors, Now Dance Korea, Charlotte Church, Tommy Fleming, and Stockton's Wing and in Malmo at the 2013 Eurovision Song Contest.

Banville, Breda, née O'Gorman, Camross, Caroreigh, President of the Wexford Federation of ICA; member of the nursing staff of Wexford General Hospital working in Phlebotomy; married to Denis, with two children, David who passed away in 2007 and Ann Marie. Apart from her busy schedule as Wexford ICA President, Breda's hobbies include drama, reading, walking and gardening.

Banville, John, born 1945, was sub-editor with the *Irish Press* and later became Literary Editor of the *Irish Times*. His first book *Long Lankin*, published in 1970, was a collection of short stories. This was followed by a number of novels, including: *Nightspawn, Birchwood, Doctor Copernicus, Kepler, The Newton Letter, Mefisto* and *The Book of Evidence*, which was shortlisted for the Booker Prize and won the Guinness Peat Aviation Book Award. In 2005 Banville won the Man Booker Prize for his novel *The Sea*. He has also written a play and a screenplay and, under the pen name of Benjamin Black, has published a number of thrillers.

Banville, Tom, Hayestown, Taghmon, son of Paddy and the late Mary, he is one of eleven children; was appointed CEO of County Wexford Enterprise Board in 2013, having been with the board since May 2002; educated at Caroreigh National School and St. Peter's College, he holds an MBA from WIT and a Graduate Diploma in Business Studies from UCD; married to Elva, née Moriarty, they have one son and a daughter.

Banville Evans, Vonnie, born in Wexford 1941, grew up in The Faythe area; sister of writers Vincent and John; married Wexford man Jim Evans, who died in 2005. She wrote *The House in the Faythe*, a childhood memoir, in 1994; *Anna's Dream*, 1995, described as an historic adventure, and *What the Green Rushes Whisper*, a novel. She is also an accomplished artist and several books of her artwork have been published under the title *The Artist's Eye.* Her son, Barry, has also published a number of books, including *Under the Surface: A New Perspective*, and *Symphony of the Wind.*

Barnwell, Jim, Ballinruane, Ballycullane, born in Wexford 1945, worked with horses for the late Stephen Codd of Clonmines; now retired; married to Una, née Barnwell, Ballymitty. Jim is an accomplished musician providing entertainment for the community throughout the last 40 years on harmonica and keyboards.

Barrington, Ted, Rosslare, native of Gorey; former Irish Ambassador to the UK. His father ran the well-known Eddie Barrington's tailor business on Gorey's Main Street. Ted joined the Civil Service in the Department of Foreign Affairs in 1971, and rose through the ranks in the department and served as Irish Ambassador to London for six years between 1995 and 2001. He was there through the tense and torturous negotiations of the 1998 Good Friday Agreement on Northern Ireland. He served with two British Prime Ministers, John Major and Tony Blair, and has met Queen Elizabeth on a number of occasions. He is currently on a sabbatical from the Department. He is married to Claire.

Barron, Ann, Rathnure, née Cullen, Knoxtown, Clonroche; married to Seamus, Rathnure, they have one daughter and two sons; trained as General Nurse in Dublin, went on to nurse in Brownswood, Enniscorthy, and the Haughton Hospital, New Ross, where she was Clinical Nurse Manager; helped establish Rathnure Senior Social Club in 2009; husband Seamus was a good hurler and one of the selectors of Wexford All-Ireland-winning hurling team of 1996.

Barron, Fr. Frank, Enniscorthy, was editor of *St. Senan's Parish Journal* published in 1985 and 1987, and he was the author of *Short and Sweet – Stories for Teachers and Preachers*, which was published in 1991.

Barron, John, architect; well-known hurler for Wexford and the Glynn-Barntown club; current manager of the Ferns-St. Aidan's senior hurling team, whom he coached to beat his native Glynn-Barntown in the county semi-final 2013. However, Ferns-St. Aidan's lost to Oulart-The Ballagh in the county final.

Barron, Leon, London, formerly New Ross; lecturer in forensic science in King's College in London; son of PJ and Angela, brother of Laura and married to Wendy Heim, Berlin; educated New Ross CBS and Good Counsel College, Leon is a graduate of DCU School of Analytical Science, and after post-graduate studies, was EPA research fellow and part-time lecturer within DCU for 10 years; now works in Analytical and Environmental Science Division of King's College.

Barron, Martin, Poulpeasty, Taghmon, born Wexford 1944; retired mixed farmer; married to Kathleen, née Doyle, Tomcoole, with one daughter and four sons; maintains grounds of Caroreigh church and Kilgarvan graveyard; underwent pioneering surgery in the Richmond Hospital in Dublin in 1970 and made full recovery.

Barry, Commodore John, born in Ballysampson, about ten miles from Wexford town, in 1745, rose from cabin boy to senior commander of the entire United States fleet and became one of the greatest heroes of his adopted country. Indeed, very few Irishmen have matched his achievements. His contribution to the American War of Independence was immense. He was the first to capture a British war vessel on the high seas, and he fought on land in the battles of Trenton and Princeton. In the course of the war, he captured more than twenty ships, he wrote a book that established a set of signals for effective communication between ships, and he fought in the last naval battle of the American Revolution in 1783. Following the war, President Washington summoned him to the President's mansion to receive Commission Number One in the navy, and he is rightly regarded as the Father of the U.S. Navy.

Barry, Redmond, Gibberpatrick, Duncormick, born Wexford 1981; Agricultural Consultant; married to Lisa, née Codd, Mayglass, they have two children; son of Geoffrey and Mary, née Maher, Thurles; dual football and hurling player for Wexford, from the St. Anne's Rathangan club, County football captain in 2013. He lined out with the hurlers from 2002-2005, and made his debut with the footballers in 2001. He has been playing at a successful time for Wexford football, helping them reach a Division 1 National league final for the first time in over 50 years in 2005, losing to Armagh; in 2008, Wexford reached the Leinster final for the first time since 1956 but lost to Dublin, and got to the All-Ireland semi-final for the first time since 1945, but lost to Tyrone. A very skillful forward, he has won a Dublin hurling title with UCD, did the senior double in Wexford with St. Anne's in 2000, and won two more football titles in 2001 and 2012.

Bates, Declan John, Tullibards, Bridgetown; jockey; currently campaigning in Britain, mainly with the David Evans' yard in Abergavenny, Wales.

> **Members of the 22nd Dáil appointed 30 June 1981:**
>
> Fine Gael and Labour back in power after four years in opposition. Garrett Fitzgerald, leader of Fine Gael since 1977, was nominated Taoiseach by 81 votes to 78 votes. In addition to the 65 votes of his own Fine Gael party, he received the 15 votes of the Labour Party and also the vote of Jim Kemmy (Ind). He was opposed by the 78 votes of Fianna Fáil. Deputies Blaney (ind), Browne (SLP), Dublin Bay Loftus (Ind) and Sherlock (SWFP) abstained. The H-Block deputies, Paddy Agnew and Kevin Doherty were absent (prisoners in the Maze Prison, Northern Ireland).
>
> Earlier the nomination of the outgoing Taoiseach, Charles Haughey, was defeated on a vote of 79 to 83. The Fianna Fáil Government was in office since 5 July 1977.
>
> Eoin Ryan (FF), a senator since 1977 and son of James Ryan, a Government minister from 1932 to 48, 1951–54 and 1957–65, was elected to the Senate on the Industrial and Commercial Panel. Deirdre Bolger (FG) of Millmount, Gorey and of John Bolger Ltd. Ferns was elected to the Industrial and Commercial Panel also.
>
> – Nealon's Guide, 22nd Dáil and Seanad.

Bates, Leslie, Kilmore Quay, Managing Director Sofrimar, and along with other shareholder, Lorcan Barden, are finalists in the Ernst and Young Entrepreneur of the Year 2013 Award. Sofrimar is involved in shellfish processing and was originally set up in April 1979 by three French men as the Société France-Irelande de Mare which gave rise to the acronym "Sofrimar". It was acquired by Leslie Bates and Lorcan Barden in a management buyout in 2000. Sofrimar received the Seafood Exporter of the Year award in 2007 and again in 2011 and employs 105 people on land with a further 200 people working on boats who supply shellfish and whitefish. France and South Korea are the main exporting countries.

Bates, Professor Ray, originally Kilmore Quay, Adjunct Professor of Meteorology at Meteorology and Climate Centre, School of Mathematical Sciences, University College, Dublin; formerly Professor of Meteorology at the Niels Bohr Institute of the University of Copenhagen and a Senior Scientist at NASA's Goddard Space Flight Centre; presented with the Vilhelm Bjerknes Medal of the European Geosciences Union at a ceremony in Vienna in 2009 - the first time the medal has been given to an Irishman.

Beasley, Bobby, 1935-2008, lived for some years in Camolin, National Hunt Jockey; won a Cheltenham Champion Hurdle, Another Flash, in 1960, a Grand National, Nicolaus Silver, 1961, and a Cheltenham Gold Cup, Captain Christy, 1974. He battled with alcoholism and had to retire in 1969; he fought the good fight, assisted by Wexford hurling legend and friend, Nickey Rackard. He was five years sober when Pat Taaffe gave him the Cheltenham ride on Captain Christy and he beat reigning champion The Dikler, to win the Gold Cup, having already taken a number of important races on the horse, including the Irish Sweeps Hurdle in 1972 and Irish Champion Hurdle in 1973. His grandfather, Harry, trained and rode the 1891 Grand National winner, Come Away, and his father, H.H. Beasley, won two Irish derbies.

Begley, Seamus, Dubai UAE, formerly Rosslare Harbour, Head of Finance, Kinnarps Project Solutions LLC, Dubai. Kinnarps is a Swedish multi-national providing interior workspace solutions for offices and public environments; educated in Saint Peter's College and UCD, Seamus is a member of the Institute of Chartered Accountants in Ireland. He is current chairman of the Dubai Celts GAA Club which was founded in 1995 to foster GAA games and sport amongst the Irish living in Dubai. Another committee member in 2013 is Shane Rackard from the well-known Wexford sporting family.

Behan, Matty, Ballinastragh, Gorey, published a book of poetry entitled *Eyes Awaken* in 1987.

Bell, Maura, St. John's Road, Wexford, General Manager of the Irish National Heritage Park at Ferrycarrig, Wexford, for the past twelve years. Before taking up the job of running what has been described as Wexford's Disneyland, Maura gained considerable experience working in the hotel and catering business. She worked in White's Hotel, Wexford, and was General Manager of the Cedars Hotel, Rosslare. After spending time in London, she decided to return to Wexford, where she took up the responsibility of running the Heritage Park, which was recently the recipient of a Customer Service Award. A grant of more than €1 million from Fáilte Ireland has been used to re-develop the park, which attracts around 50,000 visitors from all over the world each year.

Bennett, Fiona, Rathangan, member of lrish ladies' soccer team and also plays ladies' football with her local St. Anne's GAA club, daughter of Anne White Bennett, Killag, long-standing secretary of Bannow and Rathangan show committee.

Bennett, Mary, Ballywilliam, nurse, manager of Hope Cancer Support Centre, Weafer Street, Enniscorthy. The Centre was founded in 1999 by a group of people who were affected by cancer. Operating from the former Doctor Cuddigan's Nursing Home, where many in Enniscorthy were born in bygone days, Mary is at the forefront of maintaining the centre which relies in the main on voluntary contributions.

Bent, Barbara, Lough Broadway, Chairperson of the Irish Society for the Prevention of Cruelty to Animals. For more than forty years Barbara has worked tirelessly to improve animal welfare and has been involved with many local and national associations to further that work. She serves on the Veterinary Council of Ireland and for more than a decade has been a member of the Animal Welfare Advisory Council to the Minister of Agriculture. She has a particular interest in everything equine and has been deeply involved in the campaign to abolish the use of sulkies on our roads. She has also been involved in the Early Warning Intervention System to provide a framework within which farm animal welfare problems can be identified before they become critical.

Bentley Gordon, Rev. James, lived at Boro Lodge Ballymackessy, Clonroche, and died on April 19, 1819. He was a prolific author and wrote, inter alia, a moderate history of the 1798 Rebellion plus other histories and a geographical work. He was the second rector of Killegney.

> There were 874 County Wexford men killed in World War I.

Bermingham, Tom, Crossabeg, Project Officer with Wexford Local Development. A native of Mullinahone, Co. Tipperary, he moved to County Wexford in 1987. Having initially trained in both farm management and personnel management, he went on to be instrumental in the growth and diversification of Wexford Farm Relief Services (FRS) over a twenty-year period. In recent years, Tom graduated with a BSc (Hons) Degree in Rural Development through UCD and subsequently took up employment with Wexford Local Development – the agency responsible for the delivery of the National Rural Development Programme (LEADER) 2007-2013. Tom is actively involved in a range of community activities. He is married to Kathryn and has two daughters, Sarah and Rachel.

Berney, Joe, St. Anthony's, Crossabeg, born Wexford 1952, landscape gardener; married to Catherine, née Lacey, Monamolin, they have one daughter and one son; maintains the `98 monument in the village free of charge; climbed Kilimanjaro to raise parish funds in 2004.

Berney, Father Matthew, a native of Monaseed, compiled and edited the Centenary Record in 1958 to mark the centenary of Wexford's twin churches.

Berney, Mark, Kilmurry, Gorey, born 1994; son of Joe, Co. Kildare, and Nicola, née Deacon, Courtown; achieved Ireland's best leaving certificate results 2013 getting nine A1s; currently studying Science in Trinity College Dublin; has won numerous national chess titles and represented Ireland at the World Youth Chess Championships 2010 in Greece at U-16 level.

Bernie, Dave, Dublin, formerly Ferns, one of County Wexford's best known hurlers. He won an All-Ireland title when, at twenty years of age, he played a starring role at midfield in the defeat of Tipperary in the 1968 final in Croke Park. Just two Ferns' GAA men hold All-Ireland senior medals. Sean English won the first as a substitute on the 1960 team. Dave Bernie has four Leinster senior hurling titles and played for Wexford for ten years from 1968 to 1978. Although living in Dublin for many years, Dave never lost his Ferns and Wexford connections. He served as a selector under two senior hurling managers and was a prime mover in the formation of the Wexford Hurling Supporters' Club. In 1998 Dave Bernie set up Filter International based in Cabinteely in Dublin where he lives. He is married to Ena, née English, Tomfarney, Adamstown.

Berridge, Patrick, Ballyshannon, Carrigbyrne, Adamstown, born Germany 1956; intensive dairy farmer and Carrigbyrne Cheese maker; married to Julie née Roche, they have three sons and one daughter; one of the pioneers of the revival of Irish farmhouse cheese making and founder members of Cáis.

Berry, Jack, Bunclody, born Wexford 1936, retired, married to Ann, née Galvin, Cork, they have two children; former ship's radio operator, subsequently worked in Bunclody Co-op and with Wexford Corporation. Jack is a life governor of Irish Water Safety and has given 50 years' voluntary service to the body which promotes water safety in Ireland and educates people in water safety best practices.

Berry, Jack, RIP, member of the famous family from Scar, Duncormick; a leading dual player with Wexford, he lined out 67 times with the senior hurlers; won an All-Ireland U21 hurling medal in 1965; was a key member of the 1968 All-Ireland senior hurling winning team, contributing two goals; played 41 times with the senior footballers and holds individual scoring record for his 3-10 in a League match against Kilkenny.

Berry, Jim, Inishere, Murrintown, served as Wexford County Board chairman 1980, 1984, including the Centenary Year celebrations; Leinster Council chairman, 1996–1998; of the famous family from Scar, Duncormick; played hurling and football for Wexford and for the St. Anne's Rathangan Club; captained the Wexford team beaten by Cork in the 1964 All-Ireland U21 final.

Berry, Paddy, Rosemount, Drinagh, builder, developer, balladeer and songwriter; married to Mary, née Power, they have two sons and one daughter, who went to live in Abu Dhabi along with her husband in 2013. A native of Duncormick, Paddy has built hundreds of houses around County Wexford through his company, Bawn Developments, but has taken a back seat now as his sons run the business, so he has more time to concentrate on singing in the traditional sean nós style and he has taken up playing the mouth organ. He has published numerous recordings and two highly-regarded books entitled *County Wexford Ballads*, 1982 and *More Wexford Ballads*, 1987 and he has won All-Ireland Fleadh Ceoil competitions. Paddy was given a special lifetime achievement award by the then President of Ireland, Mary McAleese, in 2003. Paddy is the second of nine children and his youngest brother Phil is also a well-known traditional singer. Other brothers, Jim and Jack, have been prominent in GAA.

Binions, Gloria, née Hurley, Killanne, Enniscorthy, born Cork 1941; married to Neville RIP, they have one son; historian and writer, with particular interest in 1798; made Wexford Senator of Wexford's reconvened senate for 1798 bicentenary; most recent written work *The Bi-centenary of Christchurch, Kilmeen 1811-2011*; ecumenist; lover of the Arts.

Bird, Wallis, Galbally, Enniscorthy, born Wexford 1982, singer/songwriter; one of seven children of Gerard and Joan. Wallis got her first guitar when she was six months old. She was born left-handed but she lost five fingers of her left hand in a lawnmower accident; four were successfully reattached. She plays a right-handed guitar upside-down, which contributes to her unique style of playing and sound. She studied song writing at Ballyfermot Rock School, Dublin; has released three albums: *Spoons*, 2007, *New Boots*, 2009, *Wallis Bird*, 2012, and was winner of Meteor Music Awards: Hope for 2009 and Best Irish Female 2010. Accompanied by her band which comprises the brothers Christian and Michael, Vinnie and Aoife O'Sullivan, she frequently tours throughout Europe.

Bishop, Joe, Ballymurn, the Elder Statesman of the Parish. Joe was involved in every non-sporting organisation in Ballymurn and further afield for many years; was a prime mover in the setting up of the Strawberry Fair in Enniscorthy; was involved in Macra na Tuaithe. Joe's greatest achievement was the setting up of Ballymurn Credit Union, which, without his guidance in difficult times, would not have survived and continued to serve the people of Ballymurn and surrounding parishes today.

Boggan, Fintan, Silverspring, Ballycogley, born Wexford 1946, retired Post Office worker; married to Mary, née Parle, Ballycogley, they have one son and two grandchildren; Director of Piercestown Credit Union and current league supervisor of the Irish League of Credit Unions.

Boggan, Hugh, 1935-2013, Crossabeg. One of county Wexord's best known motor dealers, former chairman of the SIMI, he had Toyota dealership for the past forty years with showrooms in Wexford and Gorey. Started car business in a premises on Wexford's Quays with his father Matt and then bought former Sherrard's Agricultural Machinery premises at Carricklawn outside Wexford from where the busness still operates. The business is being carried on by his family. Married to Joan, he has three sons Hugh Junior, Rev. Fr. Matt and Mark.

Boland, Maurice, Naas, Co. Kildare, formerly Kilanerin, born Wexford 1947; University Professor now retired and currently Research Director with Alltech Ireland; received Wexford County Council Scholarship to UCD in 1966 and graduated with first class honours in 1970; Head of Department of Animal Science and Production in UCD 1992-2001 and Professor of Animal husbandry up to 2012; Principal of College of Life Sciences and Vice President of UCD up to 2012; joined Alltech in 2013. Maurice is married with three daughters.

Blake, Ann Marie, Garryvadden, Blackwater attended World Youth Day in Rio de Janeiro 2013.

One of the Beatles, George Harrison can trace his ancestry back to Wexford and a small farm at Corah in Ferns. His great grandparents were James Darby Ffrench and Ellen Whelan.

Boland, James and John, Whitechurch, New Ross, owners of Boland's Motors Wexford. Their father, Andrew, General Merchant, Whitechurch, in 1923 expanded his existing business to include a motorcar hire service. He bought one Ford Model T lorry and one Ford Model T car and set up the service. His sons, James and John, came into the business in the 1940s and began selling second-hand cars and later opened a filling station in New Ross. Ninety years later, Boland's Motors has state-of-the-art premises on the Waterford Road, New Ross and at Ardcavan Wexford and is the main Ford Dealership in the county.

Bolger, Dan, Ballyconran, Askamore; farmer; married to Cecilia, née Doyle, Knockbrandon; emigrated to New Zealand 1930; they had five children, including Jim, who became the 35th Prime Minister of New Zealand 1990-1997 and New Zealand's ambassador to the US. Jim entered New Zealand politics in 1972 and retired in 1998.

Bolger, Deirdre, Gorey, born 1938; former Fine Gael politician. She was elected to Seanad Éireann on the Industrial and Commercial Panel in 1981 and was re-elected in 1982. Deirdre was also a member of Wexford County Council and retired in 2004.

Bolger, Jim, born Oylegate 1941; thoroughbred racehorse trainer and breeder, based in Glebe House, Coolcullen, on the Carlow/Kilkenny border. For many years he has been recognised as one of the racing greats in Europe. He took out his first training licence in 1976, and is probably at the height of his career at this time. Jim is recognised as being a perfectionist in his business and many of the people who trained under him have gone on to achieve great success themselves, including fellow Wexford man Aidan O'Brien, world famous trainer at Ballydoyle; eighteen times English champion jockey, Tony (A.P.), McCoy; Paul Carberry, one of the most stylish Irish jumps jockeys; Jimmy Fortune from Ferns, successful flat jockey in England, and others. This is a real family business - he is married to Jackie from Wexford town, in whose colours many of his horses run; his daughter, Una, is involved closely in the business, and is married to the highly-regarded stable jockey, Kevin Manning. He has one other daughter, Fiona. Jim maintains part of his breeding operation in his native Oylegate. He is a passionate Wexford man, and is very keenly interested in all things connected with the county, especially hurling. His Classic wins include English Derby with New Approach, 2008; Irish Derby twice with St. Jovite, 1992 and Trading Leather, 2013; 1000 Guineas – Finsceal Beo, Irish and English, 2007; 2000 Guineas – Dawn Approach, English, 2013; The Irish Oaks – Give Thanks, 1982 and Margarula, 2002; English – Jetski Lady, 1991. He has won a host of other important Group 1 races in Ireland, Britain and all over Europe, and notably won the Hong Kong Cup with Alexander Goldrun in 2004.

> The Village Bank at Killurin. An exclusive bank was formed in County Wexford in 1902. "Farmers have always has special problems over money. Their business requires large capital, but the turnover is nearly always slow and frequently uncertain. Therefore their income is often irregular and peaks at certain periods of the year...
>
> The Killurin Agricultural and Fisherman's Bank had a membership of thirty smallholders and cottiers who earned most of their income by net-fishing on the river Slaney."
>
> From *The Irish Co-operative Movement- Its history and development* by Patrick Bolger. Patrick Bolger, born in Kilmore, Victoria, Australia, of Irish emigrant parents was educated at the Christian Brothers Schools, Enniscorthy and at University College Dublin where he obtained a degree in Agriculture in 1949.

Bolger, Peter, New Ross, President of the Agricultural Science Association 2012-2013; joint managing director of the family agri-business and hardware company, John Bolger and Co. Ltd., which has branches in Ferns and Ballycogley. He and his brother, David, are the fifth generation of Bolgers to take the helm. He worked as a farm manager in Australia, New Zealand and Wicklow and also worked as a consultant with Keenans. He studied agricultural science as a mature student graduating from UCD in 2001. Peter worked as journalist with the *Irish*

Farmers' Journal and took up management at Bolger's in 2004. He is married to Kate and they have three sons. He is the fourth Wexford president of the ASA, following in the footsteps of Dr Tom Walsh from Piercestown during the 1950s; Martin McDonald from Crossabeg, 1965-66; and Dr Paddy Barry from Our Lady's Island, 1985-86.

Bolger, Phyllis, née Doyle, Marshalstown, known nationally for her involvement in Macra na Tuaithe and Macra na Feirme and nationally and internationally for her achievements in sheep-shearing and as a national sheep-shearing judge. She won the Macra Na Tuaithe U17 All-Ireland sheep-shearing championship in 1963 and won the All-Ireland senior championship, organised by Macra na Feirme, in 1964, 1968, and 1972. The President of Ireland, Cearbhaill Ó Dálaigh, in one of his last acts before his retirement from the presidency, presented the All-Ireland trophy to her at the final at Hollymount, Co. Mayo. She was a finalist in all All-Ireland finals for ten years from 1963 to her retirement from shearing in 1972 when she was appointed a sheep shearing judge. She was the only female to win three senior All Irelands. She has shorn 300 sheep in a ten-hour day. Her late husband Jack who died in 2006; was a member of Wexford County Council for ninteen years and never lost an election. Their five children are Anne, Kate, Joan, Jack and Pat.

Bolger, Tim, Castledockerell, Ballycarney, born Wexford 1923; married Bridget 'Babs', née O'Connor, Ivy House, Clohamon, 1946; they purchased a small farm, started a haulage business and founded Bunclody Sheep Producers' Group. With his brother, David, they built and established, on Tim's land, Slaney Meat Packers in 1968. After struggling initially, it began to grow in the 1970s, became Slaney Meats and is now home to one of Wexford's biggest exporters, the Slaney Foods Group.

Booth, Evelyn, Bunclody, was the author of a book entitled *The Flora of Carlow*.

Bowe, Mary, née Murphy, Marlfield House Hotel, Gorey, daughter of farmers, Larry and Marjorie, Gillardstown House, Castlepollard, Co. Westmeath; studied in Domestic Science College in Navan then in Shannon College of Hotel Management; opened Marlfield House Hotel in April 1977 with husband, Raymond, and has retained 'Blue Book' and 'Relais & Chateaux' badge since 1980; retired from the day-to day operation three years ago and the hotel is now run by her two daughters, Laura and Margaret.

There's a 1,500 yew-tree maze in Dunbrody Abbey Visitor Centre in Campile.

Bourke, Mary, Clonegal, born 1946, née Goodall, Market Square, Enniscorthy, retail jeweller in the family's business and gemmologist; married to Nicholas, they have four children and eight grandchildren; Fellow of The Gemmological Association of Great Britain and Ireland. Mary has a keen interest in and has written articles on the Brownswood-born architect and designer Eileen Gray.

Boyse, Tom, proprietor of estates at Bannow and in Kilkenny, died at Roebuck House in Co. Dublin on the 15th of January 1854 aged 72. He was a hugely influential figure in the Co. Wexford; huge crowds attended anti-tithe meetings addressed by him. He detested oppression of the Catholic community.

Bradish, Colonel William Bolton, 1916-1996, Crossabeg, Lieutenant in British Army; married to Bridget, née Strutt, 1917-2012, Derbyshire, England, one of the Industrial Revolution cotton-milling dynasty; having three daughters and one son; member of very first Airborne Division; ran W.B.Nunn Malthouses in Castlebridge after WWII for his uncle, Joshua Nunn, following the death of John Nunn who was killed in action; was present at the dinner in Castlebridge House which led to the establishing of the Guinness Book of World Records; played a key role in having Kilpatrick Church of Ireland church handed over to the parish for use as a community centre having financed the repair of the building himself.

Brady, Enda, London, formerly Enniscorthy, Sky News and Sports reporter; eldest son of retired detective garda, Longford man, Michael and Margaret from the Milehouse Road. Enda started his journalism career with *The Echo* in Enniscorthy in 1992, going on to study journalism in Preston in England. He went on to work for the Press Association and the *Yorkshire Evening Post* where he won BT Young Journalist of the Year in 1997. He then became one of the elite reporters working with ITV Central in Oxford. Enda Brady joined Sky News in 2005 and is one of their most high-profile reporters based in London. He is married to Josella and they have two children, Saoirse and Donnacha.

Bradley, Josie, 1933-2008, Newbawn, post mistress; married to Charles, they have five daughters and three sons; a committed community worker involved in most committees in the village, Josie had a special interest in the I.C.A. and the stage. The ICA instituted an award in her honour, The Josie Bradley Inspiration Award, in Newbawn NS for the 'Most Upstanding Student of the year.'

Breen, Annastasia, born Co. Wexford 1999, Rathimney, Gusserane, New Ross; daughter of Bridget, née Whelan, Ballycullane, and Tom, agricultural contractor; she has one brother, John; currently studying for her Junior Certificate in St. Mary's Secondary School in New Ross; winner U8 Bungrad 2008 and U12 Ardgrad 2010 All-Ireland dancing competitions; member of St. Leonard's FC team which won the All-Ireland U12 Community Games soccer final 2010; captained the Wexford U14 ladies' football team to All-Ireland victory in 2013.

Breen, Eddie, a native of Enniscorthy, and graduate of the CBS there, retired as Wexford county manager in November 2012 having served there for nine years and a total of 45 years in the public service. Before that, he was manager of Waterford city. He served in Castlebar, Macroom, and with Meath County Council and was town clerk in Wexford for five years in the 1970s. Highly regarded by councillors and by fellow staff members of the County Council for his courtesy, he became known as 'Mr. Build' having sourced funding and managed the building of new public buildings to replace old stock across the county. He, and his team of directors at Wexford County Council, are credited with focusing on national road infrastructure for economic gain and to improve communications overall and between towns; the building of the new County Council offices at Carricklawn; managing the development of the Wexford Library service at Gorey and Bunclody; overseeing the provision of improved swimming pools in New Ross and Wexford and better sports facilities countywide; rejuvenating the quays at New Ross; overseeing supporting developments in Enniscorthy Castle and the Presentation Centre and the development of the new state-of-the-art Library in Mallin St., Wexford town. He began his public service career in Wexford County Council in the 1960s. He and his wife, Pauline, live in Wexford town.

Breen, Gerard Anthony 'Gerry', Rocksborough, Wexford town, journalist. He spent most of his working life with *People Newspapers*, Wexford, rising through the ranks to become Group Editor; served as editor of *Ireland's Own* magazine prior to his retirement and still contributes regularly to the magazine; edited all four journals published by the Rosslare Historical Society, *Rosslare in History*. Gerry is married to Marie, née Kelly, from Wexford, a talented musician and artist.

Breen, Joe, Tinnashrule, Ferns, son of Michael and Stephanie, née Duffy; played the part of Frank McCourt aged 5-8 years in the 1999 film drama *Angela's Ashes* and featured with Frank McCourt in *Time* magazine and on the David Letterman Show.

Breen, Maggie, born in Monageer, her debut collection of poetry is *Other Things I Didn't Tell* published in 2013 Scallta Media.

Breen, Martin, Staplestown, Murrintown, born Wexford 1982; son of Michael and Maria; graduated with a degree in Agricultural Science specialising in Animal Science(UCD), then took a post-graduate Veterinary course (UCD) and is now working in practice in Wexford. He appeared in the RTÉ documentary series *Junior Vet* in 2013.

Breen, P.D., Castlebridge, formerly Carrig-on-Bannow, national teacher; Wexford's first President of the GAA, serving from 1924 to 1926; Wexford's representative on the Central and Leinster Councils 1914 to 1952, and was Chairman of the Leinster Council from 1921-23. He served as Chairman/or Secretary of Wexford Co. Board during the famous period when the county won six Leinster titles in a row and four All-Irelands in a row (from 1911 to 1918); and chairman for ten years in the 1930s and 40s. He also served as an officer with Wexford and Leinster National Athletics and Cycling Association and with the Central Handball Council. He was also a very good football player and won an All-Ireland senior football medal with Dublin in 1902, played for Leinster and won club titles at all adult grades in Dublin while studying at St. Patrick's College, Drumcondra. On his return to Wexford, he won titles with Castlebridge; played with county hurling and football teams from 1904 to 1914; he gave up his place on the 1910 hurling team to what he considered a better player, and missed out on an All-Ireland medal; was on football team beaten by Kerry in the 1914 All-Ireland final.

Breen, Rose from Monageer, née Cullen from Ballyfad, very actively involved in local and county GAA; former poultry instructress with Wexford County Committee of Agriculture; member of parish committee and involved in all community initiatives.

Breen, Jim, Monageer, married to Martha, née Murphy, Blackwater, they have four children; works as an agronomist with UN in North Africa and has spent all his working life helping farmers in the developing world including Malawi, Samoa, Ethiopia and Sudan. Returned briefly to Monageer in 1983 and established Breen Agricultural Services with his brother, Tom.

Brennan, Bishop Denis, born in the Parish of Rathnure, Enniscorthy, on 20 June 1945, he was ordained on 31 May 1970 at St. Peter's College, Wexford. He was appointed to the House of Missions in 1970 and Administrator of St. Senan's Parish, Enniscorthy from 1986 until his appointment as parish priest of Taghmon in 1997. He served as Vicar Forane for Wexford Deanery and as diocesan child protection delegate. He was ordained Bishop of Ferns on 23 April 2006.

Brennan, Elizabeth, New Ross, who died in 1995, was the author of a number of books, including: *Out of Darkness, Am I My Brother's Keeper?, The Wind Fairies,* and *The Wind Fairies Again.*

A number of Palatine families settled in County Wexford most notably in the Old Ross area three hundred years ago. They were brought here by Queen Anne to support Protestant landlords.

Brennan, Joe, born Wexford 1968. His play *The Witchin' Well* was produced by An Grianán Productions, Letterkenny, Co. Donegal, in 2005 and 2006. The play toured nationally twice and featured at the Junction Festival, Clonmel, 2005, the Cork Midsummer Festival, 2005 and at a Bucharest Stories' Festival in 2006.

Brennan, John N. H., born Wexford 1914, wrote under the name of John Welcome. A Wexford solicitor, he edited several collections of crime, legal and other stories, and wrote a number of well-regarded thrillers many of them associated with the world of horseracing, including *Run for Cover, Stop at Nothing, Beware of Midnight, Hard to Handle and Wanted for Killing.* His many novels included: *On the Search, Go for Broke, Grand National, Bellary Bay* and *A Call to Arms. He also wrote The Life and Times of Fred Archer, Neck or Nothing, The Life of Bob Sievier, The Sporting Empress and Infamous Occasions.*

Brennan, Maeve, 1917–1993, daughter of Robert and Una, Wexford and Dublin; moved to the United States in 1934 when her father Robert was appointed to the Irish Legation in Washington; she remained in the United States when her parents and brother returned to Ireland in 1944. She worked for *Harper's Bazaar* and the *New Yorker*. She was recognised as a brilliant writer and collections of her articles, short stories and a novella have been published. Although she was widely read in the United States in the 1950s and 1960s, she was almost unknown in Ireland, even though Dublin was the setting for many of her short stories. In a review of one of her short story collections, *The Springs of Affection*, John Updike stated that 'she was sharp-eyed as a sparrow for the crumbs of human events, the overheard and the glimpsed and guessed at.' She had a rather sad end, suffering from alcoholism and became a lonely destitute. In September 2013 Eamon Morrissey wrote and performed the one-man play "Maeve's House" at the Abbey Theatre in Dublin. The play is about Maeve, her work, her house in Dublin where Morrissey later lived, and their fleeting meeting.

① Arts

Writers, actors, singers, directors, musicians, entertainers, painters, sculptors. County Wexford is teeming with talent that is acknowledged across the world. The main venues are Wexford Opera House, Wexford Arts Centre, Gorey Little Theatre, St. Michael's Theatre, New Ross and The Athenaeum, Enniscorthy.

ENTERTAINMENT IN WEXFORD

The entertainment industry is a fundamental component of the social, cultural, economic life of any community and in County Wexford we have an outstanding tradition of producing quality entertainment in myriad guises. A generation ago, dance halls were what people wanted and there were ballrooms everywhere, in Adamstown, Camross, Bunclody, The Castle in Enniscorthy, the Barrowland in New Ross, the Tara Ballroom in Courtown, the Unyoke and countless parish halls, community centres, and hay barns, where we could show how well we could disco, jive, twist or do the Hucklebuck. Or you could see a Tops show or a school show or the local-lads-in-a-band show. The names of impresarios such Danny Doyle, Adamstown, Paddy Doyle, Bunclody and Frank Sinnott in Wexford town became household names. Some venues survived; others went the way of the Hucklebuck.

Today, County Wexford boasts a €33 million, world-class Opera House; theatres in all of the four main towns that can host any A-list entertainer and so many parish halls and smaller, more intimate venues like The Bailey and The Stores. But most important in Wexford is that there are groups, societies and individuals who make things happen – drama, music, poetry, dance, comedy, debate, public speaking, the full spectrum of what entertains us – singers, actors, dancers, musicians and poets. Wexford's entertainment scene is vibrant.

Traditionalists, who enjoyed the dancing scene over the years, remember The Supreme Showband, The Kinsellas, The Emeralds and others. One favourite is Teresa and The Stars who in 2013 is forty years in the business.

Rehearsal of *The Nutcracker Suite* in the O'Reilly Theatre at Wexford Opera House in High Street.

New Ross Pipe Band has won two World championships in 2012 and 2013, a remarkable feat for this enthusiastic local marching band. Leo Rowsome from Monageer became the internationally famed Uilleann Pipes Master. Choral concerts in churches throughout the county provide uplifting musical and spiritual experiences, inspiring noteworthy performances from local singers and choral groups such as the Wexford Festival Singers, Valda and the Carrigbyrne Pike Choir. Art Sinnott of Boolavogue, Paddy Berry of Duncormick and John Roche from Wexford town are outstanding singers of traditional songs. Not forgetting Anthony Kearns from Kiltealy.

County Wexford's prowess in musicals and light opera is manifest in the presentation of the prestigious AIMS awards to members of Wexford Musical Society for its production of *The Witches of Eastwick* in 2013. Celtic Roots from Bree, an Irish Céilí and dance group, founded by Kay Keeley McKelvie, is hugely popular.

Amateur drama is once more in its ascendancy in Wexford. Award-winning groups in the county include Bridge Drama Group, Ballycogley Players, Camross Drama Group, Kilmuckridge Drama Group, along with groups in Wexford, Gorey and Enniscorthy. Another phenomenon of the past decade is the renaissance of the South East Tops competition brainchild of Fr. David Murphy, CC, Caroreigh and Trinity, held in Taghmon Community Centre annually.

Mumming continues to be a unique part of Wexford culture with Adamstown man and member of Drinagh Mummers, Michael O'Brien, crowned King of the Mummers in 2013. The county adopted its own anthem, *Dancing at the Crossroads,* by local band the Wild Swans, following the All-Ireland Senior Hurling win of 1996.

County Wexford is a hotbed for festivals too, the obvious being the Festival Opera, but others are the Strawberry, New Ross Drama, Street Rhythms, Riverside Jump, Blackstairs Blues, Phil Murphy Weekend, Piano, AIMS, Choral, Dunbrody, Seafood. The county caters for every taste.

Cat sitting - oil on canvas by Paddy Darigan.

SYNONYMOUS WITH MUSIC

By Jackie Hayden

Long before I took up residence in County Wexford in 1996, the town and county had a well-established national and international reputation as a vibrant musical centre of excellence.

The international music community already knew Wexford for its annual Opera Festival that attracted visitors and music fans from all over the world to relish the atmosphere of the town, and the natural bonhomie of its people, not to mention the quality of the productions on offer. Meanwhile, local artists as varied and as talented as Pierce Turner, Larry Kirwan, Cry Before Dawn, Chris de Burgh, Declan Sinnott, Leslie Dowdall and Pip and John Murphy in Carrick-on-Bannow had carved enviable reputations for themselves in the fields of pop, rock and trad.

And let's not forget that Beatle George Harrison had strong Wexford connections, as his great-grandparents James Darby Ffrench and Ellen Whelan owned a small farm in Corah.

The combined successes of those artists have since inspired younger generations to follow suit, so now the Wexford scene can boast an array of vital musical talent that includes Eleanor McEvoy, Clive Barnes, Wallis Bird, The Man Whom, Maverick Sabre, George Lawlor, Kevin Whelan, Dave Clark, Leni Morrison, Aileen Mythen, Corner Boy, Jimi Cullen, Paul Creane, Tanya Murphy, Donna Marie Sludds, SIL, Shane Kenny, Nick Day and Niall Colfer. I could go on.

The name Colfer reminds me of the redoubtable Eoin, who, not a man to rest on the laurels earned by his immense international successes as an author, has brought his skills as a wordsmith to the writing of lyrics for locally-created musicals.

Yes, there's as much music in Wexford as there are nuts in Brazil. But little of this happens by accident. It's often been said that all politics is local, but I believe that all music is local, or at least it starts out that way. Most musicians and singers get their first chance to perform in school events, busking on the streets or playing in community centres, pubs, clubs, theatres, churches and private houses.

To that end, Wexford is endowed with two venues of international calibre, The Opera House and Wexford Arts Centre. The former has been acknowledged abroad for the quality of its sound, lighting and production values, while the latter has showcased an endless parade of renowned artists from home and abroad. The *Cáca Milis Cabaret* at the same venue has always presented a stimulating mix of performance art, including music of various genres. Its on-going success proves that the perceptive Wexford audience is not fazed by a potpourri of musical styles that can range from burlesque, continental cabaret and belly dancing to less eyebrow-raising forms.

Alongside the Opera Festival there are other festivals spread around the county, including the Blackstairs Blues festival, which attracts performers and fans for the USA, The Riverside Jump Festival also in Enniscorthy, and the Gorey Market House Festival.

Venues of the calibre of The Sky and The Ground and Greenacres in Wexford town, as well as Colfers in Carrick-On-Bannow, and the Talbot, Whites, Riverbank and Riverside hotels, are as popular with musicians as they are with the fans. Long before live music become the main focus of the music industry, sessions in pubs had become part of the local cultural and social fabric, and the envy of visitors. Indeed, the importance of impromptu trad gigs might be best exemplified by Eleanor McEvoy who so enjoyed contributing to sessions in Butlers in Lady's Island that she was inspired to write a delightful piece for fiddle called 'Driving Home From Butlers' which she subsequently recorded.

Choral concerts in churches, including Rowe Street, Bride Street, the Franciscan Friary, St Iberius and Barntown, as well as St. Aidan's Cathedral, Enniscorthy, provide uplifting musical and spiritual experiences, inspiring noteworthy performances from local singers and choral groups such as the Wexford Festival Singers and Valda.

The Red Chair song club, now settled in the Potato Market under the tireless stewardship of Alan Byrne, serves as an invaluable focal point for songwriters of to-morrow to gain valuable experience and pick up tips and advice with their more experienced counterparts. A quick glance down through any of Senan O'Reilly's weekly Wexlive listings reveals the quantity and diversity of musical experiences on offer across the county. Both local papers, *The People* and *The Echo*, dedicate generous space to local musical happenings, while broadcasters of the calibre of Alan Corcoran, Tony Kehoe and Alan Maguire regularly fly the flag for Wexford music on South East Radio.

The relatively recent introduction of the annual Spiegeltent Festival by local promoters Barry Ennis and Brian Byrne has transformed Wexford quay into a lively entertainment environment, providing a hitherto unknown musical experience for Wexford's music community.

One final thought: 2013 saw the death of Jim Golden, one of the volunteer stalwarts of the Wexford Opera Festival and for whom the event was his life-blood. Wouldn't it be a fitting memorial to Jim if the Wexford authorities could see their way to honouring his generous contribution to the county in some meaningful way, such as an annual musical bursary in his name?

CULTIVATING THE ARTS

By Sinéad Barden, County Arts Officer

What is it about County Wexford that gives it its distinctive character? What is the abstract alchemy that lifts it above the conventional? I suggest that the secret behind our county's uniqueness is the power of our inherent, evolving and ever-developing Arts sector.

County Wexford can boast a rich diversity of artform provision, including dance, theatre, visual arts, literature, music, opera, film, circus and architecture. No matter what

Twilight.

your artistic interest there is an avenue for participation and engagement, which makes for a rich, deep artistic environment. Whether assertively or passively, every member of our society and every visitor to our county has the opportunity to become involved. Be it on the local stage, on the step-dancing platform, in one of our many storyhouses; you'll find open doors that welcome friends and strangers into ever expanding artistic folds.

Widening our geographic lens to the four corners of County Wexford, one is struck by the wealth of artistic heritage and infrastructure on our doorstep. Our artistic forebears include Eileen Gray, Frances Danby and John Willis. Our artistic infrastructural heritage includes St. Michael's Theatre and Wexford Arts Centre. Within and beyond town walls lie gems of permanent artwork enhancing and enriching our environment. Sculptures which respond to the physical, social, historical and cultural characteristics of an area, thereby not only relating to place, but responding to it and engaging with it.

The voluntary, amateur, commercial and professional arts sector makes a significant contribution to the artistic life of County Wexford. As a consequence of their dedication, there is an abundance of arts activity programmed throughout the county annually, ranging from exhibitions, concerts, screenings, theatre productions and literary sessions. Festivals in particular make up a significant part of the county's artistic calendar. Throughout each season festivals act as a focal point for those living in and visiting an area, creating a sense of identity and adding to Wexford's unique and vibrant artistic landscape. Undeniably, Wexford Opera Festival and the accompanying Fringe Festival are jewels in the artistic calendar. Every autumn, the streets of Wexford Town are electrified with the tangible: lights, banners and decoration, and the intangible: a sense of anticipation and a unique, magical atmosphere. As people meander through our historical town, baritones, tenors, sopranos can be heard rehearsing their scales and roles.

Wexford County Council plays a part in cultivating a rich artistic environment by delivering a strategically planned arts service with a commitment to long-term investment and sustainable development. We recognise the intrinsic value of the arts, and importantly, value the role of the arts in providing a means for fostering and supporting innovation, whilst also contributing to economic development and cultural tourism.

The arts are alive and well in County Wexford, and with the push and vigour of everyone who believes in their cause, we can be assured of a lively and dynamic sector in perpetuity.

WEXFORD SINFONIA

Founded in 1993 by a group of local enthusiasts and had its first concert in January 1994. Since then it has held four concerts every year, and in 2008 undertook a two-concert tour to France. It is unique in Ireland, being the only symphony orchestra based in a country town. The players are mostly from the Wexford area, though a number of loyal members regularly travel from Dublin and other places. Some of the members are music teachers, but mostly they are amateurs drawn from all walks of life. It is generously supported by Wexford County Council.

SOME WEXFORD BANDS
DO YOU REMEMBER?

Tru'penny Opera, Enniscorthy, Michael Egan, Peter Murphy, Noel Quaid

LaDV8, Wexford town band fronted by Mick Murphy

Leper Messiah, Bunclody

Touchstone/Strange Fruit, Clem Dake and Brendan Keane, Nick Bailey

Local Contract, Wexford town, Michael Benson

D'harma Bums, Wexford

Doozer, fronted by Justin Cullen

Cousin Bill, Ian 'Mocha' Maloney and Tommy Mahoney

Salthouse, the Colfer family from 'The Hook'

Immodium

Dorchadas Wexford town Slogadh group.

Sonas traditional group with Brendan Wade

Freres Jackman, Pat and Martin Jackman, out of 'Yellow Moriah', also featuring Eamon Murphy, Philip O Brien, and Robbie McGrath.

The Major Thinkers, Larry Kirwin and Pierce Turner.

The Wild Swans, Wexford, Paul Bell and Brendan Wade

MacMurrough, Paul Kavanagh, Gorey, and sisters, Mary and Josephine O Neill from Ferns.

The Dust Devils formerly Tasmanian Dust Devils, featured Cormac O Toole, Gerry O Callaghan, Jay Livingston, Mick Acton and Mandy Kinsella.

The Emeralds, New Ross, Patsy Cleary, John Aspels, Paddy Ryan and Michael Murray

The Kinsellas, singers of *Slaney Valley.*

Martin Codd and the Herdsmen.

George 'Gunner' Hess, played with the 'Clipper Carlton Showband', 'Premier Aces' and 'Lowney's Band'.

The Palladium

The Supreme

The Sutherlands

The Visitors

Waiting for action on Omaha Beach, Curracloe, during the shooting of Steven Spielberg film *Saving Private Ryan* in June 1997 – photograph by Noel Murphy.

Opposite: Buí Bolg preparing for the Special Olympics.

Some Wexford Vocalists

Packie Hayden; the McCracken Family, Duncannon; Ger Busher; Tony Carthy; Des Whelan; Hazel Cloney; Tony Walsh; Brid Hanton; Kathleen Tynan; Deirdre Masterson; Rita Harpur; Linda Lee; Helena Bates. David O Brien, Fergal Murphy, Tom Meehan, John and Leo Curran, Mena Murphy, John Joe Sinnott, Robbie Rae, Tommy Murphy and Sean Connick.

Some Wexford Musicians

Martin Connolly, New Ross and Jim Murphy, Knoxtown, accordion players; George Ross; Leo Carty, Broadway; Liam Gaul, Gerry Ford; The Berry Brothers; Padraig Sinnott; John Cousins; Sean and Alice Rattigan, fiddle players; Dick Boland, Ballywilliam; John Bowe, Templeudigan; Liz and Mary King; Joe Lowney and Johnny Reck; Joe Monaghan in Taghmon/Foulksmills, Paddy Hogan; bodhrán player Frank Torpey, Cullentown, member of Nomos, played with Riverdance, Micheál O Suilleabháin and Luka Bloom.

SOME BOOKS

Kilmore Parish Journal- 40 Years On, editor Hilary Murphy

Bree Parish Journal, editors Jim Doyle and Clare Doyle

Families of County Wexford by Hilary Murphy

The Year the Whales Came In by Simon Kennedy

Sacred Cows, Silent Sheep by Simon Kennedy

Inheritance and Succession, by John G. Murphy and Jason Dunne

Wexford History and Society, edited by Kevin Whelan, Associate Editor, William Nolan

A History of County Wexford by Nicholas Furlong

The Fethard-on Sea Boycott by Tim Fanning

The Moulding Shop by Philip Quirke

Its Words You Want by Patrick Kehoe

All the Bishops Men by Tom Mooney

Plough Music by David Medcalf

From Vinegar Hill to Edentubber by Ruan O'Donnell

Wexford Castles- Landscape, Context, Settlement by Billy Colfer

Tumbling Down by Billy Roche

Heather Blazing by Colm Tóibín

Jack by Blaise Brosnan

Enniscorthy- a History by Colm Tóibín and Celestine Murphy

County Wexford in the Rare old Times, Volumes 1, 2,3,4 and 5 by Nicholas Furlong

Young Farmer Seeks Wife by Nicholas Furlong

County Wexford's Macra Story by Bee McDonald

From the Hill of Wild Berries edited by Sylvia Cullen

Rebellions by Tom Dunne

Artemis Fowl by Eoin Colfer

With Heart and Hand by Tom Williams

Cúchulainn's Son- the Story of Nickey Rackard by Tom Williams

Publish and be Damned by Celestine Rafferty

Ireland's Own- an Anthology of short stories, editors Phil

Murphy and Sean Nolan

The Wexford Man- Essays in honour of Nicky Furlong

The Heather Blazing by Colm Tóibín

The Blackwater Lightship by Colm Tóibín

The Master by Colm Tóibín

The Sea by John Banville

Arrogant Trespass by Billy Colfer

1798, Tomorrow the Barrow We Cross by Joe Murphy

John, the Revelator by Peter Murphy

The Soul of Wexford by John Ironside

Bree- History of a Parish by Dan Walsh

The Battle of Oulart Hill by Brian Cleary

The Way I saw it by Martin Codd

Restless Spirit by Margaret Hawkins

Deny Me Not by Margaret Hawkins

Wexford – The American Connection by Liam Gaul

Athletics by Seamus O'Keeffe

The Lifeboats of Rosslare Harbour and Wexford by Nicholas Leach

Telling it at a Slant by Joe Neal

102 Years of Wexford ICA

A Parish and its People

My Wexford by Nicky Rossiter

Camolin Parish Gaels – 1884–2011

History of Snowcream Dairies by Jim Burke

Rosslare Harbour - Sea and Ships by John Maddock

Look Small…Pull Big – St. Ibars /Shelmalier Camogie Club

Richard Corish - A biography by Kieran S. Roche

The Hook Peninsula by Billy Colfer

Wexford Castles- Landscape, Context, Settlement by Billy Colfer

Wexford, a Town and its Landscape by Billy Colfer

Climbing Mountains in our Minds, edited by Sylvia Cullen

The Wexford War Dead by Tom Burnell and Margaret Gilbert

A Maritime History of County Wexford by John Power

History of Athletics in Kilmore – 1905–2011 by Seamus O'Keeffe

Senator Kathleen L. Browne by Mary McAuliffe

New Ross Remembers by Sean Crowley

The Rattler - Wexford Seafarers 1864-2012 by Nicholas Fortune

A History of Ferns by Christopher Power

One Shade of Green by Helen Skyrne

The People's Rising by Daniel Gahan

Sport by Jim Parle

The Irish Co-operative Movement by Patrick Bolger

Land, Lust and Gunsmoke by Peter Bacon

Houses of Wexford by David Rowe and Eithne Scallan

The GAA Bible by Dominic Williams

Hore's History of County Wexford

On Our Own Ground: County Wexford parish by parish, by Dr Ned Culleton, published by Wexford County Council Public Library Service.

Brennan, Michael, Galbally, champion Suffolk sheep breeder and secretary of County Wexford Sheep breeders' Association, which was established in 1891 and is considered to be the oldest association of its kind in Ireland. The members have been producing rams for the sheep farmers of the county and neighbouring counties for more than 121 years. Their annual sales take place in Enniscorthy Mart and they sell Charollais, Suffolk and Texel and the purchase pedigree stock from UK, Northern Ireland and the continent. Michael was a founder member of the Whirlwinds Showband which was hugely popular throughout the south east in the 1970s. Michael, an only child, is first cousin of Bishop Denis Brennan, also an only child. Michael and his wife, Mary, née Moylan, Tullow, Co. Carlow, live in Galbally. Their children are Patrick, Alicia and Denis.

Brennan, Robert, born Wexford town 1881, was a patriot, author, journalist and diplomat. He was sentenced to death for his part in the 1916 Easter Rising in Enniscorthy, but the sentence was commuted to life imprisonment. While he was in Dartmoor Prison, he wrote the novel *The False Finger, An Irish Detective*, which he published under the pen-name Selskar Kearney in 1921. He was Director of Elections for Sinn Féin in 1918 and was Under Secretary for Foreign Affairs in the Republican Government of 1921. He helped found and became a director of the *Irish Press* in 1931. Later he returned to the diplomatic service as Secretary of the Irish Legation in Washington, becoming Envoy in 1938, and remaining as Minister Plenipotentiary up to 1947. When he returned to Ireland, he became Radio Éireann's Director of Broadcasting. He wrote plays, mystery stories and reminiscences, including: *Goodnight Mr O'Donnell, The Man Who Walked like a Dancer* and *Allegiance,* his autobiography, which was published in 1950.

Brosnan, Blaise, Park, Wexford, a native of Killarney, Co. Kerry. Former chief executive of Wexford Farmers' Co-op (WFC), which he helped to build from a small mart to a business with a turnover of more than €70 million. He is an agricultural economics graduate of UCD with a Masters in Management from Trinity College, Dublin. He left WFC to found his own management consultancy/business training enterprise, the Management Resource Institute, bringing these training programmes to Russia and the USA. More than 2,000 owner-managers in the south-east region have participated in his programmes. He is also founder-director of International Dispute Resolution (Ireland) Ltd. He is a founder-member of Enniscorthy Rotary Club and board member of the world-famous Wexford Festival Opera. In 2009, he published his first book, titled *You are the limiting factor – unlocking your true business potential* and in 2011, published his second book, *Jack-Business Lessons from Life, Life Lessons from Business*. He and his wife, Delia, a well known popular community nurse in the county, live near Wexford town.

Browne, Bernard, Old Ross; personnel executive with EPA; wife Elizabeth Rose, PR Consultant; is a contributor to historical journals; has written a number of books on on county's history. Books include *Living by the Pen;* he edited *The Wexford Man,* in honour of Nicky Furlong.

Browne, Greta, Clonroche, née Murphy, Ballybrittas, Bree, born Wexford 1944, local historian, genealogist and ancestry researcher; married to Michael, they have two daughters, Sheelagh and Mary and two sons, Patrick RIP and Jim, and one granddaughter, Ciara; works with NWSPCA in animal rescue and rehousing operations; daughter Sheelagh is a well-known singer who has worked on several educational singing programmes for primary school children, she also sings at funerals and weddings.

Browne, John, who was born in Marshalstown on 1st August, 1948, is a Fianna Fáil politician who has topped the poll in the Wexford constituency on a number of occasions. He was first elected to Dáil Éireann in the November 1982, General Election and has been re-elected at every election since. He has held a number of government and opposition positions. Shortly after being elected he was appointed assistant Chief Whip. In 1992, he became Minister of State at the Department of Agriculture and Food with special responsibility for the food industry. In 1993, he was moved to the post of Minister of State at the Department of the Environment with special responsibility for Environmental Protection. He held this position until 1994. In 2002 he was appointed Minister of State at the Department of Communications, Marine and Natural Resources. In a reshuffle in 2004, he became Minister of State at the Department of Agriculture and Food. After a further reshuffle in February 2006, he became Minister of State for responsibility for Marine. He has also served as Chairman of a number of Oireachtas Committees, and is currently the Fianna Fáil spokesperson on Marine and Fisheries.

Browne, Justin, Ballybrittas, Bree; veterinary surgeon; married to Mary Jo, née Ryan, medical ophthalmologist, they have one daughter and one son.; co-founder, with Australian Simon Fahey, of Borovalley Veterinary Clinic in 2009 which provides full medical and diagnostic services for both horses and small animals along with specialist elective equine surgery equipped with on-site laboratory, pharmacy and dental clinic. David Roche, veterinary surgeon native of Oulart has joined the practice. After qualifying, Justin, spent the first five years of his professional career at the world famous Coolmore Stud, Fethard, Co. Tipperary, as a junior vet before returning to Ballybrittas to establish his own practice in 1991. A keen thoroughbred breeder himself, Justin lives nearby.

Browne, Kathleen Anne, 1876/8-1943, Rathronan Castle, Bridgetown, senator, poet, author and a founder member of the Uí Chennselaig Historical Society; was elected as a Cumann na nGaedheal member of Seanad Éireann at a by-election caused by the death of Alice Stopford Green in 1929 and she served until 1936; advocate of all things Irish; author of *Wexford a history of the county*, 1927, which became a textbook in the National Schools; widely published in historical journals; Yola dialect expert; farmer; County Councillor; Peace Commissioner; represented the Irish Farmers' Union at the World Poultry Congress in London 1930.

Browne, Mary, New Ross, born Wexford 1968, professional photographer, married to Jimmy Sinnott, Terrarath, they have two daughters. Mary is daughter of Mary Buckley, Clonroche, and PJ Browne, professional photographer, who photographed the visit of President John F Kennedy to his ancestral home in Dunganstown, New Ross, in 1963. Mary photographed The Homecoming 2013, celebrating the 50th Anniversary of the 1963 visit and the Eternal Flame on the Quay which symbolises the continuity and connectivity of JFK and his ancestors in New Ross. Mary is the President of New Ross Chamber of Commerce.

Browne, Matt, Dalkey, Dublin, formerly of Blackstoops, Enniscorthy, has played a major role in the development of the pharmaceutical industry in Ireland. A former Wexford hurler, he worked his way up through the ranks and became the first non-German to become chief executive of pharmaceutical giant Hoechst's Irish operation. Matt was awarded the Liz Herbert Memorial Lifetime Achievement Award by his colleagues in 2012. Now retired, he lives with his wife, Joan, née Bernie, originally from Ferns.

Browne, Michael, Big Barn, Ballycogley, born London 1924; married to Ann, née Muldoon, Co. Leitrim, they have four sons and two daughters; General Manager of Stafford's of Wexford for 26 years; Parish Council and Community Council member for many years; from the Browne family that produced two bishops in the 19th century.

Browne, Sean, Enniscorthy 1916–1996, County GAA Chairman during golden era of Wexford hurling, serving from 1950 to 1969. The senior hurlers won four of their six All-Ireland's during that period. He was awarded a Sealink Wexford GAA Award of the Century in 1984 on behalf of all those involved in that era. He was elected to Dáil Éireann in 1957. After losing his seat in the 1961 election, he was elected to Seanad Éireann on the Labour Panel and was re-elected to the Seanad in 1965. He regained his Dáil seat in the 1969 General Election and was re-elected to the Dáil in 1973 and 1977. However, he was defeated again in the 1981 General Election, but was re-elected in the February 1982 election. When the Dáil was dissolved later that year, he didn't contest the November 1982 election and was succeeded by his nephew, John Browne. Sean Browne served as Leas Cheann Comhairle of Dáil Éireann from 1977 to 1981. He was prominently associated with the GAA in Co. Wexford and was Chairman of the Wexford County Board for 21 years.

Buggy, world champions, see Sport

Burger-Smit, Bettie-Marie, New Ross, born South Africa 1970, General Manager Brandon House Hotel, New Ross; she has one son, Helmut, she came to Ireland in 2001 after applying for job in the Great Southern Hotel, Rosslare, her great grandfather having left Inniskeen, Co. Cork, in 1870 bound for America, but eventually ending up at the Cape of Good Hope where he met a Dutch lady so stayed and settled down.

Butler, Liam Snr and Jnr, Liam Mellows Park, Wexford, a father and son team, they have had many greyhound successes in their careers, the highlight being The Champion Stakes at Shelbourne Park with Large Mac in 2006. Liam Snr, known as Blackie, was a member of the 1964 All-Ireland intermediate hurling championship-winning Wexford team, and played with St. Martin's team, Piercestown.

Butler, Lucia, London, formerly Newcastle, Newbawn, born Wexford 1967; PRO of the London Wexford Association; professional photographer and presenter on Irish country music radio; she is the holder of two All-Ireland U16 Ladies' Football medals playing with Wexford; second youngest of a family of eleven, Lucia has a family of three.

Butler, Rev. Thomas C.,O.S.A., a native of Glynn, is the author of a history of the Augustinian priories in New Ross and Clonmines entitled *Near Restful Waters*, which was published in 1975. He also published a number of other historical works, including a history of Bannow parish.

Buttle, Eamonn, Ferrycarrig House, Crossabeg, Managing Director, South East Radio. A native of Oulart, Eamonn first got involved with the media through ownership of *The Echo* newspapers group, where he was Managing Director while his brother, Norman, was chairman of the group. The Buttles sold *The Echo* titles in 2006. Eamonn has been MD at South East Radio since it began broadcasting in 1989 and is also a former chairman of the Independent Broadcasters of Ireland and former board member of the Advertising Standards of Ireland. He is married to Mary and the couple have two daughters, Yvonne and Louise.

Buttle, Liam, Knocknasillogue, Blackwater, farmer, married to Catherine; Wexford Person of the Year 2006; former chairperson of Irish Kidney Association; treasurer Blackwater GAA Club; supporter IHCPT, the Children's Pilgrimage Trust. He has made a huge contribution to life in Blackwater with his voluntary work.

Byrne, Cathal, Moneycross, Gorey, born Wexford 1979, professional Elvis impersonator; son of Charlie and Ruth, Springmount; won National Elvis Impersonator competition in 2009 and was runner up in Ultimate Elvis Tribute Artist Contest in Gracelands 2010.

Byrne, V. Rev. Felix, Monaseed, born 1929, retired Parish Priest; son of James and Mary Catherine, née Noctor, Ballygullen, Camolin; he has two sisters and one brother; retired to Monaseed having served in Bree, Askamore, Kilmore Quay and Rathangan; very active volunteer for the Bóthar, having organised countless shipments of heifers and goats to countries such as Albania and Kosovo and all across North Africa; has also raised thousands of euro for Bóthar.

Byrne, Hugh, Gusserane, born 1943, represented Wexford as a Fianna Fáil TD for a total of eighteen years, and served as a Minister of State for Marine and Natural Resources. He lost his seat in the 1989 General Election, but was nominated by the Taoiseach to Seanad Éireann. He regained his Dáil seat in the 1992 election. And finally lost out to his party colleague, Tony Dempsey, in the 2002 General Election, when Fianna Fáil was trying to win three seats in the constituency. He played senior football for Wexford and was a member of the Kildare senior hurling team.

Byrne, Jim, Gaelic footballer, administrator and referee. A National School teacher and native of Ballymurphy, Co. Carlow, he came to teach in Poulfur in 1910 and was made principal of Kilrane NS in 1920. He played for Wexford in the six All-Ireland football finals in succession, 1913 -1918, winning the last four and being captain in 1918; was noted for the accuracy of his long-range free-taking; served as County chairman, secretary, treasurer and Leinster Council Rep. at times between 1923 and 1933; was the first 'Wexford man' to referee a senior All-Ireland final in 1923 when Dublin beat Kerry in football, and he officiated again in 1930 when Kerry beat Monaghan.

Byrne, Larry, St.Helen's, Kilrane, former Wexford inter-county hurler and footballer, schoolteacher, bookshop proprietor and owner and manager of St. Helen's Bay Golf Resort for the past twenty years. A native of Duncormick, Larry and his wife, Marie, revamped St. Helen's through participation in the RTÉ series *At Your Service* in 2012. He set up Rosslare Activity Centre and works with Club Choice Ireland which markets golf in UK and Europe. He and Marie are also involved in Sports For Africa with fund raisers at St. Helen's.

Byrne, Mick, RIP, Ballyfad, unofficial maintenance man at Ballyfad National school; won many acting awards on the Confined Drama Festival circuit; took part in many Scór and Réadóirí competitions where recitation was his forte; made stage sets for all the school plays; volunteer at all church activities and member of the local praesidium of the Legion of Mary.

Byrne, Miles, 1798 rebel, born in Ballylusk in the parish of Kilanerin. He was an only son but had two sisters, one of whom died young. At the age of 18 he joined the United Irishmen and was prominent at the Battle of Vinegar Hill. He escaped after defeat and with a few companions made his way to Glenmalure where he joined forces with the famous Michael Dwyer. Miles attempted to make his way back to Ballylusk as he was worried about his mother, but owing to the brutal

activities of the yeomen, he had to escape secretly to Dublin. In 1803 he became one of Robert Emmet's officers. Before the failure of Emmet's rising, Emmet had entrusted Miles with a message for his brother, Thomas Addis Emmet, who was the United Irishmen's agent to Napoleon in Paris. Miles carried out the task but never returned to Ireland. Following the creation of the Irish Legion, he eventually became a captain and served throughout the Napoleonic campaigns of 1804-15. An account of his experiences is set out in *Memoirs of Miles Byrne*, published in three volumes in 1863. He died in 1862 and is buried in Monmartre Cemetery, Paris. Kilanerin and Wexford are mentioned on his tombstone.

Byrne, Paddy, Scar, Duncormick, born Wexford 1947, farmer and former ESB worker; married to Eileen, née O'Keeffe, Mulrankin, they have six sons; chairman of Cleariestown Credit Union on which he wrote a treatise; produced book, *Rathangan-a parish and its people*; former chairman of local athletics club when they won National League in 1985, and former County chairman. Paddy's grandfather, Pat, was last blacksmith to work in the local forge in the 1940s, and his great great grandfather, James, worked the forge in Ballindaggin. Tradition has it that James and Pat made pikes there in 1798. Eileen's father was a founder member of the Mayglass Céilí band.

Byrne, Peter, Curraghnaboola, Bree; retired dairy farmer; married to Anne, née Kehoe, Ballybane, Davidstown, they have five daughters and one son; scriptwriter and producer of Parish Tops in 60s and 70s when there were six Tops' groups in the parish; winner of nine All-Irelands with Macra na Feirme; was involved in athletics for the Community Games but when drama section was introduced, he embraced it and Bree brought to Wexford the first drama gold medals in 1981. Wexford have been the leading lights in drama at the national finals ever since, battling it out most years against teams from Kildare and Clare for the top placings. Peter was the County Registrar for over 20 years as well. He is very involved with biennial publication of *Bree Parish Journal*, with his daughter Clare and her husband Jim. In 2005, he published book of poetry, *A View from Bree Hill.*

Byrne, Phelim, Blackwater, owner of Phelim Byrne's Seasuir Catering and Events, Wexford, Naas and Dublin. Phelim has awards with distinctions in professional cookery from City and Guilds, London, FETAC Ireland and Johnson and Wales University in the USA; honed his craft in Kelly's Hotel Rosslare, the Park Hotel Kenmare and Dunbrody Country House Hotel, Arthurstown; most recently gained a certificate in Nutrition from FETAC Ireland; contributes regularly to national TV, Radio and newspaper articles; married to Evette from Hungary, the couple currently live in Dublin.

Cahill, Breda, Ballybrittas, Bree, President of the New York-Wexford Association. She is daughter of the late William 'Grace' Cahill, well known in the GAA and Fianna Fáil, and Anna, née, Doyle of the 'Farmer' Doyle family; she has one sister, Anna, and two brothers, Martin and her twin, Bill; attended Coláiste Bríde, Enniscorthy; elected leader of the Bree Church choir at the age of 14; attended Waterford Regional Technical College and received a national certificate in law studies; holds an extra-mural diploma in social studies from St. Patrick's College, Maynooth; emigrated to the US in 1995 and now has her own catering and hospitality business; very involved in GAA in New York; elected chairperson of Éire Óg Football Club on Long Island, which won the Junior B Division title during her term of office; the only woman to be elected to the Gaelic Park Lease Committee; one of the main organisers of the Wexford Hurling Supporters' Club fundraisers in Runyan's in New York in 1996 for underage hurling and football in her native county; winner of Dreamer of Dreams business awards; former vice-president of the Irish Business Organisation of New York; is vice-president of New York Flooring.

Cahill, Ken, Taghmon, local man who has overseen the growth of Irish Pride Bakeries Taghmon to become one of the biggest bakeries in the country. He worked as bakery manager for eight years and became operations director in 2006. A new, state-of-the-art soft rolls' plant at Taghmon, was opened in 2006 following an investment of €10 million.

Callaghan, Pat, Castlehayestown, born Wexford 1965, mixed farmer; actor; traditional Irish singer; raconteur; winner of numerous Scór competitions; sang Amhrán na bhFiann at Wexford V Dublin Leinster SHC Quarter Final in Wexford Park in June 2013.

Calvert, George, the 1st Lord Baltimore, 1578/9 -1632. The man who gave his name to the city in the US state of Maryland, established a residence at Clohamon Castle prior to establishing colonies in Newfoundland and later in Maryland. He was a Member of Parliament and Secretary of State during the reign of James l of England and owned large tracts of land in the Clohamon area during the seventeenth century. The site of the castle is still visible in Clohamon and was excavated by archaeologists from Newfoundland in 2009.

Campbell-Sharpe, Noelle, née Roche, born Wexford 1943; attended St. John of God Convent, Wexford. She became known nationally as the editor of *Success* magazine and as the publisher of *Irish Tatler* magazine in Dublin in the 1970s. In the 1980s, she was featured among Ireland's 1,000 most influential people in *Who's Who in Ireland*. She is now known internationally as the founder in 1995 of Cill Rialaig Arts Centre at Ballinskelligs in south-west Kerry, where more than 2,500 professional artists, writers, poets and composers from Ireland and around the world have lived making it an important centre for creativity, contemporary art, fine craft, food and exhibitions, programmes and workshops.

Canavan Bolger, Thérèse, Enniscorthy, classically-trained mezzo-soprano; married to Pat; musical director of Enniscorthy Gospel Choir; past member of The Irish Youth Choir, Enniscorthy Choral Society, Wexford Youth Choir and St. Aidan's Cathedral Choir, she has performed as a soloist at the Wexford Opera Festival and with The Wexford Festival Singers. In 2008, Thérèse, was a soloist for three of the Easter Ceremonies which were broadcast live on RTÉ Television.

Carroll, Ann, née Foley, Fethard, married to Joe, they have three daughters, two of whom are involved in lifeboat and water boat rescue; current chairperson of community hall in Fethard and overseeing major renovations; actively involved in running water safety classes for the last twelve years; involved in running bingo every week in the hall.

Carroll, Edward, was born at Courtnacuddy and went to Mr O'Neill's school circa 1826. He trained in horticulture at Carew's of Castleboro and later at the botanical gardens in Dublin. He pioneered the introduction of fodder crops such as mangolds and edited the *Farmer's Gazette*. He adored Lord Carew of Castleboro.

Carroll, Larry, New York, born Enniscorthy 1982, real estate agent and director of the Vortex Group on Lexington Avenue in downtown Manhattan; son of Aidan and Mary, Bellefield; graduated with an engineering degree from DIT and construction management from University of Ulster. He went to New York in 2007 and is an active member of the Irish community there. His job with Vortex entails representing tenants in their commercial real estate leasing interests in Manhattan. Married to Courtney, a native New Yorker, Larry proposed to her at the top of Hook Lighthouse.

> Wexford GAA first adopted purple and gold as county colours in 1913.

Carroll, Michael, Kilmannon, Cleariestown, born in Dublin 1966, self-employed IT computer technical support; married to Bríd, née Kehoe, Laois, they have three children, Chloe, Vincent and Michael Junior. Michael but came to Wexford at a young age his mother being one of the Lett family of Wexford town. He was given a soldering iron when he was seven and has been working with electronics ever since. He studied computer programming in Waterford Regional Technical College. Michael is the technical expert with Wexford Paranormal. He is also chairman of the Joint Committee of Communities which is involved with objecting to the building of the motorway from Oylegate to Rosslare.

Carroll, Pat, RIP, Kilanerin, member of Kilanerin/Ballyfad GAA Club since 1953 and trained under-age teams for the Rackard League. He is a fondly remembered trainer, mentor and counsellor of youth in the parish.

Carthy, Jack, was a huge influence in Wexford soccer due to his work with Wexford Albion schoolboys' club, the Wexford and District Schoolboys' League, where he was secretary for many years, and also the Wexford Referees' Society, where he served first as a referee, before becoming chairman of the society, a position he also held for a long time. Jack was one of the few people from outside Dublin to be elected as president of the Schoolboys' Football Association of Ireland.

Carthy, Leo, 1929-2010, Our Lady's Island; married to Anne, née Pettitt, Moortown, Ballymitty, they have one daughter and two sons; Independent Wexford County Councillor for 49 years; played for Our Lady's Island GAA Club, coached camogie teams and refereed; served as chairman of the club and president; chairman of the County Wexford Handball Board; founder member of Comhaltas Ceoltóirí Éireann in Wexford; member of the Mayglass Céilí Band; founding member of the Carne Mummers and founded the Our Lady's Island Junior Mummers.

Carthy, Michael, GAA player with Wexford and Castletown/Liam Mellows was inducted into the Leinster Hall of Fame in 2013 to mark his years of service to club and county. He won a Leinster minor football medal with Wexford in 1969, and played U21 hurling and football for the county and played senior football for Wexford from 1971 to 1985. He won Dublin senior football medals with UCD, and captained them to All-Ireland club title in 1975 and received the Andy Merrigan Cup, named in honour of a Castletown club mate who had died in an accident. He won five Sigerson Cup University titles with UCD and six Wexford senior titles with Castletown. Michael was Wexford footballer of the year in 1973 and 76 and was a replacement All Star in 1977. He is vice-principal at St. Mary's CBS secondary school, Enniscorthy, and has coached at club and school levels.

Carthy, Mikey, from King St. in Wexford is a legendary servant to soccer in Wexford. Mikey was secretary/treasurer of Park Hotspur football club for over 40 years until the club's demise in 2013. He also served as the treasurer of the Wexford and District Schoolboys' League for many years now. A printer by trade, Mikey's day job is as a journalist with *The Echo* newspaper where he covers all sports outside of GAA, from rowing to horseshoe throwing, and everything in between.

Carton, Pat, 1939-2013, Kilanerin, ex-Sergeant Irish army and UN veteran; only son of the late Edward and Dorothy, Croghan; retired 1985 after three tours of duty – the Congo, Cyprus and Lebanon; physical trainer with Rangers wing in The Curragh; after retirement worked in Forest Park Leisure Centre before going to manage Blitzgym in Gorey Business Park; also helped train Kilanerin GAA teams for 18 years.

Carty, James, who was born in Wexford in 1901, was Assistant Librarian in the National Library and wrote two bibliographies, *Bibliography of Irish History, 1870 to 1912* and *Bibliography of Irish History 1912 to 1921*. He also wrote *Ireland from the Flight of the Earls to Grattan's Parliament, Ireland from Grattan's Parliament to the Great Famine* and *Ireland from the Great Famine to the Treaty*.

Carty, Paddy, 1907-1989, Killowen, Crossabeg, mixed farmer, married to Catherine McGinley, Glasgow, 1919-1989, they had four daughters; National Hunt horse breeder – winner of 18 silver medals at RDS; winner of several point to points, once with Denis O'Brien, Aidan's father, on board; his brother, Harry, Galbally, Crossabeg, well-known breeder of shorthorn cattle and was the winner of many prizes at the county and Spring shows.

Casey, Philip, was born to Irish parents in London in 1950 and grew up in Co. Wexford. His verse collections are *Those Distant Summers, After Thunder, The Year of the Knife* and *Dialogue in Fading Light.* His play *Cardinal* was performed in Hamburg in 1990. His novels are *The Fabulists, The Water Star* and *The Fisher Child,* which completes *The Bann River Trilogy.* He was awarded the inaugural Kerry Ingredients/ Listowel Writers' Week Novel of the Year Award 1995 for *The Fabulists.*

Caulfield, James, Slaney Manor, co-founder of Caulfield's SuperValu group; married to Ellen, née Jordan, Rathanna, Co. Carlow, they have three daughters and two sons; in 1961 he and his three brothers bought Hanlon's Pub in the Irishtown, New Ross, which became Caulfield's first Supermarket, others followed in Callan, Ballybeg, Bandon, Tipperary and Wexford; as young man joined the British army travelling to Borneo, the Phillipines and New Zealand; James was on parade in Singapore as the very last governor finished duty; met Group Captain Cheshire, founder of Cheshire Homes organisation, who was the British observer on the Enola Gay; author of *Cricket is an Ancient Irish Game* and *Secret and Silent Men Of 1798.*

Caulfield, Linda, Newtown Road, Wexford, former captain of the Irish Ladies' International Hockey team; she won 151 caps for Ireland. Linda enjoyed a distinguished international career, breaking into her first international squad at the age of 14 and played for Ireland at all levels. She was also ever present on the South East and Leinster teams at all levels. Linda earned her first cap under coach, Riet Kuiper, aged 20 against Russia in 1999 in the right back position. She became an ever-present on the team and three years later passed the first of many milestones when she lined up against England to collect her 50th cap. Her commitment and passion for the game was well known and she duly clocked up her 100th cap against China in 2005. Linda took over the Irish captaincy that year following Lynsey McVicker's retirement. She led Ireland through numerous internationals including the world cup qualifiers in Rome, the Setanta Sports Trophy and the EuroHockey Nations Championship where she earned her 150th cap against the Ukraine on 23rd August 2007. She retired in September 2007.

Caulfield, Serena, artist, owner of the Sweetshop Gallery in Rosslare Strand; graduated with a BA from the Wexford Campus School of Art and Design and an MA in Fine Art in 2009 from the University of Norwich. She has exhibited her work in the UK and Ireland.

Clancy, Sharon, born Co. Wexford 1977, actress and singer; daughter of Mary and Tony, Clonard; attended Guildford School of Acting; former member of Wexford Light Opera Society and Oyster Lane Theatre Group; performs in the West End and on tour having starred in *Jesus Christ Superstar, Mamma Mia, Tonight's the Night, Grease;* game show host on Sky; former Disney cruise performer.

Clarkin, Sean, born New Ross 1941, author of *Without Frenzy* published in 1974. He was the inaugural winner of The Patrick Kavanagh Award in 1971.

Cleary, Brian, born Wexford 1974, executive officer, Clonmel Chamber of Commerce; married to Claire, née Conran, Clonmel, they have two sons and a daughter; graduated with a BA in 1995 from UCD; former member of senior management team at international recruitment consultancy, Greythorn (London); former managing director and proprietor of The Tipperary Recruitment Company; experienced broadcaster having worked with South East Radio, Tipp FM, Clare FM.

Cleary, Eamonn, Dubai UAE, formerly Ballyanne, New Ross, senior tracks and stables manager; married to Natalie, they have three sons, Sean, Liam and Colm; played senior hurling for Wexford 1982-1995 and senior football for Wexford and won numerous county titles with Rathgarogue Cushinstown. He has won county and All-Ireland titles in handball. Eamonn also breeds racehorses. His best so far is a mare called Annie Power which has won seven out of seven to date, and he thinks she will be a superstar, trained by Willie Mullins. Eamonn loves Irish music.

Cloke, Andy, Cloheadon, Caim, Enniscorthy, owns company specialising in structural steel and cladding for the industrial and agricultural sector, which he operates with his sons. Andy and his wife, Joan, set up Chernobyl Child Aid in 2004. The charity works with communities and institutions in areas of Belarus affected by the fallout from the Chernobyl nuclear disaster. Their main projects include bringing children from the nuclear-affected area to Wexford for one month's recuperation each year, providing food and medical aid for the region, and also a number of construction projects which they have undertaken in Belarus.

Cloney, Eileen, Fethard-on-sea, born 1951, daughter of Sean and Sheila; retired farmer and artist, married to Bill Kehoe, Boley, they have one daughter and two sons; daughter of Sean Cloney and Sheila, née Kelly, she grew up in Dungulph Castle with her two sisters, Mary and Hazel; since retiring from years of tending her prized dairy herd, she can now devote more time to her art; has hosted various exhibitions of her works and also teaches art regularly with Catherine Power in Ramsgrange and in the Cockleshell Gallery in Duncannon Fort; was crowned 'Queen of the Land' in 1969 when she was 19; gives historical group talks in the Tintern and Hook area. Her family was at the centre of a notorious mixed marriage dispute in Fethard in the late 1950s when passions were inflamed over whether the Eileen and her late sister Mary should be educated in a Catholic or Protestant school. It garnered international news headlines at the time and has since been the subject of several books and a film entitled, *A Love Divided*.

Coady, Ciaran, Knockbroad, Taghmon, born 1991; plumber with H&A O'Neill, Gold Medal Winner 2013 at World Skills' Competition in Plumbing and Heating, Leipzig, Germany; one of seven children of John and Kathleen; underwent heart surgery in 2009 and has made a full recovery.

Codd Nolan, Kathleen eldest daughter of the late John and Kitty Codd, of Woodlands, Enniscorthy was elected to Wexford County Council on her first attempt on the Fine Gael party ticket for the Enniscorthy Electoral Area in June 2004. In 2009 she was re-elected topping the poll. In July 2011 she was the second woman to be elected Chairperson of Wexford County Council and the first woman to serve full term. Kathleen is married to Jim Nolan. Her hobbies include sport, reading and history.

> Napoleon's white charger Marengo, was born and bred in Kilmuckridge.

Codd, Larry, RIP 2009, Enniscorthy, Irish billiards champion six times, 1966, '67,'68, '70, '71 and '73; Honed his skill in the Athenaeum and the Working men's club, Weafer Street, both Enniscorthy; also a noted bridge player.

Codd, Martin, 1929-2008, Clonroche, hurler and singer; played for Wexford between 1949 and 1965; was on the team that beat Cork in the famous 1956 final and won National League medal in 1958, strangely, he had to wait until 1965 to win his first Leinster medal; won three senior hurling medals with Rathnure, and also captained them to a senior football title in 1952; was a popular musician and singer, fronting the Herdsmen Showband for some years, and was also a solo performer. In later years recorded Tom Williams' tribute to Nickey Rackard, Cúchulainn's Son; published his story in a memoir, *The Way I Saw It – Nickey Rackard Leads Wexford to Hurling Glory*. His son, Paul, was on the winning Wexford panel in the 1996 All-Ireland hurling final and played for Wexford and Rathnure for many years.

Codd, Martin Jnr aka 'Slim', born Wexford 1951, Corrigeen, Rathnure, stonemason, musician, married to Margaret, née Murphy, Rathnure, they have two sons and three daughters; son of Martin Codd Snr., the iconic 1950s and 60s Wexford and Rathnure hurler and accomplished musician, and Kitty née Reddy, Rathnure; his grandmother was a piano player from Albany, New York; beginning musical career at thirteen, he travelled all over Ireland and England with The Herdsmen, has produced numerous albums and has shared stages with Roger Whittaker and Hank Locklin among others; involved with numerous charitable initiatives in the parish.

Codd, Patrick 'Pat', RIP 2006, was a Fine Gael politician from Enniscorthy. He was elected to Seanad Éireann on the Agricultural Panel at a by-election in April, 1975. He was unsuccessful in the 1977 General Election and did not contest subsequent Seanad elections. He sought a Fine Gael nomination for the 1982 General Election, but, at the selection conference, he was beaten by Ivan Yates.

Codd, Pat, Dungeer, Taghmon, born 1938, Fine Gael member of Wexford County Council. Just lost out in the 1991 local elections, was then co-opted onto the council and has been re-elected in subsequent elections. A retired dairy farmer, he left school early to work on the family farm. He married Alice in 1963 and moved to Dungeer where the couple had a family of eleven. Has announced he is not seeking re-election to Wexford County Council.

Codd, Seamus, Newtown Road, Wexford, retired bank manager and consultant. A native of Drinagh, Seamus Codd began his working life as an agricultural adviser but spent most of his career working in ACC Bank where he finished up as branch manager in Wexford town. Upon retirement in 2001, he set up TUS, a rural development initiative aimed at improving farm incomes under the umbrella of the Leader Programme in Wexford. Married to Joan, née Meyler, with a grown up family, Seamus has a long time involvement with County Wexford Mental Health Association.

Cody, Liam, Ballyrue, New Ross, born 1998; swimming gold medallist 2012 Special Olympics; son of Tommy and Mary, née Hennessy; he has one brother, Brian; currently a student Our Lady of Lourdes Secondary School in Wexford; trains twice weekly with personal coach and with the national team.

Cogley, Kevin, Wexford town, athlete, son of Wally and Margaret, Liam Mellows Park; has won a string of national sprinting and long jump titles at all levels; was selected for Ireland for World Junior championships, World Senior Championships in Athens 1997 and European championships; founder member of the Menapians club and has helped them to become a major force. Kevin has also been involved in helping a number of county and club teams in various disciplines.

Colfer, Aoife, Blackhall, Bannow, born Wexford 1988; works at Special Occupational Services, Kilkenny city; daughter of Mark and Mary née Doyle, Raheen; fiddle player and member of Bannow Ceoltas Ceoltóirí Éireann; won senior lilting at All-Ireland Fleadh Cheoil in Derry 2013.

Colfer, Billy, Slade, who died in 2013, was a retired primary school teacher in Wexford. He was one of the foremost authorities on mediaeval Wexford, and his historical works earned him international acclaim. His books included: *The Promontory, The County of Wexford, Historic Hook Head, The Ethnic Mix in Medieval Wexford, Arrogant Trespass – Anglo Norman Wexford* and *Wexford's Castles*. He was also a talented artist.

Colfer, Eoin, son of Billy, born May 14, 1965 is a global phenomenon in terms of children's literature, science fiction and adventure books, being specially famous for his eight-book *Artemis Fowl* series which has sold more than 25 million copies worldwide and has been translated into 44 languages; was a school teacher before taking up writing full time. His other work includes, *Benny and Omar* (1998), *Ed's Funny Feet, Ed's Bed, The Wish List*; three books in the Eoin Colfer Legends series: *Half Moon Investigation, Airman*, etc. He was commissioned to write the sixth instalment of *The Hitchhikers' Guide to the Galaxy* in 2009, *And Another Thing*, following on from the late Douglas Adams. In 2010, *Artemis Fowl* was voted Britain's all-time favourite Puffin book. He has more recently written two books for adults, *Plugged* (2011) and *Screwed* (2013) and has started a new children's series *WARP*. It has been announced that Disney Pictures have signed a contract to film the first two *Artemis Fowl* books, supported by some of the top Hollywood talent. Eoin officially opened the 62nd Wexford Opera Festival in October 2013. He is married to Jackie and they have two sons, Sean and Finn.

Colfer, Maria, née Doyle, Camross, chairperson of Christian Media Trust, she manages radio programmes from four main churches produced for South East Radio; married to Martin, they have one son, Lloyd, who works in London. Both Maria and Martin have degrees in theology. She is the inspiration of the Camross millennium year Passion Play modelled on the Oberammergau production. She has been actively involved in subsequent productions of the play in 2006 and 2012.

② History

County Wexford's rich cultural tapestry is woven with threads of the cultures and traditions of Vikings, Normans, Celts, French, Spanish and English who invaded this strategically placed maritime county.

'The Bishop of Ferns is to inform himself of the destruction by fire of the monuments of the Priory of Saints Peter and Paul by Selskar, which is almost at the end of the world in Ireland'.

(Papal records, CPL III 565 Mandate to Bishop of Ferns on 5 Kal. January, 1355)

THE COUNTY WEXFORD, HISTORY AND HERITAGE

by Nicholas Furlong

County Wexford is possessed of properties unique in Ireland because of geological and geographic coincidence. Wexford's eastern boundary is the Irish Sea. Its southern boundary is the vast Atlantic Ocean. Wexford's earliest inhabitants left records of their hunting and fishing techniques on her south-eastern beaches nine thousand years ago.

Until the discovery of the Americas at the dawn of the sixteenth century, Ireland was the last land in the known world. The consequences for southern Ireland and County Wexford were both profitable and dire. All shipping, naval or merchant, bound for North America, in order to synchronise with the curvature of the earth, had to pass by Ireland's deep and wide harbours of enormous potential.

As we know today massive cruise vessels enter by Hook Head up to Waterford Harbour where they can enter, turn and exit with facility. Three rival naval powers, France, Spain and England, realised that whoever controlled these harbours controlled the North Atlantic.

The Crown Forces at Vinegar Hill, August 2013. Re-enactment of 1798 Rebellion 21st June.

England had a bridgehead, constantly undermined by Spain and later France. Wexford's Franciscan Friary was equal to a Spanish Embassy with intimate contact with the royal court of Spain. The perils and the stakes in the great European wars led to the ferocity of the blood and unremitting hatreds in which Ireland and Wexford suffered up to modern times.

These then were the stage sets within which County Wexford developed, a minor geographical kingdom and province where travel by water was easier, cheaper and safer. The admirable ethnic group to follow early Wexford man were the farmers who found out where the most fertile land was and studded our country with spectacularly sophisticated monuments, tombs and fortresses.

Mainland European groups, deemed Celtic, anchored in Brittany, Cornwall, Wales and Scotland. The group of peoples of Gaelic-speaking culture and language dominated Ireland's indigenous population eventually. Though culturally united, they were politically divided.

Uí Chennselaig was the Gaelic kingdom's name covering counties Wexford, Carlow, south Wicklow and east Kilkenny. Its ruling family which emerged from remote pre-history as kings were later called Mac Murrough. The soils in County Wexford, the basis of wealth and power, varied from the most fertile in Europe to a lesser type of poor draining. The powerful families are always found on rich soils, for example Mac Murroughs in Ferns.

The Norsemen arrived in Wexford, then called Loch Garman, when they raided Begerin's sacred monastic

And tomorrow the Barrow we'll cross.

island in AD 819 From that time the Annals recorded them as 'The Foreigners at Loch Garman'. From raiders they became traders in position here for 350 years. They called their citadel, south of the existing Loch Garman community, Weissfjord, the fiord of the (mud) flats.

The reports of the strange man who, after cruel execution, rose from his tomb after three days, arrived in Wexford before St. Patrick's more publicised mission. The strange man was Christ. His teaching was that human beings must love and respect each other. That earliest missioner was Ibar, in Gaelic Iúbhar, in Latin Iberius, in local dialect Iver. Though unacceptable to many Christianity made progress. The wise strategy for Ibar was to introduce the new teaching in the established sites of pre-Christian worship.

Towards the end of the seven hundreds AD, the Norsemen burst out from Scandinavia. The extent of their long reach is astonishing. For their boats they had invented the keel. It was boasted that their seamen could sail on six inches of water. They raided Ferns by the River Slaney. In time they just became part of the succession wars in Ireland. They marched as hired mercenaries in the usual tradition, whether in Wales, England or with Mac Murroughs fighting for any paymaster but especially to install a Mac Murrough to become the most powerful ruler in Ireland.

In that desperate situation, with Dermot the King only a heartbeat from ultimate power, Mac Murrough was overthrown. He sought reciprocal help from the Norman Henry II. Granted permission to recruit, he offered bribes acceptable to Flemish and Norman knights in Wales. So was introduced another foreign flavour. The Norman French were originally from Scandinavia as were the Wexford Norse. Soon they had replaced and uprooted their blood cousins from their towns and properties in Wexford. The year was 1169. Dermot Mac Murrough died on May 1, 1171. He was succeeded by his brother Murrough, but the master administrator had left a terrible void.

The course of events from the twelfth century on is known (I hope) to every school-goer. The industrious Norman policy of intermarriage with Gaelic families of substantial power and, in time co-existence with the Gaelic principles, proceeded. The Mac Murroughs claimed kingship of Leinster until the seventeenth century. The major disruption in Church and State, severe and deceptive in County Wexford, occurred with the split of Henry VIII with Rome plus the strict Reformation by his successors.

The greatest slaughter of Gaelic culture, power and property took place with the Great Rebellion (1641 – 1649) which crucially involved County Wexford, its ports and its active aggression. Cromwell's invasion in 1649 his plantations and evictions completed the devastation. Spirit and morale died until the French Revolution urged the growth of rebellion which exploded here with Vietnam-like ferocity in May, 1798.

The sea, shipping and exports to Europe's great ports as far as the Danube and Odessa showed that, as today, Wexford's soils produced world-standard malting barley. As for Wexford's inhabitants orchestrating many ethnic origins today the census records the names, Irish, Norse, French, Norman, Welsh and English to whom we now must add Chinese, African, Indian, Italian and Filipino. They are all an integral part of the County Wexford kaleidoscope.

A COMPLEX CULTURE

By Declan Lyons

Culture is the sum of all those things with which we value and define ourselves. Wexford's cultural heritage is washed by the seas and nurtured on the land. It is a rich and varied culture with complex roots and a flowering in myriad forms. The sea has had a major influence on life in Wexford. The first settlers probably arrived by sea and used the rivers Slaney and Suir to penetrate the hinterland. Others swept in from foreign shores to invade, dominate and eventually integrate. Each migratory wave has added its distinct contribution to the county's culture.

Wexford's first settlers left few remains. Portal tombs such as one found at Ballybrittas along with the other Neolithic remains scattered over the county have been incorporated into the myths, and stories of giants' beds and fairy forts still told to this day. While the myths are local, the design and construction points to people who came from the west coast of France. They are physical evidence of the close and enduring bonds between Wexford people and those in coastal France.

Christianity established an early foothold in the county. These early proselytizers absorbed Celtic myths and beliefs. Our holy wells and pilgrimage sites stretch back across the millennia to pagan times but now with a Christian brand. Christian thought, art and architecture have been subsumed into Wexford's culture and way of being.

Vikings gave us our name and influenced our culture deeply. They built our towns and brought new forms of art and technology. The Normans shaped the landscape and exploited the land in new and different ways. English forces came and went too – all influenced our culture and were eventually assimilated and made our own.

Our language is English spoken with a Gaelic twist. The Wexford rolling "r" sounds more French than English. The county had, up until two hundred years ago, its own unique Angle language, Yola, and there are relics of this in the middle of the county to this day.

Amateur dramatics capture the cultural spirit and passion of Wexford people. They foster local playwrights and Billy Roche has gone on to achieve international renown through his plays documenting and celebrating Wexford, its people, their lives and dramas. Colm Tóibín, John Banville and Eoin Colfer are authors with Wexford roots who are celebrated internationally.

Wexford's music mirrors it history. The Wexford or Enniscorthy Carol is one of the oldest carols in the western European Christian tradition. Its emphasis on the poverty of the holy family finds a resonance in the ballads commemorating 1798. Today, Wexford celebrates its musical heritage through festivals such as those held in New Ross, Enniscorthy and the internationally renowned opera festival in Wexford town.

For me, it is the architectural environment that crystallises Wexford's culture. Whether it is the majesty of Enniscorthy castle or high church splendour of that town's Pugin cathedral, the simplicity of the thatched cottages of Carne or modern farmhouses abutting the remains of a Norman keep. These buildings are physical manifestations of a culture rooted in its environment with a strong sense of place.

Declan Lyons, author and management consultant, Arthurstown and Dublin, advised on Co. Wexford's 'Strategy for Cultural Development 2001–2010.'

COUNTY WEXFORD'S NATURAL HERITAGE

by Jim Hurley

County Wexford has a very rich natural heritage, a remarkable climate and a great diversity of rocks, soils, plants and animals on land, in the coastal zone and on the surrounding sea bed.

Some would argue that the island of Ireland is too small to support different climates but the Sunny South-east is a place apart in that both its southerly location away from the direct influence of the Atlantic Ocean and its low-lying coastal plains result in it returning the highest, long-term, number of hours of bright sunshine per year of anywhere on the island together with low rainfall levels that ensure that blanket peat does not grow at sea level.

The elevated, majestic, rounded, granite domes of the Blackstairs Mountains on the north-western flank of the county give way to a gently undulating interior that in turn drops to two low-lying coastal plains one bordering the east coast and the Irish Sea, the other bordering the south coast and the Celtic Sea.

Geological sites range from the rocks at Kilmore Quay that are among the oldest found in Ireland to the amazing fossils to be found so easily and so abundantly in the limestone rocks at Hook Head.

The county's deep, rich soils are part of the legacy of the last ice age as are the fossil pingos at Camross, the kame and kettle landform around Screen, the raised beaches, eskers and moraines and the magnificent fringing barriers and their associated back-barrier, brackish, lagoons at Tachumshin Lake and Lady's Island Lake on the south coast.

A provisional list of 38 sites of geological and geomorphological interest is presented in Wexford County Council's Biodiversity Action Plan 2012-2017 and details can be accessed at http://www.wexford.ie/wex/Departments/Environment/Biodiversity/Thefile,21563,en.pdf.

Places that are legally protected because they support the very best of our wildlife heritage are called 'Natura 2000 sites'. Some 26,000 of these important sites are scattered throughout the territories of the 28 member states of the European Union; 20 of them are found in County Wexford clustered at five main locations.

The greatest concentration of Natura 2000 sites in on the South Wexford Coast. That amazing 20km coastal strip supports eight sites: Hook Head, Bannow Bay, Keeragh Islands, Ballyteige Burrow, Saltee Islands, Tachumshin Lake, Lady's Island Lake and Carnsore Point. Next comes the complex with five sites close to Wexford town comprising Wexford Harbour and Slobs, The Raven, Screen Hills, Blackwater Bank and Long Bank followed by a group of four important sites along the east coast: Cahore Marshes, Cahore Polders and Dunes, Kilmuckridge-Tinnaberna Sandhills and Kilpatrick Sandhills. The three remaining sites are the Slaney River Valley, Blackstairs Mountains and the estuary of the River Barrow.

These Natura 2000 sites support a wealth of heritage impossible to describe in this brief overview. For those who want further detail, the website of the government's National Parks and Wildlife Service (NPWS) at www.npws.ie has a full site description and conservation objectives for each of the 20 sites together with maps of the protected areas.

COUNTY WEXFORD DYNASTIES

They are families. Some have endured all kinds of difficulties to keep their roots and the family name intact in the one place or in the one skill or profession for 100 years or even 300 years. They are predominantly in farming, business, sport, politics, academia, maritime. They are not necessarily advantaged, but they are 'always there'. They are dynasties.

Ashmores of Ferns
Asples of Galbally

Banvilles of Wexford
Banvilles of Barry's Cross
Barrys of Tacumshane
Bates of Kilmore
Bolgers of Ferns
Bolgers of Oylegate
Bolgers of Marshalstown
Bowes of Ballinadara
Bowes of Kiltealy
Boxwells of Kilmore
Brownes of Mulrankin
Breens of Redmoor
Breens of Blackwater
Buggys of Wexford
Bushers of Wexford
Butlers of Broadway
Buttles of Enniscorthy
Byrnes of Bree
Byrnes of Ballyknock
Byrnes of Blackwater
Byrnes of Curraghnaboola
Byrnes of Clonmore

Cloneys of Dungulph
Codds of Clonroche
Codds of Clonmines
Colclough of Tintern
Colfers of Bannow
Colfers of Slade
Connicks of New Ross
Corishs of Wexford
Creans of Ballyhogue
Conways of Ballycullane
Cowmans of Monmore
Cullens of Ballyfad

Curtis of Garrenstackle
Darcys of Ballyhogue
D'Arcys of Gorey
Dempseys of Ballymorris
Devereaux of Wexford
Doyles of White Mountain

Egans of Barmoney
Elgee of Wexford
Englishes of Tomfarney, Camross and Newbawn

Fardys of Haresmead
Funges of Gorey
Floods of Castleboro
Foleys of Crossabeg
Foleys of Newbawn
Foleys of Templetown
Fortunes of Doonooney
Fitzhenrys of Barntown
Furlongs of Castleview, Adamstown
Furlongs of Drinagh

Grahams of Gorey

Hearnes of Fethard
Hores of Wexford

Kavanaghs of Enniscorthy
Kennedys of Sheilbaggan
Kehoes of Clonleigh
Kehoes of Boolabeg
Kellys of Kilgarvan
Kellys of Hayestown
Kennedys of Sheilbaggan
Kehoe of Boolabawn
Kehoes of Glynn
Kinsellas of Killeens

Hamiltons of Trinity

Laffans of Wexford

McCormacks of Ballymitty

McDonalds of Crossabeg
Mernaghs of Oylegate and Bree
Mernaghs of Davidstown
Meylers of Blackhall
Morrisseys of Camross
Murphys of Randlesmill
Murphys of Ballylough
Murphys of Tillidavins
Murphys of the Bridge
Murphys of Clonsharragh
Murphys of Cromogue
Murphys of Kereight
Murphys of Tomhaggard and Screen

Nevilles of Ballymitty
Nevilles of Curracloe
Nolans of Wexford town

The O Morchoe, Tara Hill
O'Connors of Wexford
O'Dwyers of Heathpark
O'Gormans of Poulpeasty
Orpens of Monksgrange

Nevilles of Ballymitty
Nevilles of Castlebridge
Nevilles of Curracloe
Nunns of Castlebridge

O'Connors of Sweetfarm
O'Briens of Cromogue
O'Briens of Monageer

Pierces of Park

Pierces of Blackhall

Quigleys of Rathnure

Rams of Gorey
Rackards of Killanne
Raths of Monageer
Redmonds of Bunclody
Roches of Garrylough
Rochfords of Camross
Rothwells of Adamstown

Seerys of Taghmon
Sidneys of Taghmon
Shannons of Newbawn
Shortles of Castlebridge
Sinnott's of Crossabeg
Sinnott's of Wexford
Staffords of Wexford
Staffords of Monageer
Sweetmans of Ballymackessy
Sweetmans of Newbawn
Sweetmans of Ballycourcey
Sweetmans of Lambstown

Youngs of Horetown

Wallaces of Wellingtonbridge
Walsh's of Coolcull, Taghmon
Warrens of Gorey
Wickhams of Rosslare
Williams of Taghmon
Whelans of Adamstown/ Barmoney
Whelans of Ballycullane
Whelans of Blackwater
Whites of Bannow

Yates of Blackstoops

THE NUNN FAMILY- LANDOWNERS, MALSTERS AND MILITARY

By Eddie Jordan, Historian

The Nunn family of Wexford are Cromwellian in origin and are descended from one Captain Richard Nunn, a Cavalry Officer. Captain Nunn was the first of seven consecutive generations of the family to be appointed High Sheriff of the County, a position of great authority and responsibility.

Following the Cromwellian Conquest, the family thrived in Wexford and established seats at St. Margaret's, Hillcastle, Silverspring in Ballycogley, Rosehill in Enniscorthy, Alma House in Ferrycarrig and Castlebridge House, to name but a few. They were among the largest landowners in the Baronies of Forth and Bargy.

The Nunns were early innovators and entrepreneurs as can be seen from their many successful business ventures. Benjamin Nunn from Hillcastle operated the largest and most modern papermill in the British Isles

On the rocks at Slade.

in the late-eighteenth century in the foothills of the Dublin Mountains at Rockbrook, while William Bolton Nunn and his descendants at Castlebridge were the main supplier of malted barley to the Guinness Company for over 150 years.

Like so many Anglo-Irish families, the Nunns were also a constant supply of mid-to high-ranking officers for the British Army and almost every generation made the ultimate sacrifice for King and Country. Nunns of Wexford fought and died in almost every conflict in which the British Army was engaged since the seventeenth century.

In addition to the military, the family also produced some of the finest medical men , church ministers and magistrates of their time. The family were among the privileged for whom education was an affordable priority and the Alumni Registers of Trinity College in Dublin bear witness to the many generations of Nunns from the different branches of the family who attended from the earliest records of the College.

In more recent times, Retired Major Joshua Anthony James Nunn, of the 10th Royal Hussars and former Bodyguard to Queen Elizabeth II, sadly passed away in April 2013 in Dorset, the last member of the family to have been born in Wexford, thus severing the centuries-old link between the family and the county.

The Nunns of Wexford are now gone from these shores but have left their mark on the local landscape and history, social, industrial and military.

The Athenaeum, Castle Street, Enniscorthy.

THE ATHENÆUM
ROMANCE, REBELS AND DREAMS

Built in 1892 as a new town hall, The Athenaeum on Castle Street in Enniscorthy was at the heart of the town in every sense of the word. People met there, danced there, laughed and cried, and fell in, and out, of love there. The theatre played host to the most wonderful travelling troubadours and opera and musical companies and produced its own award-winning actors and singers. It had a handball alley, a skating rink, a billiards room and cards and books and warm fires.

Its place in history is forever marked by the events of Easter week 1916 as Óglaigh na hÉireann made The Athenaeum their headquarters during the Rising. Distinguished visitors prior to that included Douglas Hyde and Pádraig Pearse. In 1927 the founders of The Gate Theatre, Micheál MacLiammóir and Hilton Edwards first met in The Athenaeum.

In 2004, the diocesan-owned building was closed because it did not meet fire safety criteria. In late 2008, a public meeting was held to decide its fate and from that sprung the Athenaeum Restoration Fund, a group of volunteers whose only aim was to raise enough money to see the doors of the building open again to the public. A huge fundraising campaign ensued.

Enniscorthy Athenaeum Limited, a registered charity, was incorporated in September 2010, and is run by a board of directors, all still volunteers. In 2013, the directors were granted planning permission for the necessary building works to ensure compliance with all fire safety regulations and permission from the Department of Arts, Heritage and the Gaeltacht to proceed was granted.

The directors of Enniscorthy Athenaeum Limited in 2013 are: Tony McClean, chairperson; Brendan Redmond, vice chairperson; Helen Ashdown, secretary; Josie Flood, joint treasurer; Eileen Redmond, joint treasurer; Paddy Byrne, Annette Byrne, Maura Flannery, Nancy Ashdown, Greta Browne, Maria Nolan and Ursula Clarke Everett.

CLIMBING UP A HILL

by Jacqui Hynes

It's the case that in Enniscorthy you're either physically climbing up, or going down a hill, and the knights and rebels of Enniscorthy are well on the way to the summit of our hill.

The 'Knights and Rebels' experience encompasses the visitor attractions of the National 1798 Rebellion Centre, Vinegar Hill Battlefield, and Enniscorthy Castle, and over the last three years, considerable progress has been made in developing, reinvigorating and promoting our visitor offerings, and working together throughout the town, county and region to promote our sites, the town and the tourist attractions in the county.

The award winning National 1798 Rebellion Centre officially opened in 1998 to coincide with bicentenary commemorations, has over the last two years undertaken considerable work to re-develop, re-brand, and actively promote itself. We have completed a feasibility study entitled 'How to interpret a battlefield', sourced funding to undertake a major re-development, and developed the 'Rebellion' experience, that was launched to great acclaim earlier this year. The centre now tells the emotive story of a rebellion, fanned by flames of revolution in America and France, that is forever etched on the annals of Irish

Enniscorthy Castle.

history. It is vividly retold in an exciting interpretation of events, where visitors meet General Lake, John Shehan (The Croppy Boy), and Miles Byrne, and learn in gruesome detail how some 20,000 insurgents faced the might of 10,000 well-trained and well-armed Crown Forces.

Vinegar Hill Battlefield is a battlefield of national and international significance, and one of the last relatively intact battlefields in Ireland so close to an urban area. It is the most famous site of the 1798 Rebellion, and its current peace, serenity and spectacular views belie its background as one of the bloodiest battlefields in Irish history. On 21 June 1798, the 20,000 faced 10,000 'redcoats' in a battle that lasted only four hours, but left 1,500 dead and a county distraught.

Our last site is the award-winning Enniscorthy Castle. Built in the thirteenth century, it has been 'home' to Norman knights, English armies, Irish rebels and prisoners, and local merchant families. The dungeon also hides the rare medieval wall art – The Swordsman. Our wheelchair-accessible battlements give amazing views of Vinegar Hill Battlefield, Enniscorthy town, and the flora and fauna of the surrounding countryside.

We also undertake a variety of events throughout the year, including the successful Vinegar Hill Battle re-enactment, held on the August bank holiday weekend, and events such as Murder in the Castle, Enniscorthy Castle School of Witches and Wizards, and events to coincide with Heritage Week, Wexford Day, and Strawberry and Street Rhythms Festivals.

Enniscorthy Castle also hosts the Visitor Information Point for Enniscorthy town, and both sites host events for local performers and charities, launches, fundraising and exhibitions, and civil ceremonies and partnerships.

We relish the opportunity of providing our visitors with memorable experiences, and working together as we try to climb our collective hills. However, none of this can be achieved without the support of our staff, voluntary board, colleagues in the tourism and hospitality sector and support agencies such as Wexford County Council, Enniscorthy Town Council, Wexford Local Development and Fáilte Ireland. As some wise person said 'How do you eat an elephant? Piece by piece!

TOWNLAND NAMES IN WEXFORD
A BRIEF DESCRIPTION

By Conchubhar Ó Crualaoich
An Brainse Logainmneacha
An Roinn Ealaíon, Oidhreachta and Gaeltachta

Most townland names in Wexford are from the Irish language. This is particularly the case in the northern baronies of Gorey, Scarawalsh, and Ballaghkeen North/South, where almost all English names such as *Ashwood*, *Barnland*, *Buckstown*, *Burrow*, *Beaufield*, *Hollyfort* (near Craanford), *Grove*, *Jamestown*, *Prospect*, *Corbetstown*, *Cookstown* and *Redmondstown* are either translations from Irish – as in the case of *Jamestown*, *Redmondstown* and *Hollyfort* – or post-1600 'New-English' additions to the townland nomenclature.

In the mid-Wexford baronies of Bantry, Shelmaliere East/West and Shelburne, the percentage of English place-names is much higher, doubtlessly due to the early and relatively successful Anglo-Norman colonisation of lands here. However, place-names in these baronies that contain Anglo-Norman surnames but clearly derive from Irish, such as *Polhore* < Poll an Hóraigh "*Hore's*

pill", *Ballinvegga* < Baile an Bheigigh "*Begg*'s town(land)", *Ballindinas* < Baile an Doimhnisigh "*Devenis*'s townland", and *Garrynstackle* < Garraí an Stacalaigh "*Stackpoole*'s enclosure, garden", demonstrate that the Irish language must have remained in use, or have been re-established, in large parts of these baronies after initial colonisation, before its ultimate demise as a vernacular in the nineteenth century. Even an alias found in the evidence for *Carricklawn*, a townland lying inside the modern boundary of Wexford Town, appears to be from Fearann an tSumaraigh "*Somery*'s land" which contains the Anglo-Norman surname *Somer(y)s*; the occurrence of this gaelicised form of the surname indicates that the (re)gaelicisation of areas colonised by the Anglo-Normans extended to the boundaries of Wexford Town itself.

In the southern baronies of Forth and Bargy, which essentially lie to the south of the Newline Road between Wexford Town and Wellingtonbridge, evidence for the survival of Irish after initial colonisation is much more scant, although place-names of Irish origin which contain

Galbally village in mid Co.Wexford.

Portal tomb at Ballybrittas.

borrowed Anglo-Normans elements, such as *Garryhack* < Garraí Hac and *Grascur* < Gráig Scoir (the elements in question being Hac and gráig), bear witness to the continued vitality of the Irish language in some areas of these baronies even after Anglo-Norman colonisation. In light of this it can be understood that some other place-names of Irish origin in these baronies were coined subsequent to the initial Anglo-Norman colonisation, but most were probably coined prior to this. However, most place-names in these baronies are of English provenance, many containing characteristically 'Wexford' surnames as in *Coddstown, Horetown, Lambertstown, Pettitstown, Rowestown, Rossiterstown, Sinnottstown* and *Waddingsland*, while others feature less well-known Anglo-Norman surnames such as *Dennistown* (< *Dene*), *Danescastle* (< *Dene*), *Latimerstown, Milestown* (< *Moyle*), *Rostonstown* (< *Rawsthorn*) and *Pembrokestown*. Additionally a number of place-names here contain elements of the English dialect formerly spoken in the area, often called Yola; thus while *Horesland* may seem

transparent; it is actually from Yola *hals + lone* "hazel-land". '*Holmanhill* also deceives as it probably has no connection with the surname *Holman*, but apparently consists of an English dialect word for *holly + hill*. Near *Tacumshin* one finds the name *Cotts* which is most likely from the English dialect word *cott* "cottage", and the name apparently pops up again in the well known townland name *Coolcots* "cold cottages" at Wexford Town. Notably, the townlands of *Coldcut* and *Colecot* in Dublin have similar historical forms to *Coolcots* (see *logainm.ie*), and the same construction is found in England in *Calcot* (see *DEPN*). Indeed, the evidence for many English place-names in Forth and Bargy, and occasionally also in mid-Wexford baronies, reflects English dialect traits mirrored in place-names elsewhere in the historical English Pale in Ireland, which suggests that Yola shared many features with the English of this broader area.

Notably, when it comes to Anglo-Norman surnames and English place-names elements of pre-1600 origin in the baronies of Gorey, Scarawalsh, and Ballaghkeen North/South, the well is particularly dry, with only *Brownswood, Nevillescourt* and *Courtown* (doubtlessly gaelicised as Baile na Cúirte prior to 1600) bucking the trend. In fact in the search for Anglo-Norman surnames in this area, it is to place-names of Irish origin that one must look. In doing so one can find names such as *Sinnott* in *Garryntinodagh* < Garraí an tSionóidigh; *Simons* in *Ballysimon* < Baile na Síomonach; *Elliott* in *Ballinellard* < Baile an Eileoidigh; *Wadding* in *Garryvaddenbeg* < Garraí Bhaidín Beag; *Barron* in *Garryvarren* < Garraí Bharún; *Coursey* in *Ballycourcy* < Baile an Chúrsaigh. In fact place-names of this type can be used to plot Anglo-Norman settlement in these baronies, which on occasion augments the archaeological record of such settlement (cf. *archaeology.ie*).

But it is not only numerous Anglo-Norman surnames that emerge from a closer look at the place-names of Irish origin in Wexford. Surnames of Irish origin such as *Murphy* < Ó Murchú, *Boggan* < Ó Beagáin (not Ó Bogáin), *Cogley* < Ó Coigligh, and many more which have well known 'Wexford' pedigrees, are no doubt behind place-names such as *Ballymurragh* < Baile Uí Mhurchú, *Ballyboggan* < Baile Uí Bheagáin, and *Ballycogley* < Baile Uí Choigligh. However, the current research also indicates that many surnames not heretofore given a Wexford pedigree were well established in the county at least by the sixteenth century and may have much older pedigrees in the county. Thus *Ballydarragh* near *Craanford* is not from An Baile Darach "the town(land) of oak" as might be expected at first sight, but the evidence indicates that is most likely from Baile Uí Dhorchaí "Ó Dorchaí's (*Darcy's*) town(land)", and the research indicates that the surname *Darcy* as found in north Wexford is of Gaelic Irish rather than Anglo-Norman origin, the latter being the case for many *Darcys* particularly in the region around Meath. Two further examples of surnames not usually associated with Wexford but which occur in historical place-names are *(O')Gormigan* and *(O')Canavan*; these are most likely behind the now-defunct toponyms Balliygormegan' < Baile Uí Ghormagáin, west of *Ferns*, and 'Ballycanvan' < Baile Uí Cheannabháin? south of *Courtown*, respectively. Notably the anglicised surname *Canavan* is still relatively common in the area around Gorey. In the case of the name Ó Gormagáin appears to have been first anglicised as *(O')Gormigan* or similar, but it was subsequently morphed to *(O')Gorman*, and its original Irish form disguised. While only a small taste of the nature and scope of the forthcoming volumes on the townland names of Wexford can be offered here due to restrictions of space, it would be remiss not to mention the third language from which a small handful of townland names derive, namely Norse. While the English name of the town and county itself is doubtlessly of Norse origin, very few townland names are unambiguously of Norse origin. These include *Selskar*, *Arklow* (near *Wellingtonbridge*) and *Saltee Island Great/Little*. A number of other features such as *Carnsore*, *Tuskar*, *Selskar Rock* (near *Bannow*) and *Greenore* are also of Norse origin, or contain Norse elements in their construction—while it appears that, despite suggestions to the contrary, *Cahore* is not in fact of Norse origin. It has been suggested that the element *gate* as found in *Bunargate*, *Libgate*, *Mountaingate* and *Oilgate* (locally *Oylegate*) may also be Norse. However, as the word almost certainly featured in the dialect of Anglo-Norman settlers it is most likely that it occurs in these names by way of the English language, and in fact there is no evidence to demonstrate otherwise. Indeed, in the case of *Oilgate* the evidence indicates that it is a seventeenth-century English hybrid formation of *Oil-*, an anglicised version of abhall "apple tree" as found in the neighbouring townland name *Theoil* < An Abhaill +

Crannógs at the Irish National Heritage Park, Ferrycarrig.

English *gate*. No evidence for the name exists prior to the seventeenth century, and the historical evidence indicates that the townland was known by the name *Mullinagore*, from Maolán na nGabhar "the low rounded hill of the goats" or Mullán na nGabhar "the hill, green field of the goats". The Irish name 'Bearna na hAille' is given for *Oilgate* in Laoide's *Post-seanchas*, printed in 1905, but there is absolutely no evidence that such a name ever existed when Irish was the vernacular of the area; 'Bearna na Aille' in fact appears to be a translation of *Oilgate* which is based on the incorrect assumption that the first element *Oil-* is from aill "cliff" here, and the odd use of bearna instead of geata to translate *gate*.

On the other hand, Laoide's suggested Irish form of *Barntown*, namely 'Baile Bearna' "(the town of (at the) gap" (*Post-seanchas* p.34) does find some support in the historical record. While much of the evidence is problematic, the official Irish form Baile an Bharúnaigh (the official form of the name since the passing of the *Place-Names (Irish Forms) Order* of 1975 under the *Place-Names (Irish Forms) Act* of 1973) is still satisfactory.

There are many other place-names which have surprising forerunners, both Irish and English. In some cases, of course, the original form of the name remains unclear, and in others more than one potential precursor is possible. That said, the provenance of the name Loch Garman itself at least is relatively straghtforward: garman is an Old Irish word meaning "a weaver's shuttle, club", found in Modern Irish as garma(in) meaning "sand(bar); headland"; Loch Garman can therefore be translated as "the sea-inlet of (at) the weaver's shuttles (probably referring to the shape of the sandbars, or the headlands at the mouth of the harbour)". Indeed, the Norse name for the harbour might even be a calque (loan translation)

on Loch Garman, should *Wexford* be from a Norse forerunner meaning "the inlet of marshlands, sandbars", or similar. In the Irish onomastic lore of almost one thousand years ago the name Loch Garman is explained as deriving from a character called *Garman* who, having stolen the queen of Tara's diadem, drowned after his capture at the mouth of The Slaney (Inbhear Sláine); whence Loch Garman! However, such tales, while a huge feature of the native Irish canon, cannot be taken as anything other than literary creations. The same poem provides an 'explanation' for the origin of *Raven* which is also likely to be nothing more than a literary creation, but in this case the occurrence of Rámhainn in this early text demonstrates at least that the place-name has no connection with the English word raven. The name of the county is Contae Loch Garman, based on the name of the town, but it should be noted that the county was also called An Contae Riabhach in some sources. Riabhach is an adjective with a wide range of meanings, including "brindled" as in a 'tabby cat', but I'm sure no connection with the neighbouring Kilkenny Cats was intended!

THE SEA – WAR, FOOD, RECREATION

'There is something beautiful about the town of Wexford at any time, but it is at its best … in late October and early November when the light over the harbour has a winter sharpness and, if the day becomes grey or overcast then there is a very beautiful melancholy over the water, a sense of harbour that was once great, from where ships went to Buenos Aires, with now just a line of fishing boats.'

Colm Tóibín- *Irish Times*, August 2011

53

Puffins on the Saltee Islands.

Kilmore Quay.

County Wexford is an agricultural county, a tourism county and a maritime county. Farming and fishing contribute enormously to the economy and social life of the county, as do the thousands of tourists who come to Wexford, many of them to enjoy our unmatched beaches.

The boundary of County Wexford comprises a mountain range on its north-west side but two-thirds of the entire boundary is a confluence of rivers near New Ross town, and a confluence of waters ranging from St. Georges Channel, the Irish Sea and the Atlantic Ocean.

There has been an affinity with the sea by many coastal community for centuries. Wexford and New Ross ports were thriving in the days of sail, with regular arrivals and departures from and to many exotic locations around the world. Many people fleeing famine and deprivation here at home risked all in their search for a new life and fresh hope in the New World, the coastline of Wexford being the last glimpse of their homeland for many of them.

In the seventeenth and eighteenth century, ships owned by Richard Welsh, and the Sweetmans of Newbawn laden with fresh cod left the port of New Ross and crossed the Atlantic to Newfoundland in Canada. In the nineteenth and early twentieth century, ships owned by the Devereaux family brought produce to and from Ireland and mainland Europe.

Trawlers laden with fish come into Kilmore Quay, providing traditional jobs and fresh food not just for Wexford, but many people around the world. There are many people also employed in the fish processing business, and in the leisure angling area. Names synonymous with the economic maritime life of County Wexford are Devereaux, Stafford, Wilson, Wickham, Bates, Sweetman, Saunders, of past centuries and Bates, Moore and Barden in more recent times .

The fishing community in County Wexford has interacted with fishing communities in Spain and France and across the Atlantic Ocean in Canada for centuries. Two townlands at Killurin on the banks of the River Slaney upriver from Wexford town are named Cornwall and Penzance, a tribute to their friendly fishing community neighbours across the sea.

The community of Rosslare Harbour interacts with the regular traffic of huge passenger ships and transporters coming and going from Wales, England and France, carrying everything from industrial goods to foodstuffs, often for onward delivery to the rest of the world.

Meanwhile, the sea offers great recreational and tourism opportunities to the people of the county with magnificent beaches at Courtown, Curracloe, Cullenstown and around the Hook Peninsula, created by nature and naturally appointed to be enjoyed by thousands of locals and visitors alike every year.

The sea around County Wexford too has been for centuries a focal point for battles between empires – Britain, Germany, France, Spain and America. Many historians now concur that Wexford in the south-east corner of Ireland was of even more strategic military importance to the powerful nations than it was of economic significance. During the First World War, the British established an anti-submarine base at Rosslare Harbour and a seaplane base at Ferrybank in Wexford

Gannets on the Saltee Islands.

town was built by the US Navy to combat the U-Boat threat, though it made a late and very limited entry into the war.

Artefacts of war and of want are lying conflictingly side by side on the sea bed off Hook, Duncannon, Rosslare and Carnsore Point and the appropriately named Forlorn Point looks out over an expanse of sea that contains numerous yet to be salvaged battleships and trawlers. The Mailboat Service was kept running from Rosslare at great cost during WWII, with crew being lost in several German bombing sorties.

The sea between Tuskar Rock and Hook Head has been known as 'The Graveyard' and has claimed many lives, amply illustrated by the fine memorial garden at Kilmore Quay that commemorates many of those who have lost their lives at sea.

Wexford men have not been found wanting in the constant battle to police and patrol the fickle and at times treacherous seas around our coast – there is a proud tradition of service in the Lightship, Lighthouse and Lifeboat services and heroic deeds have been performed by many of those men with little regard for their own safety in carrying out major rescue operations such as the wreck of the tanker *The World Concord* in 1955 between Rosslare and Wales and *The Mexico*, where many of the crew were saved but at the expense of nine gallant members of the Fethard lifeboat crew in Feb. 1914.

COUNTY'S HISTORIC ETHNIC MIX

By Hilary Murphy

Every county in Ireland has its distinctive family names, but none has a more historic ethnic mix than Coounty Wexford, going back to what is commonly called the Anglo-Norman Invasion of the late twelfth century. The Normans themselves were of Norse origin, long settled in Normandy in northern France. By the time of their venture into Ireland from Wales, beginning in 1169, they had largely assimilated with the Welsh in Pembrokeshire. Really, it was more a Cambro-Norman 'invasion' than Anglo-Norman. In addition, the main body of the colonising force was drawn from the Flemish colony long established in Pembrokeshire.

It is a remarkable fact that the majority of families in South Wexford continue to bear the names of this amalgam of foreign races, best summed up in these lines by the Mulrankin historian, Kathleen Browne: 'Saxon, Norman and Dane we are, Teuton or Celt or whatever we

Hook Lighthouse.

may be, we are all Irish now and have some Gaelic blood in our veins.'

So wherever in the world you come across an Irishman with surnames such as Banville, Busher, Butler, Codd, Colfer, Corish, Devereux, Esmonde, French, Furlong, Hore, Howlin, Keating, Lambert, Neville, Parle, Pettit, Roche, Rossiter, Sinnott, Stafford, Wadding, White or Whitty, he will trace his ancestral origin to South Wexford.

These are the names that have figured on school rolls, shop-fronts, commercial vehicles, on hurling and football teams and among the clergy and public representatives. This is not to overlook the small number of Gaelic names still to be found in the area. However, the colonisers were deterred from expanding into North Wexford by the fighting MacMurrough Kavanaghs and their fellow Gaels, including the O'Morchoes, Kinsellas, MacVaddocks and others.

Windmill at Tacumshane.

Several of the true Norman names can be traced to their place of origin on a map of Normandy, the best-known example, Devereux, deriving from the city of Evereux in the Department of Eure. William D'Evereux assisted William the Conqueror in the battle of Hastings in 1066. Other examples are Neville, Banville, Hays, Lacy, Tracy, Staples, Rosei (Rossiter) and Warrenne. Some of the Anglo-Normans adopted new names after settling in England, for example, the French name de Tosny became Stafford after the family settled in Staffordshire, where their castle is still to be seen.

Historians have speculated as to the ethnic origin of the colonists that settled in Wexford, whether of Anglo-Norman, Cambro-Norman, Welsh or Flemish. Surnames usually regarded as Flemish, including Cheevers, Sinnott, Siggins, and Busher, have proved to be of English origin, as verified in more recent surname studies. The most notable name of definite Flemish origin among the first invaders was Richard FitzGodebert, whose family became known as de la Roche after they had built a castle on a rock (French, roche). In the course of time the name was shortened to Roche. The Wexford name Lambert is also identified as Flemish.

Some of the Wexford names of English and French origin are descriptive, referring to a physical or personality trait, e.g. Pettit, small; Cheevers: agile, as a goat, Hore: white-haired, Whitty: White-eye, Curtis: courteous, Sinnott: bold in victory, Esmonde: east man, Colfer: Old English *culfre* 'dove, pigeon', hence the email address dovecote@eircom.net chosen by our greatly-missed historian, Billy Colfer. An amusing Forth and Bargy doggerel applied the following charactistics to some of the leading figures: 'Proud' Devereux, 'Stiff' Stafford, 'Dogged' Lambert, 'Gay' Rochford, 'Laughing' Cheevers, 'Obstinate' Hore, 'Cross Calfer', 'False' Furlong, 'Showy' Sinnott and 'Gentleman' Browne.

I conclude with this extract from *Bassett's Wexford County Guide and Directory* (1885): 'The singularity of the traditional Forth and Bargy customs seem to have long consisted of straightforwardness, thrift and energy, combined with clocklike regularity at labour. It was, and is still, in some parts, usual with the natives to arise and repair to work at 5 o'clock in the morning, and to use the middle or heat of the day for sleep, or, in the Forth and Bargy tongue, *enteete*. This reasonable arrangement aroused the wonder of the early chroniclers, one of whom, in 1682, declared that the domestic animals and births shared the noonday nap of their masters.'

Baginbun Head.

Comerford, Canon Patrick, BD, Dip Ecum, FRSAI, FASC, of Bunclody, Gorey, Wexford and Dublin family association, a canon of Christ Church Cathedral, priest in the Church of Ireland (Anglican); lecturer in Anglicanism and Liturgy in the Church of Ireland Theological Institute, adjunct assistant professor in the University of Dublin, Trinity College Dublin. He is a member of the General Synod, the Commission for Christian Unity and Dialogue, the Anglican Affairs Working Group, Dublin. In the 1970s, he was a journalist with the *Wexford People* which he left to join The *Irish Times*, where he was Foreign Desk Editor from 1994 until 2002. He is author of several books including *Embracing Difference*, 2007, *Reflections of the Bible in the Quran*, 2009 and *A Romantic Myth*, 2009. He contributed to *The Wexford Man*, 2007. He has contributed to numerous lectures on Wexford including the Dr George Hadden Memorial Lecture when he presented a paper titled 'Religion in Co. Wexford from St. Ibar to the Present Day' in 2000. He is currently writing a study of the influence of Augustus Welby Pugin on church architecture in County Wexford.

Condren, Ciaran, Castletown, Gorey, born Wexford 1961; farmer; married to Christina, née Byrne, Ballygrangans, Kilmore Quay, they have two sons; spent time drilling for oil in central Australia; with a group of friends, he has walked the entire coast of County Wexford and County Waterford, and they are currently working on County Wicklow. Ciaran is a son of Mick, born 1922, Castletown House, Castletown, retired dairy farmer, and Nancy, née Horgan, Co.Kerry, who was the local National School teacher for many years; they have three daughters and five sons; ran a Bed and Breakfast business for 45 years.

Connick, Seán, born 1963, was elected to Dáil Éireann as a Fianna Fáil candidate for Wexford in the General Election of 2007. He was the first TD in the history of the State to use a wheelchair, and he has the distinction of being the first native of New Ross to be elected to Dáil Éireann. On 23rd March, 2010, he was appointed as Minister of State at the Department of Agriculture, Fisheries and Food with special responsibility for Fisheries and Forestry. He failed to retain his seat in the General Election of 2011. He stood for election to Seanad Éireann on the Agricultural Panel in April, 2011, but was not elected.

Conran, John, born Rathnure 1957; played senior hurling for Wexford from 1975 to 1991, winning an All Star Award at left half back in 1987. Upon his retirement, served as county senior hurling manager from 2002 to 2004, succeeding Tony Dempsey. John played with Rathnure for nearly 25 years, winning eight Wexford senior titles and four Leinster senior club titles. He is a prominent businessman in Rathnure.

Conway, Arthur, 1877-1950, Ballinruane, Screen, was a world-renowned mathematician. One of the first Wexford people to attend UCD in 1892, he published numerous scholarly articles on maths. He was president of UCD from 1940-1947. He was son of Myles Conway and Teresa Harris and married Agnes Bingham from Antrim in 1903. They had four children. Arthur Conway died suddenly while preparing to attend an International Congress of Mathematicians in Harvard on 11th July 1950.

Cooney, David, secretary-general of the Department of Foreign Affairs, Iveagh House, Stephen's Green, Dublin, who was described by George Mitchell former US Secretary of State as one of the unsung heroes of the Good Friday Agreement (or Belfast Agreement) is of New Ross ancestry where his father grew up in the 1950s before going to work in London. He worked in the Department of Agriculture in Dublin from 1976 to 1978, and then the Department of the Public Service from 1978 before joining the Department of Foreign Affairs in 1979. He has held positions including those of Coordinator of White Paper on Irish Foreign Policy; Counsellor, Head of Political Section, Anglo-Irish Division, during which he participated in the negotiation of the Good Friday Agreement; Permanent Representative of Ireland to the United Nations, New York; Ambassador, Embassy of Ireland, London and was the first non-residential ambassador to the Holy See in Rome. He is an avid follower of Wexford GAA and is a regular visitor to Wexford Park, His friends include Minister Brendan Howlin TD, and Mayor of Wexford, Cllr. George Lawlor.

Corbett, Oonagh, 1923-2013, formerly Abbeybraney, Gusserane, community activist, ICA leader, member of An Taisce and the Georgian Society; married to Arthur

Corbett for sixty-seven years, a founder member of Gusserane ICA Guild; National President of ICA in 1970. Lived out her retirement years in Holy Cross in County Tipperary with Arthur. The couple had one son, Burke, and three daughters, Theo, Susan and Jenny.

Cooper, Simon, Featherbed Farm, Oylegate, born Waterford 1980, chef and ice cream manufacturer; son of Philip and Avril; graduated from DIT Cathal Brugha Street in 1998 and worked as a chef all over Dublin; in 2008 built unit on brother Paul's dairy farm and established Featherbed Farm Ice Cream – hand making luxury ice cream for the hotel and restaurant trade.

Corcoran, Alan, Wexford, Radio Presenter, Alan has presented South East Radio's flagship programme Morning Mix for the past three years; previously worked as Sports Editor and presenter of the Lunchtime Show. Before joining South East Radio, he worked in RTÉ presenting a number of radio programmes and television work for TG4. He is a noted actor, theatrical producer and runner. He is married to Anne Marie and they have two children, Alanna and Callum.

Corcoran, James, 1882-1916, Brideswell, Askamore; while serving with a section of the Irish Citizen Army in St. Stephen's Green under the command of Michael Mallin and Countess Markievicz during Easter Rising of 1916, he was mortally wounded. He is interred in Glasnevin cemetery. His son, also James, was killed in Gibraltar in August 1942, aged 30, while serving with the RAF.

Corish, Brendan, born in Wexford, was a civil servant and politician. He was elected to Dáil Éireann as a Labour Party candidate in a by-election in 1945, following the death of his father, Richard Corish, who was the sitting TD. He retained his seat in the 1948 General Election in which Fianna Fáil was returned as the largest party in the Dáil. However, Fine Gael, the Labour Party, the National Labour Party, Clann na Poblachta, Clann na Talmhan and a number of independent candidates came together to form the first inter-party government. Brendan Corish was appointed Parliamentary Secretary to the Ministers for Defence and Local Government. When the Second Inter-party Government was formed following the 1954 election, he was appointed Minister for Social Welfare. In 1960, he became Leader of the Labour Party in succession to William Norton. Fine Gael and Labour formed a coalition government between 1973 and 1977 in which Brendan Corish became Tánaiste and Minister for Health and Social Welfare. After Fianna Fáil was returned to power in a landslide victory following the General Election of 1977, he resigned as leader of the Labour Party, having indicated that he would do so prior to the election. He retired from politics at the February, 1982, General Election, and he died on 17th February, 1990, at the age of 71 years.

Corish, Richard, born in Wexford in 1889, was a trade union official and politician. As a Labour Party member of Wexford Corporation, he was elected Mayor of Wexford in 1920. However, when the Labour Party decided not to contest the 1921 elections, Richard Corish ran as a Sinn Féin candidate and was elected to Dáil Éireann for the Wexford constituency. In the 1922 General Election, he ran as a Labour Party candidate and was re-elected. He continued to represent Wexford in the Dáil for the next twenty-three years until his death in 1945, and he served a record twenty-five years as Mayor of Wexford. In the by-election which was called following his death, his seat was won by his son, Brendan, who was later to become leader of the Labour Party and Tánaiste.

Corish, Rev Monsignor Patrick, Professor Emeritus of History and former President of St. Patrick's College, Maynooth; born Ballytarsna, Ballycullane; both his parents were teachers in Gusserane National School; College archivist; author of *Maynooth College 1795-1995, The Irish Catholic Community: Seventeeth and Eighteenth Centuries, The Irish Catholic Experience*, edited and contributed to *A History of Irish Catholicism* and contributed to *A New History of Ireland;* lectured in many places, including to Old Wexford Society and Uí Chennselaig Society as well as internationally. Monsignor Corish died in 2013.

Cousins, Maurice, Barnadown Stud Farm, Gorey; Horse breeder; married to Felicity, née Holohan, Tipperary; established international standard equestrian centre and stud farm in Barnadown.

Cowman, Anne, Crossabeg, née Redmond, Gusserane, married to Nicky, Monmore, who was Wexford People of the Year Overall Award winner in 2004. Nicky devotes his time mainly to forestry, athletics and community activity. Anne has been a member of Community Games for over 30 years, County Secretary for nine of those. She is a long-standing Leinster delegate for Wexford and also a delegate to the National Games AGMs. She has also been a County Manager/PRO for the Wexford delegation travelling to Mosney and now Athlone. They have one daughter, Fiona, who is married in Australia.

Cowman, Philip, born Wexford 1918, began to write poetry when he retired in 1980. His published work includes: *Quo Vadis* and *Words*.

Crean, John, Cois Sláine, Killurin, born in Tacumshane 1957; Malting Barley Manager South, at Boortmalt, Athy, fifth largest malting company in the world with its HQ in Antwerp; worked previously with Nunns and Minch Norton. He attended St. Peter's College, Wexford and UCD. He has five children and is married to Trish, a primary school teacher in Glynn.

Creed, Fleur, Wexford, President of Wexford Chamber of Commerce. In 2000, Fleur and husband, Ted, moved to Wexford, Fleur's home county, her mother being one of the well-known Pierce family from Glynn. With the help of the County Enterprise Board they set up Genesis Business College offering a range of certificate and diploma courses to individuals and tailored corporate courses. Fleur now offers a consultancy service.

Crofton, Monica, Wexford, wrote *Memories of the Faythe School* in 1991, and she has also written a children's history of Wexford entitled *The Wexford Story*, which was published in 1997. She conducts walking tours of Wexford.

Cronin, Anthony, born in Wexford in 1926, was associate editor of *The Bell* and literary editor of *Time and Tide.* He wrote poetry, essays and novels, including *The Life of Riley, Heritage Now: Irish Literature in the English Language* and *Letter to an Englishman.* In 1976, he published *Dead as Doornails*, a memoir of literary Dublin, and he received the Marten Toonder Award in 1983 for *New and Selected Poems.* His other books include, *A Question of Modernity, An Irish Eye; Art for the People*; No *Laughing Matter: The Life and Times of Flann O'Brien,* and *Samuel Beckett The Last Modernist.* A play *The Shame of It* was produced in the Peacock Theatre in 1974. He became cultural advisor to Charles Haughey when he was Taoiseach.

The Ros Tapestry Project was started in 1998 when over 150 volunteers began working on creating fifteen large embroidered panels telling the story of the arrival of the Anglo Normans into County Wexford.

Crosbie, Michael, Wexford 1945, Ballinamona, Campile, retired Health and Safety Officer with the ESB; married to Kathleen, née Nolan, Camblin, New Ross; founder of Silver Fern Safety Consultants; joined the Boy Scouts in 1959, became in Ballykelly Scout leader twelve years later; in 1986 was Commissioner for Scouting in Wexford during which time he oversaw an old cow shed turned into a scout hall in Horeswood for the Scout Foundation; received special award for 40 years' service with the Civil Defence as Health and Safety Instructor; raised thousands of pounds and euro for charity including for Romanian Orphans and Wexford Hospital Rehab Unit.

Crowley, Brendan, Rathaspeck, Wexford, owner of Wexford Bus, which he operates with his wife, Lorene. Brendan established the business in 1996 to provide a service around Wexford Town and the surrounding towns and villages. In 2007 the Dublin Airport Express route was launched and it is now servicing Dublin and the airport twelve times daily.

Crowley, Dr Conor, Ballynagee, Wexford; place names researcher at the Department of Arts Culture and the Gaeltacht. A native of Corish Park, Wexford, Conor is son of Pete and Carrie Crowley and qualified as a plumber and worked in Ireland and abroad. He returned to education and graduated with a BA and PhD from NUI Maynooth with further studies in Albert-Ludwigs-Universität, Freiburg, Germany. Conor has won numerous academic awards including a two-year post-doctoral scholarship to study place names as a literary device in early Irish literature. Married to Anne, née Lyons, Craanford, they have two sons, Fiach and Conail. Conor is a fluent Irish speaker which he uses whenever possible and his hobbies include genealogy, GAA and cycling.

Cullen, Jason, Ballykelly, Ballymurn, born 1988; darts player; son of Johnny and Teresa. He has represented the Republic of Ireland in the World Darts Federation (WDF) Europe Youths Cup in 2004 and was runner-up in the singles. He also played in the WDF World Cup in Perth and in 2012 he was in his national team for the WDF Europe Cup and the Six Nations Cup. He qualified for the 2013 British Darts Organisation televised World Championships at the Lakeside arena. In the first televised round he played the number 11 seed, Martin Atkins and won 3-1, but lost to Paul Jennings in the second round.

Cullen, John L, from Oulart, jockey, now living in Carlow. He is regarded as one of the strongest, toughest and most consistent riders in the country. Since his first winner in 1999, he has had a steady flow of big race winners, including the Thyestes Chase at Gowran for Michael Hickey on Bob Treacy 2001, two Galway Hurdles for Paul Nolan on Say Again 2002 and Cloone River 2004, and a number of grade 1 wins for various trainers.

Cullen, Louis Michael, was born in New Ross in 1932; was Associate Lecturer in Modern History and later Professor in Trinity College Dublin. He wrote a number of books, including: *Anglo-Irish Trade 1660-1800, Life in Ireland, An Economic History of Ireland since 1660* and *The Emergence of Modern Ireland.*

Cullen, Lynda, Gorey, musician, daughter of Willie and Sandra, twin sister of Suzanne. As a member of 'Second Moon,' Lynda spent five years in South Korea where their debut album picked up three awards at the 2006 Korean Real Music Awards. Lynda had three guitar lessons at the age of fifteen, and taught herself everything else. Her sister, Suzanne, is also a talented singer and has sung with the Dublin Gospel Choir and the Arklow Gospel Choir.

Cullen, Pat, Ballyfad, born Wexford 1944; postmaster and farmer; married to Bernadette, née Byrne , Kilanerin, born in Wexford 1961, they have four daughters and two sons; Pat's mother, Margaret Mary "Molly" Cullen, was postmistress and shopkeeper for 49 years (RIP 1992). Pat and Bernadette have run the shop ever since Mrs Cullen's passing, and have kept the same friendly, traditional rural service, and are very active in many organisations in the parish. Both being great GAA fans, they manage Kilanerin ladies' football teams. Bernadette founded the underage ladies' teams in 1999. He won an All-Ireland Colleges' Senior Hurling medal with St. Peter's College in 1963.

Culleton, Dr Ned, born Piercestown, 1932, now lives in Blackrock, Co. Dublin and is a Wexford man of many sides: soils' researcher, scientific editor, University lecturer, EU Administrator, historian, curator and author. He worked in Johnstown Castle, Dublin, Brussels and was one of the instigators of the National Heritage Park in Ferrycarrig. Currently working on a major detailed book on Co. Wexford, he is also involved in Akajava Films which is owned by his son, Brendan. Their film *The Congo* won the Best Documentary Award at the IFTAS in 2013. Ned was also a GAA fan and played for both St. Fintan's and St. Martin's. He is married to Decla, née Molloy, and along with Brendan, has two daughters, Fidelma and Orlagh. He is author of *Wexford's Industrial Potential, Laboratory Analysis in Soil Survey Investigation, The South Wexford Landscape* and *Early Man in County Wexford.* He edited *Treasurers of the Landscape, County Wexford's Rural Heritage,* in 1994 and *By Bishop's Rath and Norman Fort, a history of Piercestown Parish*, which was also published in 1994. With Mary Tubridy, he edited *Guides to County Wexford.* His latest work is *On Our Own Ground: County Wexford parish by parish*, published by Wexford County Council Public Library Service first in a set of three volumes.

Cullimore, Seamus, Wexford, born 1954, is a former Fianna Fáil politician. In 1987, he was nominated by the Taoiseach, Charles Haughey, as a member of Seanad Éireann. However, in the General Election of 1989, he won a Dáil seat in the Wexford constituency, but he lost out in the 1992 General Election.

A gold bracelet, two gold dress fasteners and two gold boxes, dated to between 700 and 800 B.C. were found at Ballineskar, Curracloe. This find is known as the Ballineskar Hoard and is preserved in the National Museum.

Cunningham, David, Munny, Askamore, son of retired Teagasc adviser in Gorey, John, and Betty; graduated with BSc, Computer and Software Engineering from Athlone IT; co-founder of software company, Q-Percom Quality Performance Consultants Limited, which won a major tender with the National University of Singapore in 2013; clients include Dundee and St. Andrew's universities in Scotland, as well as the Karolinska Institute in Sweden.

Curran, Breda, from the Shelmalier Ladies' Gaelic Football Club, served as County secretary for many years and was also club secretary at the same time. Breda represents Wexford as a delegate at Leinster Council and has also served on sub committees of that body.

Curran, Dr John, Newbawn, born Kilkenny 1943, retired General Practitioner; in private practice in Newbawn 1973-2013; previously worked in hospitals in Donegal, Dublin and Waterford, now retired and enjoying golf and reading. His partner is Marie.

Curtis, Dr David, Wexford, GP, son of Dr Barty Curtis, professional cycle race medical doctor over two decades in many Irish and international professional cycle races, including the Milk Rás, Tour de France in Ireland 1998, the 2011 Tour of Beijing and the Tour of Lombardy in 2012.

Curtis, John, Garrenstackle, Ballyhogue, environmental economist with the ESRI; son of well-known Bree farmer and Wexford GAA President 2009–2010, John Curtis and Mary. He has a PhD in Environmental and Resource Economics from the University of Maryland in the USA and gained his Primary and Masters degree in economics in UCD. He has been Associate Research Professor with the ESRI since October 2012.

Curtis, Mogue, The Boola, Raheen, Newbawn, born Wexford 1936; dairy farmer; married Ann, née Kehoe, Templeudigan, they have three daughters and four sons; an historian with particular interest in vintage machinery, work horses and old farming practices.

Dalton, Ben, from New Ross, jockey, rides for Wexford trainer Conor O'Dwyer among others; had his biggest success in 2013 when piloting Dot Love's Liberty Counsel to victory at 50/1 in the Irish Grand National at Fairyhouse.

D'Arcy, Gordon, born in Ferns 1980, Irish international rugby player, son of Peggy and John, former Bank Manager in Ferns and Castlebar native. Gordon was introduced to rugby at Wexford Wanderers Rugby Club when the family moved to live in Coolree. Played schools rugby with Clongowes Wood and then for the Lansdowne club in Dublin. He has played over 70 times for Ireland and nearly 200 times for Leinster, despite suffering quite a few injuries. Gordon has been selected for the British and Irish Lions for several tours. He made his international debut against Romania in October, 1999. Highlights of his career include being part of the Irish team that won the 2009 Six Nations' championship when they completed the country's first Grand Slam since 1948,

and also being involved in Leinster's European Heineken Cup victories. He was involved in a world record breaking partnership at centre with Brian O'Driscoll. He and Irish model Aoife Cogan were married at St. Macartan's Cathedral, Monaghan, in July 2012. He has served as a Wexford Ambassador.

Daly, Gerry, native of Enniscorthy, former producer of agricultural programmes with RTE radio; presenter of popular RTE gardening programme, graduate of Trinity College Dublin; editor of Irish gardening magazine; son of chief agricultural advisor, John Daly.

Darcy McGee, Thomas, 1825-1868, was a prominent member of the Young Ireland Movement and later a leading Canadian statesman. He was born in County Louth, one of eight children of James and Dorcas McGee who moved to live in Wexford town when James was appointed Tidewaiter and Boatman with the Customs' Service in Wexford. In 1842 at age 17, McGee left Wexford due to a poor relationship with his stepmother, Margaret Day, who had married his father in 1840 after the death of his mother in 1833. He went to the US but later returned to Ireland to edit *The Nation* newspaper. He was involved in the Young Irelander Rebellion of 1848 and soon afterwards went back to the States before migrating to Canada in 1857. The following year he was elected to the Assembly of Canada and fought from there to make Canada an independent country from Britain. On April 7, 1868, McGee participated in a parliamentary debate that went on past midnight. Afterward, he walked to his lodgings and, while trying to enter the house, was assassinated. He was given a State funeral and the funeral procession in Montreal drew an estimated crowd of eighty thousand people. To date, Thomas Darcy McGee is the only Canadian politician ever to have been assassinated.

Cawdor Street in Rosslare Harbour continues on Cawdor Street in Fishguard.

Darcy, Michael, Rathmacknee, Killinick, born Wexford 1989; son of Michael and Ornagh, née O'Mahoney, Piercestown; graduated from DIT with a degree in Business Management 2013; creator of five-piece band, Corner Boy, who played Electric Picnic 2013 among other festivals and were crowned Red Bull Bedroom Jam champions in October; headline act in Whelan's of Wexford Street October 2013; filmed debut music video for their single 'Morning Morning' in Wexford; brother of Margaret "Mags" Darcy, born 1986, St. Martin's player, Wexford camogie goalie and winner of Camogie All Stars, All-Ireland senior Camogie Championship medals in 2007, 2010, 2011 and 2012, and member of the 2011 Team of the Championship.

D'Arcy, Michael, who was born in 1934, is a retired farmer and politician. He was first elected to Dáil Éireann as a Fine Gael candidate in the General Election of 1977, and he held his seat until the 1987 General Election when he lost out to Brendan Howlin of the Labour Party. He was re-elected in the 1989 General Election at the expense of his party colleague, Avril Doyle. However, he lost out again in the 1992 General Election when Avril Doyle regained her seat. He was then elected to Seanad Éireann on the Agricultural Panel. He was returned to the Dáil in the General Election of 1997 when Avril Doyle was again unseated. In the 2002 General Election D'Arcy lost out again, this time to Liam Twomey who ran as an independent candidate and later joined Fine Gael. D'Arcy served as a Minister of State for Agriculture and later was Minister of State for Fisheries. He is father of Michael W D'Arcy, born 1970, who was elected to Seanad Éireann on the Administrative Panel in April, 2011, and is the Fine Gael Seanad spokesperson on Finance. He is a former Fine Gael TD for Wexford constituency from 2007 to 2011.

Darcy, P.J., Roscora, Ballyhogue; recently retired chief executive of WFC; married to Anna, they have three daughters and one son. Their daughter Fiona is chief executive of youth radio station of RED FM in Cork. He is chairman of Green Bio-Fuels, New Ross. Established in 2004, the company now produces 30,000 tonnes of biodiesel annually. He was county chairman of Macra na Feirme in Wexford in the 1970s. He is a former All-Ireland public speaking champion and RTÉ Cross Country quiz competitor. He coached Bree branch to All-Ireland honours in public speaking and several other competitions. He is a well known community activist in his parish and in Enniscorthy. He is a director of Celtic Roots.

Darigan, Paddy, Garrycleary, Crossabeg, born Wexford 1963, artist and sculptor; married to Johanna, née Fortune, Trinity, they have four sons; founder member of Wexford Life Drawing Group and member of Waterford Live Art; works from life through many media: oil, watercolour, charcoal and sculpts from wood and stone; holds exhibitions in various galleries and during Wexford Festival Opera.

Davis, Richard, Airdownes, Broadway, born Wexford 1947, farmer; married to Lillian, née Poole, Craanford, they have two daughters and two sons; former owner of restaurant in Our Lady's Island; member of Old Folks' Committee for 42 years as Lillian has for 37; author of *Nobody Listens*, 2010, in which he reveals his ability to commune with spirits or ghosts.

Davitt, Joe, Ferns, lead singer with the Davitt Country Band. With a long tradition of the Davitt family in the music business, Joe is the lead vocalist with a new generation. Joe, and brother Tommy and Tommy's sons, Niall, Nathan, Tommy Junior, Stephen and nephew, Derek, are The Davitt Country Band. Joe's father, Christy, led the Davitt Brothers Band around the ballrooms of Ireland from the 1950s to the 1980s. Seamus Davitt, who emigrated to England, is father of Pauline, mother of international singing star Emma Bunton, formerly 'Baby Spice' of the Spice Girls who dominated the charts with a girl-power ethos.

> Wexford's coat of arms is in the county's sporting colours of purple and gold. The lion with an axe symbolises the Norman invasion of Ireland and that Wexford is a Viking town. The spear recalls the Pikemen of 1798 and the lighthouse symbolises the influence of the sea.

Dawkins, Shannen, Killesk, Campile, born Wexford 1996, fifth year student in St. Mary's Secondary School, New Ross; daughter of Chris and Katriona Shannon; she has one brother; member of St. Joseph's Athletic Club Kilkenny and this season won double gold medals for

Ireland at the Celtic Games in Wales for the high jump and the 4 x 100m relay; also won senior title in high jump at the Athletics Association of Ireland Games and four Leinster titles.

Day, Kevin, Randallstown, Bridgetown, born 1986, son of Paddy and Clare, née McCarthy, Bridgetown; won County Junior Football Championship medal in 2012, and captained the St. Fintan's Intermediate football team to victory in October 2013, qualifying them to play senior for the first time in 30 years in 2014. Kevin's parents train racehorses so he has an interest in equestrian sports also.

De Breadun, Deaglún, a native of Oylegate, was the author of a best-selling collection of short stories in Irish entitled *Scealoga* which was published in 1990. He is a respected journalist with the *Irish Times*.

De Burgh, Chris was born Christopher John Davison on 15th October, 1948, and is a singer-songwriter most famous for his 1986 love song *Lady in Red* which reached number one around the world. He was born in Venado Tuerto, Argentina, to Col. Charles Davison, a British diplomat, and Maeve Emily de Burgh, an Irish secretary, and has has strong links with Co. Wexford. His father had substantial farming interests and Chris spent much of his early years in Malta, Nigeria and Zaire, as he and his mother and brother accompanied Col. Davison on his diplomatic and engineering work. The Davisons finally settled in Bargy Castle, Co. Wexford, which had been bought by his maternal grandfather, General Sir Eric de Burgh, a former Chief of the General Staff in India. The castle was converted into a hotel where Chris gained much early experience performing to the guests, and he later assumed 'de Burgh' as his stage name. He now lives in Enniskerry, Co. Wicklow. His daughter, Rosanna, born

Dublin 1984, is a model who was crowned Ireland's first ever Miss World 2003. She has a BA from UCD and a Dip. in Event Management with PR. She has raised money for the Spinal Injuries Ireland charity.

Delaney, Nicky, Clifford Tce., Wexford, a member of the original committee of the Wexford and District Soccer League, was a very fine soccer player in his day and competed in the Waterford League with various Wexford teams before the Wexford League got going. Nicky also played a leading role on the successful St John's Athletic side. He later went on help set up the Wexford branch of the Irish Soccer Referees' Society, and was a leading referee for many years. He then turned to local "pirate" radio, CRW (Community Radio Wexford) where he reported on a match for the sports programme every Sunday evening with the late Joe Fallon.

Delaney, Padraic, Brocurra, Adamstown, born 1977, professional actor; son of Sheelagh and Michael, attended Coláiste Abbain Secondary School in Adamstown; studied acting in the Samuel Beckett Centre in Trinity College Dublin and graduated with a degree in Drama and Theatre Studies; presented with a Shooting Star Award at the Berlin Film Festival in 2007 by the European Film Promotion; acting credits include as Maurice in *Pure Mule*, Teddy O'Donovan in *The Wind that Shakes the Barley*, and George Boleyn in *The Tudors*.

Dempsey, Mary, Ballinellard, Blackwater, née McDonald of Saunderscourt, married to John who works at Cooney's of Oulart, they have three children. Mary worked in the RTÉ Newsroom and in a number of banking institutions; South Wexford Area President St. Vincent de Paul since 2009; North Wexford Area President is Edmund Roche of Davidstown. The South East Regional President of St Vincent de Paul is Rory McCauley.

Dempsey, Michael, Enniscorthy, son of Anne and Patsy, John's Street; former psychiatric nurse in the St. John of God Hospital in Stillorgan; former MD of Bristol Myers Squibb Pharmaceutical, Europe; served two terms as president of the Irish Pharmaceutical Association; was member of the State fisheries board, B.I.M.; served on health service reform review group; member of the Wexford Harbour Board and a patron of the Special Olympics. He is now a coach with the human performance group Motiv8.

Dempsey, Nick, Ballymorris, Ballyhogue, born Wexford 1940; retired mixed farmer; married to Mary, RIP, née Sinnott, they have two sons and one daughter; renowned storyteller and set dancer of note, winner of several All-Ireland Scór titles for singing, set dancing and music.

Dempsey, Peter, RIP, Ballyconnigar, Blackwater, tailor; elected to Wexford County Council as a Labour candidate in Enniscorthy District, 1950; was appointed to County Committee of Agriculture serving for 10 years; served as Chairman of Wexford County Council during 1954 1955 when he signed the contract for the "New Bridge" which was costing £350,000.

Dempsey, Róisín , soprano, and music teacher in Gorey Community School, married to Nick Bailey; graduated from NUI Maynooth with a degree in music and theology; former Anúna singer; toured Asia with Riverdance; performed with Michael Crawford, The Chieftains, Secret Garden; member of Celtic Woman show; principal female soloist on Fr. Liam Lawton's albums, *Light the Fire, Sacred Story*, and *Ancient Ways Future Days*; has released two solo albums, *Spirit of an Irish Christmas*, 2004 and *Surroundings* 2007.

Dempsey, Tom, Kilmuckridge, born 1965; Wexford and Buffers Alley hurler, now an RTÉ radio hurling analyst and columnist; played for Wexford from 1984 to 2000, scored the crucial only goal in 1996 All-Ireland hurling win over Limerick; was picked as 1996 hurling All-Star at left full forward; won two Leinster Senior medals; played 171 senior games for Wexford and scored 43 goals -344 points and is 6th in the all-time scoring lists. Tom was captain in 1993 when Wexford lost the National league final to Cork after three epic games, and then lost the Leinster final in a replay to Kilkenny. He also played football for Wexford. He won eight County hurling medals with Buffers Alley, and also an All-Ireland club and three Leinster club medals. Tom is married to Sinéad, née Codd, daughter of former Wexford camogie star, Kit, née Kehoe.

> The motto Exemplar Hiberniae on the Wexford Coat of Arms means ' A Model of Ireland'

Dempsey, Tony, from Davidstown, now Barntown, born 1944, secondary school teacher, GAA officer and Fianna Fáil politician; married to Gemma they have five children; educated at Enniscorthy CBS, UCD and St. Patrick's College, Maynooth; one of the youngest ever Chairmen of County GAA Board when serving from 1976-1979; credited with much of the groundwork on club development in Wexford prior to the GAA centenary in 1984; Wexford Rep on GAA Central Council, 1980-2002, served on many of the most important GAA committees; made unsuccessful bid for presidency of the Association; noted as an orator and motivator, and managed and trained Wexford county teams at all levels, including senior hurling team 2002-2002. Tony was elected Fianna Fáil TD at first attempt, at the expense of sitting FF TD, Hugh Byrne, and served from 2002-2007; did not stand for re-election and was succeeded by party colleague, Sean Connick. He was principal of, Enniscorthy Vocational College, at time of election. He was elected to Wexford County Council at the 2009 local elections.

Dempsey, Willie, from Hill St., Wexford, the current Wexford and District Soccer League registrar has served on the committee for nearly forty years. He has also been to the forefront for his beloved North End Utd as they have developed their terrific facilities in Belvedere Grove in Wexford town.

Denton, John, Davidstown and Wexford town, very long-serving GAA referee. Never did get All-Ireland senior final many felt he deserved after controversial 1989 All-Ireland hurling semi-final in which he sent off Galway's Sylvie Linnane and Michael McGrath and Tipperary won the game. Since 1988 he has handled more Wexford senior finals than any other referee, ten in football and four in hurling. Denton was also a very accomplished badminton player and coach.

De Val, An tAthair Séamus, Bunclody, born 1926, retired parish priest of Oulart; son of John, a noted footballer who figured on the record-breaking Wexford teams of 1916-18, and Annie Wall, née Sheridan; well-known Irish enthusiast and historian; first diocesan archivist 1997. Fr De Val published a history of Bunclody, *Bun Clóidí – A History of the District* in 1966. He also wrote *Oulart in '98*, which was published in 1986, and a biography of P.J. McCall. He is a frequent contributor to historical and scholarly journals.

Devereux, Diarmuid, Ballyoughter, born 1954, chairman of Wexford County GAA Board, succeeding Ger Doyle of Oulart-The Ballagh. He is a chartered engineer with MDK Ltd., based in Carrigtuohill, Co. Cork. He is married to Yvonne; son, Diarmuid is living in Brisbane and married; daughter, Sabrina is a doctor and living in Vienna. Before being elected County chairman, he served as Coiste na nÓg chairman. He is an active member of the St. Patrick's Club in Camolin. Prior to that played underage with Naomh Éanna, Gorey, before moving to Dublin to study. Also played club football and hurling in Dublin.

Devereux, Donal, Wexford, jockey, who mostly rides for Wales-based trainer Peter Bowen. He joined the yard as a stable conditional jockey in 2007, and has now passed a career total of 75 wins, thus ending his status as a weight-claiming conditional. Donal's first winners came as an amateur in 2008 when he won four hunter chases on the veteran Gold Cup runner-up Take The Stand. He turned professional in 2009, and the next season he rode 24 winners before his career was checked by two serious injuries. He is up and running again and had 14 winners from just 61 rides between May and August 2013.

Devereux, Fr. Sean, Ballymacane, Broadway, born Co. Wexford 1964, son of Nicholas and Phyllis; missionary priest in the Diocese of Banjul in the Gambia; involved in many projects to help fund education through fundraising in Ireland and organises for Gorey Community School Transition Year Students to travel out every year to help with this work; records public information radio programmes that are transmitted across Gambia.

Devereux, Pat, born 1939 and **Johnny Rourke,** 1940-2008, The Missioners, roofing and shed erection contractors; Pat Devereux, son of Johanna, née Power, Ballivegga. Johnny Rourke, mother was a Clegg from Saltmills, his brother died in the bomb factory explosion in Saltmills in 1922.

Devine, Alice, Ballydicken, Crossabeg, born Dublin 1953, daughter of Lily and the late James. Branch Librarian Wexford Library, recorded inscriptions on every headstone in the four graveyards in the parish with Anne Cowman and keeps the parish deaths record book. Her sister is Rhona Reck. Her brother Jim is well known farmer, fisherman and master boatbuilder.

Devoy, Frank, Riverside, Crosstown, chief executive WFC Wexford Farmers' Co-op; took over at the helm of WFC in November 2012 having been financial controller there for a number of years; long-standing volunteer with the Ferns Diocesan

Lourdes Pilgrimage; received a Bene merenti Medal for his work with them in 2010. Married to Breda, the couple have a son, Philip and daughter, Jean.

Dillon, Jim, 1922-2008, Newbawn, general merchant, married to Bridie Byrne, Gusserane, they have three daughters and two sons; very active member of Newbawn community, served at all levels for club and county as GAA selector and general advisor.

Dinan-Sinnott, Mary, Aughfad, Taghmon, born 1943, daughter of John Sinnott and Mai, née O'Connor; regarded as one of Co. Wexford's most consistent camogie players and, for a long time, was hailed as the best full-back in Ireland. She was one of two Wexford players selected on the Camogie Team of the Century in 2004, at left full back. In 1968, she put in a particularly brilliant performance to help Wexford win its first senior All-Ireland. She also played for Leinster for ten years. She retired in 1969 after the birth of her daughter. Concentrated on badminton, a sport in which she had already made a serious mark. She had married badminton player, Gay Dinan, in Taghmon in 1968. In 1967, she won Co. Wexford's badminton senior and junior singles, doubles and mixed doubles titles, all in the same evening. She went on to win Munster senior titles and played on the provincial side. She later moved to the KADCA club in Dublin with which she won the Irish Open and six national titles. She won her first international cap in 1975 against the Netherlands and went on to represent Ireland 59 times. In 1981, she was one of the seven players who made history in Norway when Ireland won the Helvetia Cup, effectively badminton's European Championships. In 1983, she announced her retirement, having just won both the ladies' doubles, with Wendy Orr and the Mixed, with John Scott, to seal Ireland's first victory over England since 1903. From 2002 to 2009, Mary was trainer of the Wexford badminton team. 'I drove down from Dublin every Friday night from October until the All-Ireland was over in May,' she says. 'But we did well. We won four All-Irelands and five Leinster titles.' Amongst those she has also coached was Sonya McGinn who became Ireland's first Olympian badminton player at the Sydney Games in 2000. She was also President of the Leinster branch of Badminton Ireland.

Dobbs, Pat, Enniscorthy, successful flat jockey in England, mainly riding as second choice for Richard Hannon and for Amanda Perrett. In the past ten years he has picked up nearly 300 winners from about 2,800 rides, including 51 winners in the 2012 season, which put him in the top 30.

Dodebier, Servaas, Artramon Farm, Crossabeg, born the Netherlands 1956, dairy farm manager, married to Frederike Frederiks, with two daughters and two sons; co-founder of Cottage Autism Network, an organisation concerned with care and development of children with autism which sees many of the children going on to mainstream education; played a major part in acquiring and developing four soccer pitches and an all-weather training ground for local soccer club; Servaas and Frederike won the Rehab Wexford People of the Year Health and Welfare Award 2008.

JFK at Dunganstown in June 1963.

③

Diaspora

They are on every continent in the world. They are in the US, Canada, South America, Britain, mainland Europe, China. They have built whole communities and they occupy some of the most influential positions. They are the Wexford diaspora.

EXILES TO ENGLAND

In the 1940s and 1950s, thousands of Wexford people made the journey from the far corners of the county by bicycle, pony and trap, or car if they were lucky to have one, taking with them perhaps the clothes they wore every day and some preciously saved or borrowed money and boarded the emigrant boat at Rosslare or Dublin. Ireland was emerging from World War II and its major impact on Europe.

From Rosslare or from Dublin they crossed the Irish sea to the ports of Fishguard or Liverpool and took the train to Paddington railway station in the heart of London, entering a life of bustle, noise and commerce in the sharpest contrast to the pace and standard of life in the small towns and rural villages and fields from which they came.

They became part of the Irish community of London then the economic capital of the world. Many stayed for their lifetime, having found jobs in the many factories in the city. Many used London and England as a springboard to the USA and other parts of the world.

THE LONDON-WEXFORD ASSOCIATION

A group of young Wexford men then living in London went on a train journey from Paddington to Fishguard and to Croke Park in Dublin in 1954 to see the All-Ireland hurling final between Cork and Wexford. On their way back to London on the train were Jim Murphy and his brother Seán from Castlebridge, Tommy Quirke, Barntown, Peter Brown, Crossabeg, Jack Carty, Bannow-Ballymitty and a few more.

A social need to keep in contact and share news and stories of home and girls and, of course, hurling and football, farming and pub-life and dances influenced their decision to form the Wexford Association.

They called a meeting in Jim Murphy's house in Cricklewood. They called a further meeting to elect officers and committee.

At this first official meeting on 6th November in 1954 in the Red Lion Pub in Kilburn, Tommy Quirke, Barntown was elected chairman, Sean Murphy was elected secretary, and his brothers Jim and Tommy Ryan of Donard and Matt Neill of Adamstown were elected to the committee. Tommy Quirke was later elected first chairman of Father Murphy's hurling club in 1958.

The association started off with fundraising dances in the Cricklewood Hotel where they used to have a whist drive. They formed a mummers set- the 'Wexford Association Mummers'. Some of the organisers were Dick Gaul, Ballyhogue; Danny O'leary, Bree; Pat McCabe, Selskar; and Martin Whitty, Peter White and Mike Meyler, Tomhaggard.

In the 1970s, they continued with concerts, fundraising dances, coaching and children's parties.

Michael Sills was chief steward of the Irish Festival in Roundwood Park.

In the mid-1970s to the 1980s, Michael Sills and Sean Devereaux formed a darts league, which is still running to this day.

Padge Reck was the first mayor of Wexford to visit the association in London. That was in 1980 starting the involvement of the Borough of Wexford with the association.

The association takes part in the Mayor of London St Patrick's Day Parade and won the prize for the Best Float, four years in a row.

Leading Wexford people were Jim Murphy, Castlebridge; Danny O'Leary, Bree, past chairman; Tomás Ó Murchu, Búnclody; Martin Whitty, Bunclody, who went back to live in Wexford; Tom Bailey, New Ross; Jim Doyle, Adamstown; Patsy Newport, Mayglass, Catherine Byrne, Taghmon, Maura Doyle, Barntown-Taghmon; Pat Clegg, Ballymitty; Martin Kirwan, Glynn; Kitty Watson, Ferrycarrig; Tom Bailey, New Ross; Anne Fitzpatrick, Oulart; Jim Ryan, Donard; Sean McGrath, Tenacre; Phil Roche, Whitechurch-Glynn; George Brown, Crossabeg and Martin Kirwan, Glynn.

Pat McCabe of Wexford Town, who went to Leeds, was head of the provincial council, and was chairman of the association. Danny O'Leary was chairman.

Kitty Watson from Ferrycarrig, elected in 1990, was chairperson for four or five years. Her brother, Sean, was also a member. Theresa Flynn, Campile, also served as chairperson.

Trevor Diviney, director of Ground Construction, sponsor, is son of Life President, Sean Diviney whose father was a Garda sergeant in Carrigbyrne.

Justin Ffrench of Clonroche, another generous sponsor, supplies the lorry for the float in the St. Patrick's Day parade. Liz and Chris Clarke are the artists from Ballindaggin, Kiltealy. Paddy Doyle from Rathnure built it. Phil Roche, who is kit manager for the London football teams and Marie Doyle helped put it together.

Among the association's memorable events was when Ned Wheeler, Damien Fitzhenry, George O'Connor, Tom Dempsey and Larry O'Connor brought over the Liam McCarthy cup.

Michael Sills went to London in February 1969 and two weeks later carried the Wexford banner in the St Patrick's Day Parade. He recalls Peter White from Kilmore saying: 'Here young fellow, you carry that banner'. Wexford County Council later donated a large banner and Wexford Borough Council donated another.

When Michael Sills first came to London, Danny O' Leary was in the chair, and the members included Jimmy Murphy, Eddie Grace, Ballinaboola, Billy Ryan, New Ross, and Tommy Harrell from Horeswood who was the Father Murphy's club secretary at the time.

Michael said: 'The reunions were the best way to meet someone from home. We had nothing then except the pub and the association and dances. The Galtymore was known as the ballroom of romance.

'We gathered in Kilburn in North London. Socialising was the main thing and charity was the next thing. There was loads of work in factories. Smiths Industries were makers of parts for cars. There was Walls, and Heinz in Harlesden and Guinness. You could walk in and out of jobs if you weren't happy.'

Other members who contributed to the working of the association over the years were Martin Kirwan, Glynn, who served as honorary treasurer of the association for twenty-three years. Sean McGrath, Tenacre, Kilmore; Senna Roche, Glynn; Sean Devereux, Ferrycarrig, P.J. Fortune, Mickey Connors, Enniscorthy; Martin Power, Cushinstown; Gordon Reid, Billy Ryan, Michael (Socks) Murphy, New Ross; Jim Howlin, Rathnure; Pat Byrne, Tinahealy, Anne and Peter Fitzpatrick, Oulart-The Ballagh, Anne Glover, Oulart; Harry Roberts, The Rower; William Clegge, London; Don Mahon, Enniscorthy and Mick Bowe, Horeswood.

In 2014, the association celebrates its sixtieth birthday. The Wexford Association, now called the London-Wexford Association, continues to fill a vital need for more than one hundred members, with a few of the early members, meeting formally and informally in the Done our Bit Club, Crown Moran Cricklewood Hotel, and the London Irish Centre in Camden.

OFFICERS AND COMMITTEE OF THE LONDON- WEXFORD ASSOCIATION IN 2013 ARE:

President -Michael Sills, Murrintown; chairman- Tommy Harrell, Horeswood; vice chairman - Phil Roche, Whitechurch, Glynn; secretary -Siobhan Talbott, daughter of Phil Roche; treasurer - Marie Doyle , Camross, sister of Sean and Pat Kavanagh; registrar- Carmel Ryan, New Ross; Public Relations Officer - Lucia Butler, Clongeen; assistant PRO- Noel Swaine, Ferns; and Life President - Sean Diviney, Carrigbyrne.

Committee members are Paddy Doyle, Rathnure; Kathleen McGrath and Nicholas McGrath, children of the late Sean McGrath, Tenacre, Kilmore, long-time president of the association; Margaret McGuinness, English born, father Jim Ryan from Rathnure; Jacqui Fortune Ryan from Enniscorthy; Nicholas McGrath, Kilmore and Noel Furlong of Adamstown ancestry who is London-born, and Breda Weller, of Rathnure ancestry, who is London-born.

Justin Ffrench from Raheen, New Ross is a generous sponsor.

DUBLIN SUPPORTERS

The Wexford Supporters' Club was founded in 1989 by a group of Wexford friends, exiles to Dublin, who met at UCD.

Since that time, the club has grown to become a world-wide network of GAA supporters and friends who meet for events including golf outings, social events and fund-raisers for the GAA.

The concept of the Dublin Wexford GAA Supporters club was handed over to the GAA and the once Dublin-Wexford Supporters Club is now the Dublin branch of

Paddy Kehoe of Glynn, racehorse owner and pundit; Moses Morrissey, Gusserane; Jimmy Roche, Oulart; Dick Bennett, Oylegate and Tom Moriarty, Bree, now MDR Consulting, Dublin

Former chairpersons of the club in Dublin include Jimmy Roche, Pat Quigley, Tom Moriarty, Bree; Matt Browne, Enniscorthy and Moses Morrissey, Gusserane, who was chairman of the club for nine years up to May 2013.

Among the events organised by the Dublin branch are an annual golf outing attracting up to 40 teams to Castlewarden Golf Club, Co. Kildare, in July. In 2013, the club members organised a dance themed 'the Purple and Gold Ball' at the Stillorgan Park Hotel, Dublin.

The Stillorgan Park Hotel is meeting place for the club members where the hotel owner, Des Pettitt of Wexford, has given meeting facilities to the club.

Jim Bolger, native of Oylegate, now world famous thoroughbred racehorse trainer and breeder, is also a patron and supporter of the club.

The founders of Dublin Wexford Supporters' Club in 1989 were Eddie Walsh, Matt Browne and Pat Quigley. Eddie Walsh, Ballyhogue, was professor of agriculture, at UCD. Matt Browne of Blackstoops, Enniscorthy, a pharmacist, became president of the Irish Pharmaceutical Society. The late Pat Quigley, native of New Ross, was a sports editor with the Sunday World newspaper, and National PRO of the GAA.

Among those who joined the club then were Peadar Murphy, Ferns, former general secretary of Macra na Feirme and later chief executive of IFAC accountants; Dave Beirne, Ferns, managing director of a refrigeration company; Ann O'Connor, Duffry Rovers, Enniscorthy; Cyril Byrne, Castletown; Jimmy Roche, Oulart and

In 2013, the officers of the Dublin Supporters' club are:

Chairman- Justin Prendergast, Oulart; Secretary- Ann O'Connor, Enniscorthy; Treasurer- John O'Neill, Wellingtonbridge.
Committee members and leading members in 2013 include: Moses Morrissey, Gusserane; Cyril Byrne, Castletown; Dave Beirne, Ferns; Tom Moriarty, Bree; Owen McCarthy, Oulart-The Ballagh; Ben Healy, Wexford; Joe Carroll, Oulart; Matt Browne, Enniscorthy and Elaine Hughes, Kilanerin, Eddie Walsh, Ballyhogue; Paddy Kehoe, Glynn; Mick Murphy, Naas; Ed Murphy, Wellingtonbridge and Joe Kinsella, Clough.

WEXFORD EXILES IN NEW YORK

The County Wexford Association of New York was founded in New York in 1907 and was incorporated in 1949.

The association's banner, called 'the Wexford Banner', made by the nuns from the Adoration Convent in Wexford town, is carried by members of the association in the annual St. Patrick's Day parade in New York.

On the front of the banner is an image of Commodore John Barry, Father of the American Navy, who was born in Wexford in 1745 and died in

Paddy Kehoe presenting cheques from the Wexford Supporters' Club (Dublin) to Michael McMahon Wexford CBS.

Philadelphia in 1803, and on the back is Vinegar Hill, iconic landmark of the 1798 Rebellion, and Father John Murphy.

The banner was completely restored in 1997 by the Adoration Nuns in Wexford for the bi-centennial commemoration of 1798 in Enniscorthy and was carried by members of the County Wexford Association, who travelled over for the bicentenary in 1998, as they marched up Vinegar Hill cheered on by more than 50,000 people.

A group of 'Pike Men' from Wexford later joined the Wexford Association in the New York St. Patrick's Day Parade. The association hosted more than 150 visitors for 10 days.

The Wexford Association organises an annual dance for members, supporters and friends.

In 2004, the association donated $10,000 to the Michael J. Quill Cultural and Sports Centre in East Durham as a contribution to the Wexford flag in the Irish Park.

In March 2007, the County Wexford Association of New York celebrated its 100th Anniversary at a celebratory dinner dance attended by four hundred people at the Astoria World Manor. The attendance, which included many public representatives from County Wexford, paid tribute to the president of the association, Breda Cahill of Ballybrittas, Bree, the guest of honour, for her major contribution to the development of the association.

The president paid tribute there to the organising committee members: Elizabeth Long, Mary and Jimmy Gleeson, Patrick Long, Eileen and Pat Howlin, Stacey Howlin and Jim Boyle and to Martin Dunne, a native of Tipperary, who was MC for the event.

She thanked representatives of Wexford County Council, Wexford Borough Council, New Ross Town Council, Wexford GAA, and the JFK Trust, New Ross for coming to New York for the celebrations. The table listings for the celebrations then included: Philomena Roche, mayor of Wexford; Kieran Roche, Pat Collins, town clerk, Noreen Collins, Harry McGrath, Jimmy Gahan, South East Radio, Mairéad Gahan, Michael Sinnott, South East Radio, Ger Griffin, county secretary, Cllr. Pat Codd, chairman, Cllr. Lorcan Allen, Pauline Quinn, Cllr. Kathleen Codd-Nolan, Cllr. Declan MacPartlin, Mrs. MacPartlin, Cllr. Sean Doyle and Cllr. Tommy Carr. She thanked also Lil Kennedy and the Ballindaggin Pipe Band, Josie Broaders and the National Pike Association and friends, Margo Murphy and her Irish School of Dancing from Adamstown, and April Coady and the Silver Spurs Line Dance Group in Wexford.

During the centenary celebrations, the association literally put Wexford on a giant map of Ireland made of bricks and the size of a football field at the Michael J. Quill Center in New York. Bricks were sold for one hundred dollars each to fund four thousand, six hundred bricks in the Wexford section of the map. Donors had their names engraved on the brick, making it a memorial in the United States for Wexford people.

Man of the Year

John O Murphy, a lawyer and native of Ramsgrange and founder of the networking groups In-NYC and IN-USA, was elected the County Wexford Association's Man of the Year at the association's annual dinner dance held at Gaelic Park. He was also honoured for his work by New York City Council. He was a leader in the Irish-American Bar Association of New York. He is a graduate of the University of Notre Dame, Indiana and of Mercyhurst College in Pennsylvania.

1938 RECORD OF SUPPORTERS OF MONUMENTS FOR THOSE WHO DIED IN THE INSURRECTION OF 1798

THE COUNTY WEXFORD MEN AND WOMEN'S PATRIOTIC, SOCIAL AND BENEVOLENT ASSOCIATION OF NEW YORK

Incorporates an image of two 1798 pikes crossed and bearing the inscription: 'Who Fears to Speak of '98 One Hundred Fortieth Anniversary'.

❛ The men and women of this association hereby unanimously commend and approved the generous noble and public-spirited co-operation of the people of Wexford to commemorate in a fitting and suitable manner by the erection of public monuments on the various battlefields of their native county, the One Hundred Fortieth Anniversary of the Insurrection of 1798 and as exiles from the most historic county in Ireland, we hereby congratulate and wish success to the various committees whose patriotic motives have evoked such a spontaneous commemoration.

In Witness whereof and in public meeting assembled on this St Patrick's Day, March 17, 1938, we hereby affix our names and places of origin.

Pres: Michael J. Mitten	Matilda Kelly	John Fleming	Patrick O'R(eilly)	Michael Harpur
Vice-Pres: James Kearney	Maurice Condon	Thomas Doran	Jo Kearns	Mrs Tom Boyle
Corr Sec'y: Michael Hynes	James Rooney	Matthew J Duggan	Ann Harney	Miss Margan [?]
Treasurer: Joseph Doyle	Patrick O'Neill	Lillian Dempsey	James A. Ryan	Catherine Murphy
Finc Sec'y: Leo Cullen	Dorthy Condon	Patrick Murphy	Harry Mullen	Mary E Maloney
Sgt. At Arms: Nicholas	Anna Murphy	Margaret Reid	Peter O'	Kathleen O'Brien
Roche	Maurice Condon	Maggie P [?]	Margaret Harney	John Sinnott
Br Aidan Whelan, O.S.F.	Anna Melia	Anna Philips	Robert Hughes	James Riley
Rev James K Morrissey	Catherine Kennedy	James Bolger	Denis O'Neill	A.N. Other
Maureen Somers	Ed Mullaney	Caroline Furlong	Patrick Whelan	John James Walsh
Kitty Cummins	Joseph Condon	Anthony Phillips	James Connelly	Katherine Walsh
Angela Lombard	Ml. J. Loughman	Mary Hoynes	May Wilson	James J. Walsh
Margaret Mitton	Mr and Mrs Kerrigan	John Fielder	William Lindsay	Minnie O'Leary
Catherine Nolan	Miss Mary Murphy	James Broaders	Mary Codd-Storey	James Murphy
Joey Daley	Thomas McCormick	Kathleen Reid	John Kehoe	Henry [?]
Patrick Martin	A Wickham Jnr	Michael O'Neill	Nancy Furlong	Mary Ryan,
Sean Cowman	Patrick Dempsey	Patrick Gregory	Ann Wilson	Graham [?]
Martin H. Doyle	Aiden Redmond	Patrick Costello	Basil Caffrey	Pierce J. Ryan
Patrick O'Neal	Mary Joe Boyle	James Murphy	James Walsh	Pierce F. Walsh
James Mooney	Joseph Nolan,	M.J. Collins	Robert J. Lee	James H [?]
Patrick O'Neill	Edmund Storey	Helen Varney	Eamon Somers	J. Walsh
Philomena Moloney	Michael Dempsey	James C. Gannon	Anastasia Doran	John Sinnott
Katherine Mullaney	Mr and Mrs Aidan Lacey	Morgan McLoughlin	John Murphy	Michael Pierce ❜

Commodore John Barry.

KENNEDY LEGACY

By Sean Reidy

In the summer of 1947, US Congressman John F Kennedy travelled from Lismore to New Ross in search of the home of his ancestor Patrick Kennedy, who left Ireland during the Great Famine in 1848. The young Congressman was staying with his sister Kathleen in Lismore Castle, the home of the aristocratic Devonshire family. Kathleen had married William Cavendish, the Marquess of Hartington, the son of the Duke of Devonshire, and heir to his title and his vast estates.

JFK's aunt Loretta had told a young John Kennedy of his grandfather Patrick Joseph Kennedy travelling to Ireland in the 1920s to meet his first cousins, and how he had helped them financially at a time when they were threatened with eviction. Loretta's stories had left an impression on him and he was determined to find out more.

He found the homestead in Dunganstown and must have been struck by the contrast between the palatial luxury of Lismore Castle and the small farmyard where he met Mrs Mary Kennedy Ryan and her children and some cousins from down the road. He was welcomed with open arms and had a cup of tea and took some photographs. These family photographs he sent back to Dunganstown once developed, and they can still be seen there today.

The 1947 encounter with his family roots in Dunganstown stayed in his memory and when he became President of the United States he determined to return. President Kennedy had a profound sense of his own destiny and his place in history. He knew how significant it was for the great grandson of an Irish Famine emigrant to become President of the United States. He stood on the Quayside in New Ross, and as a fourteen year old watching the events unfold on television in the living room in Kilkenny, I can still hear him say, 'it has taken 114 years, 6000 miles and three generations to make this journey and I am glad to be here'. With these few words, John F Kennedy laid to rest the ghost of the Great Famine and provided a transformational moment in Irish history. He also bestowed upon New Ross a priceless legacy.

He went from New Ross to Dunganstown for the iconic tea party with Mrs Ryan and her daughters, Mary Ann and Josie, and the local community. After this 1963 visit of the President, life changed forever for the Kennedys, the Ryans and the Grennans of Dunganstown. Every year thousands of people come with curiosity to see the farmyard that JFK visited in 1963. This became a significant invasion of privacy at the family farm. Ultimately, in order to manage the flow of visitors, and because he saw the importance of the story, Patrick Grennan opened an ad hoc exhibition for visitors in the farmyard to tell the remarkable story of the Kennedy family.

However nothing changed in the town of New Ross until the JFK Trust was founded in 1988 by Michael Ryan of RTÉ and local businessman Paddy Quinn, among others, in order to commemorate the Kennedy legacy by involving itself in a project that would enrich the lives of the people of the town and its environs.

I answered an advert from the JFK Trust in a local paper in 1991 looking for a project manager to develop a Heritage centre. In truth, it was the name of the organisation rather than the job description that attracted me to the position. I had been very inspired by JFK as a young man living in Kilkenny. I applied for the job and in the final interview I was asked to put forward a concept

Tallships at Duncannon.

for the proposed new centre. I proposed the building of a replica famine ship and the building of a centre that would interpret the rich maritime history of New Ross, and tell the story of nineteenth-century emigration and would have a focus on the achievement of Irish emigrants throughout the world, with the Kennedy story being the paradigm.

In 1993, we met with Senator Ted Kennedy to get the support of the family, and he introduced us to his sister Jean, who would be appointed US Ambassador to Ireland soon after. This proved to be a very happy coincidence and Jean became an enthusiastic supporter of the project. A great adventure was beginning.

More than 100,000 people came to see the *Dunbrody* being built in the late 1990s and nearly a million people have visited the ship and New Ross since it was opened as a visitor centre on the Quayside in New Ross in 2001. This has provided a very positive multimillion spin off to the local economy. A new visitor centre was added in 2011 and Jean Kennedy Smith had also persuaded the government to assist Patrick Grennan and invest in a new state of the art visitor centre in Dunganstown. Plans to develop a new Quayside infrastructure to complement the *Dunbrody* were also put in train by New Ross Town Council, the statue of JFK was unveiled in 2008 and this year the boardwalk linking the statue with the *Dunbrody* was completed, and a specially sculpted podium marking the spot that Kennedy spoke from in 1963 was erected.

As the 50th Anniversary of the '63 visit was being planned, the idea of taking a light from the Eternal Flame at President Kennedy's graveside emerged. It would light a flame dedicated to all Irish emigrants in New Ross and JFK's wish to return in the springtime would now be symbolically realised.

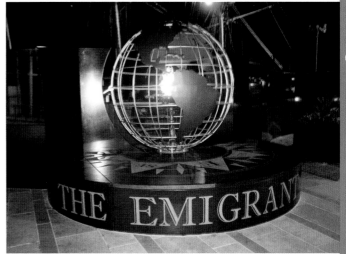

As I escorted Caroline Kennedy along the boardwalk to take her place in the VIP seating for the celebrations on that wonderful day on the 22nd of June 2013, I felt a great sense of history, and of course privilege and honour, that the daughter of the late President Kennedy would be with us, the people of New Ross, to commemorate that fateful day in 1963.

There was also a sense that the people of New Ross had finally fully embraced the Kennedy legacy and New Ross had been transformed and would never be the same again.

Dunbrody Emigrants' Eternal Flame.

William Hickey, a rector, who attended Trinty and Cambridge, and who had a pseudonym of 'Martin Doyle' founded Ireland's first agricultural school at Bannow.

"The Bannow residential school accepted boys (both Protestant and Catholic) aged between thirteen and nineteen years and thus differed from the Hofwyl school (in Berne, Switzerland) where the pupils commenced at a much younger age. It combined a literary with an agricultural education, but had a short life span, from 1820 to 1826, due to Hickey's transfer to Kilcormick. However, it served as a prototype influencing the educational structure adopted by the later and much bigger schools at Templemoye and Glasnevin. The Bannow schoolhouse is a private residence at this time and an adjacent field continues to be known locally as 'the Pelozzi' field Pestalozzi field"

- *Towards a History of Agricultural Science in Ireland*, edited by P.L. Curran, published by the Agricultural Science Association.

Donohoe, Sister Eilis Mary, formerly Furlongstown, Taghmon now Bafoussam, Cameroon. The daughter of Patrick and Annie Donohoe she joined the Sisters of Marie Auxilatrice in London in 1962, went to teach in Cameroon in Central Africa in 1980 and also worked in the transmission of radio programmes there. She did the groundwork for the visit of Pope John Paul II to the Cameroon in 1985. Devoting her life to the welfare of the poor. Now works as the director of a hostel for young girls to enable them to concentrate on their studies.

Donovan, Gerard, writer, was born in Wexford and grew up in Galway. His collections are *Columbus Rides Again, Kings and Bicycles* and *The Light House*, which was short listed for the *Irish Times* Literature Prize. His novels include *Doctor Salt* and *Schopenhauer's Telescope*, which was long listed for the Man Booker Prize, 2003, was a finalist for Irish Novel of the Year 2003, won the Kerry Group Irish Fiction Award in 2004, and represented Ireland at the European First Novel Festival in Hungary. His short stories are collected in *Country of the Grand*. He teaches at the University of Plymouth.

1,849 students sat their Leaving Certificate in Co. Wexford in 2013.

Donovan, Katie, born 1962, and spent her early childhood in Co. Wexford. Her poetry collections are: *Watermelon Man, Entering the Mare, Day of the Dead* and *Rootling: New and Selected Poems.* She is the author of a pamphlet, *Irish Women Writers: Marginalised by Whom?* With Brendan Kennelly and A. Norman Jeffares, she edited *Ireland's Women, Writings Past and Present.* She is co-editor, with Brendan Kennelly, of *Dublines,* an anthology of writings about Dublin.

Donovan, Richard, 1927-2005, Ballymore House, Camolin; lawyer, farmer; married to Margaret, they have two sons and two daughters; together with Margaret, founded Ballymore Historic Features on family lands at Ballymore; his father was a central figure in the Churchill war effort and was involved in the planning of the Normandy invasion; founder member of international aid agency, Concern; founder member of County

Wexford Mart Ltd.; treasurer of the IFA committee which challenged the Poor Law Valuation System in the High Court in the 1980s leading to the de-rating of all agricultural land in Ireland; helped found the Arts Centre in Wexford town; chairman of Katherine Howard Foundation; member North Wexford Tourism; member NWSPCA.

Doran, Ger, Craanford GAA/Community activist; married to Joan and they have three sons and one daughter; former Fr. O'Regan's player, he helped establish camogie in the parish starting off an U10 team, now there are two adult ladies' teams, one of which won a Junior B league; currently establishing an indoor playing arena for which he is fundraising; actively involved in the 'Strictly Club Dancing' initiative.

Doran, Gráinne, born 1970, Askamore, now Ballymurn, daughter of John and Mary, née Dunphy, Monasterevin; archivist at Wexford County Archives and Records Centre; graduated from UCD with BA (Hons) degree in English and Greek and Roman Civilization, 1990 and Higher Diploma in Archival Studies, 1997; attained Certificate in Local History Studies, NUI Maynooth – Rathmines; former Library Assistant with Dublin Public Library Service and Midland Regional Archivist.

Doran, John, formerly William St. in Wexford, now Dublin, born 1933, vice president of the Phoenix Cricket club in Dublin. Johnny, as he is better known in Wexford, played on the Wexford minor football team beaten 3-6 to 1-4 by Kerry in the All-Ireland final of 1950 before a crowd of more than 76,000 in Croke Park. He remains the last Wexford man to score a goal in an All-Ireland football final. Johnny continued playing soccer

throughout the fifties, mostly in the Waterford league in venues like Ozier Park and Poleberry. After he helped to start the Wexford and District League, he enjoyed a lot of success on the playing pitch with St. John's Athletic from Wexford Town who dominated in the early years. Having moved to Dublin, he also had a spell as chairman of St. Patrick's Athletic around the late 1980s, a period during which Brian Kerr led the club to a Premier League title.

Doran, Paddy, RIP 2001, Askamore, established one of the foremost country stores in Wexford where you could buy everything from the proverbial needle to an anchor; established strawberry depot for Scott's Jam Factory of Artane, Dublin, in the 1960s; he became postmaster in Askamore 1954. As well as attending to all normal post office duties, he was an unpaid social worker, form filler and counsellor for the vulnerable, the illiterate and the troubled; volunteer with Ardeen Cheshire Home, Shillelagh, Ferns Diocesan Pilgrimage to Lourdes and the Hospitalite ND de Lourdes.

> The first manager of the Shelbourne Co-op in Campile was Martin Howlett who won four All Ireland football medals with Wexford in 1915, 1916, 1917 and 1918.

Doran, Tony, Boolavogue, played senior hurling for Wexford, mainly as full forward, from 1967 until 1984, and he lined out for his Buffers Alley club for 30 years, from 1963 to 1993, when he retired at age 47 after a junior final. He was educated locally and at St. Peter's College, Wexford. He won All-Ireland Colleges' and minor hurling titles in 1963 and an U21 title in 1965, Wexford's only success at this grade. In 1966 Doran made his senior debut with Wexford and won a National League. He subsequently won his first Leinster title in 1968, before later playing against Tipperary in the All-Ireland final of 1968 where he inspired a famous second-half revival with two goals. He won three more Leinster titles but not another All-Ireland with the county, being beaten by Cork in the finals of 1970, 1976 and 1977. He won his only All-Star Award for his displays in 1976 when he was also Texaco Hurler of the Year. He shared in seven Railway Cup victories with Leinster in the 1970s. He won eleven Wexford senior hurling championship medals with his beloved Buffers Alley, and helped them to All-Ireland club final victory in 1989, the only time for this title to come to Wexford. He also won Leinster club medals, in 1985 and 89. Tony Doran played 187 times for Wexford between 1965 and 1984, including 40 championship games. He scored 131 goals, 179 points and is second only to Nickey Rackard in the all times scoring lists. What makes this remarkable is the fact that Doran was not a free-taker and almost all his huge tally was scored from play. He may have been considered an unlucky captain: he led the U21 team beaten by Cork in the 1966 final after two replays, and was captain of the senior team in 1976 and 77, again beaten by Cork on both occasions. Tony Doran's three brothers also lined out for Wexford. Bill, the oldest, played on Wexford intermediate teams beaten in All-Ireland finals by Tipperary 1963 and by Cork 1965, but he missed out on the year in between, when Wexford actually beat London to win the title. Joe Doran was on the winning U21 team in 1965, but was on the losing side against Cork in the intermediate decider of the same year. Colm Doran, youngest of the quartet, suffered quite badly at the hands of Cork in All-Ireland finals, losing to them in the 1969

and 1970, after a replay, U21 finals, and also in the 1976 and 77 senior finals when he was an outstanding right half back. He won an All-Star Award for that position in 1973, nine County Senior medals with Buffers Alley, and a Leinster club medal in 1985.

Dowdall, Elaine, Coolcotts, Wexford, golfer; daughter of Con, Wexford and Faythe Harriers hurler who was on the first Wexford teams to win minor, 1963, and U21, 1965, All-Ireland titles. Elaine represented Ireland at under-age level and was on the Irish team at the European championships at U21 level in 1994 in Vienna and 1998 in Oslo. She graduated to the senior team and competed in the Europeans in 1997 in Finland, 1999, Paris and 2001 in Spain. She was selected on the British and Irish elite squad for the Curtis Cup for 2002, but injuries ruled her out and curtailed her career at just 24 years of age.

Dowling, Mary, New Ross Golf Club, won the Ladies' Irish Close Championship in 2010 at Portstewart, beating one of the famous Cavan twins, Leona Maguire, in the final with a birdie at the last hole. She represented Ireland in the European team championships in 2009 in Slovenia and in 2010 in Sweden.

Dowling, Michael, from Gorey was Leinster Chairman of Community Games alongside Margaret McDermott as secretary and he held that position for 16 years. He was also the county Chairman and he took a keen interest in the art competition when it became part of the Games. He co-ordinated the county finals in Gorey and then the county presentation night, displaying the children's work. He acted as co-ordinator at national level and then as national judge.

Doyle, Adrian, born in Wexford, has held every position of importance in local administration and is currently Wexford County Manager. He began a distinguished career in local government when he was appointed to the staff of Wexford County Council in 1971. He was promoted to the position of Town Clerk in New Ross in 1974, and six months later moved to Midleton, Co. Cork, as Town Clerk. After two years in Midleton, he returned to Wexford Co. Council, where he filled a number of management positions, including Head of Finance, County Secretary and Director of Services for Corporate Affairs and IT. On the retirement of Eddie Breen, who had served as Wexford County Manager for nine years, Adrian Doyle was appointed Interim Manager in 2012.

Doyle, Andy, 1932-2012, Taghmon, shopkeeper; married to Eileen, née Nolan, Polehore, Glynn, they have two sons and two daughters; former Wexford inter-county hurler and footballer; organised bingo in halls across Wexford, in Kilkenny and in Clonmel; member of inaugural Community Centre committee; member Tidy Towns committee and Village and Square committee; played leading role in the Tops of the Town and Taghmon Mardi Gras.

Doyle, Anne, Ferns, born Co. Wexford 1952, journalist, retired RTÉ television and radio newsreader; youngest daughter of John, 1903-1975, and Elizabeth, née Kavanagh, 1916-1979; she has five brothers and one sister; graduated with a BA in History and English from UCD; joined RTÉ in 1978; current Wexford County Council Ambassador; presided at the Ferns Mediaeval Gathering 2013 organised by Ferns Development Association; her partner is former restaurant owner, Dan McGrattan.

Doyle, Avril, born in Dublin on 18th April, 1949; member of a well-known political family – the Beltons. Following her marriage to Fred Doyle, she came to live in Wexford, and was Wexford's first lady mayor. She was first elected to Dáil Éireann in November, 1982, as a Fine Gael TD for Wexford constituency. She lost her seat in the 1989 General Election, but was re-elected in the 1992. She again lost her seat in the 1997 election, this time to her party colleague, Michael D'Arcy. She was elected member of the Seanad on the Agricultural Panel from 1989 to 1992 and from 1997 to 2002. She was elected a Member of the European Parliament in 1999 and was re-elected in 2004. She was appointed a Minister of State in the coalition governments of 1982-87 and 1994-1997. In January, 2009, she announced that she would not be seeking re-election to the European Parliament.

Doyle, Benedict, Newbawn, building worker; married to Rita, they have three daughters; served two terms as chairman of County Wexford Macra na Feirme; great interest in vintage machinery; involved in Gathering 2013 in Ryan's farmyard at Newbawn. Their eldest daughter, Áine, was one of only three promising students in Ireland to have been awarded a scholarship to study at the prestigious Li Po Chun United World College, Hong Kong.

Doyle, Brian, Sallystown, Killinick, retired teacher St. Peter's College; married to Joan, they have four children three of which are priests. Brian joined the Grey Friars in 2013, Jim is CC in Monamolin and Rory is studying for the priesthood in Canterbury. All three are qualified engineers from NUI Galway and have worked abroad. Brian and Joan have one daughter, Judith, who is married in Cornwall.

Doyle, Eddie, Ballywilliam, born Co. Wexford 1963, singer/songwriter; son of James, Ballywilliam and Peggy, née Power, Ballybeg, Rosbercon; worked in New Orleans where he had a residency in Ryan's Irish Pub, Bourbon St. for eight years. He relocated to Nashville where he worked as a house musician in Mulligan's Irish pub on 2nd Avenue for two years; recorded five albums, one with his wife, Hazel Cloney, Fethard-on-sea. Hazel and Eddie returned to Wexford and married. They have two musical daughters, Jeanie and Róisín.

Doyle, Frances, originally from Haggard, Ramsgrange, born 1966; married to Michael, they have three children; Frances took over the care of Templetown Church from her mother-in-law, Elizabeth Doyle, née Bolger, The Dell, Ballycarney; works part time in the tourist office in Fethard and continues to be actively involved in various community affairs.

Doyle, Jim, Garrenstackle, Bree, science teacher in St. Peter's College and wife Clare, née Byrne, Curraghnaboola, principal of Crossabeg NS, they have three daughters; both are People of the Year winners 2012; both heavily involved in community activities in the parish.

Doyle, John, Fethard-on-Sea, author of *The Helen Blake – the Last Fethard Lifeboat*, 1979.

Doyle, John Joe, Kingsford, Barntown, telecommunications technician with Eircom, married to Carol, née Edmundson of Coolcotts, who played national league basketball with the Waterford team, Wildcats, they have one son, Kevin, aged 17. John is a highly successful athlete, he has been competing in cross country since 1975, and came in the top three for twenty consecutive years with thirteen wins, five silver and two bronze; represented Ireland in the world cross-country championships in Neucehatel in Switzerland in 1986; has won more than fifty senior county titles between cross country, track and road. He originally started running as fitness training for handball. He won two Powers Sports Star Awards in County Wexford in 1984 and 1988. He holds the record in the county for number of titles won. He helped raise more than a €1 million for the chemotherapy unit in Wexford General Hospital. The funds were raised mainly from the sales of a video in which he featured presented by RTÉ's Michael Ryan. The money financed the purchase of buses allowing people to get to Waterford for radiotherapy.

Doyle, John Jude, Clonroche, born Co. Carlow 1940; publican; married to Ann, née Doherty, Clonroche, they have three children. In 1976 they renovated their pub in Clonroche and renamed it The Cloch Bán. He is heavily involved in local GAA and is a leading figure in all matters equestrian. He is a director of Horse Board Ireland. He has written a number of books and presented a DVD on County Wexford.

Doyle, J. V., RIP, although not a native of Kilmore he was to become a household name in both athletics and business in the parish and beyond, one of Wexford's finest athletes, a great all-rounder on the track; set up Doyle's auto service in Bridgetown in the 1950s, importing tractors from England, doing them up and selling them on; opened garage in Redmond Road in Wexford (known as Roche's garage) and had a main car dealership; owned a number of fishing trawlers.

Doyle, Kevin, Killurin, formerly Adamstown, born 1983, Irish International and English Premier League soccer player. He is son of Paddy and Bernie, née Kehoe, one of famous Kehoe camogie playing sisters from Clonleigh. Kevin started playing soccer in Adamstown in the Schoolboys' and Wexford League. It wasn't long until his talent was spotted and he went to Saint Patrick's Athletic and then Cork City. He was then snapped up by English side Reading and helped bring them into the Premier League in 2006. He moved to Wolverhampton Wanderers in 2009 at what was then a record fee for that club £6.5 million. In recent times he has had injury problems and was dropped by Giovanni Trappatoni but is back on the Ireland team again under interim manager Noel King. At the end of September 2013, he had played 53 times for Ireland, scoring 12 goals; he also lined out 11 times for the Irish U21 team, scoring 6 goals. He had been selected on the Ireland squad for the last two games in the World Cup Qualifying campaign and was hoping his international career would be re-ignited following the departure of Giovanni Trappatoni. He was selected as Irish U21 international player of the year in 2005; Young International Player of 2006, and Senior Irish Player of the Year in 2008 and 2010; his goal against Andorra in 2010 was chosen as the Irish international goal of the year. Kevin is married to Jenny Harney, his teenage sweetheart from Wellington Bridge, and they have one son, Bennett Bernard, born 2012. He served in 2013 as a Wexford Ambassador. He commutes between England and his home in Killurin.

Doyle, Liz, Kitestown, Crossabeg, racehorse trainer; four times ladies' point-to-point champion rider in Ireland before retiring from riding in 2011. She runs a successful training outfit with her partner, Barry Murphy, son of Ferdy, a Wexford man who has trained for years in England. Liz has discovered two Cheltenham winners in recent years, Al Ferof and Cheltenian, both being sold on to English trainers. She had a fancied runner in the Cheltenham Champion bumper herself this year, Le Vent D'Antan, which finished seventh. Liz is daughter of Freddie and Avril Doyle, former TD and MEP.

Doyle, Margaret, nee O'Leary, Rosslare, county Secretary of Wexford GAA Board since 2008 and a member of St. Mary's Club. She served as assistant secretary and Bord na nÓg secretary for ten years. She follows in the tradition of Rosslare people holding this prestigious position, beginning with Liam Murphy in 1939, followed by Stephen Roche up to 1946, Liam Murphy again from 1953 to 1960, followed by Paddy Roche up to 1979.

Doyle, Michael, Cottage, Tagoat, was a farmer and politician. He was first elected to Dáil Éireann as a Farmers' Party candidate in the 1922 General Election. He was re-elected in the 1923 and June, 1927, elections, but he lost his seat in the General Election held in September, 1927. He was an unsuccessful independent candidate in the 1932 General Election and he was also unsuccessful as a National Centre Party candidate in the 1933 election. He was one of the pioneers of tobacco and beet growing in Co. Wexford.

Doyle, Mogue, Enniscorthy, born 1945. His novels are *Dancing with Minnie the Twig, A Moth at the Glass, Down a Road All Rebels Run* and *Mr Bawman Wants to Tango*.

Doyle, Paddy, born Wexford 1951. His autobiography *The God Squad,* published in 1989, was in the best-seller lists in Britain and Ireland for several weeks, and has been translated into Danish, German, Japanese and Slovenian.

> The language known as Yola was commonly spoken in south Wexford until it became extinct in the 19th century. It was the language of the people of the Baronies of Forth and Bargy which was south of a line from Wexford to Wellingtonbridge.

Doyle, Patrick, Courtown Harbour, born 1942, entrepreneur, business man; married to Therese, RIP 2005, they have four daughters; owns Doyle's garage in Courtown Harbour, a business started by his parents, John and Eileen, and also has a premises in Camolin run by his son, Paddy; owns O'Brien's Pub in Killenagh, one of the few thatched public houses remaining in the county which is run by his son, Bernard and wife, Ailish; son John runs a farm where he rears calves for beef. Patrick was stock car racing driver of the year in 1972.

Doyle, Paddy, Ferns, publican, The Thatch and the Courtyard; with Michael Nolan of S&N Granite, Camolin, and a committee, he helped raise €100,000 following the 2004 St. Stephen's Day Tsunami in South East Asia, money which was used to build a state-of-the-art orphanage/hostel for young people, called Tír na nÓg, in Sittandy, Batticaola district of Sri Lanka which was opened in November 2006.

Doyle, Rev. Philip A. , O.S.A., Maudlintown, Wellingtonbridge, wrote the three-act play *The Hook in the Harvest,* in 1881, as well as *Life of St. Nicholas of Tonentine*. He was a noted poet, playwright, historian and musician.

Doyle, Seamus, who died on 30th April, 1971, was among the leaders of the Easter Rising in Enniscorthy in 1916. He was a Sinn Féin politician, and was elected unopposed as a Sinn Féin TD to the second Dáil at the 1921 elections for the Wexford constituency. He opposed the Anglo-Irish Treaty and voted against it. He was elected as an anti-Treaty Sinn Féin TD in the 1922 General Election, but did not take his seat. He didn't contest the 1923 General Election. He wrote *The Gaelic History of Uí Chennselaig.*

Doyle, Teresa, née Peck, Ballygarrett, born 1960, music teacher and songwriter, married to Francis Doyle, Ballygarrett; daughter of Thomas Peck and Catherine, née Dunne, Ballygarrett, both National School teachers; attended Goldsmith College, University of London; established the North Wexford Youth Orchestra in 2008; currently leader of Wexford Sinfonia; teaches thirty students from 6 to 16 years of age violin, piano, guitar and recorder; author of the Primary School book *Let's Play Together* for tin whistle and recorder.

Doyle, Willie, Wexford 1923, Cooladine, Enniscorthy, mixed farmer and businessman, married to Kate, RIP 2006, née Rath, Blackwater, with five sons; established a thriving farm and milling business on which three sons still work; instrumental in building and developing the Farm Centre on the Mill Park Road, Enniscorthy; awarded honorary life membership of the IFA by unanimous vote 2006.

Dreelan, Tommy, native of Ferns, moved to Aberdeen, and with his three brothers, Michael, Sean and Ciaran, went into the oil industry. They sold their company, PSL, for £45.5million. They then developed Qserv and then sold it for £165m. They now own Dreelan Services and Tommy runs a motor racing team, Celtic Speed.

Druhan, Loughlin, Tagoat, managing director of international logistics company, Druhan Bros. Transport; married to Mary, née Fanning, Kilmuckridge, they have five sons and one daughter. Loughlin is one of the Druhan dynasty of Our Lady's Island which has been in Wexford for nine generations. His grand aunt was a abbess of Kylemore Abbey, Co. Galway. He is founder of Bargy Vintage Tractor Club.

Duffin, Annie, née Cadogan , Ballycullane, New Ross, born Wexford 1917; married to John 'Ginger' Duffin, RIP, hackney car owner, they had six sons and two daughters; has 17 grandchildren, 22 great grandchildren; the oldest lady in the parish, at 96 she does not wear glasses or a hearing aid and attends weekly bingo.

Duggan, Larry, The Moorings, Carcur, born Wexford 1927, carpenter, boat builder; married to Madge, née Farrell, William Street, they have three sons and one daughter; noted maritime historian; the son of a wheelwright, he began making boats at 14 years of age and his last boat took part in Queen Elizabeth II's Jubilee on the Thames in 2010; built 70-80 boats over his career including three Mermaids, which are no longer being made and one of the last punt gunners ever made; an uncle and aunt were living at the lifeboat station at the Fort in the mouth of Wexford harbour when it was washed away in 1925.

Duggan, Thomas, Whitehouse, Rosslare, RIP 1953; was the oldest claimant of the Argentine fortune which was known as the 'Duggan Millions'. The genealogy of the Wexford Duggans became a matter of considerable interest in the early years of this century when the story of the so-called "Duggan Millions" became known. One Alfredo Duggan of Argentina, descendant of a Wexford emigrant, had died an extremely wealthy man, with no heirs. Eventually, in 1944, a nephew then aged 72 and originally from Rosslare, inherited several million pounds.

Duggan, Peter, Whitehouse, Rosslare, who was known as 'Uncle Peter', took part in the famous gold rush to the Klondike 1896-99 and later became a paddle steamer operator on the Mississippi, plying from New Orleans before he returned to his native Rosslare.

Dunne, Jason, solicitor with John A. Sinnott of Enniscorthy, and co-author of the books *Inheritance and Succession* and also the book *Make Your Will*; has dealt with the courts and court offices on all aspects of civil litigation, conveyancing and probate. He moved from his native Dublin, where he was office manager of a law firm, to Wexford in 2004. His wife, Siobhán, née Dunne, Clonroche, is a solicitor with the firm of Huggard Brennan and Murphy, Wexford.

Dunne, Kieran, Oulart, served as Chairman of the Ladies' Gaelic Football Board for two years. He was also a mentor with the Shelmalier club and is a brother of Wexford senior hurling team manager, Liam.

Dunne, Liam, Oulart, born 1968; former star player and current manager of Wexford senior hurlers since 2011. Though small in stature, was an imperious centre back for Wexford and Oulart-The Ballagh, following in the footsteps of club mate Mick Jacob. His Wexford career spanned three decades, 1986 to 2003; he won an All-Ireland senior medal,1996, two Leinster senior, a minor and U21 medals, and three All-Star awards, 1990, 1993 and 1996. At club level, Dunne played with the Oulart-The Ballagh club for more than twenty years, winning six county senior medals before retiring in 2008. He took over as club senior manager and won three titles in a row, before taking on the Wexford job. With Damian Lawlor, he wrote an acclaimed autobiography on his life and hurling times, *Crossing the Line*. His brothers Tomás and Seán, both played senior for Wexford; brother Kieran served as chairman of the County Ladies' Football Board and was involved in the writing of the Association's first official rulebook; his sister, Siobhán was a two-times camogie All-Star and sisters, Fiona and Ailish, also lined out for the county.

Dunne, Lorcan, Clonroche, community activist involved in Clonroche Historical Society, the Penny Bank, Tidy Towns' Committee and Tops of the Town. He was secretary of Clonroche Development Society when the Millennium Park was created. In 1986 he produced a documentary *The Banks of the Boro*. In 2001 he represented Clonroche at the Nations in Bloom Awards held in China and came home with a silver award.

He hosts and produces the Clonroche website. He is an active member of Enniscorthy and Oyster Lane musical societies.

Dunne, Nicholas, Courtnacuddy, born 1969, fifth generation dairy farmer, married to Judith, née Walsh, they have two daughters and one son; owner Killowen Farm, winner of six gold stars at the Great Taste Awards 2013 for Killowen Farm Yogurt.

Dunne, Rory Jnr, Merton, Bree, student of Immunology, Biochemistry in Trinity College Dublin, son of Rory and Angela; President of the Students' Union in Trinity up to June 2013; member of the Board of TCD; member of the Finance, Human Resources and Estates Committees TCD; former PRO for the TCD Society of St Vincent de Paul.

Dunne, Prof Tom, Carrigbyrne, was a prolific writer. Books by him included *Wolfe Tone – Colonial Outsider*, published in 1986 and *Rebellions: Memoir, Memory and 1798* in 2004.

Dunphy, Mag, Spenser's Court, Enniscorthy, owner of Mags School of Motoring, she is a qualified driving instructor with the ADI. A native of Shanoule, Foulksmills, Mag competed in the Blackstairs Adventure Race in May 2013 over the Blackstairs Mountain and on to the River Barrow.

Dunphy, Shane, Wexford, born 1973, author, child care leader and family support worker. He is best known for a series of books he wrote detailing some of the situations he has worked with, including *Wednesday's Child, Crying in the Dark, Hush, Little Baby, The Boy in the Cupboard, Will Mummy be Coming Back for Me?, Little Boy Lost* and *The Girl who Couldn't Smile*. He has made a number of documentaries for radio and television.

Dunphy, Tessie, Newbawn, married to Tom, they have three sons and one daughter; a committed community worker and ICA woman, lends a hand at catering for all parish functions; lifelong member of the PTAA and has travelled widely.

Dwyer, Liam, Camblin, New Ross, general manager, South East Radio, a position he has held for the past twenty years. He has overseen the station's growth to be the most listened to radio service in Co. Wexford. Liam was instrumental in setting up the Friends of Wexford General Hospital to raise money for services and facilities there. A member of Wexford Lions Club. He is married to Vivienne who is a sales executive in South East Radio and they have one son, Cian.

Earle, Mary, Kilrush, a member of Kilrush Drama Group, which celebrates its 50th year in 2014, won Best Actress for her portrayal of Maggie Polpin in John B Keane's *Big Maggie* in the All-Ireland Confined Drama Finals in Cavan as well as numerous regional drama festival awards.

Earle, William, Seaview, Ballygarrett, born 1988, captain of the Landsdowne Rugby team with 70 caps for the club; member of Ireland U18 team; one of four children of Peter and Mary; has degree in Environmental Biology from UCD and is currently pursuing a PhD.

Egan, Babs, née Roche, from Scar, Duncormick, RIP 2007, singer/songwriter and conductor of Rathangan male voice choir; composed the air to *The Wexford Fishing Song*; wrote for the *Farmers Journal* in the 1960s; her daughter, Marian became a well-known presenter on Clare FM.

The ship *The Kerlogue*, owned by the Devereaux family, rescued 168 members of the German navy in the Bay of Biscay during World War II in 1943 and brought them to Cobh, Co. Cork. A young Malachy O'Kelly who became a Conventual 'Grey' friar missionary in Zambia for forty years was interpreter for them. Fr. Fritz O'Kelly, living in the Friary, Wexford told, aged 86, of his visits to them in the Curragh, Co. Kildare.

Egan, Elizabeth, BSc. PhD., Barmoney, Galbally, a specialist in sports physiology, she ran her first cross country race in 1993. She has since provided lifestyle support to world and Olympic medallists and today helps athletes of all levels in Ireland, the UK and Africa reach their potential. Her PhD from Liverpool John Moore's University examined the physiological aspects of the Female Athlete Triad. Her book, *Notes from Higher Grounds*, provides a guide for athletes looking to train at altitude. She is daughter of Aidan and Mary, nee Murphy.

Ellis, Ned, originally from Ferns, RIP 2013; was one of the founder members of the Wexford soccer league. Ned was a very talented sportsman, winning a Wexford Cup medal with St. Cormac's FC in 1962, before moving to Dublin where he took up ten pin bowling with great success. He won several national bowling titles as well as representing his country in two world championships, in Japan and America. He also had a great passion for horse racing, attending Cheltenham for many years. Ned is survived by wife, Nuala, son, Brendan and daughters, Sandra and Breda.

English, Jim, 1932-2008, formerly Ballindoney, Rathnure; Wexford and Leinster hurler; captained Wexford to All-Ireland victory in 1956; also won medals in 1955 and '60, and five Leinster medals; national league winner in 1956 and '58 and Railway Cup winner 1956 and 1962. Jim worked in Carlow and was elected as chairman of Carlow County Board in 1992, having served as Leinster delegate for 20 years.

English, Michael, Tinnecarrig, farmer; community activist involved with the church and local school; former chairman of Newbawn parish council and instrumental in the execution of serious roof repairs to Newbawn church and other big developments in the area during his time as treasurer of the parish council.

Enright, Michael, Killinick, was a school teacher. His book, *Men of Iron – Wexford Foundry Disputes 1890-1911,* was published in 1989.

Ensor, Tony, from Dublin but now Ballinapark, Bunclody, and Court Street, Enniscorthy, solicitor and former Irish international rugby player who assisted Enniscorthy RFC when he retired from the international scene at the young age of 28 in 1978. He won 22 Irish caps at full-back, replacing the legendary Tom Kiernan. When Tony came to Enniscorthy he played for a number of years and also coached the team to a Provincial Towns' Cup win in 1989. He was chairman during the clubhouse developments. He is married to Beatrice and they have two children.

Esmonde, Sir Anthony, 15th Baronet, Ballynastragh, Gorey, who was born on 18th January, 1899, was a medical doctor, farmer and politician. He first stood for Dáil Éireann as a Fine Gael candidate for the Tipperary constituency in the 1943 General Election, but was unsuccessful. It wasn't until the 1951 General Election that he tried again. This time he was a Fine Gael candidate for the Wexford constituency and he succeeded in winning a seat. He was re-elected in five subsequent elections until he retired from the Dáil at the 1973 General Election. He was Chairman of the Committee of Agriculture in the Council of Europe and a Member of the Consultative Assembly of the same institution. He was also a member of the Irish National Health Council and was for many years a firm advocate of Ireland's entry into the EEC.

Esmonde, Bill, Bachelor's Hall, Piercestown, was a Trustee of National Community Games and a founder in Wexford. He had been involved in sport all his life, playing in goal for Wexford in their Leinster junior hurling wins of 1940 and '41, alongside a young Nickey Rackard, Billy Keilthy and others - these teams were the harbingers of a revival in hurling in the county after a dormant period. Bill was also a great athlete, excelling in the field throwing events. He helped in the promotion of athletics and was the on-field MC for many years at events around the county, including the rural schools athletics finals. He was the first chairman of Wexford Community Games. He ran a business as a drainage and land reclamation contractor.

Esmonde, Sir John, 14th Baronet, who was born on 5th February, 1893, was an Irish nationalist politician who served as a Member of Parliament in the House of

Commons and later as a TD in Dáil Éireann. He was elected a Member of Parliament for North Tipperary on the death of his father in 1915. He withdrew without defending his seat in the 1918 General Election. He subsequently served as a Fine Gael TD for the Wexford constituency, having won a seat in the 1937 General Election. He was re-elected in the 1938 and 1943 elections, but lost his Dáil seat in 1944. He was one of the few people who served as Member of Parliament in both Westminster and as a TD of Dáil Éireann.

Esmonde, Sir John Grattan, sixteenth Baronet, who was born on 27th June, 1928, was a senior counsel and politician. He was elected to Dáil Éireann as a Fine Gael TD for the Wexford constituency in the 1973 General Election. He lost his seat in the 1977 General Election. His uncle, Sir John Esmonde, 14th Baronet, was a Fine Gael TD for Wexford and his father, Sir Anthony Esmonde, 15th Baronet, also served as a Fine Gael TD for the Wexford constituency.

Esmonde, Sir Osmond, 12th Baronet, who was born on 4th April, 1896, was an Irish diplomat and Cumann na nGaedheal, and later Fine Gael, politician. He was first elected to Dáil Éireann in the 1923 General Election as a Cumann na nGheadheal TD for Wexford constituency. He didn't contest the June, 1927, General Election, but was returned to the Dáil in the General Election of September, 1927. He was re-elected in 1932 and again in the 1933 General Election. He died on 22nd July, 1936, and the Fianna Fáil candidate, Denis Allen, won the seat in the subsequent by-election.

Esmonde, Sir Thomas Henry Grattan, Gorey, 11th Baronet, who was born on 21st September, 1862, was an Irish Home Rule nationalist politician, and was one of the few people who were elected to the British Parliament and the Oireachtas. He was an Independent senator from 1922 to 1934. He was also the first Chairman of Wexford County Council, and was author of *Hunting Memoirs of Many Lands,* in 1925 and *More Hunting Memories,* in 1930.

Etchingham, Frank, 1913-1987, Rosehill, Rosslare, P&T worker, dairy farmer; married to Breda, née Costigan, 1919-2006, Tipperary town; they had two daughters and three sons. Frank and Breda were both founder members of Rosslare Development Association which purchased the community field for £6,000 in the 1970s with a far-sighted view to provide a civic amenity for local people and visitors.

Etchingham, **Seán,** was a Sinn Féin politician, and he was a member of the Irish Volunteers, the Gaelic League and the Irish Republican Brotherhood. He was first elected as a Sinn Féin candidate for Wicklow East in the 1918 General Election. Like the other Sinn Féin MPs he refused to take his seat in the British House of Commons. Instead, he took his place in the revolutionary First Dáil, which met in the Mansion House, Dublin, in January, 1919. He was appointed Secretary for Fisheries. He was re-elected in 1921, but retired from politics at the next election. He opposed the Anglo-Irish Treaty, and was arrested during the Civil War. During his imprisonment, his health deteriorated and he died in prison in April, 1923.

Evoy, Denis, Dublin, formerly Carrigbyrne, President of the Irish Hospital Consultants Association; son of Patrick and Mary, he graduated from UCD in 1991. He became a fellow of the Royal College of Surgeons in 1994. Having worked as Consultant General Surgeon at Wexford General Hospital, he now holds the same position at St. Vincent's University Hospital in Dublin. He is a specialist in breast and endocrine surgery. He was elected President of the IHCA in June 2012.

Evoy, John, Grallagh, Raheen, born 1975; married to Sarah; founder and CEO of Men's Shed movement in Ireland, involved since 2008 when he brought the idea home from Australia; son of Ned and Christina Evoy; graduated with a Masters Degree from the School of Social Justice in UCD; grandfather was the last blacksmith to work in Evoy's forge, the historic 1798 landmark at the foot of Carrigbyrne Hill.

Fallon, Niall, born 1941, author and journalist. His writings include, *The Armada in Ireland, The Lusitania* and *Fly-fishing for Irish Trout.* Niall is the son of the poet, Padraic, who was born in 1906, and served in Wexford in the Customs and Excise Department for many years and raised his family there. He was a notable poet and his verse-play, *Diarmuid and Gráinne*, was described as Radio Éireann's best broadcast. Padraic's youngest son, Padraic also, born 1946 published a dramatized memoir of his childhood, *A Hymn of the Dawn* and one novel, *The Circles of Archimedes.*

Fanning, Fintan, Ashford, Co. Wicklow, born 1959, Assistant Garda Commissioner; one of a family of six boys, born and reared in Ahullen in Kilanerin parish, he went to national school in Ballyfad and then onto Arklow CBS. Joined the Gardaí in 1980 and married Eleanor in 1987; served as Superintendent in Enniscorthy in 1997. As Assistant Commissioner in 2008/09 he had responsibility for the Gardaí in the South Eastern Region which included County Wexford, before being transferred back to Garda HQ, assuming responsibility

nationally for human resources, professional standards, training, human rights and the Irish language. Fintan has three children, one studying for a Masters in Architecture in Oslo, another studying Journalism and the youngest in transition year in secondary school. Aside from work, Fintan's main interests are GAA and boxing.

Fanning, Rory, managing director of Slaney Foods International. He grew up on the family farm in the townland of Ahullen in Kilanerin, one of the northernmost parishes in the county. Rory graduated from UCD, having attended Ballyfad N.S. and Gorey C.B.S. His early working years were spent with the Irish Farmers' Association and with CBF, the predecessor of an Bord Bia. Having spent three years managing the CBF office in Paris, he returned in the 1980s to join Bert Allen and his team in Slaney Meats, now Slaney Foods. Rory is married to Mairéad and they have two adult sons, Robert and Michael.

Fawsitt, Siobhan née Meyler, daughter of Liam and Ann, Bayview Drive; multi-AIMS awards winner and widely acclaimed star performer on musical and light opera stage with Wexford Light Opera Society and other musical societies.

Ffrench, Aidan, 1934-2011, Rosslare, Laboratory Technician, EPA Johnstown Castle; married to Frances, née Berry, Rosslare Strand; renowned entertainer and singer at weddings, fund-raisers and funerals; member of Wexford Male Voice Choir; Nat King Cole's *Mona Lisa* was his song.

Ffrench, Jim, Wexford, was the first secretary of Community Games in Co. Wexford. He was the main organiser for years of the swimming events. He had a shop at the junction of Rowe Street and Main Street in Wexford and was attached to the Rowe Street/Bride Street Area of Community Games. He took over the coaching of swimmers for the national finals and he was also a national starter for many years.

Ffrench, Peter, Harpoonstown, Bridgetown, Member of Parliament for South Wexford 1893-1918. A National Teacher by profession, he was a fine advocate for the people of South Wexford, a lifelong Nationalist and a prominent member of the Gaelic League.

Fielding, Anna Maria, 1807-1881, Bannow, went to London where she married Samuel Carter Hall and she began a most prolific writing career. She published countless short stories, novels and travel works. Queen Victoria honoured her for her work.

Finn, Lukie, Ballygullen, Craanford, Gorey, born Wexford 1960; self-employed at Grass Machinery Limited; married to Mary née Byrne, Castletown, with two daughters; winner of All-Ireland Junior Hurling medal with Wexford in 1985.

Fitzachary, John Christopher, born in Duncannon in 1840, was best known for *The Bridal of Drimna and other poems*, published in 1882.

Fitzgerald, Mick: former top national hunt jockey and now popular presenter on Channel 4 Races and At the Races; born Co. Cork 1970, but spent most of his childhood years near The Harrow, famed in the 1798 Rebellion and in the ballad *Boolavogue*. Joined local trainer Richard Lister at 16, his career spanned 20 years until his retirement in August, 2008, after he had broken his neck for the second time in a fall from L'Ami in that year's Grand National. His career total of 1,280 winners, places him in the top ten national hunt riders of all time. His big winners included the Grand National on Rough Quest in 1996, and the Cheltenham Gold Cup on See More Business in 1999. He was leading jockey at the Cheltenham Festival in 1999 and 2000. He wrote an autobiography when he finished riding, called *Better Than Sex: my autobiography*. The title comes from his famous quote to Des Lynam live on the BBC after winning the 1996 National – "After that, Des, even sex is an anticlimax!"

Fitzgerald, Paul, London, formerly Saint John's Avenue, Wexford; son of Bridget and the late James Fitzgerald. Educated St. Peter's College and Shannon School of Hotel Management, he has worked his way up through the hospitality industry in the UK to become Director of Operations for the Crimson Hotel Group. He was selected to carry the torch for the Olympic Games in London in 2012 after receiving a corporate nomination for his contribution to the hotel industry. He is married to Jemma and they have two children. They live in Kent where he still finds time to indulge time in his favourite game tennis.

FitzGerald Molloy, Joseph, who was born in New Ross in 1858, wrote poetry and novels as well as history and biography. His best-known books are, *Court Life Below Stairs, The Life and Adventures of Peg Woffington, Royalty Restored, The Life and Adventures of Edmund Kean, The Most Gorgeous Lady Blessington, Romance of the Irish Stage, The Russian Court in the 18th Century* and Sir *Joshua and His Circle.*

4

Business

County Wexford has a reputation throughout the world for its quality workforce and its culture of entrepreneurship. Ongoing indigenous investment and Foreign Direct Investment (FDI) are necessary for increased economic growth and jobs.

LEADING BUSINESSES INCLUDE:

Waters Technologies Ireland Ltd, based in IDA Business Park, Drinagh, is a US multinational, involved in creating business advantage for laboratory-dependent organisations by delivering scientific innovation to enable advancement in healthcare delivery, environmental management, food safety and water quality industries. Operating in Wexford since 1997, the company employs 232 people. Stephen Creaner is the current manager.

Kent Engineering, Ardcavan, is a manufacturer and exporter of stainless steel products to Europe, Middle East and China. The business began as a small engineering company founded by Pat Kent of Kayle, Foulksmills in 1982. In 2013 the company employed 104 people. In the same year the company opened an office

in Qatar which is run by sales executive Billy Colfer, who relocated there with his wife Emma. Ann O'Brien, daughter of company founder Pat Kent is managing director of the company. From 2009 to 2012 the company doubled its turnover and in 2012 developed to €16 million on exports alone.

Zurich Insurance, Rosslare Road, Wexford was established in 2008. The Zurich Wexford Business Centre now employs 147 people. It is part of the multinational Zurich Insurance Group, which was founded in Switzerland in 1872. The Wexford Centre services over four hundred brokers along with direct customer contact. Robert Eden is general manager.

Slaney Foods, Clohamon is part of the Linden Food Group. Along with Slaney, the group consists of Linden

WFC, or Wexford Farmers Co-op, Old Dublin Road, Enniscorthy, originally began as County Wexford Marts in 1969 trading at its current headquarters. The business branched out into retail and property development during the Celtic Tiger era but in 2013 restructured and exited this end of the business. It now operates Enniscorthy Livestock Mart and WFC Oil Ltd, its oil distribution arm. The Co-op has around four thousand shareholders in County Wexford who elect a sixteen member management board. The chairman of the current board is Charles Kavanagh, Drumgoold House, Enniscorthy. The Chief Executive is Frank Devoy, Riverside, Crosstown, Co. Wexford.

Foods based in Dungannon, Co. Tyrone and Irish Country Meats which is based in Camolin and Navan.

The group sources prime Irish beef and lamb and sells it into some of Europe's leading supermarket chains, having achieved some notable success from the quality of their produce. In 2013, Slaney Foods was the official beef supplier to the Chefs World Championships gala dinner in Lyon, France. In 2102, Slaney Foods was the chosen supplier of beef for the state dinner in Dublin Castle to honour Queen Elizabeth and Prince Philip on their visit here. Between both plants in Clohamon and Camolin, they employ 550 people. Rory Fanning from Enniscorthy is the managing director of Slaney Foods. James Walshe from Dunganstown is the general manager of Irish Country Meats.

Nolan Transport of Oaklands, New Ross, is an international transport company celebrating fifty years in business in 2013. Involved in UK and European transport of a large range of goods and services. Now comprising a fleet of eleven-hundred trailers and four hundred and fifty tractor units. The company has one hundred employees and an annual turnover of €55 million. The managing director is Patricia Nolan.

Stafford Bakeries, based in Clonattin, Gorey, was established by Sean Stafford, a native of Wexford town who moved to Gorey in 1955 where he established his first bakery in a rented premises. It now now employs over two hundred in a new state-of-the-art bakery at Clonattin supplying bread and confectionery. Day to day

Wexford strawberries.

running of the business is now carried on by his son and daughter, Sean Stafford and Una O'Leary. The company also owns Joanne's Coffee Shops in Gorey, Arklow and Wexford.

Lake Region, Butlers land, New Ross is a medical devices company and the biggest employer in County Wexford. It was established here in 1994 and it now employs eight hundred people. Lake Region is the world's largest manufacturer of guidewire which is now used worldwide in different types of vascular access applications. The company produces six hundred thousand guidewires each week at its New Ross plant. Latest figures show Lake Region exports 63.3 million euro worth of goods annually from its New Ross base. The company is a privately held corporation with its headquarters in Minnesota in the US. Chief Executive in New Ross is Noel Hennessy who in 2013 spearheaded the company to a major industry award, winning the Pearse Walsh Award at the Irish Institute of Training and Development Awards (IITD) for its Continuous Improvement Programme.

Eishtec Contact Centre, Drinagh Business Park opened for business in January 2013. The company provides tailored solutions to fourth generation Smart Phone users in the UK. The company was set up in Waterford in 2010 by its three directors Brian Barry, Heather Reynolds and Colm Treacy who between them have sixty years' experience in the business. They set up with nine former employees following the closure of the Talk Talk Centre in Waterford. In 2013 they are employing 600 people; 400 in Waterford and 200 in Wexford.

Sulzer Pumps, Clonard Industrial Estate Wexford. Originally ABS Pumps, the company began in Wexford in 1972. It manufactures a wide range of pumps including machining, assembly, motor winding, packaging and shipping of submersible pumps. The company has a long history and began in Switzerland in 1834. In 2011 Sulzer purchased Cardo Flow Solutions, the parent company of ABS Pumps. It is one of largest producers of submersible pumps in the world. Latest annual figures for 2011 show its Wexford operation had a turnover of €64 million, and profit of almost €11 million. The company has 261 employees. Its general manager is Sean Roche. 2013 figures from the Irish Exporters Association show Sulzer Pumps to be the biggest exporter from County Wexford in monetary terms.

BNY Mellon Bank, is based in Wexford Business Park, Rochestown, Drinagh. Originally PFPC, which set up in Drinagh in March 2002, this business was bought out by BNY Mellon in February 2010. One of Wexford's only high-tech financial services' companies, it is an international corporation headquartered in Wilmington, Delaware, US. Andrew Finucane is general manager at Wexford BNY Mellon.

ClearStream Technologies, Moyne Upper, Enniscorthy, is a developer and manufacturer of minimally invasive medical devices such as catheters and stents for use in procedures such as angioplasty. They are used to clear blocked arteries and stents and are permanently implanted devices used to prevent prolapse of the artery following the angioplasty procedure. The plant was first set up in 1996 by another US company, AngioDynamics, who were persuaded by then Minister Ivan Yates to make Enniscorthy their base for manufacturing platinum stents to assist patients with heart disease. There then followed a management buyout of AngioDynamics making the company wholly Irish owned and called ClearStream. It was subsequently bought out by US Medical devices

giant, Bard in October 2011. It has a workforce of 280 in Enniscorthy. The Operations Director, a native of Wexford, is Pauline Oakes.

Celtic Linen Limited is a family-owned group of companies based outside Wexford town on the Rosslare Road at Drinagh. The managing director is Philip Scallan and the business was set up by his grandparents in 1926. Now employing three hundred people, it is one of the biggest laundries in Europe. It specialises in laundry services for the healthcare, hospitality and workwear sectors along with supplies for the janitorial, catering and textile services. Philip Scallan, a graduate of Carlow Regional Technical College and Derby Lonsdale College, has worked through all sections of the business, before becoming managing director.

Great Island Power Station. SSE is currently constructing a 460MW combined cycle gas turbine at Great Island. Expected to be commissioned in 2014, this clean gas-fired power plant will replace the existing 240MW fuel oil unit at the site significantly decarbonising electricity generation in Ireland. SSE bought the plant from Endesa in 2009 who, in turn, had bought it from the ESB who established the plant in Great Island in 1968. When complete in 2014 it will have the power to run the equivalent of half a million Irish homes. SSE is bringing a 41km gas pipeline from Bawnlusk in Co. Kilkenny which will be extended to Wexford town via Taghmon . This is the first time that natural gas will be delivered to County Wexford. Peter Gavican is SSE's Project Manager for Great Island. In 2013, there are 860 construction and maintenance workers on site.

Paganini is a family-owned Irish company. Founded in 1990 by Tomás Murphy who began making ice cream using a classic Italian recipe on his dairy farm in Wexford, the company today makes a full range of premium ice cream and desserts. The company won the Bord Bia Innovation Award for its specialist ice cream in November 2013. The company is now run by the founder's son, Barry Murphy.

BREAD, CULTURE AND BUSINESS ENTERPRISE – TOM WILLIAMS AND FRIENDS

Tom Williams grew up in Taghmon in the house attached to his parents' business, the old Williams Bakery at the front of the site currently occupied by McGee's Quickpick. He attended Taghmon national school. With him were his sister, Ann, and brothers, Dominic, Kevin and Brian.

The bakers in his youth were Jem 'The Baker' Walsh, Paddy Carton, Fintan Martin, Jem Kehoe, Paddy Walsh and Jack Walsh. The van salesmen were Jimmy Brady, Nicky Brady and Pat Kehoe. Pat Connors worked in the yard and Joe Kavanagh and later Mike Flaherty worked in the shop with Mary Whitty from Kilmannan taking care of the Post Office which was attached to the shop.

Tommy Murphy of Coolaw worked in the garage servicing the vans and the bakery machinery. Others who worked at the bakery were Dick Whelan, Seamus Seery, Jem Sinnott, Patsy Doyle, Phil Kelly and John Boland. Tom Furlong and Pat Murphy worked in the shop for many years.

Tom's first job was working for Tom O'Donnell, the chemist and next-door neighbour, every Saturday and got a sugar barley stick for payment.

When he was a young boy, he played with neighbours, Brendan Doran, Mossie Kehoe, Michael and Tom Furlong and a returned Cockney, Terry Gosby. He was also friendly with Nicholas Sinnott of Aughfad.

In primary school in Taghmon, his teachers were Miss Mai Bennett, Martin Doyle, Olga O'Malley, Tom Ryan and Mr. Buckley. Paddy Walsh of the Wexford Road and Tom achieved joint first place in the class in the Primary Certificate examination.

In September 1953 Tom Williams was enrolled in Good Counsel College, New Ross. He did his Leaving Cert in 1959. He joined the Provincial Bank of Ireland, later AIB, in 1960. He first worked in Waterford O'Connell Street, Dublin branch, Cabra and Finglas branches. Later in 1966 he was seconded to a new branch in Templeogue, Co. Dublin where the manager was Hubert Topping.

He and sister, Ann, sang in a folk duo doing gigs around Dublin. They performed on the Late Late Show on RTE presented by Gay Byrne and sang *The Chinaman,* an old song taught to them by their mother. He later wrote *Cúchullain's Son,* which became a Wexford anthem; *A Man Named McCall; A Civil War Lament;* and *Wexford – My Homeland*, all of which were recorded by various artists.

Marie and Tom married on the 7th October 1967 in St. Andrew's Church, Westland Row, Dublin. The best man was Paul Hanratty and the bridesmaids were Patricia Groarke, Marie's first cousin, and Dympna Brennan later Bramley.

During the 1970 bank strike, Tom and Marie stayed in Taghmon with Tom's parents. The bakery business began to expand under their direction. Brian Williams joined the firm about 1971. In 1970, the firm had three sales routes and ten staff consisting of bakers: foreman, Jem (the baker) Walsh, Jim Kehoe, Denny Flood, Séan Murphy, Eddie Waters, Dick Whelan, Tommy Murphy and van salesmen John Hanlon, Mossy Kehoe and Martin Doran.

By 1988 the bakery had grown. Employment figures were in excess of 150. A brand name promoted by the firm was 'Tommy Tucker'

In the 1990s Tom became involved in Wexford Enterprise Centre, a voluntary organisation set up to create jobs in Wexford. He succeeded the late Niall McConnell, as chairman in 1998. He was chairman up until his passing. Wexford Enterprise Centre, and its large premises at Wexford town, has supported the creation of over 800 jobs for Wexford.

When Wexford won the All-Ireland hurling final in 1996, he wrote the book *With Heart and Hand - the Inside Story of Wexford's Hurling Resurgence*, published by Blackwater Press. In 2006, he wrote the book *Cúchulainn's Son - the Story of Nickey Rackard* about his idol.

He was a member of Wexford Historical Society, contributing articles to the Society's journal. He was a founder of Taghmon Historical Society and edited its journal for several editions. He also wrote a history of Rosslare Golf Club entitled *Fairways of the Sea - 100 Years of Golf in Rosslare*. He was made an honorary life member of the club.

Tom Williams lived the last 27 years of his life at Park House at Wexford town, with Marie. He passed away on August 18th, 2012, after a long battle with illness. In a eulogy at this funeral in Barntown, his friend, Liam Griffin, said that he was a man of the future to whom the past really mattered.

He is survived by Marie; his eldest daughter, Joanne Powell, husband Billy and children Ben and Beth; his second-eldest daughter, Annette O'Gorman, husband Eoin and children, Ciara, Susie, Gillian and Drew; and son, David, who is engaged to Rosaleen O'Shaughnessy.

FOREIGN DIRECT INVESTMENT

by Patrick Howlin
Director North America, IDA Ireland, New York

The IDA is responsible for marketing Ireland as a location for Foreign Direct Investment (FDI) worldwide. The United States is by far the largest market for IDA, accounting for up to 65 per cent of FDI into Ireland every year.

IDA has a marketing team of 26 people in six offices throughout the US whose job it is to build relationships with companies that are growing internationally, especially in Europe, and are planning to either set up their first offshore presence or grow their existing European infrastructure.

Among the key decision factors for companies looking to invest abroad are: access to a skilled and talented workforce, ease of international access, a supportive business environment, clusters of similar businesses, proximity to Universities, availability of latest technology and communications infrastructures, an attractive international taxation regime, and cities where people will want to live and work.

The delivery of this physical, social, and economic infrastructure is key to securing inward investment and IDA is continually engaged with Wexford County Council and local business support networks and organisations in identifying and prioritising investment in these areas for the county.

While FDI companies tend to gravitate towards larger cities and centres of population, areas like Wexford still offer substantial advantages to international companies. There are 14 IDA-supported companies (9 from the US) employing 2,200 people in the county, a 6.5 per cent increase since 2009.

Based on a strong tradition in manufacturing, County Wexford has proven to be particularly effective in attracting companies in the medical technologies and the engineering industries. More recently some success has also been achieved in attracting knowledge-based industries such as financial services. The establishment of the Coca-Cola manufacturing and innovation facility was a notable recent addition to the international business community in Wexford.

Johnstown Castle.

RICH RESOURCES FOR WORLD OPPORTUNITY

In 2013, County Wexford is equipped to take advantage of the inevitable upturn in the national economy and contribute to increased national growth in the years to come.

The presence here of world-leading multinationals employing thousands of local people in IT and software development, in international call centres, film production and products ranging from foodstuffs to fashion accessories is testimony to the high regard nationally and internationally for the county's skills and talent base and the loyalty and flexibility of staff. Ireland is among the top ten in the world for availability of skilled labour, openness to new ideas, labour productivity and flexibility and adaptability of people.

The reputation abroad of Wexford manufacturing is manifest in major contracts for its products in other countries across the world. The entrepreneurial spirit of young people is based on a background of first class education, training and an agri-rural socio-economic context. All young people are English-speaking and many are fluent in French and German. Mandarin is now being taught in secondary schools and colleges.

Indigenous industry, based mainly on agriculture, construction and Government and public service organisations, is the backbone of the Wexford economy.

The government and local government officials are emphasising education, investment in research and development, and increased competitiveness in the quest to boost the county's economic growth.

Tourism thrives with many thousands of people within Ireland and from all over the world coming to the county for its amazing heritage, its sunshine, (Wexford has more hours sunshine than any other county in Ireland), its summer events and in the autumn, its world-famous Wexford Festival Opera.

Wexford is traditionally an agricultural county, for which it earned the name 'The Model County' for its superior production of quality food. The Wexford flag carries the Latin motto 'Exemplar Hiberniae' meaning 'Model of Ireland'. Farmers here have produced crops of the best barley, wheat and oats ,sugar beet, cattle, sheep and pigs and milk for food production for centuries. Ships laden with Wexford produce left ports at Wexford and Rosslare and New Ross for destinations in Wales, England, Europe and the rest of the world. Wexford is also a maritime county. Fish products made from fish harvested in the seas around the coast and from factory production are now exported to many continents.

Wexford has also an enviable reputation for its horse sport industry with some of the world's leading trainers and owners coming from the county and a world-class equine treatment centre based in the centre of the county.

Here, we now have in 2013 a mix of traditions of farming and fishing and the horse sport industry combined with the new skills and industries of the future based on new Information Technology.

Wexford is now connected to the world and the world to Wexford through high powered fibre-optic broadband. There are airstrips for private landings and an international airport is only an hour away. Road infrastructure is developing with Wexford town and Rosslare not more than two hours from the capital centre.

County Wexford with its rich resources of talent, skills and raw materials, made more valuable over many years of investment aided by the IDA and Enterprise Ireland and the County Enterprise Board is now poised for opportunity across every sector in the world.

LEGAL EAGLES

By Jason Dunne, solicitor
at John A. Sinnott and Company

What good Wexford solicitors endure as they work for their clients goes most often without recognition.

On 10 May 1916, during the 1916 Rising in Enniscorthy, John Scallan, a solicitor in the firm of John A. Sinnott's, then in Abbey Square, wrote to his uncle, also a solicitor, and also named John Scallan, in 25 Suffolk Street, Dublin as follows:

"The Rebellion or Insurrection was sprung on us very suddenly here, as all was peace and quiet on Wednesday and at 4 o'clock a.m. on Thursday, the Rebels were being posted in their several places around the town. Now that the police barracks is situated next to me, I need not tell you that my position in the Abbey Square was not what one would call pleasant as bullets were flying up and down from the top of Castle Hill and from the far side of the river to the Barrack. Some have struck the house and it was with difficulty that I succeeded in getting the family out of the place and lodged in the Hotel while the Insurrection lasted… It was I may say, an appalling time here, and what made it worse still unfortunately two of my staff were mixed up in it and I have been left short-handed as they have been arrested and taken straight away…"

That solicitor's ordeal and good deeds were not discovered until about ninety years later.

In the 1798 Rebellion, Bagenal Beauchamp Harvey, a protestant barrister found himself appointed reluctantly as commander in chief of the Irish insurgents not long after they took Wexford. He later, led an attack on New Ross. He and his aide-de-camp, Mr. Gray, a Protestant attorney, were on a neighbouring hill, almost inactive spectators of the fight.

In the retreat, on seeing the blackened walls of Scullabogue barn, he remarked to a friend: "I see now the folly of embarking in this business with these people: if I succeed, I shall be murdered by them; if they are defeated I shall be hanged." The attack was initially successful but they didn't follow through. The King's troop re-organised and then re-took the town.When Wexford was re-taken by troops, Harvey was caught, court martialed and executed on Wexford Bridge.

In 2009, a man began choking in the Wexford District courtroom in Ardcavan. Solicitor Sean Cryan, a mountaineer, who wasn't supposed to be in court that day, dashed to his side and opened the man's airway which saved his life. The members of the Press in the court created national headlines from the incident and a solicitor's good deed was recognised next day.

County Wexford solicitors have been involved in the defining moments in the history of the county. They have made their mark on the county and the law of the land and the laws of other countries for hundreds of years ever since Brehon law, the first legal system in Ireland. Well known solicitors in the county in recent times include, John Murphy, Enniscorthy; Jimmy Murphy, who represents the Earls of Portsmouth and Leinster and was the coroner for South Wexford for many years; James O'Connor, Wexford; Kevin O'Doherty, Gorey, the State Solicitor for County Wexford, Tony Ensor, rugby legend and former President of the Law Society, and Simon W. Kennedy of New Ross, who went to the United Nations with a case, then on to Rome to sue the Pope.

The Circuit Court still sits in the County Hall, formerly Wexford Gaol, where 23-year-old Daniel Handley of Wicklow, was the last man to be hanged in 1890.

For many years Judge Donnchadh OBuachalla was the District Judge for Wexford. He presided over many cases that made national headlines. The District Court is a place for the expression of all the emotions of County Wexford life. It deals with extremes from murders to fines for having no car tax displayed, bringing at times great sadness and at time great joy such as when the noted Judge Dunleavy would break into song.

The current District Judge is Judge John Coghlan from Kildare.

THE PEOPLE NEWSPAPERS GROUP

Based in Channing House in Rowe Street, Wexford, *The People Newspapers Group* is the largest regional newspaper group in Ireland; its titles include the Wexford People, Enniscorthy and Gorey Guardian, New Ross Standard, Wicklow People, Bray People, Carlow People and the Ireland's Own magazine. It is part of the Independent News and Media (INM) group, having been bought by the Irish Independent in 1971. The Wexford office is a production hub for a number of other regional papers in Cork, Kerry, Sligo and Drogheda.

The Wexford People was first published on January 8th, 1853, by editor and proprietor Edward Walsh, a founder and first president of the GAA in Co. Wexford.

The Group is headed by Michael Ryan, Operations Director for Independent News and Media's nine regional newspapers on the east coast of Ireland. From St. Mullins in Carlow, he joined People Newspapers in 1990; he was appointed Editor in 1999, became Operations Director at the company in 2007 before moving to his current position in 2011. He was preceded by Ger Walsh from Taghmon, as group editor and as Regional Managing Director with INM.

Jim Hayes is Group Editor, Alan Aherne is Group Sports Editor, and Phil Murphy and Sean Nolan are editors of Ireland's Own. Advertising Manager is Ann Jones from Taghmon. News reporters in the Wexford office are David Tucker, Maria Pepper, Brendan Furlong and Padraig Byrne, and the other towns are covered by Fintan Lambe, Gorey; David Medcalf, Enniscorthy, and David Looby, New Ross. Other editorial and production staff in Wexford include Colm Lambert, John Donoghue, Toddy Walsh, Darragh Clifford, David Devereux, Michael Harpur, Shea Tomkins, Stephen Rooney, Sinead Duffin, Emma Stafford, Peter Henry, Brendan Lawrence, Jill Acheson and Eimear Hogan.

THE ECHO

When it first appeared in Enniscorthy in 1902, *The Echo* was a weekly broadsheet carrying the iconic masthead, *The Echo* and *South Leinster Advertiser* One hundred and eleven years later, the newspaper has a more modern size and shape, and three more titles, including New Ross, Gorey and Wexford.

The Buttles, Eamonn and Norman, rescued the ailing paper in the late 80s, and sold on a flourishing buoyant set of titles to Cork-based *Irish Examiner* owners, Thomas Crosbie Holdings Ltd in 2006. Landmark Media Investments purchased *Wexford Echo Newspapers* group in 2013.

The current team at *The Echo* includes: Editor, Tom Mooney; Journalists: Mikey Carthy, Ronan Fagan, Anna Hayes, Niamh Devereux, Saoirse McGarrigle, Dan Walsh, Brendan Keane. Production team: Manager, Michelle Treacy; Louise O'Connor, Kathleen Doran, Richard Nolan, Stewart Malcolmson, Ian Lawlor. Advertising team: Manager, Ray Mahon; Darren O'Connor, Conor

Breen, Richard Thomas, Paul Kelly, Clodagh Mernagh, Evelyn McCloskey. Photographers: John Walsh, Jim Campbell, Christy Farrell. Administration team: Sarah Doyle, Sharon Murphy, reception Murry McDonald CEO; Ann Murphy, accounts manager, Sue Harpur, Karen O'Dowd.

SOUTH EAST RADIO

South East Radio is County Wexford's designated radio station. It began broadcasting under regulations brought in by the government for the establishment of local radio stations around the country in 1989. It has continued to hold the broadcasting licence since and in 2013 signed a contract with the BAI the Broadcasting Authority of Ireland to provide the service for the coming ten years.

South East Radio began broadcasting on October 20th 1989 and the first voice heard on the station was that of legendary broadcaster Noel Andrews and the first tune played was "Boolavogue". Down through the years the station has received many awards and this was capped on October 4th, 2013, when it won a PPI Award the radio "Oscars" for a programme and campaign in May 2013 entitled No Phone No Facebook. This was broadcast on the station's flagship programme, Morning Mix. in conjunction with secondary schools in Co. Wexford.

South East Radio is Wexford owned with most staff also from the county. The managing director is Eamonn Buttle while his brother Norman is company secretary. The general manager is Liam Dwyer, head of programming is Michael Sinnott, head of sales is Marian Barry, and office manager is Orla McGuinness. Alan Corcoran presents the "Morning Mix" programme. Other full-time presenters and producers are Stephen Dee, Tony Scott, Alan Maguire, Tony Kehoe, Jimmy Ryan and Lee

Hynes. South East Radio News department consists of Michael Sinnott, Michael Doyle, Jim Kealy, Janice Stafford and Emma Ní Riain. A number of part time workers complete the voices of South East Radio: sports presenter/reporter/commentator Liam Spratt, news reporter Jimmy Gahan; weekend news/sport Paul Rowley; specialist music Paddy Ryan, Brendan Walshe, Seamus Coleman; Midweek Voices Dan Walsh; GAA programme Pat Murphy and music show presenters, Lorraine Byrne and David Roche. South East Radios weekly output is complemented by programmes produced by the Christian Media Trust. This trust is run by the four main churches in County Wexford. Its chairperson and co ordinator is Maria Colfer who presents "Simply Divine".

BEEF AND LAMB AND THE SLANEY FOODS STORY

By Rory Fanning, Managing Director, Slaney foods

I have a very clear recollection of visiting my maternal grandparents every Sunday in Bolacreen just outside Gorey. While all important matters of the day were discussed during that weekly visit, farming matters dominated the conversations. I remember flicking through the pages of the *Hereford Herd Book*, a compendium showing all that was best and available in cattle breeding to the farmers of the day. Little did I know at that time that all of this was a very early preparation for a lifetime working with farmers in Wexford, in the Slaney valley and beyond, preparing the quality beef and sheep meat they produce with such attention and respect for animal welfare and our environment, dispatching the end product all over the world.

The opportunity to present beef and lamb originating in County Wexford to the world came to me through my time with Slaney Foods in Bunclody. Established by the Allen family in the late 1960s, Slaney Foods is a name trusted by retailers, restaurateurs and food manufacturers worldwide. It makes me very proud to know that brands like "Slaney Valley", "Slaney Gold" and "Wexford" are sought by premium customers in all key international markets. The foundation of this demand for Wexford beef and lamb is the Wexford family farm.

It is really fantastic to think of the teamwork involved from 'farm to plate' in building this reputation. Today we are delighted that our business has expanded to include the Irish Country Meats operation further north in Camolin. While we are a team of 370 dedicated employees in Slaney in Bunclody, the ICM team, led by Managing Director Joe Hyland, employs 425 people with its operations extending beyond Camolin to other locations, namely Navan in County Meath and Liege in Belgium. ICM specialises in lamb while Slaney can put all of its focus on beef.

As well as being a significant employer in the county, we also think a lot of the wider community in which we live and work. Beyond the most important agricultural community, we have our schools, our public services and private business, all of us linked and working so closely with one another.

In my schoolboy days, we spoke of agriculture as the most important industry in Ireland, contributing by far the majority of our GDP and especially of our exports. Everyone is rightly well pleased to see the growth in many other areas like IT and pharmaceuticals.

While we have all witnessed and pay the price for the tragedy of the national economic disarray of recent years, one compensation for those of us involved in agriculture and the food industry is to see that we have come centre stage again. Slaney Foods and Irish Country Meats are investing in the future, making sure that our production remains world class. For this journey into the future, we are also very fortunate to be at the centre of a very unique working relationship with Linden Foods of Dungannon in Northern Ireland, a reflection of modern Ireland where co-operation North and South carries so many positives for all stakeholders.

We can be confident that like in my grandfathers' time, Wexford will continue to be one of the most important regions in the country for food production. Our land, our water and our people are resources that we must nurture and that will remain. We are seven billion people in the world, with the prediction that this will grow to nine billion people by 2050. For us today and the generations that follow in our footsteps, it will be our responsibility to contribute to the well-being of humanity, no matter how small we may be on a world scale.

Fitzharris, Larry, Gusserane, was a founder member of the Wexford Ladies' Gaelic Football County Board in 1979 and served as its treasurer for many years; was a mentor on county teams at all adult and under age grades. He was President of the County Board for numerous years until his death in 2012.

Fitzhenrys, GAA family. see Sports

Fitzhenry, Jeremiah, 1774-1845, fought as a rebel officer in the 1798 Rebellion; he later went to France and became an officer in Napoleon's army in the Peninsular Wars. He defected in April 1811 to Wellington and was allowed to come home. He followed the Whig politics.

Fitzhenry, Robert, formerly of Barntown. In June 2013 retired as Head of the Press Service of the EPP European People's Party in Brussels. He spent thirty three years in Brussels, fourteen of which were acting as adviser to Fine Gael MEPs; educated at St. Peter's College Wexford, he studied Agriculture at UCD and went on to become an Inspector of abattoirs with the Department of Agriculture. He moved to Brussels in 1975 on a three-year contract to work for the European Commission and stayed. He is married to Josephine Gallagher.

Fitzpatrick, Carmel, née Kavanagh, New, Ross, born 1947; married to Willie, they have one son; daughter of Moses and Anastasia, née Whitty; has been involved with New Ross Old Folks' Club for 33 years, chairperson for 15; forty years a member of New Ross Pantomime Society, chairperson for eight; enjoys rock fishing all over Ireland with her family.

Fitzpatrick, Michael, Cluainín, Gorey, 1935, retired carpenter/joiner; married to Bridget, née Sheil, The Bridge, Gorey, they have five sons and three daughters;

served his time with carpenter Murt Whelan in Gorey before completing his apprenticeship with George Wimpy in London. An historian of note, he is author of seven books and countless articles which have been published in various historical journals. Irish music is very important to both Michael and Bridget and they have fostered a love of traditional music in all its forms in their children and grandchildren. Michael was Gorey's Person of the Year in 1983.

Flanagan, Sean, Robinstown, Palace East, Clonroche, jockey; had his first winner in 2006 and has had a steady stream of winners since. Rides regularly for Dusty Sheehy, and Wexford trainers Liz Doyle, Leonard Whitmore and Lar Byrne. His biggest win was probably the valuable Pierse Hurdle on Liz Doyle's Penny Bill in 2009 and he also won the €100,000 Ballymore 25th Anniversary Hurdle on Brave Right for Whitmore.

Fleming, Edel, Gorey, model at Prima Models Agency, Waterford; winner of Love Fashion Love Wexford 2013; took a year out of her business studies degree course in Waterford IT to concentrate on modelling. Her favourite fragrance is *Daisy* by Mark Jacobs, and her ambition is to open her own modelling agency in Wexford.

Fleming, Gerald, Wexford, well-known meteorologist and weather presenter; married to Mary Duggan, an architect; joined Met Éireann in 1980 and has worked as coordinator of the RTÉ Television weather team and is currently Head of Forecasting in Met Éireann. He has served as Chairperson of the International

Association of Broadcast Meteorology and Co-Chair of the First World Conference on Broadcast Meteorology. He has also chaired the Expert Team on Media Issues for the World Meteorological Organization. He is involved with Wexford Arts Centre and with Wexford Swimming Club. Gerald is known for his trademark wink when signing off his TV broadcasts.

> The first school bus service ever provided in Ireland was a horse-drawn service supplied by Robert Duggan under a Department of Education scheme in Rosslare in 1923. It made the journey to and from the Fort twice each day, bringing children to Rosslare Convent School.

Flood, Tim, Cloughbawn, born 1927, an ever-present forward on the great Wexford hurling team of the 1950s and 60s, he was known for his style, speed and touch; won All-Ireland medals in 1955, '56 and '60, won six Leinster medals from 1951 to 1962, and two National league titles; won two senior hurling medals with Cloughbawn, 1949 and '51. The versatile Flood was immersed in traditional music and the famous Castleboro Céilí Band, and was a champion sheep dog breeder and handler in trials at the very highest level, including the televised *One Man and His Dog*. Tim is married to Kathleen McGrath, sister of that great Wexford hurler, Oliver 'Hopper' McGrath. Tim told his story in a book entitled My Best Shot. His son, Seán, also won an All-Ireland Senior Hurling medal with Wexford in 1996.

Flynn, Kathy, 1923-2010, Aughtighmore, Clonroche, daughter of Patrick and Mary. The Flynns were farmers and had a public house. Kathy had a sister, Annie, and a brother, Paddy. Kathy took over the running of the pub from her mother and it was known far and wide as a destination for ceol, caint agus craic. She sold only bottled beer. Kathy kept an open fire with the trunk of a tree alight that would be pushed to the back of the fireplace as it burned away throughout the day – no need to chop wood in Aughtighmore. And last orders were not set in flagstone. She was an admired Wexford woman who gave all who visited her establishment a glimpse into an older world. Her cousin, Kathleen Kinsella, today continues the tradition in Aughtighmore.

Foley, Hughie, Rathduff Lane, Rathnure, born Wexford 1938, retired dairy farmer; married to Anne, née Murphy, Rathnure, they have two daughters and three sons; coached Rathnure U10-14 hurling teams with Fr. McDonald for more than thirty years; still coaches at National School level part time.

Foley, Jerry , Wexford town, managing director of television broadcast company WTV, Dublin and Wexford, and Propel Media; computer science graduate from Trinity College Dublin who has worked in the public and private sectors on large scale computer systems; involved in multimedia production since 1990s. He has produced programmes for different television stations in Ireland and the UK including a recent business series on TV3.

Foley, Jim, Ballykelly; great community man, he is involved in all aspects of life in Ballykelly. He comes up with novel ideas for fund raising and is renowned for his yarns and story telling. Widowed at a young age, he has one grown-up daughter and continues to do his daily school bus run along with other chartered runs.

109

Foley, John, Crory, Crossabeg, born 1959, farmer and part-time school bus driver; married to Julie, née Murphy, Oylegate, they have one daughter and one son; son of Seán, RIP 2010, and Anne, née Crane-Murphy, Curracloe; his father was a dedicated Pikeman, marching in 1938 as a teenager, riding a horse in the 1948 commemoration, and in the bicentenary in 1998, he rode out in Enniscorthy on Vinegar Hill; his grandfather was E.P. 'Ned' Foley, a Gaelic League supporter, and committed GAA man, who provided the field for training and competition. He fought in 1916 and the War of Independence and was interned in Frongoch.

Foley, Mick, Foley's Cross, at the intersection of Hayestown and Barmoney, was a talented footballer who gave the benefit of his skills to two parishes, Bree and Taghmon, which the farm he was raised on straddled. Mick won six senior Wexford football championship medals, two with Saint Munn's Taghmon in 1957 and '58 and four with Ballyhogue in 1963, '64, '70 and '71. He was also a member of the Wexford senior football team. He now lives in Palmerstown, Dublin and continued his footballing career with Clondalkin right into his forties; brother of Willie and Joe who were also outstanding footballers.

Foley, Willie, Brownstown, Newbawn, born Wexford 1923, farmer; married to Lilah, née Murphy, Brownstown, RIP 1976, they have two sons and four daughters; president of St. Abban's Adamstown GAA Club; won Wexford senior hurling championship title with Adamstown GAA club 1942 defeating a Nickey Rackard-led team; attends the All-Ireland finals every year; works daily on farm and continues to drive.

Forde, Gerry, 1923-2013, Ferrybank, Wexford, award-winning traditional musician and former Wexford County Engineer; married to Nellie, they had five children; graduated from UCD in 1944 with a degree in engineering and took up a position on Wexford County Council in 1949; retired from Council in 1985; with brother-in-law, Tim Flood of Clonroche, won an All-Ireland Fleadh Ceoil on the fiddle and banjo. His son, Gerry, is the current Wexford County Engineer and well-known sporting fanatic and assists with GAA commentaries on South East Radio.

Forde, Matty, Ballyfad, Wexford and Kilanerin footballer, Wexford's only Gaelic football All-Star, in 2004 at left full forward; was also Players' Association Player of the Year. He is the greatest scoring forward ever in Wexford football, with almost 700 points in total in over 100 appearances, more than double his nearest rival, Billy Dodd of Sarsfields. This includes 4-5 in a league match against Galway, 2-10 against both Sligo and Offaly. He was for a number of years the leading scorer in the National League. He represented Ireland in the International Rules series against Australia in 2004 and '05, and won Railway Cup medals with Leinster. He retired from inter-county football in early 2011 having made his senior debut in 1999. He won four Wexford senior titles with his club, Kilanerin.

Forde, Fr Walter, Bunclody, born 1943; author of *Adventuring in the Priesthood*, published in 1993, and *The Christian Marketplace*, 1994. He was associated with the publication of *The Link* in Gorey, and has acted as editor of *Tara Hill*, published in 1987, and *The Bridge,* the Castlebridge parish magazine; was involved with the foundation of the Ferns Diocesan Youth Service.

Forrest, Rev. Dean Leslie, retired Dean of Diocese of Ferns; Rector of Ferns for 16 years, retired in 2011. During his tenure, Dean Forrest became a pillar of the Ferns community and was for many years Chairman of the Ferns Development Association. In his spiritual mission, Dean Forrest, 40 years a priest, he was a major force in the Ecumenical movement and worked assiduously with Fr. Aidan Jones in building relationships between the Churches.

Forrestal, Chris, Rathnure, seanachaí tells stories, composes, recites and sings on the first Friday of every month in Conran's, Rathnure, and annually at the Old Folks' party. Chris has farmed and bred sheep in the shadow of the Blackstairs Mountains for many years.

Fortune, Jimmy, Ferns born, jockey, he learned his trade with Jim Bolger. He has been campaigning in England since 1988 with quite a lot of success. He is well-known and respected for his physical strength in the saddle. He was formerly stable jockey to John Gosden, but since 2010 has been freelance. He won the St. Leger classic on Lucarno in 2007. Rides in India during the Winter and won their Derby in 1996 and in 2013. He rode 47 winners in Britain in the 2012 season.

Fortune, John senior, Ringbawn, Ballyhealy, Kilmore, born Wexford 1940; retired farmer; married to Anne, née Sullivan, Barntown, they have six sons and one daughter; set up a thriving potato-growing business creating sustained employment and supplying supermarkets and shops all over south east and now run by two of his sons.

Fortune, Michael, a native of Bree village, became a sports journalist in the late 1960s. He joined the Irish Press in 1968. He is a well-known broadcaster on RTÉ Sports and other programmes and as a correspondent with the Racing Post. In recent years, he has specialised in reporting and commentary on greyhound racing and is regarded around the world as an expert on the sport and on the greyhound industry in Ireland. One of his favourite places is Shelbourne Park in Dublin.

> Thirty six is the number of stud farms in Co. Wexford in 2013.

Fortune, Michael, Curragraigue, Ballindaggin, born Ballygarrett 1975, filmmaker and assistant lecturer at the Limerick School of Art; studied Fine Art, specialising in video and performance, at the Limerick School of Art, where he graduated with a First Class Honours Degree in 1999; following the completion of his MA with the Dun Laoghaire School of Film, he has established himself as an independent film producer based in rural Co. Wexford. This year, as part of the 'JFK 50 - The Homecoming ' Programme, the Arts Department of Wexford County Council commissioned Michael to produce a series of short films based on the undocumented histories and stories surrounding the visit of the late John F. Kennedy to Co. Wexford in June

1963. He is currently completing two new projects based on old crafts and field/place names of interest in Castlebridge and Grantstown in Co. Wexford which have also been commissioned by the Arts Department of Wexford County Council. He is married to artist Aileen Lambert.

Fortune, Paul, Kereight, farmer, married to Nellie, they have four children; was recognised and honoured by Dawn Meats as an outstanding beef cattle producer. He is an IFA activist,and promoter of progressive farming.

Fox, Billy and Josie, née Broaders, Bree; Carrigmannon, Glynn. Billy, worked with Coillte for half a century. Was a founder with Nick Casey of Credit Union in Glynn As a young woman Josie worked in Castleknock in Dublin. She is a well-known member of the ICA and a noted artist.

French, Nicholas, born Wexford 1604, became Bishop of Ferns in 1643, and was one of the Wexford representatives at the Confederation of Kilkenny in 1645. He became President of the Irish College in Louvain, where he published *The Settlement and Sale of Ireland*.

French O'Neill, Bessie, 1925-2010, Carrigbyrne, née Banville, Shanoule; married to Nick, having two sons, Ger and Eugene; B&B owner; co-ordinator of ladies' knitting co-op; ICA guild activist; pilgrimage organiser, participant and producer of parish entertainment shows, founder member of Newbawn Tidy Towns group; recipient County Wexford People of the Year, Hall of Fame Award 2008.

Fuhrmann, Siegfried, Horeswood, born former DDR, Republic of East Germany, now Poland, in 1942; married to Anastasia, née Rowe, Conna, Fethard on Sea; they have six children; studied farm management and came to Ballyhogue in 1964 as assistant farm manager for a German family; when farm was sold, and his employment ended, he started to repair shopping trolleys, out of which evolved Mann Engineering and almost thirty years later, Mann has contracts with Dunnes Stores, Pettitt's in Wexford and some of the SuperValu chain.

Fulham, Brendan, RIP, Rosbercon, New Ross, native of Ardagh in County Limerick, had a banking career that took him to many towns in Ireland. He played Gaelic games in Killorglin, Kilrush, Clifden, Ballyshannon, Tralee and Wexford; author of eight bestselling books on hurling, including, *Lest We Forget, Giants of the Ash* and *Hurling Giants*.

Furlong, Dr Brendan, New Jersey, owns BW Furlong Equine Clinic. A native of Brocurra, Adamstown, Brendan Furlong is one of the foremost sport horse experts in the United States. He graduated from the Veterinary College of Ireland with honours in 1976, and in 1977 went to the United States for a two-year internship. He never left. In 1980 he founded the practice that bears his name, and over 30 years has built it into one of the premier equine clinics in the United States and he served the Three-day Eventing Team as US team veterinarian at Olympic Games, Pan American Games, and World Championship Games. Brendan is married to Dr Wendy Leich, who is also a vet in the practice. They have two sons, Adam, who runs Furlong's Healthy Horse, and Jonathan, who graduated from the University of Virginia in 2013 and is now pursuing studies in veterinary school. Brendan and Wendy breed and train sport horses on their farms in Pittstown, New Jersey and he is a Joint Master of the Amwell Valley Hounds and a member of the Essex Fox Hounds.

Furlong, Daniel, Castle Court, Taghmon, born 1998, student in St. Peter's College, Wexford; son of Thomas and Teresa, née Stafford, Kilmore; winner of the RTÉ All-Ireland Talent competition 2011; toured in the United States with Phil Coulter; has performed with Celtic Thunder.

Furlong, James, Palace West, Clonroche, farmer with a keen interest in the environment. James is fourth generation of Furlong on his farm. In 2013 he was the overall national winner of the Best Kept Farm competition sponsored by the *Irish Farmers' Journal* Teagasc and FBD. Judges complimented him on the excellent maintenance and upkeep of his farm with an eye on safety also. Married to Una, née Murphy, a nurse, they have two sons and one daughter.

Furlong, Jimmy, Ballinaboola, Newbawn, born 1946, former ACC bank manager and retired publican; married to Mary, née Casey, Clongeen, they have two daughters and two sons; studied Agricultural Science in UCD; long-time, full-time hurling coach for Co. Wexford having played senior hurling for Wexford late '60s-'70s; former proprietor of The Camolin Inn; treasurer of the New Ross golf club.

Furlong, Neville, Ferrybank, Wexford, son of Colette and Ronan, former regional manager, Bank of Ireland, based in Wexford; played rugby twice for Ireland. He was selected on the Ireland team for 1992 rugby tour to New Zealand and played in both test matches, at Dunedin and Wellington. In the second game, he scored Ireland's only try in heroic fashion, limping over the line with a bad leg injury which caused him to leave the field immediately after. He was playing with UCG and Connacht at the time and is the last player to be capped for Ireland while actually a student at the Galway College. He is currently chief executive responsible for the overall running of the Park Village residential retirement centre, Castletroy, Co. Limerick.

Furlong, Nicholas, Nicky; Drinagh Lodge, Rosslare road, Wexford, born in Mulgannon, in 1929, historian, lecturer, playwright, newspaper columnist and author of twenty-four books. Nicky is married to Mairéad, née Breslin, Dublin, twin sister of Dr. Muriel McCarthy, curator of Marsh's Library, Dublin, whose husband, Professor Charles McCarthy, wrote the ground-breaking book *A Distasteful Challenge* in the 1970s. He became a dairy farmer on the family farm at Mulgannon. His father owned a pub on Main Street, Wexford. He attended St. Peter's College, Wexford, the Salesian Agricultural College, Warrenstown, Co. Meath, and University College Dublin. He is a member of the Royal Society of Antiquaries of Ireland. For many years he wrote a satirical column for the *Wexford People* under the pen name 'Pat O'Leary'. He wrote regular features in *The Irish Press*, the *Irish Farmers' Journal* and the Irish Sugar Company magazine, *Biatas* and was a contributor to the RTÉ Television series Halls Pictorial Weekly, to The Late Late

Show and to several RTÉ Radio programmes. He later became a columnist with *The Echo* newspaper in which he wrote fearlessly about social and historic matters in a weekly two page column titled 'Furlong at Large'. His stage production *Lunatic Fringe* was condemned by clergy of the time and subsequently made international headlines. He has, through his vast works, brought County Wexford and Ireland's past to life contributing to an understanding among non-historians of the complexities of three defining events especially, the coming of the Normans in the 12th Century , the Rebellion of 1798 and the Rising of 1916. He has become synonymous with a dramatic narrative sweep of history as first pursued by Herodotus, achieved in his many books by means of digression. He brings tapestries of the past alive, embellishing his impeccable gift for story telling with a style that is unique. His novel *Young Farmer Seeks Wife*, has been described as the outstanding classic Irish novel of the 20th Century. He is the author of books including: *Dermot King of Leinster and The Foreigners; The Mighty Wave* with Dr Daire Kehoe; *Fr. John Murphy of Boolavogue 1753-1798; The Women of 1798*, with Dr Daire Keogh; *A History of County Wexford; County Wexford in the Rare Oul' Times* Volumes I-IV and a sequel, *County Wexford in the Rare Old Times 1880-1980;* a novel titled, *Young Farmer Seeks Wife*; a novel for schoolchildren titled, *A foster son for a King*, 1986; *The Greatest Hurling Decade; By Bishop's Rath and Norman Fort,* Wexford 1994, with Dr Edward Culleton and Patrick Sills. A Festschrift, titled *The Wexford Man*, ed. Bernard Browne, a collection of twenty-two essays addressed to him, comprised contributions written by distinguished scholars, colleagues and friends and was published as a befitting and long-standing tribute to him for his outstanding service to his native county. He received a Rehab People of the Year Award for his contribution to literature.

Furlong, Sonny, Corrigeen, Rathnure, born 1925, married to Winnie, née Murphy, Rathnure; avid reader and historian; accomplished musician, he plays both a Paolo Soprani two-row button accordion and a piano accordion.

> The parish of Clonegal straddles three counties with an equal portion in counties Wexford, Wicklow and Carlow but it belongs to the Diocese of Kildare and Leighlin.

Furlong, Thomas, Scarawalsh, born 1894, was a prolific writer and is considered to be one of Co. Wexford's foremost poets.

Furlong, Walter, Dranagh, Caim, Enniscorthy, managing director, Cooney Furlong Grain Company; married to Marguerite, née Crosbie, a secondary school teacher, they have one daughter and one son; farms in excess of 2,500 acres of cereals in County Wexford. His daughter, Bronagh, is one of Wexford's best known track and field athletes.

Furlong, William, Butlerstown, Broadway, born Wexford 1947; mixed farmer; married to Beetie, née Stafford, Kilmore; they have two sons and two daughters; member of Our Lady's Island Helpers' Group which organises the annual 15 August to 8 September pilgrimage and maintains the Island year round.

Furniss, Harry, born Anne Street, Wexford, in 1854, was a famous cartoonist. He illustrated for *Punch* magazine and for Lewis Carroll and Charles Dickens. He published a book entitled *Confessions of a Caricaturist.*

Gahan, Dr Daniel, Ballycarney, Ferns, wrote *The People's Rising, Wexford 1798*, which was published in 1995. It is widely considered to be the most complete account of the 1798 Rising in Wexford.

Gahan, Jimmy, Brownswood, Enniscorthy, journalist, retailer, and broadcaster; former editor of *The Echo* group of newspapers; regular reporter to South East Radio newsroom. He also does some freelance PR work and runs a grocery and service station business at Chapel Lane, Enniscorthy. He is married to Dr Mairéad Kelly and the couple have three children.

Gahan, Canon John V., a native of Ferns and a former President of St. Peter's College, published *The Secular Priests of the Diocese of Ferns*.

Galvin, Margaret, Wexford-town-based award-winning poet, native of Co. Tipperary, former Editor of *Ireland's Own*; awarded degree in Professional Social Care at IT Carlow, Wexford Campus. She has always been concerned with profiling life lived on the margins, seeking wisdom and story in the unlikeliest places. Her work has been commended for its celebration of the vital life of the moment. Margaret is married to Philip Quirke, also a writer, and secondary school teacher. His first poetry collection entitled *Journey to the Shore* was published in 2008, and *The Moulding Shop*, a fictionalized memoir of a child's growing up in Wexford, was published in 2011. They have one son, Ibar, who has had his poetry published also.

Godkin, James, born Gorey 1806, was a distinguished author and historian. His best-known books are *Ireland and her Churches, The Land War in Ireland* and *The Religious History of Ireland*.

Gilligan, William, Ballinabarney, Gorey, architect and owner of Mr DJ Wedding and Corporate Events and Audio Visual Hire. The origins of the deejaying business lie in William's secondary school days in Carnew. After his Leaving Certificate, he went on to WIT and qualified as an architect and then went to Trinity and studied for a postgraduate diploma in Fire Safety and Project Management. Outside of his work, his interests are martial arts, motor cycling and overland travel. Lives with his partner where he was born in Ballinabarney.

Gleeson, Willie, Ballygow, Fethard-on-sea, born 1960; farmer of pedigree Suffolk and Charollais sheep, and horse breeder; former National president of Macra na Feirme; currently the southeast regional organiser of Fine Gael; former chairman of Wexford Partnership, 1996-2009; played polocross with Horetown at local, national and international level, as well as badminton and underage Gaelic football for Fethard.

Goff, Dr Henry, Lower Shannon Hill, retired principal St. Senan's Primary School, Enniscorthy, son of Patsy and Mary Ellen; historian specialising in the 1916 Rebellion; author of *Wexford has Risen*.

Goggins, Rodney, born Wexford town, 1978, Irish professional snooker player. He earned his place on the 2007/08 professional tour by finishing top of the Irish senior rankings in the previous season. Goggins won the International Billiards and Snooker Federation World U21 Championship in 1999 when he beat Rolf de Jong of the Netherlands 11–4 in the final in Egypt.

Goodison, **Willie,** Wexford town, an outstanding Gaelic football centre-back, one of the best not to win a senior All-Ireland medal; won Leinster senior football honours in 1945 and won four County senior medals with Volunteers; played on the Ireland team in representative games 1950 and 1952; refereed the 1955 Kerry-Dublin All-Ireland senior final; was a well-known publican in Wexford town for many years running The Gaelic Bar, Bishopswater.

Graham, George, Ballyoughter, world champion sheep shearer, began shearing at eight years of age and is a third generation shearer; organiser of the world championships in Gorey 2014.

Grant, Padraig, professional photographer, from High Street, Wexford, has specialised in the photographing famine and war-torn areas and has published four books. As a freelance photo-journalist he spent ten years working for all the major Irish and international newspapers and magazines. His sister, Deirdre, is a Wexford-based choreographer.

Grattan Flood, **Canon William,** author of *History of Hooke (Templetown) Parish*, published in 1970.

Gray, Kathleen Eileen Moray, born at Brownswood House, Enniscorthy on 9 August 1878, died 31 October 1976 in Paris, has been recognised as one of the most influential and revolutionary furniture designers, a pioneer of the Modern Movement in architecture, and also as an artist. She was the youngest of five children. Her father, James McLaren Smith, was a painter who encouraged his daughter's artistic interests. Her mother was Eveleen Pounden, a granddaughter of the 10th Earl of Moray who became the 19th Baroness Gray in 1895, upon the death of her own mother. After

that, Lady Gray, who had separated from her husband in 1888, changed her children's surname to Gray. Her childhood was spent between the Brownswood house and Kensington in London. She left Ireland for Paris in 1900 after her father's death and never returned, as far as is known. For many years she won little recognition in her native country but this is now being redressed with some major exhibitions. The *Eileen Gray* exhibition is on permanent display at the Decorative Arts and History site of the National Museum of Ireland, Collins Barracks, Dublin. The exhibition includes many important items but also values Gray on a personal level, including family photographs, her lacquering tools, and personal ephemera The Irish Museum of Modern Art (IMMA) presented in the second half of 2013 a major retrospective of the work of Eileen Gray, designed and produced by the Centre Pompidou, Paris, in collaboration with IMMA. This exhibition is a tribute to Gray's career and also celebrates Gray's Irish roots. It includes a number of previously unseen works that offer new insights into Gray's extraordinary career. A major focus is given to her landmark piece of modernist architecture, the French villa E-1027, built in Roquebrune-Cap-Martin in 1926-1929, in close collaboration with Romanian architect ,Jean Badovici. The exhibition includes examples of furniture for E-1027, including the tubular steel designs with which Gray's name has become synonymous. As an example of the value now being placed on this extraordinary Enniscorthy woman's work, in February 2009, a "Dragons" armchair made by Gray between 1917 was sold at auction in Paris for €21.9 million, setting an auction record for 20th century decorative art.

Greene, John, Inch, born Co. Wexford 1955, fruit farmer, at Green's Berry Farm; married to Paula née

Breen, B.Sc., Ballydonegan, Monageer, they have one daughter Nicola, currently working on Ph.D in Engineering and one son, Conor who works in the family business at Ballinacoola, Gorey. Having graduated with a B.Comm and an H.Dip from UCD, John has built up the family fruit farm into a thriving business and is an accomplished grower of seasonal fruits. He is the son of Sean, RIP, and Kathleen, née Mordaunt, born County Wexford 1933, retired housewife. Kathleen has been a volunteer at Craanford Community Centre for more than thirty years. John has one sister, Mary Brown who works at Aer Lingus.

Grennan, Patrick, Dunganstown; in mixed farming; married to Siobhán, they have two sons; he is third cousin of President John F. Kennedy and lives in the Kennedy ancestral home in Dungansatown. He is curator of the exhibition at the new Kennedy Homestead Visitor Centre.

Griffin, Liam, hotelier, business leader and radio and television pundit on business, sport and in particular the game of hurling. He is a native of Rosslare where his father, Michael, a former Garda from Co. Clare and his mother Jenny, née Hall of Gorey, founded the Harbour View Hotel overlooking Rosslare harbour and port. His wife, Mary, née Lambert, is from a well-known Wexford town business family. Their son, Niall, an equestrian three-day eventing competitor, was the leader of the Irish Olympics team in Athens in 2004. Their sons, Michael and Liam Anthony, are also involved in the management of the Griffin Group. He was manager of the Wexford team that won the All-Ireland Hurling final and the Liam McCarthy Cup in 1996. In his early career, he trained in hotel management in Shannon College of Hotel Management. He worked in hotels in Switzerland and Wales before returning to Ireland where he joined Inter Continental Hotels followed by a period with the State tourism body Bord Fáilte. He left there to work in the family hotel business. The Griffin Group now comprising the Ferrycarrig Hotel, the Hotel Kilkenny and Monart Destination Spa, one of the top spas in the world, is the biggest hotel group in the south east of Ireland.

Griffin, Niall, son of Liam and Mary, he competed in the Olympic three-day eventing on Lorgaine in 2004 in Greece and 2008 in Beijing. He had the honour of carrying the Irish flag at the opening ceremony in Athens. He finished in 23rd place from over 70 riders and helped Ireland to 8th place in the team event. In Beijing, he completed in 41st place and helped Ireland to 10th place. He also represented Ireland in the World Equestrian Games at Aachen and twice in the European championships. He now operates the top class Monart Equestrian Centre with Polly Jackson.

Gaul, Liam, Wexford, is an historian and author who has contributed numerous articles to Co. Wexford's historical journals. His books include *Masters of Irish Music, Glory O! Glory O! The Life of P.J. McCall* and *A Window on the Past*, forgotten tales behind some of Wexford's landmark features; *Wexford: The American Connection*, published by Wexford County Council 2013.

Hadden, Francis J., who resided at Springfield, Wexford, wrote a number of books, including *The Clock with Four Faces.*

Hall, Jim, Woodstown Road, Rosslare, born Wexford 1943; retired Laboratory Technician in EPA Johnstown Castle; married to Bena, née Furlong, Adamstown, they have a son and a daughter and two grandchildren; Rosslare Golf Club's first secretary/manager 1992-2003, Hon. Sec. for 12 years; represented Wexford on senior golf team.

Hannon, Eileen, née Campbell, Carrig on Bannow, accomplished actress on the amateur drama circuit and involved in community activities; married to Paddy Hannon, building contractor, they have a grown-up family.

Hanrahan, Fionnuala, County Librarian, originally from Dublin, she came to Wexford in 1996. She has served on the boards of the Irish Library Council and the Library Association of Ireland, and is a former President of the latter. Currently she is on the Library Development Committee, Local Government Development Agency, and is a board member of Age and Opportunity.

Hanrahan, P.R. was an author and poet who lived in Farnogue Cottage, Wexford, in 1817. He wrote *Eva, or The Buried City of Bannow, a historical tale of the early English invaders,* 1866.

Harrington, Carmel, Screen, author, originally from The Ballagh, went to school in Blackwater. Her favourite pastime as a child was going to Wexford library to read. In 2013 she published a novel *Beyond Grace's Rainbow* as an eBook which won the March 2013 Kindle Book Award and Harper Collins have agreed terms to publish it as a book. Carmel says she has an idyllic lifestyle writing and living in the Wexford countryside along with husband, Roger and children, Nate and Amelia.

Harvey, Robert, Broomley, Kyle, Crossabeg, noted for his contribution to was parish enterprises; instrumental in getting the history of the parish into book form. His father, made land available for a school playground at Kyle Robert, himself, has provided land for other community activities in the area.

Harvey, Beauchamp Bagenal, 1762-1798, Bargy Castle, Tomhaggard, barrister and one of the commanders of the United Irishmen in the Battle of New Ross during the 1798 Rebellion. After Vinegar Hill was lost, Harvey took refuge on one of the Saltee Islands with John Henry Colclough and his wife. They were pursued, and after a long search were found concealed in a cave, disguised as peasants. Harvey was tried by court-martial and executed on Wexford Bridge on the 28th June.

Haughton, Joseph, Ferns, member of the Quaker community and trader in the Main Street, Ferns and is reputed to have publicly destroyed his fowler's gun as tensions mounted in the lead up to the 1798 Rebellion. He refused to sell rope to a yeoman knowing it was going to be used to hang rebels. The inscription on the wall of the former Haughton shop in Ferns refers to his 'Christian example in providing shelter, food and care to the many destitute and wounded in the conflict of 1798'.

Hawkshaw, Travers R., died at Hillburn, Taghmon on May 3rd 1857, aged 60. He was a magistrate, farmer, County Coroner and a leading figure in the Whig Party. His father was a Protestant clergyman as was his brother but Mr Hawkshaw famously campaigned against the tithes most vociferously. Hawkshaw clearly took the line most favourable to Catholics on a number of issues and showed leniency to them in court. He was slightly rude in manner to opponents.

Hay, Edward, Ballinakeele, Crossabeg, born 1761, was tried for complicity in the '98 Rising, but was acquitted. His brother John was found guilty and was executed on Wexford Bridge for his part in the Rebellion. He wrote *History of the Insurrection of the County of Wexford*.

Hayden, Jackie, Dublin-born has been living in Wexford since 1996. He has published 10 books, including *A Map of Love*, about the poet Dylan Thomas, and *My Boy*, the number one bestselling story of rock star Phil Lynott based on interviews with Lynott's mother, Philomena. He has also edited four books and, as contributing Editor to *Hot Press* wrote literally thousands of reviews and news stories, while also interviewing a wide range of subjects, including Bob Geldof, Michael D Higgins, The Corrs, Johnny Giles, Liam Clancy, Glen Campbell, Kenny Rogers, Donovan and Gerry Adams. As Marketing Manager with Sony Music, Hayden signed U2 to their first record contract. He served on the Government's Task Force on Irish Music and still lectures regularly on music careers and on writing.

Hayes, Jim, Group Editor of *People Newspapers*, Wexford; a native of Wexford town, he is son of the late Pat Hayes, well-known photographer, and Mary; he is married to Maire, née Gibbons, from Piercestown, Wexford; they have three sons; educated at Wexford CBS and Waterford IT; since leaving college he has worked in various editorial roles before being appointed to his current position. He

has written a music column in *The People* newspapers since 1981. He is brother of Pat Hayes, drummer with Cry Before Dawn.

Hayes, Rosemary, a legal secretary; former president of Wexford Lions' Club, who during her time in office spearheaded many projects to raise funds for a variety of worthy causes to support local people and national and international projects.She is an acknowledged expert on the business use of social media. She was inaugurated as the 29th President of the club in July 2011, and served for two years. She handed over the chains of office to the club's new President, Seamus Murphy, in July. Wexford will host the 2014 District Convention of Lions' Clubs.

Hayes, Tomás, Wexford, co-authored *Walk Wexford Ways* with William Roche, Nicky Rossiter and Kevin Hurley in 1988, and he also co-authored *A Wexford Miscellany*, 1994.

Hearne, Ian, Crossabeg, of the Wexford Star Plough engineering family, was a member of the staff of CNN, the global television broadcaster, during 'Operation Desert Fox', the Anglo-American bombing of Iraq in 1998.

Heffernan, Noel, Coolree, Wexford, managing director of Perennial Freight, Poulmarle, Taghmon, which he founded in 1998 and which is now one of the largest transport companies in Ireland with depots in the UK, France, Germany, The Netherlands, Belgium and Poland, with plans to open an office in Romania in 2014. The company employs eighty-eight people and has a fleet of five hundred and fifty trailers. A native of Waterford,

Noel has been in Wexford since 1982 has a son and daughter and his son now works in the business with him in Taghmon.

Hegarty, David, George Street, Wexford, published novel entitled *Three-Day Break* in 1986 as well as short stories. He also wrote *Dynamic Health*, published 1997.

> " ...a number of private schools such as that at Ramsgrange, Co. Wexford for teaching practical farmhouse management "to farmers' daughters of the better class", were in operation early in the present century, and some such as St. Martha's near Navan, continued to function into the 1980s."
> —*Towards A History of Agricultural Science in Ireland,* edited by P.L. Curran

Hegarty, John, born in Ballyfad in 1975; topped the poll for the county in first council election 2009; founded annual Wexford Day and Wexford Ambassador Programme. He is chairman of the Gathering 2013 in Wexford. He played intercounty football for Wexford over 100 times (1995-2007). Honours include Railway cup(Leinster) Sigerson cup , All Ireland colleges hurling (both UCD), Leinster U21 hurling and six senior football titles with Kilanerin GAA club. Dept Principal at Coláiste Éamon Rís, CBS secondary school, Wexford.

Herron, John, former Australian Ambassador to Ireland and former cabinet minister, is of Wexford descent. His ancestor, English-born Nicholas Herron was sent to Ireland in the 1500s to "subjugate the Irish." He married Cecily Moore a daughter of Sir Thomas Moore. John Herron's father left Glenbrien in the 1920s and settled in Queensland. John became a doctor and rose through the ranks of medicine to become Chief Surgeon at the Mater Misericordiae Hospital in Brisbane prior to his entry into politics. He was first elected to parliament in 1990 as a Senator for Queensland. He resigned from parliament in 2002 and took up diplomatic postings as ambassador to Ireland and then to the Holy See between 2002 and 2006. John Herron and his wife, Jan, visited his ancestral home in Wexford in August 2005. He is currently chairman of the National Drugs Council in Australia and Jan and he have six daughters and three sons.

Hill, Jeremy, Monksgrange, Rathnure, born 1943; married to Rosemary, they have one daughter and two sons; landlord of Orpen Estate; owner of Monksgrange Gardens, Monksgrange Stud and the Norman Gallery; chairperson Wexford Garden Trail; hosts Blackstairs Opera in Monksgrange grounds. Jeremy's mother, Charmain was owner of Dawn Run, the only horse to win both the Champion Hurdle and Gold Cup at Cheltenham, trained by Paddy Mullins.

Hodgins, Bill, 1894-1920, the son of Peter Hodgins and Mary, née Scully of Brideswell, Askamore; long-time secretary of Brideswell Gaelic Football Club, he won All-Ireland senior medals in 1917 and 1918 for Wexford; Bill's most prized possession was the county junior medal he won with Brideswell in 1918; died suddenly after injuries sustained in a Leinster football championship match against Kildare.

Holden, Jim, Ferns, was the Hon. Treasurer elected to the first committee of the Wexford and District Soccer League. He played with St. Cormac's of Boolavogue, Ferns Athletic and later still with Ferns Utd as a centre forward, often travelling to matches by bicycle. He also enjoyed playing hurling with the local club, Ferns St. Aidan's during the 60s.

Holohan, Jimmy, Rathnure, hurler, lined out 112 times for Wexford senior hurlers in all competitions and stands third in the county's all-time scoring lists, behind only Nickey Rackard and Tony Doran. He notched up 44 goals and 432 points and is ahead of Padge Kehoe and Ned Buggy in the rankings. He was a replacement All-Star in 1986 and he won eight Wexford senior hurling titles with Rathnure.

Hore, Gerard, South Main Street, Wexford and Clearies town, professional photographer celebrating thirty years in business in 2013. Known throughout the county as photographer with *People Newspapers.* He has photographed more than two thousand weddings. He is married to Jackie née Ryan who runs the studio with him.

Hore, Harry, Kennedy Park, Wexford, and Sean Cullen, Belvedere Grove, Wexford, bred the Irish coursing derby winner, Danaghers Best, by Ballyshannon May, and Harry was chairman of Wexford Coursing Club for many years.

Hore, Philip Herbert, Wexford, born 1841. The first volume of his monumental work *History of County Wexford* was published in 1900. The sixth and final volume was published in 1910. His work was based largely on papers and documents gathered by his father, Herbert Francis Hore over many years.

Howell, Denis, Gorey, auctioneer at Warren Estates, noted actor in Gorey Little Theatre Group productions, renowned for comic acting ability; native of Camolin. Denis was a very good hurler in his youth with St. Patrick's, Ballyoughter.

Howlin, Brendan, a former school teacher, was born into a well-known Wexford political family on 9th May, 1956, and has served as a Labour Party TD for Wexford constituency since 1987. He has been the Minister for Public Expenditure and Reform since March 2011, and has previously served as Leas-Cheann Comhairle, Minister for the Environment and Minister for Health. He was named after Brendan Corish, for whom his father, John, was election agent. He contested his first national election in November 1982. He ran as a Labour candidate, but was not elected. Following this election, a Fine Gael-Labour Party Government came to power and he was nominated by the Taoiseach, Garret FitzGerald, to serve in Seanad Éireann. He again contested the 1987 General Election, and this time he was successful in securing a seat. He was subsequently elected Chief Whip of the Labour Party, a position he held until 1993. Following the resignation of Dick Spring as leader of the Labour Party in 1997, he lost out to Ruairí Quinn in the subsequent leadership election, but was later named deputy leader of the party. In 2002, he again stood for the party leadership when Ruairí Quinn resigned, and this time he was defeated by Pat Rabbitte.

Howlin, Gerard, his father's family are from Rochestown, Ballymitty and his mother's are Sinnotts of Blackmoor, Cleariestown. Gerard who was raised and educated Dublin, graduated with a degree in history from Trinity College and returned there in 2009 for his Master's degree. He was a special adviser at the Department of Tourism and Sport 1997-1999 and at the Department of Taoiseach 1999-2007. Always loyal to his Wexford roots he collaborated closely with the late Jerome Hynes to secure state funding for the new Wexford Opera House. He is now a Public Affairs consultant, a frequent media contributor and has returned again to Trinity to embark on a PhD.

Howlin, Patrick M., Courtnacuddy was appointed Executive Vice President and Director North America for IDA Ireland in January 2013. He is the third son of George and Peggy. He has been with IDA Ireland since 1980 and has wide experience of the organization's activities at regional, national and international levels. Previous US assignments include five years in the IDA's New York Office. In 1999 he was appointed Senior Vice President and Director US West Coast Operations. He returned to IDA Headquarters in Dublin in 2002 as Business Development Manager in the ICT Division. From 2005 to 2008 he led the team that developed a new model for Industry-Academic Research collaboration that still serves the need of multinational investors. Appointed Head of Information and Communications Technologies for the organization in 2008, he has overseen some of the most significant ICT multinational investments in Ireland in recent years. He attended St. Peter's College, Wexford and is a graduate of University College Dublin. He also holds qualifications from the Institute of Public Administration, the Irish Management Institute and Columbia Business School, New York. Before joining IDA Ireland, he spent five years with the Department of Agriculture following a brief stint as a secondary school teacher. While currently living in Manhattan, he and his wife, Mary, have a home in Milltown in Dublin.

Howlin, Sheamus, Rathmacknee, Killinick, Piercestown; businessman and GAA official; married to Vera; from St. Martin's club, served as Wexford County Board chairman 2001 and 2002; Leinster GAA chairman 2008 - 2011; has announced his intention to run for President of the GAA in 2014. Involved with Transkon Logistics, Freight Forwarders and Shipping Services.

Twelve members of the Somers family of Coolroe were evicted from their home at Coolroe, Ballycullane in 1888. Six thousand supporters came to Arthurstown village for a six-day trial.

Howlin, Tommy, RIP, Crossfarnogue, Kilmore Quay; life-long member of Fianna Fáil and member of Wexford County Council; member of the Sugar Beet Growers' Association; founder member of the Kilmore Athletic club; his granddaughter, Deirdre Howlin, won a FBD Women and Agriculture Award 2013 for her Grange Green Garden Centre at Grange, Kilmore.

Huberman, Amy, Dublin, professional actress, daughter of Sandra Morris, Wexford, whose parents were May and William Morris from King Street. Sandra married clothes designer Harold Huberman, a Jewish emigrant to Dublin, in 1975. They have a daughter, Amy and two sons. Daughter Amy is herself an acclaimed actress of stage and screen and is married to Irish rugby international, Brian O'Driscoll. Her uncle Billy was a well-known Fine Gael and RNLI activist in Wexford.

Hughes, Benjamin, was born in 1825 and he was Mayor of Wexford in 1900 and 1901. He compiled the *Wexford Almanack* and *Notebook of County Jottings*, which was published in 1910. He also compiled a topographical dictionary of place names in the county in 1880.

Hughes, Carmel, Kilanerin; organist in Kilanerin Church and occasionally in Ballyfad; former treasurer of Kilanerin/Ballyfad GAA Club; active member of the Tidy Towns' committee.

Hughes, Méabh, Kilanerin; represented Wexford at all under age grades in camogie and Gaelic football and has been a prominent member of Kilanerin ladies' senior teams for last six years; while in UCC, captained college football team that won All-Ireland in 2008; every summer organises 'Cúl Camp' for children aged 5-14 years.

Hughes, Peter, Galbally, recently qualified primary school teacher, handballer, won his first title in the U10 county singles and has won several titles at county, Leinster and All-Ireland levels since then; travelled to the US on six different occasions competing in handball events, both with the local club and in college events in Chicago, San Diego, Minnesota, Portland and Arizona. His granduncle Ben was a handballer of note also.

Hurley, Jim, Grange, Kilmore, born Dublin 1943, retired teacher of Biology and Deputy Principal at Bridgetown Vocational College, married to Rose, née Howlin, Wexford, they have two sons and two daughters; BP Science Educator of the Year 1987, Ford Motor Company Conservation Award 1993 and CIWEM Environmental Merit Award 1999; columnist with *People Newspaper* Group; naturalist with special interest in the south Wexford coast; author of *A Guide to Nature in the Irish National Heritage Park,* 1988, *South Wexford Coast National Park*, 1991, *The South Wexford Coast – a Natural Heritage Coastline,* 1994.

Hyland, John Joe, Kilnamanagh, Oulart, born Wexford, 1970; married to Aisling, née Osbourne, Clonegal, they have two sons and two daughters; studied at Kildalton Agricultural College, and is the fourth generation of Hylands in the plant and garden business, set up by his grandfather, William Hyland, in 1945 on a 20-acre site in Oulart Village; he is the son of Joe and Kathleen, née O'Reilly, Blackwater, who established the Garden Centre in 1986. Kathleen O'Reilly is the name used by his mother when writing – she has had three books published: *A Village Curate, Times & Tides Of Uppertown* and *Profile Of A Parish.*

⑤
Agriculture

County Wexford earned the name the 'Model County' from its reputation in Europe as a producer of quality food. Today the county's leading farmers and agri-business are supplying food products across the world.

A HAND ON THE LAND

The farmland of County Wexford produces some of the finest foodstuffs and produce in the world.

Farmers use best farming practices and the most up-to date technology to produce 100 per cent quality produce. They have built upon the county's reputation as the 'Model County', a reputation earned more than 100 years ago for production of the best quality food in Europe.

The agricultural advisory services and research facilities of Teagasc at Johnstown Castle support this endeavour. These organisations manage and protect the thousands of acres of land in their care, ever mindful of the protection of the natural environment.

Thanks to a legacy dating back to the Ice Age, County Wexford is blessed with the best of land from the sweep of the Blackstairs Mountains to the rolling farmland that brushes the sea along Bannow Bay. The farmers of County Wexford have capitalised on this. Many of them have won national and international recognition for their management and production.

In the past fifty years, farming has been transformed from a way of life to a sophisticated business in which food production is traced from farm to the tables of the world.

In 2013, agriculture in County Wexford is owned and managed by thousands of farmers who have trained in management and the use of the most modern methods of farming. The agriculture business in the county now comprises individual farmers, family farms, farm service businesses, farm co-ops, farming organisations, artisan food producers, and agri-multinationals.

Looking south from Carrigbyrne Hill after the harvest.

Raheen, Davidstown; Liam O'Byrne, Churchtown, Kilrane; Issac Wheelock, Moneyhore, Enniscorthy; Mark Browne, Broomlands, Caim; Paul Kehoe, Glascarrig, Ballygarrett; Sean Grace, Ballyanne, New Ross; Joe Healy, Ballinastraw, Glenbrien; Larry Whelan, Rospile, Foulksmills; Ned Lyng, Ballygalvert,Ballywilliam, and James Kehoe, Balllymurtagh, Enniscorthy.

Serving Wexford at national level in IFA in 2013 are Tom Doyle, Ballyoughter who is chairman of the IFA Farm Business committee and JJ Kavanagh, Ballywilliam. Adrian King is the IFA regional development officer. He is based in the IFA Farm Centre in Enniscorthy.

The fifty three branches of IFA in County Wexford are led by the following chairpersons in 2013:

Adamstown- Michael Moore, Tomgarrow;

Askamore- James Tomkins, Askamore;

Ballindaggin- Justin Sutton, Wheelagower;

Ballycanew- John Rothwell, Tomduff;

Ballycullane-James J Murphy, Yoletown;

Ballygarrett- Patrick Darcy, Roney Point;

Ballymore/Mayglass, John Cleary, Coddstown;

Ballymurn- Denis Kehoe, Ballykelly;

Ballywilliam/Templeudigan- Edward Lyng, Ballygalvert;

Bannow- John Cullen, Maxboley;

THE IFA

The biggest association representing farmers in Wexford is the IFA. It has fifty-three branches servicing the length and breadth of the county.

In 2013, the leader of the organisation is Pat Murray, Knocknagapple, Monaseed, who was elected county chairman in January 2013. County secretary is Bob Mackey from Effernogue, Ferns, vice-chairman is Michael Doran of Johnstown Duncormick and county treasurer is Ger Lyons, Ballygullen,Craanford.

The County Executive is serviced by a number of commodity committees who look after the specialist interests of members.

The chairpersons of the various commodity committees in 2013 are John Fitzgerald, Gobbinstown, New Ross; Gerald Dunne, Merton, Bree; Marie Redmond,

Farmers' Mart Enniscorthy.

Barntown- Anthony Whelan, Holmestown;

Blackwater- Simon Neville, Ballyroe;

Boolavogue -Fergus Redmond, Raheendarrig;

Bree/Galbally - Padraig Doyle, Coolteigue;

Broadway- James Butler, Airhill;

Bunclody -Simon Byrne, Ballinavocran;

Caim- John J Doyle, Kiltrea;

Camolin -Patrick Murphy, Medophall;

Campile/Ballykelly -Padraig Hearn, Ballykelly;

Camross - Patrick Banville, Barrys Cross;

Castletown -Tom Keyes, Castletown;

Clongeen- Frank Whelan, Loughnageer;

Clonroche- James Kehoe, Castleboro;

Cushinstown- Seamus Ryan Rochestown;

Davidstown- David Reck, Courtnacuddy;

Ferns- Donal Murphy, Ballyduff House, Ballycarney;

Fethard-On-Sea - James Walsh, Lewistown;

Glenbrien -John Doran, Cranrue;

Glynn- Brendan A Keane, Davidstown;

Gorey- Kevin Murphy, Corriganeagh;

Kilanerin -Sam Rose, Linnanagh;

Kilmore-Martin Power, Sarshill;

Kilmuckridge- James Walsh, Island Farm;

Kiltealy- Michael Mooney, Askinvilla;

Marshalstown- Frank Morris, Ballyorrell;

Monageer -William O'Brien, Monageer;

Monamolin- John Donohoe, Baraglen;

Monaseed- James Osbourne, Ballylusk;

Nash -Patrick Ryan, Nash;

New Ross- Eugene Murphy, Lacken;

Newbawn-James Murphy, Grallagh;

Oulart- Stephen Graham, Wells Hill;

Oylegate- Martin Nolan, Garrynisk;

Piercestown- Frank Cardiff, Sunrise, Murrintown;

Poulpeasty -John F Murphy, Clonleigh;

Ramsgrange- Conor Murphy, Clonsharra;

Rathangan- Padraig Banville, Gibberpatrick;

Rathgarogue- Padraig O'Keeffe, Robinstown;

Rathnure -James Brennan, Larkfield;

Shelmalier-Ian Hawkins, Hollyview, Crory;

Taghmon -Karl Winters Ballintartin;

Tagoat -David Hemmingway, Cottage Farm, Rosslare Harbour;

Trinity- Philip Rochford, Coolsallagh.

FARM ADVISORY SERVICES

Wexford farmers are served by the state-run Teagasc advisory service, which has four offices in the county serviced by thirteen farm advisers. These are:

Enniscorthy Teagasc office: Tim Morrissey, Michael Fitzgerald, Phelim McDonald, Martina Harrington and James Doran.

New Ross Teagasc office: Catherine Colfer, Larry Murphy and Peader Finn.

Johnstown Castle Teagasc office: Nelius Nunan, John Pettit and Ciara Byrne.

Gorey Teagasc office: Eoin Woulfe and Kay O'Connell.

John Keating is the Teagasc Regional Area Manager.

Two agricultural consultants and members of the ACA who service the advisory interests of Wexford farmers are Geoff Barry, Ballingly, Wellingtonbridge and Laura Johnston, Kirwan Agri Consultants, Monamolin, Gorey.

The decentralised Department of Agriculture is located in Johnstown Castle. It houses fourteen administrative sections operated by the Department. These include Forestry, Wildlife Unit, Export Refunds Division, Fallen Animals Payments, Milk Subsidies, Alternative Farm Enterprises, Dairy Hygiene, Farm Waste Management Scheme, Installation Aid, Organic Farming, Aids for Private Storage, Environment, Rural Environment Protection Scheme and Farm Retirement Scheme.

The regional office of the Department of Agriculture's Veterinary and Livestock Section is located at Vinegar Hill Lane in Enniscorthy. In 2013 the Department announced it was removing the administrative section of the office from Enniscorthy but technical and support staff would remain to look after the needs of the 3,091 herds in County Wexford.

THE FARMING MEDIA

Farming is served by South East Radio's long established *Farming Forum*, broadcast each Friday at 8p.m. Presented by Michael Doyle, the programme provides the latest farming news and views from around the region. Nicky Cowman provides weekly commentary on the programme. A daily farming news bulletin is broadcast on South East Radio each day after the 7a.m. and 6p.m. news.

Most farm households in County Wexford read the *Irish Farmers Journal* every week. Journalists from County Wexford are Andy Doyle from Haggard, Ramsgrange and Pat O'Toole from Ballingale, Ferns. Margaret Hawkins, Broadway, journalist and author, is health correspondent.

The *People* newspapers and the *Echo* newspapers carry farming features.

GLANBIA – A CENTURY OF BUSINESS FOR FARMER AND COMMUNITY

Glanbia, with its origins in the co-operative movement, has a proud history and tradition of playing a central role in local communities. With 490 tillage and 466 milk suppliers here, Glanbia is an integral part of the entire County Wexford.

The Glanbia history in Wexford dates back almost a century and new developments and changes continue. The Glanbia Campile branch was established in the early twentieth century. In contrast, Bunclody branch opened under Glanbia ownership for the first time in September 2013.

Glanbia has eight locations in Wexford with AgriBusiness and CountryLife branches.

The managers of the Glanbia Agribusiness branches are Theresa Nolan – Ballycanew branch; Joe Quigley – Ballywilliam branch; James Kinsella – Bunclody branch; and Marks Morrissey – Taghmon branch.

The managers of the Glanbia CountryLife branches are Robert Furlong - Campile, Brian Molloy -New Ross; Les Rothwell - Kilmuckridge and Michael Redmond Clonroche.

The Glanbia mill in Clonroche started production in 1981. Producing over 30 tonnes of feed per hour, it was the biggest and most high tech mill in the country.

Today, Clonroche Mill remains one of Glanbia's key grain processing plants. Glanbia is the biggest assembler, processor and user of Irish grain, with an intake of c. 200,000 tonne per annum.

The removal of the European Union milk quota system in 2015 has been a catalyst of change and growth in the Irish dairy industry. At the time of print, discussions are taking place between Glanbia Ingredients Ireland (GIIL) and Wexford Milk Producers Limited (WMP) in relation to the sale of Wexford Creamery Limited to GIIL.

Glanbia is also constructing a new greenfield dairy processing plant in Ireland, which is a first in 40 years, adjacent to the county bounds in Belview Port. All produce from the new facility will be destined for export markets and the new facility is expected to begin production in spring 2015.

This is very significant for the rural community in the south east of Ireland. Our suppliers expect to increase output by up to 50 per cent. The dairy industry purchases

Harvesting vintage style at the Hook.

90 per cent of its inputs from the domestic economy so the new processing plant will provide a huge boost to the local rural economy and the local industries that will service on-farm expansion.

Glanbia's focus is on building strong relationships with the customers and suppliers of County Wexford for the future growth and development of dairy and tillage farming. There has been a steady agricultural tradition to date and we are proud of our rich heritage in the county that can trace its roots back to over a century of business. We look forward to continued involvement and the exploration of future opportunities in the region for many years to come.

Eamon Power, a dairy farmer from Fethard-on-Sea, is a current Glanbia Board member.

Marty Murphy, Killihile, Arthurstown, chairman of Wexford Milk Producers, is leading the negotiations between Wexford Creamery and Glanbia.

ICMSA

The ICMSA, representing in the main the interests of dairy farmers, has a county executive in Wexford and four regional branches

The Wexford county chairman in 2013 is Sam Rose, Linnanagh Kilanerin and the county secretary is Michael Murphy, Kilscanlon, Foulksmills.

Wexford has six members on the National council of the ICMSA and along with the chairman and secretary they are: James Turner Junior, Tomnaboley Boolavogue; PJ Wall, Linden Farm Ballinamona, Newbawn; Michael Barron, Ballygarvan, Gusserane and Frank Kennedy, Boley, Craanford.

The four area chairmen are North Wexford – Sam Rose, Linnanagh Kilanerin, Enniscorthy – James Turner Senior, Tomnaboley Lower, Boolavogue, New Ross – Michael Murphy, Kilscanlon, Foulksmills and South Wexford – Michael Barron, Ballygarvan Gusserane.

ICMSA Regional Officer for County Wexford is John Quigley of Rosbercon, New Ross.

MACRA NA FEIRME

Macra na Feirme was founded by a group of young agricultural advisers and vocational teachers at Newman House, St. Stephen's Green, Dublin, in September 1944, to promote the educational, social and cultural needs of young people in rural Ireland.

The first county executive in Wexford was formed at the Railway Hotel, now Treacy's Hotel, Templeshannon, Enniscorthy, on 16th March 1949. James Scully of New Ross Young Farmers' Club was elected first chairman, Frank Barry, a teacher and member of Adamstown Young Farmers' Club was elected secretary and Pat O'Connor of Kiltealy Young Farmers Clubs was elected treasurer.

Over the next sixty years, the organisation became the great open university of the country, developing the leadership talents of its members, equipping them for roles in their community and in business and other fields.

Members brought many honours to County Wexford which included 144 national titles. These ranged from public speaking, debating, farm skills and home skills, make and model, stockjudging, quizzes, acting and entertainment.

At one stage in the late 1970s to early 1980s there were twenty-five active branches and more than 1,000 members in the county.

From its foundation and over the next thirty years Macra na Feirme was the mainstay in providing for the educational, social and cultural needs of many of the young people of rural Wexford.

In 2013 the five branches in the county and their chairpersons are: Cushinstown Terrerath- Eric Wickham; Bree- Mark Waters; Blackwater- Joe Warren; Kiltealy/Ballindaggin- Patrick Hipwell; Kilrush Askamore- Eugene Sheridan.

Richard Dempsey, Cushinstown, is county chairman and Mairéad McCabe, Blackwater, is county secretary.

In 2013, the county national award winners were Leanne Brennan, Kilrush-Askamore, winner of the Ms Blue Jeans final and John Forrestal of Cushinstown-Terrerath, beef judging winner.

National titles brought back to the county for its first thirty years:

1953 Dairy judging: Thomas Roche, Shelmalier; stock judging: Sean Kavanagh, Shelmalier; Club Efficiency: Bunclody.

1954 Club Efficiency: Bunclody.

1956 Poultry judging: Anna Fortune, Shelmalier, Alice Kavanagh, Shelmalier and Babs Naughton, Marshalstown.

1960/1962 Queen of the Shears: Beatrice Orr, Bunclody

1962 Debating: Gorey - Edward O'Reilly, Matthew Maguire, Brendan Devereaux and Samuel Slater; farm management: Michael Lyons, Gorey.

1963 Question Time: Pat Rath and Nicholas Rath, Monageer. Thomas Kennedy, Ferns, John Breen, Bannow-Rathangan and Brendan Hamilton, Trinity; Queen of the Shears: Bridie O'Leary, Bree.

1964 Drama: Monaseed; Sheep-shearing- junior, senior and ladies': Phyllis Doyle, Gorey,

1965 Dairy-judging: Pat Rath, Monageer; Public Speaking: Fethard - Hugh Byrne, Fintan Chapman, Patrick Colfer and Gerard Maguire; Bacon Carcase competition: Luke Murphy, Trinity; Poultry Judging: Statia Roche, Shelmalier.

Strawberry promotion at Clogh roundabout.

Steam-powered at Loftus Hall.

1966 Question-time: Brendan Hamilton, Trinity, John Breen, Bannow/Rathangan, Imelda Doyle, Clongeen, Edward O'Reilly, Gorey and Tommy Kennedy, Ferns; sheep judging: Patrick Weafer, Carnew.

1967 Question Time: Brendan Hamilton, Trinity; Imelda Doyle, Clongeen, Tommy Kennedy, Ferns, Nicky Cowman, Shelmalier and Pat Rath, Monageer; Gaelic Cabaret: Monageer; dairy judging: Michael Casey, Clongeen.

1968 Question Time: Imelda Doyle, Clongeen, Michael Casey, Clongeen, Jim Breen, Monageer; Brendan Hamilton, Trinity and Pat Rath, Monageer; sheep shearing junior, senior and ladies': Phyllis Doyle, Gorey; Queen of the Land: Eileen Cloney, Fethard; Gaelic Cabaret: Monageer; stock judging: Winston Ashmore, Ferns; poultry trussing: Evelyn Dowse, Carnew.

1969 Question Time: Michael Kent, Clongeen, Ann Kent, Clongeen, Willie Boggan, Kilmore, Pat O'Connor, Bannow/Rathangan and Joe Monaghan, Kilmore.

1970 Public Relations' Officer award: Michael Freeman, Bree; sheep shearing: Tom Hatton, Bunclody; Gaelic Cabaret: Poulpeasty; Public Speaking: Bree- P.J. D'Arcy, Michael Freeman, Michael O'Leary and Breda Brophy; Cross Country Quiz: Sean Barry, Kilmore; Philomena Monaghan, Kilmore; Frank Rath, Monageer; Willie Considine, Bannow/Rathangan and Martha Murphy, Blackwater.

1971 Public Relations Officer award: Michael Freeman; Bree; Showcase award: Bree- Mary Curtis, Catherine Creane and Elizabeth Creane.

1972 Sheep shearing- junior, senior and ladies': Phyllis Doyle, Gorey; Make and Model: Ann McCabe, Raheen;

Light Entertainment: Cushinstown; Public Speaking: Ballycullane- Anne Redmond, Mary Wallace, Stasia White and Tom Corcoran.

1973 Make and Model: Nancy Kinsella, Ballycullane; Sheep Judging: Eugene Murphy, Blackwater; Ideal Bachelor: Joe Byrne, Bunclody.

1974 Light Entertainment: Camross.

1975 Dairy Judging : Donal Moran, Bree; Farm Tasks: Bree- John Crean, Michael Foley and Willie French; Public Speaking: Cushinstown- Luke Grace, Michael Kent, Ann Stacey and Joan O'Dwyer; Cross Country Quiz- Michael Kent, Clongeen, Philomena Monaghan, Kilmore,Willie Considine, Bannow/Rathangan and Michael Sinnott, Clongeen.

1976 Public Speaking: Camross-Michael Doyle, Breda Banville, Maria Doyle and Ann Somers; beef judging: Tom Shannon, Newbawn; Debating: Clongeen, Martin Colfer, Michael Casey, John Sane and Tom Sinnott.

1977 Public Speaking: Clongeen – Tom Sinnott, John Sane, Bridget Casey and Martin Culleton; Debating: Shelmalier, Tom O'Donoghue, Eileen Shaughnessy, Margaret Doyle and Jim Corcoran.

1979 Miss Macra: Elizabeth Conroy, Inch.

ICSA

The Irish Cattle and Sheep Farmers' Association was set up in 1993 to serve the interests of those in the beef and lamb sectors.

It has a national structure with five sectoral committees representing varying interests.

In 2013 a Wexford man, Terrerath farmer Paddy Kent, is standing for the position of National President of the organisation. Another prominent member of the ICSA in Wexford is Frank Kehoe from Marshalstown.

MUINTIR NA TÍRE

The organisation had a number of branches in County Wexford at one time. One of them, Askamore Muintir na Tíre, first affiliated in the mid-1960s. The first chairman was Fr. Felix Byrne and the first project was a group water scheme that provided water on tap to approximately forty houses. Muintir is again enhancing the promotion of a Rural Development Programme in Askamore with Paddy Byrne becoming a board member of the organisation in 2010. He was elected vice-president in 2012. Margaret Quinn from Bree also works for Muintir na Tíre in Wexford

THE ICA

Breda Banville.
Federation President

ICA, founded in Bree, celebrated its centenary in 2010 and has gone from strength to strength with 32 very vibrant guilds and a membership of almost 600 women in 2013. The ICA has been at the heart of every community over the past hundred years and is building on this valuable heritage in the 21st century. Its key values today, as always, are family and community, social justice, accountability, integrity and leadership.

Into its second century now, the ICA continues to be at the forefront in looking after the needs of its members. In 2011 the Wexford Federation was selected as a pilot area to implement a computer training programme for members. Up to mid-2013 one hundred and forty nine members had been trained.

In March 2012, ICA secured space in the newly refurbished Enniscorthy Castle for the 'Deeds Not Words' exhibition. The exhibition focused on the famous women of Wexford ICA and their contribution to the association locally and nationally over the past century.

A 'One Day Craft School' and Cookery demonstrations are held annually for all guilds. A 'Knitathon' was held in 2011/2012 to raise funds for the Irish Heart Foundation. Members and their families knitted over 150 sets of scarves, caps and mittens which were then sold in Kilkenny Design shops nationally. At the National Ploughing Championships held in Heathpark, Ballinboola, in September 2012, the busy ICA members excelled in arts and crafts exhibitions and demonstrations and provided 1,468 cups of tea and coffee with Wexford Hospice Homecare benefiting from donations.

Liz Wall, the National President of the ICA, launched the County Wexford book *102 Years of ICA* at the National Ploughing Championships. The book was the brainchild of Mary Somers, competition's secretary.

ICA was involved in 'The Gathering' throughout 2013. Twenty ladies from the Pembrokeshire Women's Institute visited Wexford ICA for four days in June. The members stayed with host families in Davidstown, Camross, Wexford Town, Bree and Kilrane/Rosslare Harbour guilds. International officer, Breda Whelan took them on bus tours, which included visits to Clonmore cemetery, where Anita Lett, the founder of ICA is buried and Bree Garden, the site where the first ICA meeting was held.

In 2013 Wexford Federation was invited by Wexford Creamery to participate in the compilation of their commemorative recipe collection marking 50 years of Wexford Cheddar and were also involved with Wexford Festival Opera and Wexford Creamery in 'A Taste of the Opera'.

Wexford Federation of ICA had three National winners in 2013, Mella Winters, Taghmon guild, winner of Gempack baking; Josephine Keane, Wexford Town guild; photography winner and Barbara McGranaghan, Kilmore Quay guild; reporting winner, her subject being 'The Gathering'.

As always, the guild members have a number of projects in the pipeline, in keeping with our motto of "Deeds not Words", so 'Go for it now as the future is promised to no one'.

WEXFORD FEDERATION COMMITTEE 2013/2014

President–Breda Banville.
Vice President and Competitions Secretary–Mary Somers
Vice President–Marie Foley
Secretary–Mary Fitzgerald
Treasurer–Eileen Creevey
An Grianan Rep–Breda Roch.
Timire–Deirdre Connery
Sports Officer and Assistant Treasurer–Mary Nolan
Arts and Crafts Rep–Mary Darcy
Produce Rep–Emily Murphy
International Rep–Breda Whelan
Womens Refuge Rep–Joan Furlong
Development and Information officer–Delores Devereux

Information officer–Breda Dunne
Water Quality Rep–Geraldine McCarthy
Guild Presidents 2013/2014
Sheila Delaney, Adamstown
Ann Young, Ballyanne
Mary Darcy, Ballyfad
Eilish McCann, Ballyoughter
Kit Mackey, Boolavogue
Catherine Dunleavey, Bree
Clare Brennan, Bunclody
Marian Donnelly, Camross
Anne Crosbie, Carrig on Bannow
Emily Murphy, Clonroche
Sarah Buckley, Cushinstown
Eithne Cosgrave, Davidstown
Louie Clement, Duncannon
Susan Danielson, Enniscorthy
Norah Clifford Kelly, Gorey
Statia Fuhrmann, Horeswood
Eithne Lee, Inch
Geraldine O'Connor, Kilanerin
Margaret Keane, Killinick
Myriam Duggan, Kilmore Quay
Kathleen Creane, Kilmyshall
Betty Halligan, Kilrane/Rosslare Harbour
Eileen Brennan, Kiltealy
Marie Foley, Marshalstown
Mary Walsh, Maudlins
Mary Fisher, Monaseed
Mary Crotty, Murrintown/Piercestown
Ellen McCallion, Oulart
Delores Devereux, Our Lady's Island
Anne Doran, Oylegate
Mary Monaghan, Taghmon
Breda Meagher, Wexford Town

Hynes, Jacqui, née Sidney, Duncormick, manager of the National 1798 Rebellion Centre, and Enniscorthy Castle Knights and Rebels experience, married to Paddy with two children, Muireann and Ronan. She has a Master of Literature in the Folklore of the 1798 Rebellion, and recently graduated with a Higher Diploma in Primary Education. Jacqui has worked since her appointment in 2010 to redevelop and reinterpret key Enniscorthy tourist attractions to give them wider appeal. This work has flourished with the annual Battle of Vinegar Hill re-enactment, Enniscorthy Castle School of Witches and Wizards and the redevelopment of the 1798 Centre. She also has responsibility for Vinegar Hill as a tourist attraction and for The Presentation Centre, Enniscorthy.

Jackson, Charles, Wexford, published a book on the '98 Rebellion which went into many editions. It was called *Wexford Cruelties*, and was an account of the rebellion from the loyalist side.

Jacob, Daryl, from Davidstown, Enniscorthy, jockey; winning rider on Neptune Collonges in the 2012 Aintree Grand National. They beat Sunnyhillboy in the closest ever finish to the great race. He has been second jockey to English champion trainer, Paul Nicholls, for some years, behind Ruby Walsh, but is moving up to No. 1 after Walsh has decided to concentrate on Ireland. He has ridden quite a few big-race winners in both Ireland and Britain and can expect many more now that he is the top man in one of the top stables in these islands. He rode 73 winners for the 2012-13 season.

Jaycock, Margaret, Ballybeg, Screen, was a community nurse in Bristol in England for over forty years. Formerly Margaret O'Reilly from Ballinroade, Oulart, she delivered over eleven thousand babies in their own homes in Bristol without one loss. She was awarded an MBE by Queen Elizabeth in 1987.

Jeacle, George, Rathnure, Coiste Seana Ghael recipient, entertainer in drama and Tops of the Parish. In the Athenaeum in the 60s, the late Harry Ringwood proclaimed that George's face was the greatest he had ever seen in Irish entertainment.

Jenkins, James, was a well-known Wexford businessman and, when he retired, he wrote a number of books on Wexford town, including *Retailing in Wexford*. He was Mayor of Wexford in 1968.

Jones, Mervyn, Killowen, Gorey, born 1947, retired dairy farmer; married to Joyce, née Dixon, Killowen, with three sons and one daughter; World champion Holstein dairy cow breeder (Hallow Herd), sons now running the farm and showing internationally in 37 countries.

Jones, Kay, Kilcullen, Ballindaggin, who died in 1990, wrote a number of plays, which were performed mainly by Kiltealy Players. She also published *Templeshambo, A Country Waterway.*

Jordan, Michael, farmer, entered politics in the interests of his fellow farmers. He was unsuccessful as a candidate in the 1922, 1923 and June, 1927 General Elections. He was first elected to the Dáil in the General Election of September, 1927, as a Farmers' Party TD for Wexford. He stood as a Cumann na nGaedheal candidate in the 1932 General Election, but failed to win a seat.

Kane, Seamus, Whitechurch, New Ross, married to Margie, raised over €10,000 for charity through their Steam Rallies and barn dance with funds being distributed to: Fr. Michael Kane, African Water Project, Ballykelly Church Fund, Rehab, St. Patrick's Special School, Enniscorthy and the Church of Ireland, Whitechurch.

Karllson, Geraldine, née Cullen, formerly Ballymitty, now Whiterock Hill, Wexford, co-founder and director of Done Deal classified ads website with husband Fred. Geraldine met Fred, a Swedish national, through a mutual friend while studying in Dublin. Done Deal now employs 25 people at its headquarters in Wexford and also employs five people in Dublin. The website has been a phenomenal success and now has 600,000 daily hits.

Kavanagh, Chris, Tomnalosset Enniscorthy, owner of Parnell Antiques since 1991. Involved in the sale of antiques and collectables with his wife, Helen. Originally from The Moyne, Enniscorthy, he is from a family of eleven and he and Helen have four children.

Kavanagh, Crystina, born 1988, daughter of Joseph and Joan, née Hussey, Roscommon; she has one brother; Christina attended Equine studies in Kildalton in 2006-08, and subsequently graduated with an Honours Degree in business management from Carlow I.T. Wexford campus; avid horse riding enthusiast; she was diagnosed with leukaemia when she was a year old and had a bone-marrow transplant in 1998.

Kavanagh, JJ, Ballinabanogue, Ballywilliam, Irish Farmers' Association activist and in 2013 announced his candidature for deputy president of the IFA at national level; served as national treasurer, returning officer and Leinster vice president along with chairmanship of the Wexford County Executive. A national figure in farming politics he carries on a mixed farming enterprise in the Ballywilliam area. Married to Geraldine, they have one son and one daughter.

Kavanagh, Michael, along with Dan Walsh, edited the *First Annual Journal of the Kavanagh Clan* in 1993.

Kavanagh, Patrick, who was born in 1834, was ordained to the priesthood in Rome in 1856. He was a grand-nephew of Father Michael Murphy, the famous priest of 1798, and he wrote *A Popular History of the Insurrection of 1798*, based on family traditions.

Kavanagh, Paddy, Craanford, Gorey, born 1942; owner Kavanagh Crane Hire; married to Maeve, née O'Connor, Kilmuckridge, they have one daughter and three sons; established Kavanagh Crane Hire in 1973 and it is now the largest company of its kind in the country; first man to captain Craanford to hurling championship victory in 1965.

Kavanagh, Dr. Siobhán, Ballydonfin, Glenbrien, Master's Degree in Agricultural Science from NUI Dublin, 1994; Masters and PhD in Feed Evaluating Systems, followed by a post doctorate in UCD and a Diploma in financial Management from WIT; appointed Chief Ruminant Nutrition Specialist with Teagasc.

Kavanagh, Tomás, born 1963, Artistic Director of St Michael's Theatre, New Ross; plays trumpet, keyboard/piano and percussion; has a strong traditional music background, his father being a percussionist and his mother, Bridget, is a Murphy of Carrig on Bannow; played in the Point Depot on several occasions and with Celine Dion in Lansdowne Road; played salsa music with a Cuban band in the 90s for six years with whom he travelled to the Middle East and all over Europe and Ireland.

> Fortunes Woollen Mills at Brownscastle Taghmon won a silver medal at the Dublin Textile Exhibition in 1897.

Keane, John, The Elms, Bridgetown, Auctioneer and Property Valuer, based at Custom House Quay, Wexford. Born into a butchery business on South Main Street, he began his auctioneering career with WFC Property Division thirty-three years ago. Established his own practice twenty three years ago and was joined in the business for the past seven years by his daughter, Edel. Married to the former Marian Cullen of Cullen's Baby Clothes Shop in Wexford, they have three other daughters Laura, Alison and Jenna. John's other passion in life is horses, hunting and three-day eventing.

Kearns, Anthony, Kiltealy, born 1971, one of six children of Mogue and Betty; one of Ireland's best known classical tenors. Anthony was "discovered" when he entered a singing competition on the Gay Byrne Radio Show in 1993 called "Search for a Tenor" held in conjunction with the launch of the new Irish ten pound note. This led on to professional training under Veronica Dunne. In 1998 he joined the Irish Tenors and the group has performed in many major venues across the world. Anthony has been named as the Best Living Tenor in Ireland.

Keating, John, who was born on 2nd August, 1869, at Sarshill, Kilmore, was a politician and farmer, and he was first elected to Dáil Éireann as a member of the National League Party for the Wexford constituency in the June 1927. He lost his seat in the September 1927 General Election, but was re-elected as a Cumann na nGaedheal TD in 1932 and retained his seat in the 1933 General Election. He was elected as a Fine Gael TD in the 1937 and 1938 General Elections. He lost his seat again in 1943, but was re-elected in 1944. He stood as an independent candidate in 1948, but was not elected. He died on 8th July 1956.

Keegan, Claire, born Wexford 1968. Her story collections are: *Antarctica, Walk the Blue Fields* and the single story *Foster.* Her awards include The Francis MacManus Award, The William Trevor Prize, the Olive Cook Award, the *Los Angeles Times* Book of the Year award, the Rooney Prize for Literature, Davy Byrnes Irish Writing Award 2009, The Tom Gallon Award, and the Edge Hill Prize.

Keevans, Seamus, 1933-2008, Garda Sergeant, Kinnagh, Ballycullane, born in Taghmon to Michael and Elizabeth, née O'Connor; married to Ann, Munster Hill, Enniscorthy. Seamus was a talented player and devoted promoter of Gaelic football and all things Irish. He played inter-county at various levels in all four provinces, for Sligo, Cork, Cavan, Waterford and Wexford; won seven County. senior football titles in three different counties – Taghmon, Wexford, 1956–57; Cavan Gaels, 1965; Kill,

Waterford 1966, '67, 68, and Gusserane, Wexford, at 42 years of age, 1975; managed Wexford senior football team in 1976 and '77; was chairman/secretary of the County Football Board for over twenty years, refereed seven county senior finals in Wexford; served as chairman of the County Camogie Board and as a county selector. He established and organised numerous football competitions for schools (Corn Uí Chaomhain, the Keevans Cup), and U18 club players (the Jim Byrne Cup), and many more. He retired from the Gardaí in April 1993, having served for 40 years.

Kehoe, Billy, Oakwood, Milehouse Road, Enniscorthy, has seen his dream come true in greyhound coursing. He purchased a dog named Carrigtobin Lad for small money and went to Limerick with him and won the biggest prize of all, the €70,000 Irish Cup. Billy only has a few dogs, but is a true lover of the game and proved that the small man can reach the stars.

Kehoe, Brian, Glencarrig, Enniscorthy, chief executive Wexford Local Development (WLD) is the company responsible for the operation of the EU Leader Programme in Co. Wexford. He is one of two sons of one of Wexford's hurling greats of the 1950s and 60s the late Padge Kehoe. He is grandson of the late Padraig Kehoe, politician, poet, author, and composer. Brian Kehoe took the top job in WLD in 2011. Educated at Good Counsel College, New Ross, and UCC, he previously worked with the County Wicklow Partnership. He is married to Deirdre, née Kavanagh, daughter of Toss Kavanagh, Templeshannon, Enniscorthy, and they have two daughters.

The Fair of Clohamon held every year on the 11th of June, was renowned for its faction fights.

Kehoe, Denis, Camolin, born 1960, is married with three children. He is a Wexford businessman and started an agricultural machinery company Kehoe Bros. in 1984 with his three brothers Joe, Laurence and Noel.

Kehoe, Eugene, Kilmore Quay, born Wexford 1959; married to Sylvia née Whitford, they have two children; former fisherman and present coxswain of Kilmore Quay lifeboat; owner Kehoe Marine Ltd., Hardware and Marine Supplies est. 1987.

Kehoe, Ian, Enniscorthy-born journalist, the son of Carmel and Peader Kehoe. He graduated with a BA in Journalism from DCU, and also obtained an MA in International Relations. Upon graduation, he worked with the *Sunday Business Post*, and was later appointed the paper's Chief News Correspondent. In 2010, he was appointed reporter/presenter with RTÉ's *Prime Time* programme, covering a range of economic and business issues. After two years, he returned to the *Sunday Business Post* as assistant editor. In 2013 he co-wrote and published *Citizen Quinn: A Man, An Empire and A family,* a book on the life and times of Sean Quinn.

Kehoe, Joseph, Blackwater, well-known general merchant, set up a family business in Blackwater and also had a business in Selskar, Wexford town. The Blackwater store is still thriving today, having been handed down to his son, George, and now to his grandson.

Kehoe, Monsignor Lory, born 1935; native of Glynn, was ordained at St. Peter's College, Wexford in 1959; served as curate in Ballycanew, 1959 to 1969; spiritual director in St. Peter's College, 1969 to 1976; CC New Ross, 1976 to 1985; PP Clonard, 1985 to 1994; PP Craanford, 1994 to 1999, and PP Gorey, 1995 to 2010. He was appointed Vicar General of the Ferns diocese in 1995 and in 2009 was made an Apostolic Protonary Supernumerary by Pope Benedict, the highest rank of Monsignor. In 2010 he was given a Civic Reception in Gorey for his years of service to the town. He edited a history of Glynn parish which was published in 1989; wrote *County Wexford and Savannah, Georgia 1848-1860*, published 2013. He is now retired and lives in Wexford town. He is the son of Micheál Kehoe, National School teacher and president of the GAA 1950-52.

> Two hundred years ago in 1813 a barrel of barley in County Wexford was making forty two shillings.

Kehoe, Martin, Ballybrack, Foulksmills, New Ross; married to Karen, RIP, they have five children; three times World ploughing champion and 16 times national champion, 12 times on the trot, hailed as 'a ploughing icon'; each of their children has competed successfully in ploughing matches; sons Willie John and Martin Jnr have won national titles; Michelle won the 'Queen of the Plough' title on four occasions while her sisters, Christine and Eleanor, have won one each. Martin and his sons set up a milling business, Kehoe Farms. He was also a member of Boley Tug-of-War team that won various world, international and national titles.

Kehoe, Micheál, Glynn, national school teacher; second Wexford man to be President of the GAA, serving from 1950 to 1952; educated at his local school, Enniscorthy CBS, De La Salle College, Waterford, and at UCD where he played hurling and football; served on Laois County Board while teaching in Emo from 1922 until his return to Wexford as principal at Glynn NS in 1929; member of the Leinster GAA Council for 55 years, Wexford County Secretary in the mid-1930s, and Leinster Chairman from 1942-44. He participated in the 1916 Rising at Enniscorthy as a captain in Fianna Éireann. He had a great love of the Irish language and local history. He was secretary of the 1798 Commemoration Association that had many memorials erected around the county and helped organise the great demonstrations of 1938 and 48. He served as president of the Uí Chennselaig Historical Society and was a life member of the Royal Society of Antiquarians of Ireland.

Kehoe, Mick, Slaney Lodge, Crossabeg, fruit and vegetable grower/wholesaler; married to Annis, née Lancaster; their sons, Paddy and Michael help with the business; Mick is chairman and coach of St. Killian`s Athletics Club with accomplished athlete Annis. They are both always to the fore in fund-raising for charity and parish projects.

Kehoe, Paddy, Gusserane, Wexford hurler and footballer: accepted as one of the best dual players of all time; played for his county in all grades of hurling and football and also for Leinster. He first played senior hurling for the county in 1943 and senior football in 1944, and lined out 135 times for the county in both codes; scored a total of 38 goals 143 points for Wexford; won a Leinster senior football medal in 1945; played with

Wexford in three hurling finals, 1951, '54 and '55, and was a substitute in '56; also on team beaten in Leinster football final in 1956. One of the great footballing forwards never to win an All-Ireland.

Kehoe, Paddy, born in Enniscorthy in 1956. Formerly a teacher, he has been a journalist in Dublin for 25 years. Currently works for RTÉ 10 the Entertainment Network. He is also a guitarist and songwriter. His debut collection of poems is *Its Words You Want.* His first poems were published by the late James Liddy in broadsheets and issues of *The Gorey Detail.*

Kehoe, Padraig, Glencarrig, Enniscorthy, RIP 1959; farmer and a poet and was associated with Arthur Griffith in launching the Sinn Féin movement; played a prominent part in the Gaelic revival and was elected to Dáil Éireann as a Fianna Fáil TD for the Wexford constituency in the 1933 General Election. He didn't contest the 1937 election, but he was elected to the Seanad on the Agricultural Panel in 1938. He lost his seat in the 1948 Seanad election. His son, Padge was a hurling star of the 1950s and 60s.

Kehoe, Padge, 1926-2007 Enniscorthy. Wexford has won six All-Ireland Senior hurling titles; Padge has the unique distinction of being involved in four of them – as a player in 1955, '56 and '60, and as team manager in 1968. He was on the losing side in the finals of 1951, '54 and '62, but won six Leinster titles in all. Kehoe could lay claim to being one of Wexford's most decorated GAA players. His other medals include two National Hurling League, four Oireachtas hurling, nine county senior hurling with St. Aidan's, one junior and one minor hurling; three senior and one junior football.

Kehoe, Paul, TD, Minister of State Bree, born 1973. He was first elected to Dáil Éireann in the 2002 General Election as a Fine Gael TD for Wexford; appointed by Enda Kenny as Fine Gael spokesperson for Communications, Marine and Natural Resources, and he has served as Fine Gael assistant chief whip; re-elected in the 2011 General Election, was appointed government chief whip and Minister of State at the Department of Defence.

Kehoe, Siobhán, Ballywilliam, acupuncturist and herbalist based at the Slaney Medical Centre in Templeshannon, Enniscorthy. a nurse and midwife who went to study eastern medicine practice in China. A native of Castleboro, Siobhán lives with her partner, Jimmy O'Gorman, and has three daughters, Katie, Millie and Sarah.

Kehoe, Tony, Screen, one of County Wexford's best known musicians. Drummer and vocalist with Teresa and The Stars since 1973, he has recorded a number of country music favourites during this time. Tony presents daily country and Irish music programme on South East Radio since the station opened in 1989. He played drums for Johnny Cash at his concert in the Cork Opera House in 1987 and has a collection of fifteen thousand CDs. Loves horses and animals which keeps him busy when not playing music.

Keilthy, Billy, New Ross and Wexford town, RIP; played hurling and football for Wexford; one of the first team managers in the 1950s; famous for his hospital visits to former players and was largely responsible for setting up Sean Gael Loch Garman, a group that helps to maintain contact between older former players and officials, along with then County Secretary Tomás Ó Murchú, New Ross and Bunclody, and Canon William Mernagh, President of the County Board; was succeeded as chairman by Art Bennett, Oylegate and Oulart. Billy was well known throughout the county for his travelling shop. He was married to Patsy, daughter of Sean O'Kennedy, leader of the 1914-18 Wexford football team.

Kelly, Alex, New Ross, born 1974; daughter of Chris, Howth, and Eva Cullen, Taghmon; has been with the sea scouts since she was ten years old; organised River festivals on the, Barrow, Nore and Suir as well as The New Ross Celtic River Festival; member of the Harbour Board in New Ross; author of guide on *The Three Sisters* for The Rising Tide, as part of a European Exchange Programme.

Kelly, Billy, owner of Kelly's Resort Hotel, Rosslare; married to Isabelle, from Provence, and they have six daughters. He is the fourth generation of Kellys to run what his great-grandfather opened as a tea room in 1895 to cater for visitors who arrived by train for day trips to the beach. His father, Bill, expanded the business greatly during the 1960s but died young in 1977 and Billy's mother, Breda, kept the hotel going for years. She also contributes unselfishly to the community through sponsorship of various events every year. She is a great supporter of the arts and the hotel houses an impressive fine art collection.

In 2011, 183,000 overseas tourists visited County Wexford of which 83,000 were from Britain, 68,000 from mainland Europe, 22,000 from North America and 10,000 from other parts of the world. They spent more than Euro 40 million in the county during their stay.

Kelly, John, was born in Enniscorthy. His debut collection is *Gathering the Dead in the Garden.* He lives and works in North County Dublin.

Kelly, Julie, Kilpierce, Enniscorthy, born 1970, daughter of Andy and Sheila; winner of seven All-Ireland snooker titles; moved to the US to pursue a career in professional ladies American pool and became a major player on the Women's Professional Billiards Association circuit. Julie won the World Championship in Quebec 2000. She has also won numerous other competitions, most notably the Canadian Classic and the Florida Classic.

Kelly, Mick, Newtown Road, Wexford, owner of Total Fitness Systems, Clonard. A native of Bishopswater, he is an amateur boxer with fourteen years' experience and is boxing coach/tutor with the Irish Amateur Boxing Association. He is also the main man behind the sport of Kettlebell in the country having been the first Irish man to win the World Kettlebell championships in November 2012 in Latvia. Wexford hosted the European Kettlebell Championships in May 2013 and Mick again was the winner. He is married to Pamela and they have two teenage sons.

Kelly, Paddy, Cornmarket, Wexford, established well-known furniture and workwear store in 1929; his son, Paddy 'Junior', now runs the store assisted by his daughter, Mary, an outstanding Gaelic football and soccer player.

Kelly, Seamus, 1931-2012, Ferrybank, Wexford; married to Margaret, they had four children, Amanda, Patrick, Barry and Peter. He played at out-half five times for Ireland and was a great servant to Lansdowne and Wexford Wanderers rugby clubs. He was the first Irish player to top 1000 points in senior and representative rugby. He played his schools' rugby with Clongowes Wood College. He retired from the game in 1961 to concentrate on the family drapery and retail business, with headquarters at Cornmarket, Wexford. He was very interested in all sports and acted as a judge on the *People Newspapers* Hotel Rosslare Sports Star Awards scheme. His brother, Patrick 'Junior' Kelly currently runs the family business and was himself an outstanding athlete in his youth.

Kennedy, Dan, 1932-2013, Ballynaberny, Kilrush, was a member of Wexford minor football squad beaten by Kerry in the 1950 All-Ireland final. He played right half-forward on the Kilrush team that won the Gorey District junior football championship for the first time in 1950 also. Dan was equally adept at hurling and was on the Askamore team that gained the county junior hurling crown in 1969.

Kennedy, Denis, Palace East, Clonroche, born 1944, Fine Gael member of Wexford County Council, first elected in 1999; retired soft fruit growing specialist at Teagasc Research Centre, Clonroche. Denis got the last seat in the New Ross District in 2004 but reversed his place in 2009 when he topped the poll. Married to Anna, née Kehoe, the couple have a grown-up family. Denis is also a very active member of his local community

Kennedy, James J., born 1909, farmer and politician. He was a member of Dáil Éireann for one term. Representing the New Ross District, he won a seat on the Fianna Fáil ticket in the 1965 General Election. He served as a TD until his death on 13th September, 1968. Because a General Election was due to take place in June, 1969, no by-election was held to fill the vacancy.

Kennedy, Michael, Courtnacuddy, born 1945, retired Principal of Courtnacuddy N.S., married to Eilish née Dunne, they have two sons and a daughter. He helped school to win £75,000 in *Independent Newspaper* competition, 'Building for the future,' in 2001.

Kennedy, Patrick, 1801-1873, Bunclody; attended Mr O'Neill's school at Cloughbawn and trained as a teacher in Dublin; wrote for *Dublin University Magazine* and published a number of popular books of legends, stories and folk tales, including *Fictions of our Forefathers, Legendary Fictions of the Irish Celts, The Fireside Stories of Ireland, Banks of the Boro, Evenings in the Duffry* and *The Bardic Stories of Ireland*. Kennedy's writings are a hybrid of fact and fiction; he implies that the estates of Whig landlords such as Carew of Castleboro of Clonroche are paradigms of perfect social order.

Kennedy, Simon W, Duncannon, a former seminarian who left his studies for the priesthood to train as a lawyer, became internationally known in 1983 for his defence of the teacher Eileen Flynn, now deceased, who was sacked from the convent school where she taught because of her relationship with a married man. He made further international headlines when in the clerical sex abuse scandals in the Diocese of Ferns in 1998, he sued the Papal Nuncio. He is author of the book *The Year the Whales Came In*, in 2004, a novel based on the Fethard-on-Sea boycott of the 1950s in which Catholics were accused of boycotting Protestant businesses in Fethard-on-Sea, in a dispute over the schooling of children in a mixed marriage. The affair generated international media coverage. His book, *Sacred Cows Silent Sheep*, comprises twelve short stories about defining incidents and events in Co. Wexford and elsewhere over the past six decades giving insights from his work as a solicitor in Wexford and Dublin. He was chairman of Co. Wexford GAA in 1985, 1986, 1987. He lives in Duncannon with his wife, Lilian.

Kenny, Paraic, Craanford , born 1996, show jumping rider; member of the Irish national pony team, winner of Young Riders' Bursary and named *The Irish Field Junior Show Jumper of the Year* 2013; currently working with trainer Anthony Conlon in Manchester.

Keogh, Christy, 1943–2002, Enniscorthy, played hurling for Wexford from 1969 to 1979, winning three Leinster medals and taking part in the All-Ireland finals of 1976 and '77 against Cork. Christy is famous for almost winning the '77 final with a blistering late shot that was brilliantly saved by Martin Coleman in the Cork goal. A noted stickman, he won an All-Star Award at right half forward in 1977. He managed Wexford county hurling team 1992-94. He won two Wexford hurling medals, with Shamrocks, 1969 and Rapparees, 1978.

Keough, Donald, retired president of Coca Cola. In 2013 he was inducted to the Irish American Hall of Fame at the Dunbrody Famine Ship in New Ross, in recognition of his Wexford ancestry. His great grandfather, Michael Keough, left Co. Wexford in the 1840s; married Hanora Burke in America. They settled in the prairies of Iowa and had nine children becoming farmers and cattlemen. One of their sons, John, continued farming and married Kate Foley and they had four sons, the eldest of whom was Leo, father of Donald Keough. Donald was born on the farm in 1926, the youngest of Leo and his wife, Veronica's three sons. After a fire destroyed the family home, they moved to Sioux City where Leo found work in a stockyard. Donald at the age of fifteen knew how to close a deal on livestock; at eighteen he joined the American Navy. After graduating from Creighton University in Omaha, Nebraska, he started a career as a talk show host at WOR in Omaha where he became a life-long friend of American chat show host, Johnny Carson. Donald at this stage changed career to work for Butternut Coffee. Within a few years that company was acquired by Duncan Foods which in turn was taken over by Coca Cola. Donald Keough was appointed Head of the Americas for Coca Cola in 1976 and by 1981 he was appointed president, chief operating officer and director. He retired in 1993. After this he turned his attention to his Irish roots and Notre Dame. With an endowment of $2.5million, he established the Keough Institute of Irish Studies and the Keough Notre Dame Centre in Dublin. In 2007, he was granted Irish citizenship. He was instrumental in bringing the Coca

Cola Innovation and Flavour manufacturing facility to Drinagh Business Park Wexford. It opened September 2011 and now employs 100. Donald Keough married Marilyn Mulhall in 1949.

Keyes, Tom, Tomnahealy, Castletown, Inch, born 1946; retired dairy farmer; married to Anne, née Griffin, Dingle, Co. Kerry, with two daughters; current chairman of Castletown IFA; member of Teagasc Macamore group; helps maintain Tara Hill graveyard; helped with the gardens at Tara Hill NS where they won the All-Ireland School Garden competition five years in a row.

Kickham, Dan, Enniscorthy, managing director DKG Group, Quarrypark, Enniscorthy, one of Enniscorthy's oldest and biggest employers. The Kickham family are the latest in the long line involved in this business which began in 1876 when James Donohoe returned from Australia to Enniscorthy and set up J Donohoe Ltd to produce mineral water. The firm has remained Enniscorthy-based and Dan Kickham has expanded and relocated the group to a new site at Quarrypark beside the Blackstoops Roundabout. DKG now includes the Donohoe Motor Group and Datapac and has offices in Dublin and Belfast.

Kiely, Evan, Kilbraney, Gusserane, born 2002, sixth class student at Gusserane N.S., son of Michael, from Waterford, and Maria, née Gill, Kilbraney; an avid reader and Liverpool FC supporter, having won the county title against much older students, he represented Wexford in the Leinster final of the Easons Spelling Bee.

Kiernan, Dominic M, Wexford town, former Mayor of Wexford, retired auctioneer, born 1937, to Patrick and Gretta, one of a family of seven boys and three girls. His father was posted to Wexford as a Detective Garda Officer in 1923, where he met Gretta Morris of Grogan's Road, Wexford and they married in 1931. Dominic was always interested in sport and had a long and varied career. As national secretary of the Irish Amateur Wrestling Association, he was a member of the Irish Olympic Council and took an active part in all Olympic matters. In July 1963, he married Betty Wade, a near neighbour, and they moved to Wexford to work with his mother's brother, Kevin C. Morris, at the auctioneering business. He was asked by Fr. Harry Sinnott of St. Joseph's Boys' Club, to help train the boys; these included future sports stars Ned Buggy, Denny Grannell, Eddie "Heffo" Walsh, Ger Howlin, Shamie Edwards and a host of others. He became trainer of the Wexford senior and junior camogie teams in 1967 and they won Wexford's first senior All-Ireland in 1968 and retained the title a year later. Dominic was then asked by Wexford football manager, Fr. Jackie McCabe, to be physiotherapist to that team, and served the same role later with the county hurlers. He was also involved with many other sporting clubs and organisations all over Wexford, serving as chairman of the Wexford and District Soccer League. Dominic ran the Wexford Health and Fitness Centre at his premises at George Street, Wexford, which was also an injuries clinic, used by most of the county's leading sports people. He served as Hon. Secretary of Wexford County Boxing Board, then Hon. Secretary of Leinster Council and later assistant Hon. Secretary to the Irish Amateur

Boxing Association. He managed International teams to many venues in Europe and the United States, including world boxing championships in Milan, Italy and Chicago. He followed his uncle Kevin C. Morris into politics as a Fianna Fáil member of Wexford Corporation. Kevin had served as Mayor of Wexford seven times from 1954 and died in office in 1984. Dominic was Mayor in 1987, 1996 and 2003.

Kingsmill Moore, Mr Justice Theodore Conyngham, 1893-1979, lived at The Mill House, Bunclody; judge, politician and author; wrote the highly regarded book on fly fishing, *A Man May Fish*, 1960; Independent member of Seanad Éireann 1943 to 1948. He resigned from the Seanad in 1947 on his appointment as a judge of the High Court, where he served from 1947 to 1951 and in the Supreme Court from 1951 to 1966. A Kingsmill Moore Memorial Prize is given to students of Law at Trinity College, Dublin, scoring the highest marks of the first and second divisions

Kinnaird, Mattie, 1919-2003, St. Aidan's Villas, Enniscorthy, entertainer and musician, actor, teacher and author, one of Enniscorthy's greatest sons; married to Ita, he had three sons, John, Matthew and Noel and daughter, Mary.

Sixty-one passengers and crew were lost in the air tragedy near Tuskar Rock on Sunday 24 March 1968.

Kinsella, Anna, Courtown, wrote *The Windswept Shore*, a history of Courtown area, and *County Wexford in the Famine Years 1845 to 1849*, published in 1995.

Kinsella, Michael, former Wexford hurler and County GAA Board Secretary; member of famous Gorey hurling family. Michael was first Wexford coaching officer, and first full-time paid secretary of the County Board, serving from 1993-2007; won All-Ireland minor, 1963, and U21, 1965, medals with Wexford hurlers, representing Wolfe Tones, Gorey; won county senior medals with Buffers Alley; was on the 1962 St. Peter's team that won the county's first All-Ireland senior colleges' hurling title. Michael's brothers, Rory and Seanie, also played for Wexford up to senior level. Rory also served as Wexford senior hurling selector for 1996 All-Ireland win, and took over as manager in 1997 after departure of Liam Griffin, winning the Leinster final against Kilkenny. They are sons of Padraig, Principal of Gorey Vocational School in the 1960s.

Kinsella, Paul, Killowen, Crossabeg, born 1944; retired dairy farmer; married to Lorna, née O'Connor, Bunclody, they have one daughter and three sons; formerly with the Department of Agriculture; involved in setting up of Slaneyside Dairies and Killowen Farm Products; winner of three county championships in a row with Oulart; trainer at Bree Athletics Club; trained Clara Thomspon, youngest athlete to win National British U17 senior hammer.

Kinsella, Pat, Kilgorman, Castletown, developed one of County Wexford's first caravan parks at Kilgorman, recently sold the business and has retired; very interested in local history, the Irish language and the GAA.

Kinsella, Stephanie, Clonleigh, Palace, Enniscorthy, born 1999, daughter of Barry and Jacinta, née Kehoe, Clonleigh, she has one sister, Clodagh and one brother, Robert; attends Ceol Loch Gorman studying classical and musical theatre and singing, under the tuition of

Deirdre Masterson; she performed with Opera In The Open on three occasions in Dublin; has won solo singing competitions for two years running at the AIMS choral festival in New Ross and has won numerous awards from the Dublin Feis Ceoil; she appeared as the young Vreli in the Wexford Festival Opera production of Delius' *A Village Romeo and Juliet,* 2012. Her sister, Clodagh, who also trained under Deirdre Masterson and performs as a duet with Stephanie most of the time, is in her first year of study in Trinity College Dublin and the Royal Irish Academy of Music.

Kinsella, Dr William, Dublin lecturer and Director of the MA in Educational Psychology in UCD School of Education. A native of Ballycullane, having qualified as a secondary school teacher, Billy graduated from the Open University with a First Class Honours Degree in Psychology in 1999 and he attained a Master's Degree in Educational Psychology, with First Class Honours, from UCD in 2000. He has a keen interest in special needs' teaching and was instrumental in the design and establishment of the Master's degree course in Special Needs Education. From a farming background, he is married to Catherine and they have three sons.

Kirwan, Daniel J., a native of Bunclody, died in New York in 1876, was a journalist and the author of a book called *Palace and Hovel.*

Kirwan, Larry, born in Wexford, is a writer and musician best known as the lead singer on the New York-based Irish rock band, Black 47. He has written and produced eleven plays and musicals, some of which have been performed in the United States and Europe. The plays, which include the successful *Liverpool Fantasy*, mostly deal with Irish history and politics. Five of the

plays have been published in a book entitled *Mad Angels*. Larry Kirwan formed the band Black 47 with Chris Byrne in late 1989 following a session in Paddy Reilly's Pub in Manhattan. The band has released thirteen CDs and has performed in more than 2,000 shows. Since April 2005, Larry Kirwan has hosted 'Celtic Crush', a radio show on Sinius Satellite Radio, and he also writes a weekly column for the *Irish Echo* newspaper. He has published several books.

Kirwan, Seamus, from Boolavogue, was elected the first Hon Secretary of the Wexford Soccer League and is a man of many skills. He was a very talented player for many years, winning Wexford Cup medals with St. Cormac's of Boolavogue; refereed games in Wexford and Wicklow. He served as secretary to the Wexford Amateur Boxing Board, was a show-band promoter for many years, and beauty pageant organiser among other interests. Without his persistent efforts, particularly in going to Dublin and pushing the case for a Wexford League to both the LFA and FAI, the League wouldn't have started when it did.

The first train travelled from Wexford to Rosslare on the 26th of July 1876. It was called The Jupiter.

Lacey, Bill, 1889-1969, Ross Road, Enniscorthy, soccer legend. Wexford has produced many great soccer players and while Kevin Doyle may be the south east's brightest star in recent years, undoubtedly the individual who first blazed a trail in the professional ranks was Bill Lacey, from the Ross Road, Enniscorthy. Born in September 1889, he carved out a stellar career that even the passage of time cannot diminish. Lacey had signed from Shelbourne for

Everton in February 1909 and transferred to Liverpool three years later, becoming, it is claimed, the first Irishman to play for them; won back-to-back league titles in 1921 and 1922 and made some 257 appearances for the club, scoring 18 goals. A league title winner with Shelbourne in 1926, he also managed Bohemians to the League of Ireland and League of Ireland Shield double in 1934 and the following year in 1935 led the club to the FAI Cup. Lacey played for the IFA on 23 occasions between 1909 and 1924. Even more remarkable was the fact that at the age of 37, he became the oldest player to make his FAI international debut when he lined out against Italy B in April 1927. A plaque in Bill's honour was unveiled on the Ross Road in August 2010 by the FAI's president, David Blood.

Lacey, Ian, Gorey, born 1986; son of John and Emilie, née McGrath, Limerick; past pupil of Gorey CBS and Community Schools; graduated from UCD with a BA in Geography and Archaeology and subsequently an MSc in World Heritage Management; cycled the Pan American highway from Alaska to Tierre del Fuego, Argentina, in 2012; currently living in Laos where girlfriend Áine Lynch, Cois Linne, Gorey, is working with UNICEF; he is working for a local newspaper and is writing a book about his experiences over 15 months and 17,006 miles.

Lacey, Thomas, born in Wexford, wrote *England and Ireland: Home Sketches, on Both Sides of the Channel,* published in 1852, and he also wrote *Sights and Scenes of the Fatherland,* an account of his tours in Ireland, which was published in 1863.

> Kings in Wexford were Dermot Mac Mael na mBó- 1032;Dermot Mac Enna MacMurrogh – 1125 and Dermot Mac Donncha MacMurrogh -1126.

Lambert, Dick, 1933-2008, Rathangan, married to Anna, née Furlong, they have two sons and one daughter; son of Joseph and Mary Anne, née Kelly, from Trimmer in Tagoat; researched and wrote a great deal about the history of Rathangan: *Rathangan - a Co. Wexford parish,* and *Norman to Pikeman.*

Lambert, Robert 'Bob', Kyle, Crossabeg, was the leader of a flying column during the Civil War and a Sinn Féin politician. He was elected to Dáil Éireann as a Sinn Féin TD for Wexford in the 1923 General Election, but he did not take his seat in the Dáil due to Sinn Féin's abstentionist policy. He did not contest the September 1923, General Election.

Larkin, Mick "Wee", Enniscorthy, tasted success in his very first year in the job as Wexford youth team soccer manager. When Mick Wallace retired from that post after 21 very successful years at the helm, Larkin was his successor and his team again beat Waterford in Ozier Park to win the county's fifth National Youth Inter-League title. Larkin gave outstanding service as a player, manager and committee member.

Lawlor, Councillor George, is Mayor of Wexford, the last in a 700-year succession of mayors of the town since the first years of the 14th century. He is a special adviser to Brendan Howlin, TD Minister for Public Expenditure and Reform. He is a popular singer and entertainer and has performed in numerous stage shows and musicals as a member of Wexford Light Opera Society in the Wexford Opera House. He has been nominated for a number of awards, including several AIMS awards. In June 2004, as a Labour candidate, he was elected to become the youngest member of Wexford Borough Council. Like his late grandfather, Eddie Hall, he has been mayor of the town twice. In June 2009, he topped the poll in elections to both Wexford Borough and County Council, winning more than 2,000 first preference votes. He has served on several boards since his election in 2004 including Wexford Area Partnership, South East Regional Authority Consultative Committee and Wexford County Council's Housing committee. He is owner-manager of the printing company Impression Print. He is a former player with Sarsfields GFC and Faythe Harriers Hurling Club.

Lawlor, Ger, Killcarrig House, Park, Wexford, photographer organist, choirmaster and current chairman of Wexford Festival Opera and of Wexford Festival Trust which has responsibility for running Wexford Opera House.

Lawlor, Tracey, 1983-2007, Castlebridge, music teacher and singer, daughter of Ian and Philomena, sister of Joseph and Brian; graduated with a BA in English and Music from UCD, and went on to become a secondary school teacher; she travelled to China and Spain, and sang with Phil Coulter in New York. Tracey had cystic fibrosis and died aged 24 years. Her family set up the Tracey Lawlor Trust in her honour and they have raised thousands of euro to help people who have cystic fibrosis and to lobby the government and public service on their behalf.

Leacy, Noreen, née Cullen, Ballyclemock, Newbawn, born Wexford 1940, retired community worker, married to Michael, RIP 1993, with one son, Mick; former caretaker of Newbawn NS; noted ballad singer and leading member of Newbawn choir; winner of Bene Merenti papal medal.

Leared, Arthur, was born in Wexford in 1822. A doctor, he invented the binaural stethoscope, and wrote on the circulation of the blood and on digestion. He also wrote a medical treatise in Icelandic. He travelled widely and his travel books include *Morocco and the Moors* and *A Visit to the Court of Morocco.*

Le Mesurier McClure, Sir Robert John, born Wexford 1807, was an Arctic explorer and first discovered the waterway known as the North-West Passage, linking the Pacific and Atlantic oceans. He entered the navy in 1824 and had taken part in a number of Arctic expeditions before taking command of the 'Investigator', one of two ships sent to rescue the British explorer, Sir John Franklin, who was missing. The 'Investigator' became trapped in the ice, forcing McClure to abandon the ship. Two ships sent to rescue McClure and his party had to be abandoned too and the party proceeded on foot. McClure received a knighthood in 1854. He published two volumes dealing with the expeditions under the title *The Discovery of a North-West Passage* (1856).

Lett, Anita, Enniscorthy, wife of local businessman, Harold Lett. She lived near Borodale and was a pioneer in the formation of the United Irishwomen's Organization. The first branch of the organization in Ireland was founded at Bree on 15th June, 1910. As vice-president of the County Wexford Farmers' Association, Anita Lett was in close touch with the needs of farming wives. She invited interested women to a meeting in Dublin to discuss the desirability of forming an all-Ireland society for their benefit. A provisional committee was set up and Anita Lett was elected as its president. The name of the organization was changed to the Irish Countrywomen's Association in 1935.

Letts, Winifred, was born in Co. Wexford in 1882, and she wrote plays that were produced on the Abbey stage. Her novels included *Christina's Son*. She also wrote poetry and her best-known volume was *Songs from Leinster*.

Lewis, Kevin, Wexford, his home was for many years next door to the Theatre Royal in High Street. Kevin has written a number of books about Wexford Opera Festival, including *Memories of Wexford Festival Opera*, 1984. He is also a talented artist.

Lombard, Garrett, Gorey, actor, graduated from the Samuel Beckett Centre, Trinity College Dublin in 2000. Since graduation he has had numerous television and theatre credits to his name including *Pure Mule* and *Love is the drug* on TV and in Oliver Stone's blockbuster, *Alexander*. He also starred opposite Brian Denehy in *The Field* at the Olympia. He is son of Veronica and Garry, who have both been heavily involved in Gorey Little Theatre for many years, as actors, producers and directors as well as in administrative capacities. Garry has adjudicated at drama festivals across Ireland over the last 20 years.

Londra, Michael, Wexford, singer; decided in his early thirties to pursue a career as a professional singer and is now an international star; lead singer with Riverdance in the U.S. National Tour and also in the new production of Riverdance on Broadway. He has also had a successful recording and producing career, and he has worked as an arranger and co-producer for Bette Midler and Celine Dion. He appears with Pavarotti, Bocelli, Il Divo, Sarah Brightman and Kathryn Jenkins on the Universal Records Asia 2009 release *Arias: Ancora*. In June, 2012, he was named Wexford Ambassador along with Man Booker Prizewinner John Banville and X Factor host, Dermot O'Leary.

Lowney, Declan, born Wexford 1960, and is now an internationally renowned film and television director. Cut his teeth in RTÉ directing the Eurovision Song Contest in 1988. Then went on to direct BBC sitcom, *Father Ted* and more recently *Moone Boy* for which he won an IFTA Award in 2013. In 2013 He also directed the feature film *Alan Partridge: Alpha Papa*; is director of Hungry Hill Ltd Media production company in Brighton; he is married to Jenny, and they have two sons, Danny and Ted.

Lydon, Gary, actor, born as Gary O'Brien, in London 1963, to Jimmy O'Brien from Wexford and Londoner Julie Lydon; the family came to live in Wexford when Gary was nine. He began his acting career with Wexford Theatre Co-Op and collaborated in many early stage productions of his work with Wexford writer Billy Roche. One of his early breaks was playing Jimmy Brady in the Bush Theatre, London, production of Roche's *A Handful of Stars*. He won best supporting actor Irish Film and Television Awards in 2005 and 2007 for his role as counsellor Patrick Murray in the RTÉ drama series, *The Clinic*. He has appeared in many other film, TV and stage roles, including in an acclaimed production of Samuel Beckett's *Waiting for Godot* at the 2013 Dublin Theatre Festival. He is married to Kara, daughter of Roscommon Fianna Fáil TD, the late Sean Doherty, and they have two sons, Luke and James.

Lynskey, Alice, A Dubliner living in Ferns, songwriter finalist in the RTÉ series, The Hit in August 2013. Awarded the Recording Development Bursary by Wexford County Council and the Arts Council.

Lyons, Michael Snr, Craanford Mills, born Wexford 1925, retired miller; married to Anna, née Kavanagh, Craanford; with three sons and three daughters; oversaw the restoration of 17th-century watermill in the village, creating an impressive tourist attraction.

MacPartlin, Declan, is a Dublin-born, son of a Ferns woman, Margaret Maguire of Ballinakill. For many years he was a public relations consultant specialising in the agri-sector. He represented Dublin on the National Council of Macra na Feirme in the 1960s and his grá for the land developed from his annual summer holidays from school with his relatives – the O'Learys of Clonee and the Maguires of Ballinakill. He moved to Baylands in the 1970s and when, as he says 'a horse came right' for him he bought, with his wife Catherine, née Cousins, from Barnadown, Gorey, the farm which had been owned by the late Matt Galavan; elected to Wexford County Council as an Independent in 2004 and re-elected in 2009. Promoted the campaigns of Independent member of the European Parliament, Marian Harkin, and served as her

advisor during her career; played hurling for Dublin and won National League and Walsh cup medals; won county junior championship with Clonee in 1984 at 44 years of age.

McCann, Eilish, Ballinclare, Gorey, greyhound owner/breeder has enjoyed great success over the years. She bred and reared the very impressive 2003 Irish Derby winner Climate Control, which also won the Consolation Derby in 2002, the ultimate for any breeder. Her Ballinclare prefix is highly respected throughout the greyhound industry. Eilish's father, Dinny, was a well-known figure on both sides of the Irish sea, buying and selling greyhounds.

McCarthy, Áine, who was brought up in Murrintown, Wexford, has written a number of books, including: *Body Matters for Women, How to Lose Weight and Stay Fit*, as well as a travel guide for women in 1992.

McCarthy, Maurice, Branch Manager, MJ Flood Ireland Ltd, for over 40 years; impresario and musician, got his first guitar when he was 16 and has never looked back, appearing on Opportunity Knocks in the UK in the 70s and The Late Late Show twice and once in Boston Symphony Hall. Regular MC at the opening of the Wexford Festival and other events, Maurice is widely recognised as the sixth Beatle and was responsible for bringing fifth Beatle, Pete Best, to Wexford, to be part of his Beatlemania show.

6

Religion

County Wexford's priests, brothers and nuns have influenced and inspired the lives of the people for centuries. Many of them in their capacity as teachers, nurses and evangelists, have changed whole communities and societies.

GIVING HOPE, SPIRITUAL LEADERSHIP AND INSPIRATION

The spires of magnificently designed and built churches can be seen for miles across the landscapes of County Wexford. They indicate the places of worship for thousands of people.

The dominant religions in the county today are Christian. The Catholic religion, with Bishop Denis Brennan as its head in the Diocese of Ferns, accounts for the faith of more than 90 per cent of the population. The Protestant, or Church of Ireland religion with its leaders, Bishop Michael Burrows, bishop of the Church of Ireland Diocese of Cashel, Ferns and Ossary and the Venerable. Chris Long in Enniscorthy as the Archdeacon of the Diocese, is the faith of seven per cent.

According to the central statistics office (CSO) in the 2011 Census, in a population of 145,320, there were 127,842 Roman Catholics in County Wexford. 'A further 9,659 were adherents of other stated religions e.g. Church of Ireland, Islam, Presbyterian, Orthodox, while 6,204 persons indicated that they had no religion'.

Other Christian faiths include Anglican, Presbyterian, and Wesleyan/Methodist. The Coptic Orthodox religion, ministered by one priest, Fr. Tom Flanagan, has a tiny community here from Egypt, Romania, the Sudan and Syria. The Society of Friends or Quakers in Wexford, who meet in Enniscorthy, have been close friends of the Catholic and Church of Ireland communities for hundreds of years.

The different Christian religions in Wexford are members of a coalition of Catholic and Protestant,

Faith and History rhyme - Corpus Christi, Enniscorthy.

Methodist and Presbyterian in a grouping called the Christian Media Trust (CMT), of which the chairperson is broadcaster Maria Colfer. CMT promulgates their ecumenical and interdenominational messages to the people of Wexford and surrounding counties. CMT has 4.5 hours per week for its programmes, which are heard through regional radio broadcasts on South East Radio.

County Wexford's Catholic missionary priests, nuns, brothers and lay missionaries, are trained as teachers, nurses, philosophers, spiritual advisers community development leaders and managers. They are noted for bringing the Catholic faith to people on every continent and almost every country in the world.

In bringing the faith, they have also inspired, educated and guided people to become independent and self-sufficient, fight for their human rights and oppose slavery and oppression. They became noted for intervening beyond their spiritual leadership and caring remit to influence economic , political and legal decisions at local and national government levels in order to promote a better quality of life and living for people of all persuasions everywhere.

Historically, many bishops, priests and other religious figureheads suffered great personal loss and even death in defence of the faith and of their followers. In October 1649 Oliver Cromwell, regarding the Franciscan priests and brothers of Wexford as dangerous enemies, put six men to death. In June 1798, British yeomen put to death Father John Murphy of Boolavogue and his colleague Fr. Michael Murphy, who served in Ballycanew. In that case, the cause may not have been religious bigotry, because Protestant and Catholic fought side by side and in opposition depending on whether they favoured the Yeomen or United Irishmen.

Wexford missionaries working in other countries from Africa to China have suffered too. In recent times, Fr. Michael 'Mal' Sinnott of Wexford was held hostage by rebels in the Philippines for a month in 2009.

Christianity has influenced and shaped the way of life of Wexford people for thousands of years. Saints most credited with the introduction of Christianity to County Wexford include Saint Aidan, Saint Ibar, Saint Patrick and Saint Munn. Churches are named after saints and Pattern days or Patron days commemorate the saints in every parish. Saint Aidan or Mogue or Maedoc, a native of Cavan, was first bishop of Ferns around AD500. Before the arrival of the saints, Ireland and Wexford was said to have been mainly pagan.

The influence of religion on communities is evidenced by the number of grottos, holy wells and sites of mass rocks. In Penal Law times, in the sixteenth and seventeenth centuries, Catholic priests brought their flocks to secret locations marked out only by a rock on which they said Mass. In recent years on Christmas morning Mass is celebrated at an open-air Mass rock in Tomhaggard, attracting huge crowds annually.

Up to recent times the Catholic Church has had major influence on political, economic, education, social, community and individual decisions and behaviour. That influence continues to this day, in varying degrees, but to a much lesser extent than fifty years ago.

DIOCESE OF FERNS

Bishop

Bishop Denis Brennan was consecrated Bishop of Ferns 23rd April, 2006. He was born in the Parish of Rathnure, Enniscorthy, on 23rd June, 1945, and the first native of the county to be appointed Bishop in seventy years.

He was ordained on 31st May, 1970 at St. Peter's College, Wexford. He was appointed to the House of Missions in 1970 and Administrator of St Senan's Parish, Enniscorthy, from 1986 until his appointment as Parish Priest of Taghmon in 1997.

He served as Vicar Forane for Wexford Deanery.

Vicar General

Rt Rev Mgr Joseph McGrath, PP VF VG, Parochial House, New Ross, Co. Wexford.
The Vicar General is appointed by the Bishop, under his authority from Canon Law, to attend to assigned executive duties within the diocese.

Episcopal Vicar for Clergy

Rt Rev Mgr Denis Lennon, PP VF, 39 Beechlawn, Wexford. The Episcopal Vicar for Clergy is appointed by the Bishop, under his authority from Canon Law, to promote and support development of priests.
Diocesan Secretary and Diocesan Communications Officer: Rev John Carroll, CC, Barntown, Wexford.

Parish Priests of the Ferns Diocese in 2013

Adamstown Rev Robert Nolan
Annacurra Rev James Hammill
Ballindaggin Rev John Sinnott
Ballycullane Rev Wm Byrne
Ballygarrett Rev James Butler
Ballymore Rev Martin Byrne
Crossabeg Rev James Finn
Bannow Rev James Kehoe
Blackwater Rev HughO'Byrne
Bree Rev Francis Murphy
Bunclody Rev Laurence O'Connor
Camolin Rev Joseph Kavanagh
Carnew Rev Martin Casey

Castlebridge Rev Walter Forde
Clonard Rev Denis Lennon
Clongeen Rev Colm Murphy
Cloughbawn Rev Richard Hayes
Craanford Rev Thomas Doyle
Cushinstown Rev Michael Byrne
Davidstown Rev James Nolan
Duncannon Rev John Nolan
Enniscorthy, Saint Aidans, Rev Richard Lawless
Enniscorthy, Saint Senans, Rev Brian Broaders
Ferns Rev Patrick Cushen
Glynn Rev Patrick Stafford
Gorey Rev Wm Howell
Horeswood Rev Gerald O'Leary
Kilanerin Rev Patrick OBrien
Killaveney Rev Raymond Gahan
Kilmore Rev Denis Doyle
Kilmuckridge Rev Seamus Larkin
Kilrane Rev Diarmuid Desmond
Kilrush Rev Joseph Power
Marshalstown Rev Daniel McDonald
Monageer Rev Wm Cosgrave
New Ross Rev Joseph McGrath
Newbawn Rev James Furlong
Oulart Rev Patrick Browne
Our Lady's Island Rev Brendan Nolan
Oylegate Rev James Cogley
Piercestown Rev John O'Reilly
Ramsgrange Rev Bernard Cushen
Rathangan Rev Kevin Cahill
Rathnure Rev Anthony O'Connell
Riverchapel Rev Thomas Dalton
Taghmon Rev Sean O'Gorman
Tagoat Rev Matthias Glynn
Templetown Rev Oliver Sweeney
Wexford Rev James Fegan

Clergy of the Church of Ireland, Ferns

Bishop Michael Burrows is bishop of the Church of Ireland Diocese of Cashel, Ferns and Ossary.
The Ven Chris Long in Enniscorthy is the Archdeacon of the Diocese.

The parishes of the diocese are Ardamine, Bunclody, Enniscorthy and Monart, Ferns, Gorey, Killanne, Killegney, Tinahely/Carnew and Wexford and Kilscoran.

The rectors of the nine parishes in the county of which seven are unions are as follows:

The Revd Paul Mooney, Dean of Ferns, who ministered in Korea.
The Revd Canon R.Harmsworth - Killanne/Killegney Union
The Revd Canon Bob Gray - Ardamine Group Kilnamanagh
The Revd Richard Greene (Priest-in-charge) - New Ross/Fethard-on-Sea Union
The Revd Michael Stevenson; The Revd R, Stotesbury (Non Stipendiary Priest) - Bunclody Union
The Revd Ruth Elmes - Tinahely /Carnew Union
The Ven Chris Long; The Revd R, Stotesbury, (Non Stipendiary Priest)-Enniscorthy/Monart Union
The Revd Arthur Minon; The Revd Nicola Halford (Curate Assistant) - Wexford/Kilscoran Union
The Revd Canon Mark Hayden - Gorey Group
Georgina Rothwell is Diocesan Secretary for Ferns District.

Sisters of Perpetual Adoration, Wexford

A Wexford-founded order of nuns known popularly as the Sisters of Perpetual Adoration, and more formally as The Institute of Perpetual Adoration of the Most Holy Sacrament, is a small enclosed order which was founded by the then bishop of Ferns Most Rev. Dr. Thomas Furlong and an English nun, Mother Mary Joseph Bennett, in 1875.

The convent of the order was built twelve years later beside the Church of the Assumption in Bride Street, Wexford.

This small order which once numbered thirty-nine nuns has continued their unbroken adoration of the Blessed Sacrament from 1st January 1875 to March of this year 2013, more than 138 years, when they reduced their 24-hour vigil to 13 hours per day because of declining years of the nuns.

Eight members of the order come from Cavan, Louth, Limerick and Tipperary and two members, Sr. Agnes McCormack and Sr. Dominic O'Neill, are from Wexford.

Priestly support for the Sisters of Perpetual Adoration, Bride Street, Wexford.

McCauley, Sam, pharmacist and businessman. He and wife, Leslie, are the principals in one of the country's most successful enterprises. Sam McCauley Chemists was founded in 1953 by the late G.B. McCauley, M.P.S.I., who acquired the Brooke Kelly Pharmacy at 21 Rafter Street, Enniscorthy, which operated since the early 1900s. Over the next forty years McCauley Chemists grew into a thriving enterprise. Sam and Leslie, joined the family business in 1978 and, under their direction, the business has continued to expand. Sam McCauley Chemists Group currently operates twenty-eight stores nationally, with a strong presence in counties Carlow, Cavan, Cork, Dublin, Kerry, Kilkenny, Tipperary, Waterford, Wexford and Wicklow. The group employs over 570 staff and has an annual turnover in excess of €80 million.

McClean, Colin, Carrigabruce, Enniscorthy, born 1984; son of Tony and Anne, née Donohoe, Clondaw, Ferns; partner of Li Hua Zou; currently studying for PhD in Biomedical Engineering in Beijing having received primary degrees from University of Limerick, University of Glasgow, Taiwan University; his grandmother on his father's side, Lizzie Murphy, is directly related to Fr. John Murphy, Boolavogue, and his paternal grandfather was related to the MacLeans of Duart Castle, Mull of Kintyre. He has two brothers, Alan, chartered accountant with Ernst and Young, Dublin, and Tony, who teaches English in China. His only sister, Donna, is a full-time mother to Ryan.

McCullagh, Patrick, Ferns, GAA administrator and first Wexford man to referee an All-Ireland senior hurling final. He took charge in 1925 when Tipperary beat Galway, and in 1926 when Cork beat Kilkenny. No other Wexford man was appointed until Dickie Murphy in 1992, a gap of 66 years. He filled all the top County Board posts at various times from 1916-1945 and refereed six Wexford senior hurling finals.

McCutcheon, **John Charles,** who was born in 1925 in Ballymitty, was a prodigious composer of ballads, and a posthumous collection of his work, *Where the Silvery Corach Flows*, was published in 1992.

McCutcheon, **Sam**, spent many years in Cork, and was author of *A History of St. Finbarr's Cathedral* and *History of Douglas, Co. Cork*.

McDermott, Kevin, born 1936, retired fireman, Kyle, Crossabeg, married to Noreen, née Cronin, Cork, with two sons; percussionist; accordion player and teacher; singer; actor; poet; writer of *The year of the Corncrake;* a verse from one of his poems is inscribed on commemorative plaque in Cavan town; is regular performer and MC for the Wexford Folk Orchestra.

McDermott, Margaret, Five Acres, Busherstown, became involved in Wexford Community Games in 1977 and is the current County president. She held the position of county secretary for four years and was appointed Leinster secretary 1978/79 , a position she held for sixteen years. She served as county chairperson on and off for eighteen years and was the first National Executive Committee delegate for Wexford. Margaret was elected to the National Standing Orders committee in 1982 and then she was elected National Treasurer, a position she held for 20 years.

McDonald, Damian, Stradbally, Co Laois, chief executive Horse Sport Ireland. Formerly from Crossabeg, only son of Albert and Angela, but has six younger sisters, Aideen, Sarah, Sinéad, Laura, Susie and Niamh; graduated with a Masters in Economics in 1995 from UCD and became CEO of Macra na Feirme in 2001; appointed first CEO of Sport Horse Ireland in 2007 and was Irish Equestrian Team Manager at the London 2012 Olympics; married to Siobhán with three children Mark, Kate and Sean.

> There were monasteries at Adamstown, Clonmines, New Ross and Taghmon.

McDonald, Edward, Newbawn, born 1978, primary school teacher, Cushinstown NS, and qualified architect; while travelling the world, witnessed and aided Red Cross work in Indonesia after earthquake 2005-6; plays guitar and accordion.

McDonald- Gayer, Bee, Crossabeg; teacher, Loreto Secondary School, Wexford, married to Danny. Having completed her education with a B.A. and H.Dip, she joined the local Shelmalier Macra na Feirme branch where she proved herself to be an effective and strong leader. Author of *County Wexford's Macra Story, 1949 to 1989.*

McDonald, Darragh, Gorey, born 1994, won a silver swimming medal at the 2008 Beijing Paralympics at the age of 14. In the 2012 Games in London when he won a gold in the Men's 400m freestyle event. He won another gold medal at the 2013 Paralympic World Swimming Championships in Montreal in Canada, finishing in 20 seconds in front. Darragh's Montreal success was all the more remarkable as his training had to be combined with studies at Gorey Community School for his Leaving Cert. He actually checked his results on computer while in Canada and was pleased with the outcome. He is studying Commerce at UCD where the swimming facilities are very good and he is already turning his attentions to the Rio Olympics in 2016.

McDonald, Jimmy, New Ross, and Menapians AC. Jimmy finished sixth in the 20k walk in Barcelona Olympics in 1992, arguably the best ever performance by a Wexford athlete in the able-bodied Games; Irish record holder; finished eighth in the World Indoor championships in 1991; competed in Seoul in 1988 when coming in seventeenth. He scored a great double in the World Masters' Track and Field Championships in Lahti, Finland, 2009, winning the 5k and 10k races in the over-45 category.

McDonald, Lisa, born 1974, solicitor with a practice in Wexford town. Former member of Seanad Éireann, Lisa served on the Fianna Fáil National Executive from 1995 to 2004. She was an unsuccessful candidate in the 2007 General Election, and was nominated by the Taoiseach, Bertie Ahern, to the Seanad 2007. She was the Fianna Fáil Seanad spokesperson for Equality and Law Reform from 2007 to 2011. Also a former member of Wexford County Council, Lisa is married to Richard Simpson and the couple have two children.

McDonald, P.J., Monastery Avenue, Taghmon; jockey; son of Mary and Paddy, has been successfully plying his trade in England; rode Hot Weld to victory for fellow Wexford man Ferdy Murphy in the Scottish Grand National of 2007; rode 37 winners in the 2012 season but has been riding exceptionally well in 2013 and at the time of writing was just outside the top 20 riders in Britain.

McDonald, Tom, Ballymackessey, Clonroche, born 1951, historian, native of Barrystown, Carrig on Bannow; son of Martin, Clongeen, and Mary, née Murphy, Ballycrinnegan, Co. Carlow; studied history in UCD for five years in the 1970s, specialising in County Wexford during the nineteenth century. Writing predominantly on religious and land issues in the 1800s, he has had articles published in many journals and newspapers including the *Journal of the Wexford Historical Society*, The Past and the Kilmore, Taghmon Historical Society, and Bannow Historical Society and Bree Journals. He is also a well-known lecturer.

McGovern, Cian, Gurtins, Cleariestown, born 1987, singer/songwriter; son of Liam and Doreen, née Cogley, Kilmore, he has one brother and one sister; currently in Wellington, New Zealand, on the back of a busking tour that has taken him through India, Vietnam and the Phillipines. Cian started playing music at four years of age and plays guitar, piano and keyboard. Liam is a former member of Cornerboy.

McGovern, James, Killurin, teacher in CBS Enniscorthy; native of Co. Longford. He attended St. Mel's College and later graduated from NUI Maynooth with a degree in history and philosophy. He then went on to study theology at the Gregorian University in Rome. He later returned to Maynooth to complete his B.D. degree and also did the H. Dip. there.

He arrived in CBS Enniscorthy in 1982 as a teacher of history, religion and public speaking. He has taken a keen interest in the personal development of young people and has tutored the school's public speaking and debating teams for the past thirty years, as well as coaching football teams. He has been a member of the Central Executive Council of the A.S.T.I. for many years and has always equated trade unionism with professionalism. He played for the Wexford senior football team during the 1980s and has also trained Wexford Minor and U21 teams as well as managing the Wexford ladies' football team. He founded the Purple and Gold Stars and worked on the fixtures problem in Wexford GAA in the first half of the 1990s. He is the author of *Coming of Age in Wexford GAA 1982-2003* and co-authored *The Gallant Boys of Glynn-Barntown*, in 2010. James lives with his wife, Bernadette, née Randall, in Killurin. They have three daughters, Claire, Susan and Eimear.

McGrath, Eamonn, born Wexford 1929. His novels are, *Honour Thy Father*, *The Charnel House* and *The Fish in the Stone*. Both *Honour Thy Father* and *The Charnel House* were serialised on the *Book Time* programme on RTÉ radio read by his son, Garvan.

McGuinness, Seamus, New Ross, owner of Prim Ed Publishing, Marshmeadows. A native of the town, Seamus has built a successful publishing company over the last 20 years, selling into the schools of Ireland and the UK. He and his wife Pauline live in New Ross. Their five daughters are pursuing careers or studying in America and Europe.

McLoughlin, Anne, from Kilmuckridge, published *Macamore Miscellany* in 1987.

McMahon, Brian, born Co.Wicklow 1953, principal of CBS Primary School, New Ross; married to Ann, née Bennett, New Ross, they have three sons; director of New Ross and District Pipe Band - world champions for 2012 and 2013, Scottish champions 2013 and three time All-Ireland champions; his sons also play with the pipe band. Brian has been instrumental in helping to bring a newly-built primary school to New Ross which will amalgamate three New Ross primary schools.

McNamara, Sarah, a native of Davidstown, Enniscorthy, wrote *Those Intrepid United Irishwomen, Pioneers of the Irish Countrywomen's Association*, which was edited by Dr Austin O'Sullivan, and published in 1995.

Mackey, Paddy, New Ross, one of only two Wexford players to win All-Ireland senior medals in both codes; he won all four football titles from 1915 to 1918 inclusive, and he also played on the Wexford team that won the 1910 hurling title, the county's first. A native of Kylmore, The Rower, and therefore a Kilkennyman, he had to sleep on the Wexford side of the Barrow to qualify for Wexford; Sean O'Kennedy, the Wexford captain and team leader, provided him with that bed at his home at Quay Street, New Ross.

Maddock, John, native of Rosslare Harbour; journalist with *Independent* Newspapers until his retirement. He has written two books on Rosslare Harbour, *Rosslare Harbour: Past and Present*, 1986, and *Rosslare Harbour: Sea and Ships*, 1996. His father, also John, was a freelance journalist working out of Rosslare for many years.

Marconi, Guglielmo, 1874-1937, inventor of radio. He was born in Bologna in Italy to father local landowner Guisseppe Marconi, who was married to Annie Jameson, Daphne Castle, Enniscorthy. She was granddaughter of John Jameson, founder of the Whiskey Distillers. It is believed Marconi along with his mother spent many summers at Daphne Castle in Fairfield in the parish of Monart. The world's first commercial wireless telegraph transmission was performed by Marconi's employees, on 6 July 1898. His company established a wireless transmitting station at Marconi House, at Rosslare Strand. He was awarded the Nobel Prize for Physics in 1909 and he was married twice.

Masterson, Anthony, Castletown and Wexford senior football goalie; selected on 2008 Gaelic Players' Association national team of the year; son of Tommy, who also played in the goal for Wexford and Castletown for many years. He has been part of Wexford's football resurgence in the past decade.

Masterson, Deirdre, Ballycanew, Gorey, award-winning mezzo soprano and vocal coach; proprietor and director of Ceol Loch Garman prestigious vocal and dance academy; founding member of The Irish Sopranos. Deirdre along with her brother, Gary and sisters, Aisling and Kelli Ann perform together as The Masterson Clan. They are children of Frank and Lilli, Brackernagh, Ballycanew.

There were 1,018 planning applications approved in County Wexford in 2010.

Meleady, Rosie, Oylegate, wedding planner, born 1972; married to Ronan Skelly, Dublin, they have one son and one daughter; established business organising complete weddings in Johnstown Castle and other venues, since 2009 for locals and couples from as far away as

Georgia, LA, New York, Boston, Beirut, Canada, New Zealand – including several those who have no familial connection to Wexford; publishes online magazine 'lifeisshortmagazine.com.'

Mernagh, George, 1955-2011, late of Balrath, County Meath and a native of Castledockrell, Enniscorthy. George was managing director of Tattersalls up to the time of his death, a position he had held for four years. Educated at Rockwell Agricultural College, he was stable jockey at British trainer, John Webber for five years. He joined Tatttersalls in 1989 and became a member of the board in 1999 and managing director in 2007. Widely recognised as a gifted horseman, his untimely death came at the age of 56.

Merrigan, Andy, Monareigh, Castletown, a barnstorming Wexford and Castletown Gaelic football midfielder - the man with the cap on backwards - died in 1973 and the All-Ireland Club Football Championship Cup was donated and named in his honour. It is played for at Croke Park every St. Patrick's Day. The Cup was first played for in 1974 and fittingly, it was won by UCD who were captained by a Castletown club mate of Andy's, Michael Carty, the only Wexford player ever to accept the Andy Merrigan Cup.

Meyler, Gerry, Tacumshane, publican; married to Teresa, proprietors of Meyler's Millhouse Bar and Restaurant which is located beside the only surviving complete windmill in the Republic of Ireland. Built in 1846 by the Rotterdam-trained millwright Nicolas Moran, Thw Windmill has a rare, revolving, straw-thatched cap. Virtually all the timber used in the building was driftwood or timber from shipwrecks off local shores. It is now a designated national monument.

Middleton, Karl, Our House, Monbay Lower, Craanford, born 1966, landscape gardener, married to Marina, née Oldfield, Mirfield, Yorkshire; chairperson of multi-award-winning Craanford Tidy Towns; Secretary of Craanford Askamore Kilrush Community Employment Scheme.

Minias, Simon, Gorey, born 1997, a native of Poland, pupil at Gorey Community School; won Texaco Art Competition 2013 with a portrait of his sister Sophie which, according to the adjudicators was 'wonderfully composed and superbly executed.'

Molloy, Graeme, Duncannon, Seashells Guest house, woodwork teacher at St. David's Secondary School in Artane, Dublin; Wexford senior county footballer, acknowledged for his defensive skills in the full-back line.

Molloy, Philip, native of Wexford town carved out a distinguished career in national newspaper journalism, first with the *Irish Press* and then the *Irish Independent*. He began his career with the *Wexford People* before becoming district reporter with the *New Ross Standard*.He later moved to the *Irish Press* before taking up the post of News Editor with the *Irish Independent*. All through his career he has maintained his interest in movies. He is now film critic with NewstalkFM.

Molloy, Richard, Kinnagh, Ballycullane, born 1989, Business Market Analyst, Erie Insurance, Pennsylvania; single; past pupil Good Counsel College, won scholarship to Mercyhurst University in 2009; graduated with honours degree in Business Competitive Intelligence May 2013; first Irish student to be Mercyhurst Student Government President; received the Frank Barry leadership award.

Moloney, Michael, Raheen, married to Margaret, née Evoy, Tinnecarrig, owner of Moloney Windows Company, in business for more than twenty years, gives valuable local employment in the manufacture of windows and doors. They have five grown-up children and both are well-known on the dance floor.

Mooney, Tom, Ballylucas, Ballymurn, born 1964; Editor *Wexford Echo* Newspaper Group; son of Tom and Christine; studied Journalism at the College of Commerce, Rathmines, and in Toulouse. In 1989, he was appointed Wexford reporter with the *Wexford Echo* Group, and was appointed Group Editor in 1995. During that time the newspaper has won numerous awards: he was the first provincial journalist to win The Law Society Media Justice Award. He has published several books including, *All The Bishops Men,* 2011, an investigation into three decades of clerical abuse in an Irish diocese, *Battleground: The Making of Saving Private Ryan in Ireland,* with Stephen Eustace, and a book of his own poetry with photography by Pádraig Grant, *With This, or Upon This;* edited *Dust motes Dancing in the Sunbeams*, an anthology of fifteen Wexford writers, 2013.

Moore, Jim, Crionna, Kilmore Quay, Fine Gael member of Wexford County Council, elected at his first attempt in 2009 became chairman in 2010. Returned to Kilmore from a career at sea in the late 1980s and started his own engineering services business. Qualifications include engineering, industrial management and rural development. In 2013 was elected chief executive of the National Parents' Council Post Primary Section. He is married to Lucy and they have two children, Sarah and Jaimie. Jim's other passion in life is sport.

Moore, Lily, The Old Pound, Wexford, a popular corner shop owner for many years. The shop was run up to 2009 by Lily's nephew, Hugh, who, along with his wife, Stella, has now retired. Lily's was known in times gone for its broken biscuit and sweet collection.

Moore, Michael, a native of New Ross, compiled T*he Archaeological Inventory of Co. Wexford,* which was published by the Office of Public Works in 1996.

The extraction of silver at Clonmines began in 1550.

Moore, Toddy, born Wexford 1931, Rackardstown, Kilmore, married to Eileen, née Sheil, RIP 1988, with three sons and four daughters, two of whom died young; later married to Betty Byrne, Knockboyne, Ballymitty, RIP 2008; carpenter for CIE in Rosslare Port 1961-1996; a founder member of Community Games in Wexford; secretary Kilmore Athletics Club for 30 years, County Board of Athletics for 30 years and chairperson of Leinster Athletics Council for 14 years; currently enjoying life with partner, Pam Kehoe, Bridgetown, participating in the Active Retirement Group; won a Rehab People of the Year Award and Hotel Rosslare Annual Sports Award; represented Wexford in the Go for Life initiative playing skittles, horseshoes and lobbers. Toddy has never retired. The highlight of his sporting career was being present to see Jimmy McDonald of New Ross finishing sixth in the 20km walk at the Barcelona Olympics 1992.

Moriarty, Jonathan, Knocknagross, Bree, RIP 1999. A primary school teacher and native of Kerry, he first taught in Galbally, but he was best known as The Master, principal of Bree NS for many years. He retired in 1978. Very actively involved in GAA, particularly Bord na nÓg. He was predeceased by his wife, Nancy, and they had four sons, Tom, Sean, Seamus and Paud.

Morris, Anthony, Verneglye, Bannow, actor; graduated with a degree in Theatre Studies from Samuel Beckett Centre, Trinity College Dublin; has appeared in a number of TV programmes including *Killinascully* and *Titanic: Blood and Steel.* Star of the famous Weetabix racecourse TV advert.

Morris, Fr. Fintan, born 1966, CC Caim, noted historian, has studied Church history and archaeology in Rome; son of Des and Mary, née Donohoe, Ballinacor, Tinahely; former member of the teaching staff of St. Peter's Seminary; lectured in Church history in St. Patrick's College, Maynooth; before his appointment to Caim, he was curate in Cleariestown.

Morrissey, Jim, Cherryorchard, Enniscorthy. One of Wexford's great inter-county hurling stars of the 1950s; member of the Wexford All-Ireland-winning team of 1955-1956 and 1960; played club hurling in his native Camross, where he was one of thirteen children of the late Jim and Catherine. Jim and his late wife, Gaye, née Doyle, Broadway, had eleven children. One of his daughters, Dorothy, is Humanitarian Aid Officer with the EU in Brussels and works in the ECHO programme which specializes in disaster zones in South America; well known in later life as farmer and oil distributor, Jim Morrissey died in 1997.

Morrissey, Moses, native of Nash, Gusserane, a retired Garda detective sergeant, who has worked on many of Ireland's high-profile criminal cases; son of Michael and Mary, née McCabe. He and his wife, Eleanor, née English, live at Straffan, Co. Kildare. He was for 25 years a member of the Technical Bureau at Garda HQ in Dublin, where he became a fingerprints' expert. He has worked on more than 150 murder cases. He is a past pupil of CBS, New Ross, and of St. Peter's College. On St. Peter's teams, he played centre-field. His team-mates included Dan Quigley, Vinny Staples, Jim O'Neill, Eamon Doyle, Michael Jordan and John Murphy of Blackwater. He is a trustee of Castlewarden Golf Club in Co. Kildare and was researcher on the book *Trees of Castlewarden* by Eddie Walsh.

Moynihan, Dave, RIP, Ferns, led a very successful band which toured Ireland and the UK for many years and was extremely popular with emigrants, especially those from Co. Wexford. As a family the Moynihans have also been identified with voluntary church music and David's widow, Patty, who played with the band, was organist in Ferns and Ballyduff for many years, until her recent retirement. Currently David and Patty's son, Arthur, is organist in Ferns Parish Church, while brothers, David and Tommy, are also active in the music scene.

Mullen, Dr Karl Daniel, 1926-2009, born near Courtown, consultant gynaecologist, and Irish rugby international hooker; won 25 caps for Ireland from 1947 to 1952, and captained the country to its first Grand Slam (wins over all the other teams in a single season) in 1948; this was not repeated for 61 years until the current team's Slam in 2009. He was also selected to captain the

1950 Lions Tour to Australia and New Zealand, during which the Lions lost the Test series against the All Blacks 3-0, with one game drawn, but won the test series against Australia 2-0. He played four tests for the Lions on that tour; two against New Zealand and two against Australia. He missed the third and fourth tests against New Zealand through injury. Played some of his early rugby with New Ross RFC and his senior club was Old Belvedere.

Mullery, Ger, Horeswood, was County ladies' Gaelic football chairman for three years and was also a mentor on county teams. He continued his involvement until his untimely death in 2012.

Mulrennan, Frank, born Bunclody, now living in Glenageary, Dublin, Managing Director of Celtic Media Group, publishers of the *Anglo-Celt, Meath Chronicle, Westmeath Examiner* and *Westmeath Independent.* He is a member of The Press Council of Ireland, the independent public complaints body established by the Minister for Justice in 2007. He was previously MD of the *Drogheda Independent* Group, business editor of the *Irish Independent,* editor of the *Farming Independent,* and both producer and presenter of programmes with RTÉ Radio.

Murphy, Breda, Barntown, has served Wexford Ladies' Football Board with distinction; was County chairperson for two years and was also President of Leinster Council. She played her football with Forth Celtic and Shelmalier Club and also represented Wexford county teams at many levels. Breda was also involved in the setting up of a club in her native St. Martin's Piercestown parish.

Murphy, Brian, Drimagh, Rosslare, born 1952; married to Gabrielle, née Wickham, Rosslare Harbour, they have two sons; former Irish Ferries' purchasing and catering manager; former chairperson Wexford Festival Singers,

has appeared in a number of light operas and during the Festival Opera ; member of the Lifeboat Memorial Committee.

Murphy, Celestine, was born in Wexford, historian and librarian with Wexford Public Library Service. She is a graduate of NUI Maynooth and University College Cork. A long-time member of Wexford Historical Society, she has served as chairman, secretary and journal editor. She has also acted as editor of a number of other historical journals and publications. Her particular area of interest is in 17th century Wexford and part of her undergraduate thesis on this period appeared in *Religion, conflict and co-existence,* 1990, a collection of essays in honour of her former history professor and fellow Wexfordian, Dr Patrick J. Corish. In 2010, she was assistant editor with Colm Tóibín of the book *Enniscorthy – a history,* published by Wexford County Library Service for 'Enniscorthy 1500'. She is well-known as a lecturer and researcher and has contributed a number of well-regarded essays on a range of historical subjects to various publications. She is the author of *Publish and be damned: some practical advice for the community publisher,* 2002 and *Between place and parish, a guide to the historical administrative divisions of County Wexford,* 2004.

Murphy, Charlie, Wexford, actress, graduate of the Gaiety School of Acting; daughter of Pat and Brenda, owners of Scissors Empire Hairdressers, South Main Street, Wexford; plays starring role of Siobhán in RTÉ drama series *Love/Hate* for which she won best Television Actress at the IFTAs awards, 2013. At 26, she has also appeared in British TV series *Misfits, The Village* and *Ripper Street.* Charlie has also toured Ireland with the Druid Theatre playing the part of Kate in *Big Maggie.*

Murphy, Colm A, Ballinadrummin, Killenagh, Ballycanew, horse trainer, commenced training in 2000, having worked with Aidan O Brien for 6 years, as rider and in the office. He comes from an equestrian background, his father, Pat, having been a rider and having a few horses. Colm has had remarkable success with a relatively small stable of horses – including the Supreme Novice Hurdle and Champion Hurdle at Cheltenham in 2004 and 2006, with Brave Inca, who won 10 Grade 1 races in an illustrious career, never being outside the first three in 27 completed starts. Big Zeb also won nine top class races for Murphy. Other stable stars include Fethard Lady, Volder la Vedette and Quito de la Roque.

Murphy, Colette, born 1975, formerly New Ross, now Brooklyn, New York, artist, daughter of Michael and Maire. After finishing school, emigrated to US and got a Masters Degree in Fine Art from Hunter College in New York. Her paintings have been bought up by art collectors and she has exhibited in Dublin, New York, London, Berlin and Venice. Many of her paintings feature the perils faced by emigrants from New Ross in the 18th and 19th centuries.

Murphy, Dickie, Enniscorthy Rapparees/Starlights GAA Club, one of the best referees in recent years. Took charge of 1992, 1995, 1997 and 1998 All-Ireland senior hurling finals, and the U21 finals of 1998 and 2002; holds the record for handling eight Wexford senior hurling finals; member of the Central Referees Applications' Committee at Croke Park.

Murphy, **Ferdy**, Forrestalstown, Clonroche, racehorse trainer, from the same area of Wexford as Aidan O'Brien, has been one of the leading jumps trainers in the North of England since moving there in 1990, taking up residence in North Yorkshire in the year 2000. He has had ten winners at the Cheltenham Festival, a Hennessy Gold Cup, three Scottish and an Irish Grand National. He shocked racing in 2013 when he announced he was selling up and intended to continue his career in France. He had begun his career in Ireland, serving five years as stable jockey to the great Paddy Mullins.

Murphy, Fintan, RIP, Enniscorthy, curator of the former County Museum which was housed in the 13th century Norman castle in Enniscorthy for many years, and during that time compiled the book, *The County Museum, Enniscorthy*. The castle and museum exhibits have recently been refurbished and it is now simply called Enniscorthy Castle.

Murphy, Fintan, Mayglass, has written a number of plays and, under his direction, Ballycogley Players have won many awards. His first collection of poetry was published by Wexford publishers, THE WORKS, in 2006. Fintan's poems range across tradition forms, performance poems and intense personal reflections. Whether rambling through the lanes and fields of rural Wexford or exploring themes as diverse as depression, books, Shakespeare and addiction.

Murphy, Gráinne, Ballinaboola, New Ross, born 1993, swimmer, daughter of Brendan and Mary, owners of the Horse and Hound Hotel. Qualified for the 2012 Summer Olympics in London, although due to glandular fever, she only swam the heats of the 400m freestyle. She was forced to withdraw from the rest of the meet, including her main event, the 800m freestyle. This was a major disappointment to Gráinne and her family who have devoted much of their lives to her swimming career for ten years. When she was 12, she relocated with her mother to Limerick to avail of the high-class facilities and coaching available at the University of Limerick, while dad, Brendan, continued to run the business at Ballinaboola, commuting to Limerick on a regular basis. In the European junior championships in Prague in 2009 she won three gold medals and a bronze in events from 200m to 1500m, which earned her the Irish Texaco Young Sport star of the Year Award; won silver medal in the 1500m at the European long course championships in Budapest in 2010, and two bronze medals in the Euro short course championships at Eindhoven, at 400m and 800m, in the same year; shortlisted for the RTÉ Irish Sports Person of the Year.

Murphy, Hilary, Parklands, Wexford town, journalist, editor, genealogist, historian, a native of Tilladavins, Tomhaggard; married to Bernadette, née Ryan, from Irishtown, New Ross. He began his journalistic career with the former *Free Press* in Wexford, and New Ross, before joining *The People* Newspapers group as district reporter in Arklow and later on the editorial team at head office in Wexford, retiring in 1997. Among the many assignments he covered were the visits to Wexford in 1962 and 1963, of the American Presidents Dwight D. Eisenhower and John F. Kennedy. In 1976 he published *The Kynoch Era in Arklow,* an account of the factory that was transformed into a major munitions producer during the First World War, employing up to 4,000 people. In 1986 his book *Families of County Wexford* received national acclaim. His interest in family history led to contributing a surnames column to the weekly magazine, *Ireland's Own*, which is sold across the world. He was founding editor in 1972 of the *Kilmore Parish Journal,* and continued as editor for forty-one years, as well as editing and contributing articles to the journals of the Wexford, Taghmon and Bannow Historical Societies. He received the County Wexford Rehab People of the Year award for literature in 2013.

Murphy, Imelda, Clongeen, compiled *Clongeen Through the Ages,* which was published in 1993.

Murphy, Kevin, Ballygarrett, born 1964; dairy farmer; married to Ann, they have four children; Kevin's mother, Mai, née Kehoe, Co. Carlow, has worked very hard in helping to build up a dairy herd after being widowed at an early age. Kevin is a strong supporter of Wexford GAA.

Murphy, Fr John, 1753-1798, one of the leaders of the 1798 Rebellion, was a Catholic curate at Boolavogue. He was the youngest son of farmers and bacon-curers Thomas Murphy and Johanna Whitty of Tincurry, near Scarawalsh. He was described as 'a quiet, inoffensive' curate who became incensed at the brutal treatment of his parishioners by supporters of the British forces in Ireland. He defied the orders of bishop of Ferns, James Caulfield, and led his supporters, described as 'rebels' armed mainly with home-made pikes, in attacks on the British and Yeomen. He and the rebels defeated more than 100 soldiers of the North Cork Militia at the Battle of Oulart. He later led the rebels, many of whom were members of the United Irishmen, in battles with the British forces across the county and neighbouring counties culminating with defeat and the death of many thousands of rebels and Yeomen at the Battle of Vinegar Hill, at Enniscorthy town on 21st June, 1798. British soldiers caught fellow leader James Gallagher and Fr. Murphy following further battles in July. They flogged, hanged and beheaded them at the Market Square at Tullow, Co. Carlow. They burned the body of Fr. Murphy in a barrel of pitch. They were unaware of his identity until after the event. His body is buried in the cemetery at the Mullaun near the square. Part of his remains are said to have been brought by his sister to Ferns for burial. A statue by Oliver Sheppard in Enniscorthy Market Square shows Father John Murphy with a young 1798 pikeman pointing towards Vinegar Hill.

Murphy, John, Poulpeasty, owner of Uncle Aidan's Flour, manufacturer of traditional stoneground wholemeal at Ballyminane Mills, Ballindaggin. John's uncle, Aidan Murphy, is the master miller who, with his sister, Kathleen, live in the home place at Ballyminane. John's partner is Maya Breitendach from Germany, and they have two daughters. He is a keen GAA fan particularly of his beloved Cloughbawn.

Murphy, John, formerly Ramsgrange, now New York, one of eleven in the family of Paddy and Breda. After helping lead Good Counsel to All-Ireland senior colleges' football championship victory and St, James's to a minor title in 1993, he availed of a scholarship opportunity to attend Mercyhurst College, in Erie, Pennsylvania. After graduating with honours in 1997, he went on to achieve his law degree at the University of Notre Dame. He practised law at global law firms White & Case and Linklaters, and more recently, global bank, UBS. In July 2013 he opened his own law firm, John Murphy and Associates. He also serves as President of the Irish-American Bar Association and the recently founded Manhattan Gaels Gaelic football team. In 2012, he was recognized as the New York County Wexford Association's Man of the Year. He lives in Glen Ridge, New Jersey, with his wife, Carly and their sons, James and Nathaniel.

Murphy, John, Randalsmills, Crossabeg, dairy farmer; along with daughters, Mary and Judy, he is planning further expansion. He served for years as a member of the Board of Wexford Farmers' Co-op. He is a keen follower of the GAA and was solid in the full back while playing for his local club.

Murphy, John G., Cornamona, Enniscorthy, solicitor, is the principal of the law practice of John A. Sinnott and Co., Enniscorthy. He is a member of the criminal legal aid panel and of the civil legal aid panel. He is co-author of the book *Inheritance and Succession* and also the book *Make Your Will.* He researched and co-authored the nationally acclaimed book *Farm Family Partnerships* published by Macra na Feirme and the Law Society in 1981. He is well-known sportsman having been an international oarsman with UCG and a rugby player with UCG and with various clubs in his adopted Wexford.

Murphy, Martin, Corderraun, native of Saltmills, New Ross; joined the Commissioners of Irish Lights in 1973 and trained as a supernumerary assistant lighthouse keeper, he was made permanent in 1976 and served on lighthouses around the Irish coast until made redundant under the programme for the automation of light houses in 1994. He worked for a number of years as a tour guide/ information officer at John F Kennedy Arboretum, New Ross; was co-opted to Wexford County Council in 2007 and subsequently elected in 2009.

Murphy, Matthew, Coolcotts, Wexford, RIP 2013, husband of the late Eileen, RIP 2009, they had eight children. He was long-time Chairman of Dun Mhuire, Wexford's parish hall, on South Main Street, the home of many great nights of entertainment over the years from the showband era to the present day.

Murphy, **Michael,** Roseville, New Ross, managing director of Wexford racecourse since 1989, having become a director in 1981. Racing has been taking place at Bettyville, Wexford, since the 15th of October 1951 when a bumper attendance, estimated at 17,000, attended the first meeting. Michael Murphy's father, also Michael, was one of the founding board members, along with Dr. Jim Pierse, Dr. Toddy Pierse and TD Sinnott, County Manager at the time. Clerk of the course at Wexford is Val O'Connell; Chairman of the stewards is Walter Hally, Tramore, and Jim Mernagh of Templescoby, Enniscorthy, is chairman of the supporters' club.

Murphy, Michael, native of Oulart, Director of Markets at Bord Bia, responsible for leading Bord Bia market development programmes and services across ten overseas' offices. He has worked with Bord Bia since 1995. Prior to that, he worked with Departments of Agriculture and Environment, the Irish Farmers' Association and a public relations company. Michael is an Agricultural Economics graduate from University College Dublin and has undertaken further studies in Marketing and Management. Michael has a strong interest in international affairs, hurling and golf. He has travelled extensively, and lived in London for six years and worked in the United States.

Murphy, Michael, Tinnock, Gorey, wood turner and carver using both pole lathe and electric lathe; owner Woodlands arts and crafts gallery in Tinnock; commissioned by Gorey Town Council to make pieces for presentation to Presidents Mary Robinson and later Mary McAleese, on their visits to the town; Gorey Town Council also presented a piece of Michael's work to Gorey's twin town of Oban in Scotland.

Murphy, Noel, Kilanerin, grocer, publican, postmaster, married to Emi; Noel, Emi and Barbara, their daughter, facilitate all fundraising activities in the pub providing party food free of charge. Noel is a clay-pigeon shoot enthusiast.

Murphy, Peadar, native of Ballylough,Ferns, a former student at St. Peter's College and graduate of UCD with a B.Agr. Science degree in the 1960s. A noted hurler and team captain and later founding member of Dublin-Wexford Supporters Club. Was an agricultural adviser in Waterford before his appointment as General Secretary of Macra na Feirme. Was part of Ireland's EEC entry campaign during which the organisation controversially hosted the visit of European Commissioner Sicco Mansholt, architect of the Mansholt Plan. Was part of the organisation of the NFA, Irish Farmers' Journal and farming and rural organisations into the Irish Farm Centre, at Bluebell, Dublin. He was also part of the Law Society and Agricultural Institute group that published the landmark survey on farm inheritance. Was elected president of the European Young Farmers organisation. He later became the founding chief executive of IFAC accountants, the farmer's accounting service, making it one of the largest accountancy practices in Ireland. He and his wife Bríd, nee Dempsey, a former Revenue official, of Ballymorris, Galbally live in Dublin.

Murphy, Peter, born Milehouse, Enniscorthy 1968, now living in Dublin, writer; released his second novel *Shall We Gather at the River* in 2013. His first book *John the Revelator* was shortlisted for the 2011 IMPAC Literary Award, the Kerry Group Fiction Prize and Costa First Novel Award. At the age of seventeen, he won the EU-sponsored Michael Sweetman Award for Young Writers. One of five children, he is son of Peader and Betty Murphy. Peter is also a musician of note, while his father, Peader, was a national amateur boxing champion.

Murphy, Phil, 1917-1989, Carrig on Bannow, renowned for his unique style of traditional Irish music on the mouth organ; passed on his passion to his two sons John and Pip, he is now immortalised in the Phil Murphy Weekend Musical Festival, held every summer in Carrig. Phil recorded an album weeks before his death in 1989 on which he was composer and performer of *The Trip to Cullenstown.* He won three All-Irelands in Senior Mouth Organ while both his sons also won the same competition during their musical careers. John and Pip are now part of a musical group called the Tin Sandwich Band.

Murphy, Phil, Piercestown, Wexford, monthly editor, *Ireland's Own* magazine, published in Wexford by *People Newspapers*; from Ballinamona, Ballycanew, son the late Michael and Lizzie Murphy; married to Nuala, née Kehoe, the Dirr, Trinity. He has spent all 45 years of his working life with *People Newspapers*, filling various roles from junior reporter to sports editor and assistant group editor, before being appointed to *Ireland's Own* twelve years ago.

Murphy, Rory, 1927-2003, Ballinavocran, married to Nancy, née Kelly, Bunclody, they had six children; County Councillor over many years; secretary Kilmyshall Cumann Fianna Fáil as teenager; founding member of local Macra na Feirme and Bunclody Co-op, and National President of Macra in 1959; held chair of Macra na Tuaithe and An Foras Talúntais, and was appointed Chair of Teagasc by Jack Lynch in 1979; held positions on RTÉ Authority, Board of CERT, Irish Sugar Company; founding member of Bunclody Historical Society, and member of

reconvened Wexford Senate 1998; author and co-author of several books and articles; and very involved in GAA at local and county level.

Murphy, Stephen, Wilton, Bree, singer; married to Majella, Glenbrien, they have four children; former manager in Smyth's Hardware, Rafter Street, Enniscorthy, he embarked on a solo singing career in 2001 and since that time he has raised thousands of euro for charities through concerts and CD sales.

Murphy, Willie, B.Agr.Sc., a native of Tomhaggard, is an internationally known agricultural scientist whose tests decided the optimum quality and quantity of fertiliser to be used on grassland throughout Ireland from the 1950s to 1990s. He was, for many years, head of the Grassland Department at the Agricultural Institute, Johnstown Castle. He spent many years working in the Azores. He is a graduate of the Albert College, UCD and qualified with first class honours in Agricultural Science in 1956. In 2010, the president of the Fertilizer Association of Ireland presented the association's special recognition award to him.

Murray Ryan, Bernie, Rathurtin, Clonroche, born 1970; National School teacher in Raheen, leader of the Carrigbyrne Pike Choir and creator and owner of *Singing Made Easy* and *Music Made Easy* music resources for primary school teachers; married to Joe, Coolhill, The Rower, Co. Kilkenny, they have one daughter, Katie.

Murray, Bill, Templenacroha, Clonroche, Enniscorthy, born 1934; retired mixed farmer, writer, historian, filmmaker, married to Margaret née Foley, Newbawn, they have four daughters; founder of Carrigbyrne Pike Group and Choir, who participated in the making of five films on 1798 as well as making four films of their own; spent 10 days in jail in Limerick, January 1963, when, the farmers were demanding that the government take action after two disastrous harvests 1961 and 1962, and they put up road blocks as part of the protest. Bill wouldn't pay the £1 fine on principle and spent ten days in prison. On his release he was given 6d for each day of his incarceration. In 2012 Bill and the Carrigbyrne Pike Group were given the Key of the city of Savannah and the Key of Chatham County, Georgia.

Murray, Paddy 'The Boxer', 1945-2013, Ferns, married to Alice, née Dwyer, Ferns; they have six children; founding member of St. Aidan's Boxing Club in Ferns; former chairman of the Parc Mhuire Residents' Association; supporter of many local organisations including Ferns St. Aidan's GAA Clubs, Ferns United FC, the local horseshoes clubs, the Ferns and Clologue Field Day committees; a committed parish and community fundraiser.

Murray, Patsy, author of *A History of Coolgreany* which was published in 1993; former chairman of the Wexford County Handball Board and leading light in the successful Coolgreaney Handball Club.

Murray, Pat, Knocknagapple, Monaseed, farmer, elected chairman of County Wexford Executive of IFA in January 2013 for a four-year term; runs a suckler and sheep farm in one the most northerly townlands in County Wexford. He is the fourth generation of Murrays in Knocknagapple and farms with his wife, Mary, mother and two daughters.

Mythen, Billy, Longraigue, Foulksmills, Managing Director Mythen Construction, one of Ireland's top one thousand companies. Latest figures show the company had a turnover of €11.2million with forty employees. Work completed in 2013 included New Ross Swimming Pool and Leisure Centre and the Kennedy Homestead Visitors' Centre at Dunganstown. Mythen Construction were finalists in three categories for the Irish Building and Design Awards 2013, including the Architectural Award for Wexford County Library.

Mythen, Paddy, Enniscorthy, has an unusual link with Roscommon football. They have won only two All-Ireland senior football finals, beating Cavan in a replay in 1943, and beating Kerry in 1944 , and Mythen was the referee on both occasions. He was also in charge for the 1946 final replay, and this time Roscommon lost out to Kerry. Mythen was a good player with Wexford and was on the team beaten by Dublin in a Leinster final replay in 1932; he won Wexford titles with Clann Loinsigh and Starlights, Enniscorthy.

Nally, Derek, Tipperary and Bunclody, former County Wexford youth leader and a former Garda detective sergeant who served for thirty years in An Garda Siochana, he was a candidate in the 1997 Presidential election won by President Mary McAleese. He secured 59,000 votes in the election. He was General Secretary of the Association of Garda Sergeants and Inspectors for ten years. He retired from the Gardai in 1987 and set up a security and private investigations business. He was later elected president of the Council of International Investigators (CII). He was elected Investigator of the Year in 1996. He brought the international conference of the CII to Enniscorthy in 2013.

Neal, Joe, born North Wales, now lives in Edenvale, Castlebridge; poet and actor on stage, radio and television; former journalist; graduate of Nottingham University; he has one son, daughter-in-law and one grandson; first book of poems *Telling it at a Slant* published 2013.

Neville, Colm, Wexford, owner-manager Riverside Park Hotel, The Promenade, Enniscorthy; one of eight children of Cathy and the late William Neville; announced in October 2013 a €1.4 million extension to the 48-bedroom four-star establishment, citing 'green shoots' of economic recovery, as the reason for his decision to expand the business. He is chairman of Enniscorthy Tourism.

Neville, Pat, Fontjoncousse, France, formerly Danescastle, Carrig on Bannow. Pat is living his dream having purchased an eight hectare vineyard in the tiny hillside area overlooking the Mediterranean Sea. In the 1970s Pat got a job with the ESB and played football for Wexford and Starlights. Later returned to education, getting a degree in English, Greek and Classical Civilisation followed by a Masters in Old English. During the 1990s he went to work with UN and Dutch forces as a language consultant in war-torn Sarajevo. He, along with wife, Catherine, née McGuinness, Wexford, bought and set up the vineyard Domaine Aonghusa in 2001 which they have since expanded and run as a family business

Neville, Tom, New Ross, now living in Carlow town, very reliable hurling defender with Wexford and his club, Geraldine O'Hanrahan's, New Ross, all through the 1960s; usually had his club mate, Ned Colfer, as a companion in the full-back line. Tom won two All-Ireland medals, 1960 and 1968, five Leinsters and one National League; won county senior championship with his club in 1966, beating Enniscorthy Shamrocks in a replay. He was picked on the National hurling team of the year, Cúchulainn Awards, for three years in a row, from 1963 and managed the county hurling team and St. Martin's (Kilkenny) and Oulart-The Ballagh club teams, among others, to great success.

Neville, Dr W E, whose family comes from Bawnmore, New Ross, founded the Geology Department of University College, Cork. He has written many books, including *Geology in Ireland*, which was published in 1963.

Nolan, Adam, The Ballagh, boxer; son of John and Anne; became the second boxer from Wexford to represent Ireland at the Olympics, following on from Billy Walsh. He worked his way through a tough qualifying regime to earn his place, winning the European qualification tournament against top opposition in Turkey. He won his first bout of the 2012 Olympics 14-8 against Ecuador's Carlos Sanchez but lost to Russia's Andrey Zamkovoy in the round of 16. He has won three Irish senior titles, in 2011, 2012 and 2013. A Garda, he is coached by Pete Taylor in Bray in the same gym as Peter's legendary daughter, Katie. He learned his boxing with the The Ballagh Club from a very young age under his father, John, and Martin O'Connor; he also trained with the St. Ibar's Club in Wexford under Billy Walsh and won his first All-Ireland title with him in 1999 when just 11 years old. He recently represented Ireland in the World championships at Almaty, Kazakhstan. He hurled with the Oulart-The Ballagh club for a number of years before concentrating exclusively on boxing since 2009. Adam's brother, Darren, has also won titles in boxing and hurling, and his younger sister, Leanne, plays camogie for Oulart.

The new Wexford Library, Mallin Street.

7

Civics

The people of County Wexford are served by excellent governance which overseas infrastructural development, library services, and other amenities.

GREAT PLACES - OUR SPACE: WEXFORD'S PUBLIC LIBRARIES

Fionnuala Hanrahan, County Librarian

Wexford people love their libraries. Buzzing from morning to night, six days a week, visitors always meet a neighbour, a friend, or enjoy an encounter with someone interesting when they call in to read the papers, swap their books, attend a talk, shoot the breeze or check their emails. The local library is the best meeting place in town - free, comfortable and friendly. It's no wonder they are so popular.

Library membership and services are free, provided for local people by Wexford County Council. Many people dip in and out of the library throughout their lives; transitions, from school to work, parenthood, career changes, health issues, trigger the need for information to support decisions and new circumstances. For many others the library is a part of the steady formula of their week. Whatever the pattern, in the library different zones suit children, families, adults and researchers.

Activities, for every age and interest, introduce the information stock and bring people with similar interests together. Health, science, careers and employment support, travel, foreign languages, leisure pursuits like gardening or sport, effective communications, e-learning, legal issues made easier, reading for pleasure, author visits – everything our hearts desire is offered.

The library is the *go-to* place for information about Wexford, today and from older times: staff are expert researchers and love a challenge.

Eileen Morrissey, Senior Executive Librarian, Library Management

Sinead O'Gorman, Senior Executive Librarian, County Library; Nicola McGrath, Executive Librarian – Community Liaison and Programming, County Library; Linda Horan, Executive Librarian – Research and e-services, County Library; Hazel Percival, Executive Librarian, Gorey; Jarlath Glynn, Executive Librarian, Enniscorthy; Patricia Keenan, Executive Librarian, New Ross; Dearbhla Ní Laighin, A/Executive Librarian, Bunclody; Gráinne Doran, Archivist

REHAB PEOPLE OF THE YEAR AWARDS

2003

Billy Woods -Community Development
Slaney Search and Rescue Team- Humanitarian
Willie Doyle - Business and Enterprise
Sr. Valerian - Community Service
Tommy McElwaine - Voluntary Achievement
Josephine Casey - Health and Well-being
Harry Ringwood -Arts and Culture
Fr. Tony Scallan - Hall of Fame
County Wexford Person of the Year - Josephine Casey

2004

Nicky Cowman- Sport and Heritage
Rev. J. O'Brien- Music and Art
Kitty Warren- Youth Work
Ray and Gretta Quigley- Community Service
Kevin Leacy- Voluntary Endeavor
Mogue Curtis- Community Enterprise
Anne O'Neill- Courage
Toddy Moore- Hall of Fame
County Wexford Person of the Year - Nicky Cowman

With technology and know-how, every interest is just a click away. However, skills in judging the reliability of information are essential. Research skills are taught in the library. E-resources are explained in straight-forward, step by step, workshops. More and more, digitised information and e-courses are made available through Wexford public library services' website and through its social media presence.

An energising service for a modern society, Wexford's public libraries mix curiosity with identity, community with heritage, and technology with expertise and learning to engage our interest and create opportunities as rewarding and as wonder full as our imaginations can soar.

2005

M.J. Booth -Arts and Culture
Peter Byrne -Community Service
Vivian Rath - Courage
Aileen Kennedy -Youth Work
Eoin Nolan -Sports
Paddy Berry -Music
RNLI ,Wexford Inshore Lifeboat -
Voluntary Endeavour
**County Wexford Person of the
Year- Peter Byrne**

2006

Maureen O'Connor -Hall of Fame
Liam Griffin - Enterprise
Liam Buttle -Community
Development
Martin Kehoe - Achievement
Breda Banville -Youth
Michael Byrne - Art and Drama
Dan McLean -Voluntary
Endeavour
Abraham Bolan Laval
-Community Integration-
**County Wexford Person of the
Year- Liam Buttle**

2007

Denis Cadogan -Community
Service
Alice Mernagh - Community
Development
Aaron Gaffney - Achievement
Dr. Paddy McKiernan - Medicine
John Joe Nolan - Humanitarian
Shirley O'Connor - Youth Work-
Stan Scanlan - Courage
**County Wexford Person of the
Year- John Joe Nolan**

2008

Seamus O'Beirne – Business and
Enterprise
Frederikeand Servaas Dodebier –
Health and Welfare
Bishop Denis Brennan –
Leadership
CWCW Enniscorthy, Team
Ireland Special Olympics –
Achievement
Nicky Furlong – Arts and
Heritage
Wexford All Ireland Senior
Camogie Team – Sports
Brigid Cullen, Wexford Society
for the Prevention of Cruelty to
Animals – Environment
Bessie French– Hall of Fame
**County Wexford Person of the
Year – Frederike and Servaas
Dodebier**

2009

Michael Sills - Leadership
Paul Hennessy – Arts and Culture
Edward Milbourne – Youth Work
Betty Breen – Community Service
Sarah and Michelle Kavanagh-
Courage
Ivan Yates – Enterprise
Billy Walsh – Sports
Noel Dillon- Hall of Fame
**County Wexford Person of the
Year- Michael Sills**

2010

Brian McKenna- Achievement
Andy and Joan Cloke-
Humanitarian
Coast to Coast – Voluntary Group

The J.F.K. Trust – Business and
Enterprise
Seamus O'Keeffe- Community
Service
Camross Drama Group – Arts
and Culture
Emer Lovett – Leadership
Steve Martin – Hall of Fame
**County Wexford Person of the
Year- Andy and Joan Cloke**

2011

Enniscorthy Choral Society –
Entertainment
Sean Stafford (Snr) – Business
Barbara Byrne – Arts and Culture
Paddy Byrne – Community
Services
Michael Cloney and Jenny
Quigley – Voluntary Endeavour
Michael Hayes – Enterprise
Jim Bolger – Leadership
Stan Blanche – Sport
Billie O'Donnell – Hall of Fame
**County Wexford Person of the
Year -Jim Bolger**

2012

Jim and Clare Doyle –
Community Development
Seamus Kane – Humanitarian
Boolavogue Foroige Group –
Youth
Bannow Rathangan Show
committee- Rural Development
Danescastle Music Group – Music
Anne Doyle – Communications
Fr. Jim Fegan – Leadership
Sofrimar – Business and
Enterprise

**County Wexford Person of the
Year**- Bannow Rathangan Show
committee

2013

Darragh McDonald -Youth
Mary Fitzgerald-Community
Service
Ann Furlong - Voluntary
Endeavour
Enniscorthy Castle and the 1798
Rebellion Centre- Culture
Celtic Roots and Kay McKelvie,
Bree- Entertainment
Hilary Murphy- Literature
Maureen Rossiter – Hall of Fame
New Ross and District Pipe and
District Band - Music
John Whelan – Achievement

**County Wexford Person of the
Year**- Darragh McDonald

The People of the Year awards
honour people who have made a
significant contribution to their
community either professionally
or in a personal capacity.

Organised by Rehab People of the
Year in association with Wexford
County Council and The Wexford
People. Category sponsors are
Property Team M.A. O'Leary,
Riverside Park Hotel and Leisure
Club, and John A. Sinnott and Co.
Solicitors.

STATISTICS 2011

Population – 145,320, Males - 71,909, Females- 73,411

Of the 112,256 persons aged 15 years and over:
Married –55,723, Divorced –3,132, Separated- 4,305
Pre-school (0-4yrs) – 11,539
School (5-12yrs)- 17,405
Secondary School (13-18yrs) - 11,570
Number of persons aged 18 yrs or over - 106,478
Number of persons aged 65 yrs and over - 18,367

Non-Irish nationals accounted for 9.4 per cent of the
population compared with a national average figure of
12.0 per cent. UK nationals (4,604 persons) were the
largest group, followed by Polish (4,010 persons).
Roman Catholics - 127,842
Other stated religions (e.g. Church of Ireland, Islam,
Presbyterian, Orthodox) - 9,659
No religion- 6,204

Household Disposable Income – Euro 19,000-19,622
Index of Disposable Household Income 2009 - 92.8%

Housing, internet and cars

More than 95 per cent of households lived in houses or
bungalows while a further 3.9 per cent lived in apartments,
flats or bedsits. 38,526 dwellings (73.6 per cent) were
owner occupied while 13,257 dwellings (25.3 per cent)
were rented. 33.5 per cent of the dwellings in this area
were built in the ten years before the census.
More than 56 per cent of households had broadband
connectivity compared with 63.8 per cent
nationally. 44.4 per cent of households had two or more
cars.

WEXFORD IN NATIONAL POLITICS

By Gerry Breen

A significant number of politicians from Co. Wexford
have achieved high office and have made their mark in the
service of their constituency and their country. Foremost
among them must be John Edward Redmond from
Ballytrent House who came from a family of distinguished
parliamentarians and was one of the outstanding figures in
Irish political history.

He was the Leader of the Irish Parliamentary Party
in the House of Commons, and, following the death of
Parnell, reunited the Irish Party and pursued his dream
of a unified self-governing Ireland. The outbreak of
World War One and his campaign for the recruitment of
Irishmen to fight in the British army shattered that dream
and his party lost the support of the Irish people.

The Irish General Election of 1918 was a pivotal event
in modern Irish political history, resulting in a landslide
victory for Sinn Féin. One of those elected was Dr.
James Ryan from Tomcoole, near Taghmon, and he was
subsequently to play a commanding role in the political
life of Wexford and Ireland until his retirement in 1969.

Dr. James Ryan was a founder member of Fianna Fáil,
and another Wexford man, Richard Corish, was a founder
member of the Labour Party and another towering figure
on the political landscape in the county for more than
thirty years. He first came to prominence as a young man
during the infamous Wexford lock-out between August,
1911, and February, 1912, which affected more than 700
workers. In association with James Larkin and James
Connolly, he played an important role in bringing about
an end to the lock-out.

He became a leading member of the new Labour Party
which he helped to found in 1912, and he was the first
member of the Party to become mayor of an Irish city or

town when he was elected Mayor of Wexford in 1920 and retained the position until his death in 1945. He served in as a TD in Dáil Éireann from 1921 to 1945.

He was succeeded in the Dáil by his son, Brendan, who became Leader of the Labour Party, a member of the cabinet and Tanaiste in the Coalition Government in 1973–74. Both Richard and Brendan Corish had the distinction of being made Freemen of the Borough of Wexford.

Another son, Des Corish, became Mayor of Wexford in 1973, and Helen Corish followed in the footsteps of her father, Des, and grandfather, Richard, when she became Mayor of Wexford in 1991.

Another notable Wexford family with an impeccable political pedigree is the Esmonde family from Ballynastragh, Gorey. Sir Thomas Esmond was the first chairman of Wexford County Council and MP for North Wexford, from 1900 to 1918.

Sir Osmond Esmonde was a Fine Gael TD for Wexford from 1923 to 1926. He was succeeded in Dáil Éireann by his cousin, St. John L. Esmonde, S.C., who represented the Wexford constituency in the Dáil from 1937 to 1944 and from 1948 to 1951. He was succeeded by his brother, Sir Anthony Esmonde, who was, in turn, succeeded by his son, John Grattan Esmonde, B.L., who later became a Judge of the Circuit Court.

Currently representing the Wexford constituency in the Dáil and Seanad are: John Browne, TD, Enniscorthy (Fianna Fáil); Brendan Howlin, TD, Wexford, Minister for Public Expenditure and Reform (Labour); Paul Kehoe, TD, Enniscorthy, Minister of State and Government Chief Whip (Fine Gael); Liam Twomey, TD, Wexford, (Fine Gael); Mick Wallace, TD, (Independent); Senator Michael W. D'Arcy, Gorey (Fine Gael) and Senator Jim Walsh, New Ross (Fianna Fáil).

Mick Wallace, well known as a builder/developer and soccer enthusiast and promoter, caused one of the biggest upsets ever in Wexford politics when he belatedly entered the 2011 election and astounded all and sundry by topping the poll, a remarkable performance. Sean Connick, New Ross, outgoing Fianna Fáil, was the one to lose out.

COUNCILLORS

County Councillors will take over authority of urban and rural areas following the Local Elections in 2014. The current Wexford Borough Council and the town councils of Enniscorthy, Gorey and New Ross will cease to exist. The current councillors as listed below are the last ever to be elected to those bodies. Wexford County Council membership will increase from twenty one members to thirty four members under the new local government

The new Wexford County Council offices, County Hall, Carriglawn, Wexford.

administration as set out in the Local Government Bill of 2013.

Chairman, Ted Howlin, Labour
Vice-Chairman, Robert Ireton, Labour

Wexford Electoral Area Committee:
Pat Codd, Fine Gael; Tony Dempsey, Fianna Fáil; Anna Fenlon, Fine Gael; George Lawlor, Labour; Jim Moore, Fine Gael;Padge Reck, Non Party.

Enniscorthy Electoral Area Committee:
Kathleen Codd-Nolan, Fine Gael; Keith Doyle, Fianna Fáil; Paddy Kavanagh, Fine Gael; Oliver Walsh, Fine Gael; Martin Storey, Labour.

New Ross Electoral Area Committee:
Denis Kennedy, Fine Gael; Martin Murphy, Fianna Fáil; Larry O'Brien, Fine Gael; Michael Sheehan, Fianna Fáil.

Gorey Electoral Area Committee:
Malcolm Byrne, Fianna Fáil; John Hegarty, Fine Gael Michael Kinsella, Fine Gael;Declan MacPartlin, Non Party.

Wexford Borough Council

Mayor-George Lawlor, Labour; Deputy Mayor- Joe Ryan, Labour; Councillors: Jim Allen, P.C., Fine Gael; Anna Fenlon, Fine Gael; Danny Forde, Green party; Ted Howlin, Labour; David Hynes, Labour; Fergie Kehoe, Fianna Fáil; Anthony Kelly, Sinn Féin; Paddy Nolan, Fianna Fáil; Padge Reck, Non-Party; Philomena Roche, Fine Gael.

Enniscorthy Town Council

James Browne, Fianna Fáil; Keith Doyle, Fianna Fáil; Sean Doyle, Non-Party; Paddy Kavanagh, Fine Gael; Jackser Owens, Non-Party; Tom Moorehouse, Fine Gael; Johnny Mythen, Sinn Féin; John O'Rourke, Non- Party. Pat Cody, RIP, Labour, was elected chairman and Francis O'Connor, Labour was co-opted to the council following Pat Cody's death.

New Ross Town Council

NiamH Fitzgibbon, An Cathaoirleach, Green Party; Victor Furness, Leas Cathaoirleach, Fine Gael; Anthony Connick, Fianna Fáil; Paul Crowdle, Labour; John Dwyer, Éirigí; Annette Larkin, Fine Gael; Jas O'Callaghan, Fianna Fáil; Michael Sheehan, Fianna Fáil; Ollie Somers, Labour. Kevin Dwyer, Fianna Fáil, stood down and Jas O'Callaghan was co-opted to replace him. Bobby Dunphy, Labour stood down and Ollie Somers, Labour, was co-opted to replace him.

Gorey Town Council

Michael D'Arcy, Snr. Cathaoirleach, Fine Gael; Robert Ireton, leas Cathaoirleach, Labour; Lorcan Allen, Fianna Fáil; Malcolm Byrne, Fianna Fáil; Bernard Crosbie, Fianna Fáil; Angie Dooley, Fine Gael; Darren Keegan, Fine Gael; Patricia Quinn, Fianna Fáil; Colin Webb, Fine Gael.

Matt Travers, Fianna Fáil was elected to the council. He in turn was replaced by Bernard Crosbie, Fianna Fáil. Jimmy Fleming was elected for Sinn Féin. Patricia Quinn was co-opted in his place.

Nolan, James, born 1995, Gorey, current captain of Ireland's U18s rugby team; son of Terry and Maria and brother of Bill who is an accomplished golfer and three-year-old sister, Madeline. He attended Carnew Community School and also attained grade seven on piano. He first played U7s rugby with Carlow. James' father, Terry, was also a rugby player and played with Bective Rangers.

Nolan, John, The Forge House, Whitechurch, New Ross, co-founder of The Street Children of Bucharest in 1994; married to Margaret, together they have raised €150,000 for the charity. John's unrelenting commitment to the poor in Romania has been of enormous benefit to the people there.

Nolan, Martin, Circuit Court Judge; son of Ned and Margaret, Ballinastraw, Glenbrien; educated locally and at Enniscorthy CBS. As a teenager, he represented his county at both hurling and football, before becoming a garda, and was subsequently stationed in Dublin. He studied law at night, and was called to the Bar in 1989. He practised on the South eastern circuit until his appointment as a Judge of the Circuit Court in May 2007. Martin is married to Anne and they have four children, Laura, Anna, Jane and John. He is a frequent visitor to his native Glenbrien.

Nolan, Mary, Camross, née Murphy, Rathgarogue; very involved in Wexford GAA Ladies' football, serving as treasurer and register; married to Denis, who has also been involved with Wexford GAA on the field and at Board level, for many years, they have two sons and two daughters.

Nolan, John and Pat, Ballinastraw, Glenbrien, All-Ireland hurling champions. Pat is the holder of three All-Ireland and three National League medals, earned during almost two decades in goal for Wexford. John's greatest hour was undoubtedly his superb display at half-back when as a newcomer to the Wexford team, he held scoreless the great Tipperary forward, Jimmy Doyle, in the 1960 All-Ireland final in which Wexford shocked Tipperary.

Nolan, Paddy, The Moyne, Enniscorthy, is the last Wexford person to own an Irish Greyhound Derby winner, Táin Mór in 1973. He and his late brother, Jack, will always be associated with this great dog which also won the Leger, a rare feat indeed. His wife, Mary, ran Enniscorthy greyhound track for many years and was a great woman for bringing sponsorship to the track.

Nolan, Paul, Toberona House, Davidstown, Enniscorthy, born 1969; racehorse trainer jumps and flat; married to Catherine, née Byrne, they have two children, Barry and Sarah. Major races won include three Galway Hurdles, two Swordlestown Cups, Greatwood Hurdle, Fortria Chase, Hennessy Gold Cup, Galmoy Hurdle, John Durcan Memorial Chase, Michael Purcell Hurdle. Best horses trained include Accordion Etoile, Cloone River, Kill Devil Hill, Say Again, Shinrock Paddy, Joncol. He is assisted by his brother, James. Paul was a good hurler in his younger days, winning junior honours with Wexford.

Nolan, Sean, Enniscorthy, weekly editor of *Ireland's Own* magazine, published in Wexford by *People Newspapers*; married to Mary, née Breen, from Rosslare, recently retired after 35 years teaching at Monageer National School. Sean has spent all his working life with *People Newspapers*, serving as district reporter in Enniscorthy before filling various editorial roles in head office, up to deputy editor. A county senior football medal winner with Starlights of Enniscorthy, Sean has served as public relations officer for Wexford County GAA Board.

Norton, Clody Elizabeth, Bunclody, born Dublin 1938, artist, owner of Newtownbarry Stud and Newtownbarry House gallery and gardens; daughter of Robert Westley Hall-Dare; studied at Byam Shore School of Art, Postgraduate in Art and Design; opened art gallery in London 'Do Not Bend'; oversaw the extensive restoration of the house and gardens.

The first car with a Co. Wexford registration was owned Col. JR McGrath of Ferrybank who lived at the site of the present Riverbank Hotel. It was a single cylinder open car registration number MI 1.

Nugent, P.J., Adamstown, born Cork 1960, GAA coach throughout South Wexford in hurling, football and camogie; wildlife photographer, and overall winner at the Bannow-Rathangan Show 2013 in Killag.

Ó Braonáin, Donal, Fisherstown, Campile , born Wexford 1943, retired teacher; married to Patricia, née Boardman, Dublin, having four sons and one daughter; qualified as a primary school teacher, then, ten years later, as a secondary school teacher after which he taught English, Irish and History through Irish and subsequently graduated from NCAD with an Art teaching qualification; paints now in oils, acrylics and watercolours and exhibits twice a year during the Kilkenny Arts Festival and Wexford Festival Opera; following the loss of his son, Conor, ten years ago, Donal, through 'Painting the Light', aims to raise awareness of suicide and endeavours to show those in despair that there is light at the end of the tunnel.

O'Brien, Aidan, Wexford senior football team manager, and deputy principal of Good Counsel College, New Ross; was appointed to succeed Jason Ryan in 2012. He brought Good Counsel College to an All-Ireland Colleges title in 1999, and looked after the County U21 side for some years. He managed Adamstown from junior to senior in three successive years, and guided Horeswood to two senior titles in succession.

O'Brien, Aidan, Killegney, Clonroche, born 1969, one of six children of Denis, RIP 2008 and Stella, née Doyle. Denis was a farmer and small-scale horse trainer in the townland of Killegney, near Poulpeasty, Clonroche, where Aidan grew up. He attended Donard National School, and Good Counsel College, New Ross. He first started working professionally with horses at P.J. Finn's racing stables at the Curragh, County Kildare, and then with Jim Bolger, at Coolcullen, Co. Carlow, where he spent four years. Aidan O'Brien is married to Anne-Marie, daughter of Joe Crowley, who trained horses at Piltown, Co. Kilkenny. Anne-Marie was champion National Hunt trainer during her brief time at the helm before husband Aidan took over the licence in 1993. He also became champion National Hunt trainer, with record numbers of winners. Aidan switched to the flat scene when was appointed trainer at the world-famous Ballydoyle operation in 1996, in succession to the legendary Vincent O'Brien (no relation), at just 27 years of age. O'Brien and Anne-Marie have four children: Joseph, Irish champion jockey in 2012 and 2013; Sarah and Ana, who have ridden in equestrian events and on the track, and Donnacha. In 2012 Aidan and Joseph, aged 19, became the first father-son/trainer-jockey combination to win the Epsom Derby with Camelot. They also combined to win a Breeders' Cup in America on St. Nicholas Abbey. It is impossible to list O'Brien's major successes, they are so numerous. In Ireland he has won 29 Classics, including ten Derbies; in England he has won 20 Classics, including four Epsom Derbies; he has picked up major prizes in America, including eight Breeders' Cups and the Arlington Million twice; in France including the Prix de l'Arc de Triomphe, Canada, United Arab Emirates, Italy, etc. Before he concentrated totally on the flat racing, he won three Cheltenham Champion Hurdles with the legendary Istabraq and set records for the number of winners in a year only recently beaten by Willie Mullins. This unassuming man is heading up a worldwide Bloodstock operation that is worth billions, but always seems to remain calm in the eye of any storm. A great family man, Ann Marie and all the children are also intimately involved in the Ballydoyle operations. Many people around the world watching Aidan being interviewed have wondered about the significance of the pin he wears in his lapel at all times – it is a Pioneer Pin, symbol of the Pioneer Total Abstinence Association and a sign that he does not drink alcohol.

O'Brien, Billy, Ballycogley, coach hire business owner, married to Ella, née Furlong, Rathaspeck, they have four children; son of William and Una. Billy has a place in the Guinness Book of Records for the longest career as an international darts player, 34 years. He first played for Ireland as an 18-year-old in September 1968 and he last represented his country in June 2002. His best period came from 1975 to '80 when he played for Ireland for six consecutive years, coming up against some of the legends of the game. Though he continued win countless tournaments, Billy then went 17 years without an international cap until he made a memorable comeback in 1997 and lined out on the national side once again in 2002. He was a member of the only Wexford darts team to win an All-Ireland in 1988. An all-round sportsman, he won Wexford hurling and football titles as a goalie with his local St. Fintan's Club and won a Masters All-Ireland Hurling Championship with Wexford in 1991. He won county and Leinster badminton medals with his daughter, Karen, in 1991.

O'Brien, George, Enniscorthy, born 1945; Professor of English at Georgetown University, Washington. His books, which include *The Village of Longing, Dancehall Days* and *Out of Our Minds*, have received a number of prestigious literary awards.

O'Brien, **James J.,** born New Ross 1792, was Bishop of Ossory, Ferns and Leighlin. He wrote and preached against the disestablishment of the Church of Ireland. His *Attempt to Explain the Doctrine of Justification* ran to five editions. He also wrote: *The Irish Education Question, The Case of the Established Church in Ireland,* and *The Disestablishment and Disendowment of the Irish Branch of the United Church.*

Songwriter PJ Mc Call wrote the famous Wexford songs *Boolavogue* and *Kelly the Boy from Killanne*. His mother was Eliza Newport from Rathangan.

O'Brien, Jennifer, New Ross, founder of 2Cubed Web Design based at Enniscorthy Enterprise Centre on the Milehouse Road. A native of Glynn, Jennifer heads up the Development studio and is joined by Ronan Murphy in the business. Married to Sean, from Barntown, the couple have two young sons.

O'Brien, Fr John, 1937-2013, son of Michael and Bridget, née Hughes, New Ross; taught maths and applied maths in St. Peter's College; started painting in 1981 as a pastime but quickly established himself as one of Wexford's most accomplished landscape artists producing many fine pieces. He exhibited annually during Wexford Festival Opera. He was an award-winning musical director with Wexford Light Opera Society and combined with Ned Power to produce some memorable operas at St. Peter's College. He also had a great interest in the GAA, especially hurling.

Richard de Clare, Earl of Pembroke known as Strongbow, a leader of the Anglo-Norman mercenaries who arrived in Ireland in 1170, and his wife Aoife, daughter of Dermot McMorrough, King of Leinster are buried at Christ Church Cathedral in Dublin.

O'Brien, Kathleen, née O'Shea, principal of Blackwater primary school; she took over from her late father, Thomas, who was also Principal therefore marking 50 years unbroken tutelage by the O'Shea family. She is sister of Sean O'Shea noted footballer.

O'Brien, Lar, RIP 2011, Monageer, married to Ciss, née Breen, they had ten children, he was predeceased by their daughter, Mary, RIP, 2000; former county chairman Macra na Feirme also involved in numerous other organisations including the founding of Monageer-Boolavogue-Monamolin Marching Band; a well-known historian and after retiring from farming, he embarked on promoting the Father Murphy Centre in Boolavogue as a qualified tour guide. His daughter, Ann, returned from Australia and set up a crèche which has become a vital part of Monageer community.

O'Brien, Larry, Ballinamona, Campile, Fine Gael County Councillor, married to Cindy, née Furlong, Adamstown, they have two sons and a daughter. Larry survived the Herald of Free Enterprise ferry disaster at Zeebrugge in 1987, and also helped 30 other passengers to safety, in an accident that claimed 193 lives.

O'Brien, Martin, New Ross, was probably Wexford's most successful golfer. He won the Irish Amateur Close championship twice and was beaten in the final on a third occasion. This is event that has been a springboard for nearly all of Ireland's top professionals, including Padraig Harrington, Rory McIlroy and Graham McDowell. In 1968 O'Brien succeeded the legendary Joe Carr as champion, beating Frankie McCarroll in the final at Royal Portrush; he was beaten in the final by Raymond Kane at Ballybunion in 1971 and had a runaway 5 and 4 win over JA Byrne in the 1975 final at Cork GC. Martin represented his country on a number of occasions.

O'Brien, Tom, born 1986, jockey, son of Wexford-born Jim, and nephew of world class trainer, Aidan O'Brien. After riding in point-to-points, O'Brien moved to England in 2004 and in the 2005-06 season, he was crowned champion amateur rider with 32 winners; he turned professional in June of that year. In 2007 and 2008, O'Brien rode McKelvey in the Grand National, coming second to Silver Birch in 2007. O'Brien is a regular jockey for Philip Hobbs and Peter Bowen and is based in the South West of England. He finished eighth in the British Jump Jockey's championship in 2012 with 70 winners.

O'Brien, Tony, native of Kevin Barry Street, Wexford, now Shankill, Co. Dublin. Public Relations Consultant, journalist, author, editor; married to Claire née Lambert, formerly of Rivertown, Murrintown, they have two children, Conor and Niamh; former award-winning environment correspondent with *Irish Independent;* author of *Going Green – The Irish Guide to Living a Greener Life*; has advised Government Departments, semi-State agencies and local authorities on communications issues as well as working in PR capacity with Michael Flatley's *Lord of the Dance* and Ticketmaster amongst others.

O'Byrne, Rev. J. W., author of *History of the Wexford Men's Confraternity of the Holy Family*, which was published in 1910.

O'Byrne, Rev. Canon Mark, born New Ross 1874 and he was a close friend of President Sean T. O'Kelly. He wrote a number of books, including *Thunder an' Turf*, which was published in 1916 and *Off and On* and *Heaps of Money*. He also wrote a number of plays.

O'Byrne, Rev. Thomas, who was born in New Ross in 1873, was a founder member of the Uí Chennselaig Historical Society. He was highly acclaimed for a broadcast he made from Enniscorthy in 1936, in which he outlined the history of Co. Wexford.

O'Byrne, Terence, Java, Harristown, Rosslare Harbour, farmer, actor, well-known community activist, has appeared in numerous tops competitions. Both he and his wife, Mary, née Kavanagh, who works in the Bank of Ireland Taghmon, were very prominent in Macra na Feirme in County Wexford.

143 the number of acres on which the Great Island Power Staton is built.

O'Callaghan, Daniel, was a Labour Party politician. He was a running mate with Richard Corish in the 1922 General Election and was elected as a Labour Party TD for Wexford. He failed to retain his seat in the 1923 General Election.

O'Callaghan, May, Curracloe, born Wexford 1881; lived in Vienna before returning to Curracloe, Wexford, in 1939. She published a number of travel books, and translated *Dreams by a French Fireside* from the German. She died in 1973.

Ó Catháin, Diarmaid, born New Ross 1951. He wrote *Eachtra sa Bhlascaod, a children's story,* when he was 14, it was published in 1975, and his *Caoimhin Abú* won an Oireachtas Prize.

Ó Cléirigh, Brian, Oulart, historian, B.Ag.Sc. (UCD) BA history and Irish (UCG); a fluent Irish speaker, he was translator in the Houses of the Oireachtas; was member of Agricultural Advisory Service in Wexford; author of *Battle of Oulart Hill: Context and Strategy* and the articles *The Story of the Wexford Republic* and *Sowing the Whirlwind*; member of Comóradh '98 Committee; chairman of Tulach a' tSolais; chairman of the Robert Emmet Commemoration Association in 2003; chairman of ad hoc committee for the reinterment of Mountjoy Ten, 2003; member of the Dublin branch of the Wexford Hurling Supporters' Club; a founder member of County Wexford Community Workshops; member of County and National Development Committees of the GAA 1980-84; presently secretary of the Oulart Hill 1798 Battlefield Walking Hub.

O'Connell, Emmet, Horetown, Foulksmills, mining company executive, farmer. Emmet is current chairman of Great Western Mining. He has been a promoter and investor in a number of technology and exploration companies for over thirty years. His son, Oisín, will be a candidate for Sinn Féin in the Wexford local elections in 2014.

O'Connor, Adrian, Southknock, New Ross, born 1972; swam in the 100 and 200m backstroke at the Atlanta Olympic Games, 1996. In 2010 he took a silver medal in the World Master Swimming Championships in Gothenburg, Sweden. He was one of a very talented family of swimmers - Adrian, his sisters, Gráinne, Paula and Niamh, and brother, Hugh, all won Irish titles, setting scores of records. They had great encouragement from mother, Peggy, and father, Hugh, who was an Irish international shooter. Niamh had reached sixteenth place in the world rankings when she retired in 1994.

O'Connor, Claire, Grange, Rathnure, born Wexford 1980; Primary School teacher, Gaelscoil Inis Corthaidh, daughter of Teddy and Anne, Rathnure; engaged to be married to Pierce White, Killag, April 2014; winner of three All-Ireland senior camogie championships and three All Star Awards as well as numerous Leinster and club titles at all grades; member of St. Michael's Theatre Musical Society New Ross; camogie commentator for TG4.

> Bob Lambert of Kyle, Crossabeg was a leader in the IRA during the Civil War in Ireland in 1922 and was said to have been captain of a military unit called the Kyle Flying Column, which ambushed British soldiers at Ferrycarrig and at Killurin.

O'Connor, David, Ferns, singer, horse trainer; David sprang to national fame when he won the You're A Star Talent Show on RTÉ in 2007. Son of Willie and Martina, David has never forgotten his love of horses and continues to combine his work with them and singing.

O'Connor, Dennis, Ballygarvan, Gusserane, born Wexford 1953, farmer, married to Jane née Colfer, they have two sons; successfully executed emergency landing of two-seater single-engine light aircraft he was piloting, near Foulksmills, after smoke began to fill the cockpit, thus saving the life of passenger and airplane owner, 80-year-old John Duggan, Newlands, Wexford.

O'Connor, Denis, Rathnure, practising counsellor and psychotherapist for the past fifteen years. He established Console House in Wexford town three years ago and it has played a huge role in the lives of bereaved families throughout the county. Involved in community and charitable work for the past quarter of a century, Denis won the South East Radio Person of the Year Award for 2013.

O'Connor, George, Piercestown, born 1959, iconic figure on the Wexford GAA scene for over 20 years and was a hurling All-Star in 1981, at centre forward and 1988, midfield. From 1979 to 1995 Wexford suffered an horrendous period, losing all eighteen provincial and league finals in which they appeared. Salvation came under Liam Griffin in 1996 in the twilight of his career when Wexford beat Limerick. O'Connor had got his All-Ireland medal after seventeen years in the senior jersey, at the age of almost 37 years. He retired after this game. He was also a gifted footballer and all-round sportsman, being especially strong in athletics when young, and appeared on a Sporting Superstars series on RTÉ television. He played 184 senior games for Wexford, 149 in hurling and 43 times in football. He is now director of hurling for Wexford. His brothers, James, John and Arthur, also played for Wexford, and their father, Paddy, played in an All-Ireland junior final in 1940, the first real signs of a revival in Wexford's hurling fortunes after a long blank spell.

O'Connor, Michael, Oylegate, runs his greyhounds under the Whitefort prefix and has been very much to the fore over the last twenty five years. Brown Dot was a bitch which brought Michael success and he has bred some top dogs over the years. Michael bred Fatzboz Nodrog which won the Champion Stakes at Shelbourne Park, trained by Enniscorthy man, Pat Gordon.

O'Connor, Peadar, Crossabeg, has served as ladies' Gaelic football county chairman, vice chairman and PRO; is also assistant PRO for Leinster Council and is a delegate to Leinster and Central Councils.

O'Donohoe, Liam, a native of Corry's Villas, Wexford town, attended St. Peter's College, then UCD and later Stanford University in the US where he specialised in psychology and business. In his early career, he worked in the Middle East. He was appointed HR Director at the formation of Enterprise Ireland in the late 1990s. As a senior member of the Enterprise Ireland management team, he led the development of world-class innovative long-term leadership development and international selling programmes for the CEOs and senior teams of more than 500 leading Irish exporting companies to help them to compete and succeed in world markets thereby building and sustaining employment in Ireland. This work in collaboration with institutions including Stanford University, continues to significantly impact on software, construction, engineering and food companies and other key sectors in Irish industry. He and his wife, Celine, have

four adult children. His main passions include scuba diving, Rosslare beach, the Wexford hurling team and Liverpool FC.

O'Donovan Power, Victor, Rosbercon, was a prolific writer of stories, novels and plays. He was the author of the famous *Kitty the Hare* stories which appeared for many years in *Ireland's Own* magazine. Amongst his many books were: *Bonnie Dunraven: a Story of Kilcarrick, The Footsteps of Fate, The Heir of Liscarragh, The Secret of Sheila* and *The Banshee's Cry*.

O'Dwyer, Alan, Ballygow, Carrig on Bannow, Fleadh Cheoil na hÉireann All-Ireland champion whistler 2013, learned his musical craft from the legendary Phil Murphy.

O'Dwyer, Conor, formerly Clonard, born Wexford 1967, very successful national hunt jockey, riding more than 600 winners, and currently doing well as a trainer, having taken out his licence in 2007. He is based at Rossmore House, Friarstown, Kildare. Conor has a remarkable record at the Cheltenham Festival, the Olympics of National Hunt racing. He won the Gold Cup on Imperial Call in 1996. He was pipped to Champion Hurdle success on War of Attrition in 2004 by Colm Murphy's Wexford-trained Brave Inca, but he came back two years later to win the Gold Cup again on the horse, owned by Ryanair boss, Michael O'Leary. O'Dwyer also won the Champion Hurdle twice, on Hardy Eustace, 2004 and 2005. His most famous partnership at home was with the Arthur Moore-trained Native Upmanship, on which he scored 12 wins.

O'Flaherty Michael, Chapel Gardens, Kilmore Quay, seafood businessman and a director of Celtic Link Ferries. The ferry company was launched in 2005 and serves the

Rosslare-Cherbourg route. In October 2012 organised for free fish to be handed out on Kilmore Quay in protest at EU policy of discarding fish back into the sea. Michael is manager of the family-owned business, Saltees Fish and, along with his brothers, Seamus, Brendan, John and Denis, markets and exports locally-landed fish. He is married to Kira and they have two daughters and two sons.

O'Gorman, Colm, Wexford 1966, Adamstown, now Gorey; qualified physical therapist and psychotherapist, current Executive Director of Amnesty International Ireland; founder of One in Four Ireland, and through his role as director of One in Four, was instrumental in the establishment of the *Ferns Inquiry*, the first state investigation into clerical sexual abuse in Ireland; helped to found Gorey Educate Together School; author of bestselling book, *Beyond Belief.* Appointed to Seanad Éireann 2007 to fill the vacancy caused by the death of Senator Kate Walsh and held the seat for a number of weeks until the General Election was held.

> Fifty years ago this year was the only time Oylegate Glenbrien won the Wexford senior hurling title.

O'Gorman, Larry, born Wexford 1967, played hurling for Wexford 1987-2004, and for Faythe Harriers; his big year was 1996 when Wexford beat Limerick to win their first All-Ireland title for 28 years. His swashbuckling style and exciting runs earned him the Texaco Hurler of the Year Award, one of only four Wexford hurlers ever to be so honoured, and the Gaelic Players' Association Player of the Year and an All-Star Award at left full back. Known as 'The Brother', Larry was noted as one of the 'characters' of the team. He won a county senior medal with Faythe Harriers. His brother Paddy also played for Wexford.

O'Gorman, Mairéad, Poulpeasty, Taghmon, née Cullen, Duncormick, married to Noel, they have three daughters and one son; former Miss Ireland, she represented the country in the 1964 Miss World pageant in London; was an air hostess with BOAC and internationally known expert in the craft of Irish quilting. David Blake Knox featured her in his book, *Hands*. Her mother was a native of the Blasket Islands.

O'Gorman, John, Kilkenny, formerly Poulpeasty, Taghmon, one of Wexford's most consistent footballers of the modern era. The Taghmon-Camross clubman played in the backs for the county team from the mid-1980s to mid-1990s. He was also joined on the Wexford team on occasions by his twin brothers, Bernard and Padraig. Married to Siobhán, the couple have three children and live in Kilkenny where John is an accountant.

O'Hanlon-Walsh, Fr Davey, was born at Knocktarton, Ballymitty in 1844. His mother refused to pay her rent and was evicted from her farm in June 1881. Fr Davey became a mesmerising personality in the Land League, in conflict to some extent with Church authority. He died in Kiltealy in 1899.

O'Hanrahan, Michael, born New Ross 1877, played a leading role in the Easter Rising of 1916 and was executed in Dublin. He was a published author and his novels include *A Swordsman of the Brigade* and *When the Normans Came.* The railway station in Wexford is named in his honour, as is the bridge across the river Barrow in his home town of New Ross.

O'Kennedy, Gus, New Ross, brother of Sean, played in all four of the 1915-18 All-Ireland finals. O'Kennedy Park GAA Grounds in New Ross is called after the O'Kennedy brothers, Sean and Gus, and not after President Kennedy as some people think.

O'Kennedy, Sean, New Ross, captain of three of the four-in-a-row Wexford All-Ireland winning football teams, 1915-1918, the first time that the four-in-a-row had been done; was not available for the 1918 team. He is one of just a handful of players to have won All-Ireland senior medals in both codes as he was also a member of the 1910 hurling winners. O'Kennedy really was the leader of the county as he served as County chairman, secretary and treasurer in 1915; was chairman also from 1911 to 1914; secretary from 1907 to 1910 and also acted as Leinster and Central Council Representative at times. He was recipient of a Sealink Wexford GAA Personality of the Century Award in 1984.

26-the number of tries Wexford Rugby player Gordon Darcy scored in the Heineken Cup.

O'Leary, Aisling, daughter Frank and Mrs O'Leary, Mulgannon, Wexford, was born within a good driver shot of Wexford Golf Club. She represented Ireland at girls and U21 levels at the European team championships and in 1994 she was number 1 in the Irish girls' Order of Merit table.

O'Leary, Dermot, born in Colchester 1973, television presenter, X Factor host. The younger of two children born to Sean and Marie, both natives of Wexford town. Sean was a well-known player for the Faythe Harriers in the 1960s while working in Fine Wool. They emigrated to UK where Sean worked his way up to a management position in BT. Dermot spent many holidays in Wexford during his childhood and continues to hold dual Irish and British citizenship. Dermot began his career in radio and television as a DJ on Essex Radio Then on to "Big Brother's Little Brother" on Channel 4 and in 2007 he became host of the X Factor on ITV. In September 2012 he married long-time girlfriend, TV producer/director Dee Koppang.

O'Leary, Diarmuid, born Fethard on Sea; lead singer with the Bards; became very well-known after their single, Lanigan's Ball, won them a Gold Disc Award and their follow-up comedy single, The Oldest Swinger in Town, is a classic.

O'Leary, Ellen, née Roche, Garrvadden Blackwater, born 1920; through her father, Ellen has a direct link with famine times. She is the daughter of James and Alice Roche. James was 77 years of age when Ellen was born, he himself having been born on the 1st April 1843. She was married to Thomas they had four sons; Jack was very well known in GAA circles but was killed in road accident in Wexford in 2006. Her other sons are Michael, Bobby and Eamonn.

O'Leary, John 'Johnny', who was born on 1st September, 1894, was a Labour Party politician from Enniscorthy and he served in the Oireachtas for nearly twenty years, first as a TD and then as a Senator. He was first elected as a TD on the Labour Party ticket for Wexford in 1943; re-elected in the 1944 and 1948 General Elections as a National Labour Party TD. In the 1951 and 1954 General Elections, he was once again elected as a Labour Party candidate. He was defeated in the 1957 General Election, but was elected to Seanad Éireann on the Administrative Panel.

O'Leary, Liam, Clonee, Camolin, comes from a highly respected farming family. Liam's uncles in various branches of the family operated retail businesses in Bunclody and Enniscorthy. Liam left Clonee with a horse bought by an American who facilitated the progress of Liam's education. Having graduated from Ballyduff primary school, it is an indication of Liam's dedication that he was capable of skipping secondary school but still subsequently qualified as a veterinary surgeon. Liam was a very good hurler and won a County minor championship with Ferns in 1958. Liam returned to Ferns to marry Josephine O'Toole of Ballingale, Ballycarney, and they have reared their family in Connecticut where he is an eminently successful veterinary surgeon.

O'Leary, Michael, Redinagh, Killurin, 1951, accountant, estate agent, native of Tomfarney, Adamstown; married to Dolores, former nurse; worked with Smith Group in Wexford and County Wexford Farmers' Marts before setting up his own accountancy firm in 1980 with offices in Wexford, Enniscorthy and New Ross. He now employs 16 people. He is a member of the Institute Professional Auctioneers and Valuers and the Institute of Finanicial Accountants. He ran track and field and cross country for the county in the 70s. He ran all distances from 100m to intermediate cross country with brother, Pat, recent winner of achievement award for his services to athletics as a member of Bree AC. He was Macra na Feirme All-Ireland public speaking champion, 1970. Founder member of Enniscorthy Lions Club in the 1980s; chairman Rehab County Wexford People of the Year Awards for 11 years; member of organising committee of Glynn church centenary celebrations, 1980; raised funds for Belarus orphanage. His son, Andrew, is operations manager, United Technologies, and daughter, Sinéad Bolger, a Registered European Valuer, is one of the leaders of Killurin Rowing Club.

O'Leary, Dr Olivia, Monagreaney, Monamolin, Chiropractor partner in Gorey Family Chiropractic Clinic on Railway Road. A native of Camolin, Olivia qualified as a chiropractor in 2001 following a four-year degree course in the University of Glamorgan. Olivia completed the final year of her training in Cornwall where she met her husband, Dr. Michael Veal, who is now a partner in the Gorey Clinic with her. The couple have three sons and she describes her family as being sports mad. Her brother, Dermot O'Leary, is a member the Wexford U21 hurling team, Leinster champions in 2013.

O'Leary, Paddy, Gurrawn, Rathnure, born 1923, retired farm worker, married to Elizabeth Quigley, Rathfylane, with one son and one daughter; his father, also Paddy, worked in Castleboro and Coolbawn estates around the time they were burnt during the Civil War 1923.

Castletown and Duffry Rovers players dominate the leading medal winners list in senior football. Leading with 9 medals are Joe O'Shaughnessy and Oliver Cullen; second on 8 medals each are Sean Sheridan and Fran Molloy (Castletown, all between 1965 and 81), Louis Rafter, Noel Fitzhenry, Jay Mernagh, Ger O'Connor, John Casey and Seamus Fitzhenry of Duffry Rovers (between 1986 and 94, including seven in a row from 1986), and John O'Connor of Volunteers, Wexford (between 1939 and 56).

O Morchoe, David The, Ardgarry, Gorey, born Dublin 1928, Major General Rtd. David Nial Creagh, CB, CBE, KLJ, the hereditary Chief and Prince of the Ó Murchadha (Murphy) Sept, a cadet line of the ancient Irish dynasty the Uí Chennselaig, who were Kings of Leinster. He is head of the O Morchoe clan.

Ó Muirithe, Diarmuid, born and reared in New Ross, he became a Primary teacher and taught for a time in Caroreigh National School. Later, while working as a freelance writer and journalist at RTÉ, he won the first Jacob's Radio Award and scripted the award-winning pan-European Nordring Prize programme for the station. He wrote the scripts for many cultural series, and has twelve radio plays to his credit. He gained his doctorate for a thesis on the old dialect of Forth and Bargy, Yola. He edited *The English Language in Ireland* in 1977 and published *The Wexford Carols* in 1982. He edited *A Seat Behind the Coachman – Travellers in Ireland 1800-1900*, which was published in 1995, and he published *The Dialect of Forth and Bargy* in 1996 with T.P. Dolan. His *The Words We Use column* has been appearing in the *Irish Times* for twenty years. His academic publications have influenced other scholars, and he has lectured on the Gaelic influence in major seats of learning from Oxford to Vienna.

O'Neill, Hugh, born at Rathfylane, Courtnacuddy, was master of the school at Cloughbawn established by Mr Carew of Castleboro. It attracted pupils from all over Ireland and Mr O'Neill became legendary. He was principal of the first National School in Clonroche. He passionately supported the Carews and died on August 8th 1859.

O'Neill, Catherine, paralympian from Caisleán Maol, New Ross, born Ramsgrange, 1976, won silver medal at the London 2012 games in the her class in the women's discus; she was the world champion and record holder and in her third Games; she threw a season's best effort and it took a new world record throw by Britain's Josie Pearson to deny her gold. She had finished fourth in the club throw event earlier in the week. One of Ireland's most experienced paralympians, Catherine had already competed at the Games of 2000 in Sydney, fourth in discus and 2008 Beijing, fifth in discus, and was happy to win her first Olympic medal at last. She had already won gold in discus at the World Championships in Birmingham in1998 and she won gold in discus and silver in club event in the IPC World Athletic Championships in Christchurch, New Zealand in 2011.

John Casey from Caim has a unique distinction – he captained the winning team in seven successive county senior football championships. This was the Duffry Rovers during their run from 1986 to 1992. The Rovers did not make the final the next year but were back again in 1994 and they won their 8th (and last to date) senior title; Casey was on the team but the captaincy had passed to Louis Rafter, the elegant midfielder and county player who also lined out in all 8 winning finals.

O'Neill, John, formerly Whitty's Hill, Wellingtonbridge, trained as an engineer with Radio Éireann in the 1950s. He worked at the then broadcasting studios at the GPO in Henry Street, Dublin. In 1961, he moved from there to the newly- built broadcasting premises at Donnybrook, where he was one of the team of ten engineers involved in the setting up of the RTÉ Television station. He is treasurer of the Dublin branch of the Wexford Supporters' Club.

O'Neill, Julie, formerly of Wexford town now an Independent Management Consultant and Director of Ryanair. She was educated at Loreto Wexford, UCD and Trinity College and spent seven years in the top job in the Department of Transport as its Secretary General. Julie is also Director of Sustainable Energy Ireland and the Irish Museum of Modern Art. Formerly Julie Corcoran, she is sister of South East Radio presenter, Alan. Her son, Shane, is married and has set up his own business in China and on a visit there it was an inspiration for Julie to set up shananigansblog.com which is about connecting Ireland with China and Australia, where Julie's daughter is married, through a love of food.

O'Neill, Martin, the O'Neills of Ferns have been steeped in the GAA since its inception. Martin was a member of the Wexford County Committee in 1886 and 87, and represented Wexford at the Annual Congress in Thurles in 1887. His grandson, also named Martin, was one of nine brothers, six of whom played for Wexford, and he has an unmatched record of service to the GAA. He was a talented player of hurling, football and handball, notable referee and an incredibly long-serving official; he died aged 87 years in 1991. He entered St. Peter's College, Wexford, in 1915; he won a Leinster senior football medal with Wexford in 1925, and junior hurling in 1926; won three Railway Cup medals with Leinster footballers, 1928-1930, and was picked on the Ireland team for the Tailteann Games of 1924, 1928 and 1932. The family moved to Bray and Martin won two All-Ireland handball doubles titles for Wicklow, with Luke Sherry. He won a Wicklow senior football medal with Bray Emmets in 1935 and captained

Wicklow to All-Ireland junior football title in 1936. He refereed three All-Ireland senior football finals, in 1932, '33 and the unique final of 1947 played at the Polo Grounds in New York – the only final played outside Ireland, in which Cavan beat Kerry.

He became Leinster GAA Secretary in 1927 and became the Council's first full-time official. He served until 1969 and was recognised as forward-thinking innovator. He was succeeded by his son, Ciaran, who later became Financial Controller at Croke Park. He was secretary of Leinster Handball Council from 1927 to 1947 and served as secretary of Leinster Colleges' GAA for 50 years up to 1977.

He was awarded the Cúchulainn Trophy in 1966, and an All-Star Award in GAA Centenary Year, 1984, in recognition of his service. Also in 1984 he was the recipient of a Sealink Wexford GAA Personality of the Century Award. The Corn Uí Neill is presented to the Leinster senior club hurling champions each year in Martin's memory.

O'Neill, Matt, Adamstown, Matt was ever present on Wexford Ladies' Gaelic Football County Board over the first twenty years; was a mentor at adult and underage levels and represented Wexford as a delegate to Leinster and Central Councils. He also refereed a senior All-Ireland Final in Croke Park.

O'Neill, Pat, 1928-1976, and **Mogue**, 1920-2002, were born in Bolinadrum in Kilrush Parish. From an early age they made their names in the athletic tracks, sports meetings and cross-country races all over the county from 1947 to 1958. Another set of Kilrush brothers made a name for themselves in athletic circles also. Dan, Patsy, and Johnny Donohue were known for their endurance and competed with Sliabh Buidhe on the cross-country circuit.

O'Reilly, John, Corrigeen, Rathnure, born Wexford 1969, pantomime and musical producer, scriptwriter, actor, married to Fiona, née Reilly, Rathnure, they have two sons and two daughters. John has collaborated on numerous musical projects with Liam Sharkey, including, pantomimes: *Shrek: The Quest for Cinderella, Shrek and the Secret of the North Pole, The Fairest of them All, Pinocchio: Return to Oz, A Winter's Tale, Sulkyella and the Highland Adventure, Dorothy Rocks, Merlin and the Legend of the Golden Key* and *Goldilocks and the 3 Sisters*. Musicals: *Torn Dreams, Fallen Angel, When I Grow Up and Eternal Flame*. John was in Giants' Stadium, New York, to see Ireland beat Italy 1-0 in the 1994 World Cup finals.

O'Reilly, Seamus, formerly Camross, born 1943, Ballyglissane, Bartlemy, Co. Cork, joined the Army Apprentice School in Naas in 1958 and served with Irish troops in Congo in 1962. Joined An Garda Siochána and served in Dublin and Templemore. Married Rose in 1966 and had a family of three sons and one daughter. Started in business in Cork and opened his first petrol station there in 1977. Now owns and runs three service stations and convenience stores in Cork city. Rose died in 2003. He married Bernie in 2008.

O'Rourke, Eamonn, Horetown, married to Peg, with a grown-up family of daughters. The O'Rourke family have been involved in cattle dealing for many years and in his younger days spent time in marts and fairs all over the country; great community man formerly involved with farming issues in ICMSA at national level; a member of Clongeen Ploughing Association.

O'Shaughnessy, Joe, Coolroe, Castletown, born 1943; dairy farmer, GAA player and official; married to Ann, née Carroll, Ballycanew; they have five daughters

and two sons. Played football for Wexford and Castletown; won nine county senior football medals with Castletown between 1965 and '81, he shares the honour of winning the most in Wexford GAA history with his club mate, Oliver Cullen; chairman of Wexford County GAA Board from 1990 to '93 inclusive; has been Wexford's Rep. on GAA Central Council in Croke Park since 2002. His brother, Larry, also played senior football for Wexford and Castletown.

O'Sullivan, Dr Austin, Coolballow, Wexford, was born in 1940 and grew up in Co. Meath. He was the driving force behind the foundation of the National Agricultural Museum at Johnstown Castle, which was opened in 1979. He was the museum's first curator. Dr. O'Sullivan obtained his PhD in Plant Ecology in UCD and also studied in Germany. He is the author of numerous scientific papers and articles. Many of his articles have been published in the Journal of the Wexford Historical Society, and his *Guide to Johnstown Castle and Nature Trails* was published in 1978. Other publications by Dr. O'Sullivan include: *Johnstown Castle Estate and Research Centre* and *Tacumshane Windmill, its History and Mode of Operations*.

O'Sullivan, Kathleen, Carrigbyrne, retired a few years ago after spending many years at work in St. Senan's Hospital, Enniscorthy, now very much involved in work for the Newbawn community; played a big part in the recent successful "Gathering" events in the Newbawn area.

Parker, Dr. Pamela, a member of a long-established Oylegate family from Martingale. She has a BA in psychology from UCD, and an MSc in health psychology from the University of the West of England. She now works as a clinical psychologist for Cambridgeshire Children's Social Care.

Parle, James, Drinagh, Wexford, born 1932, is the author of the best-selling book *The Mummers of Wexford,* and he has also published *Our Sporting Past, a history of track and field athletics, cross-country, cycling and tug-o'-war in Co. Wexford from 1877 to 1967.*

Parle, Paddy, Spawell Road, Wexford, 1917-1998, married to Maureen, née Lawlor, The Faythe; managing director of William Walker's, North Main St; conductor of the Holy Family Confraternity Band for many years, his brother, Tom, was manager of the band and worked as a manager with *People Newspapers* along with his wife Una. Paddy and Maureen had four children, Mary, Anne, Pat and Teresa.

Pettitt, Des, Wexford, comes from a family with a long history of retailing in Wexford town. His great grandfather and great-great grandfather ran a grocery, wine and spirit business on Wexford's Main Street. In 1946 his father, Jack, took over the Beechville Dairy, one of the premises formerly owned by his grandfather. Less than ten years later, he bought the premises next door and opened the first self-service store in Wexford. Over the years, the business has expanded, and now there are Pettitt's SuperValu stores in Wexford, Gorey, Arklow and Athy. The family also owns the Talbot Hotels in Wexford and Carlow and the Stillorgan Park Hotel, Dublin. In the list of Ireland's top 250 rich people, Des Pettitt is listed in 127th place with €61 million. His sons John and Cormac are directors of the company.

Sr. Philip, Saint John of God Order, Newtown Road, Wexford. This order of nuns was established in Wexford in 1871 by Bishop of Ferns, Thomas Furlong. The order has now become established internationally and also runs the Ballyvaloo Retreat Centre in Blackwater. Sister Philip was a very familiar figure in Wexford town in the 1960s and 70s as she helped the poor and needy of the town through the establishment of the Sick Poor Fund.

Pierce, John W., Arthurstown, published *Arthurstown, the story of a Village* in 1986. He also wrote *Dunbrody Abbey – Monastery and Monument* in 1994.

Popplewell, Nick, born 1964 in Dublin, living in Killinick, Wexford; former Irish rugby international, works with the auctioneering firm Sherry-Fitzgerald Haythornthwaite in Wexford town. His parents moved to live in Ballyoughter, north Wexford, when he was seven. Nick played some of his early rugby with Gorey RFC. He won 48 Irish caps between 1989 and 1998 and was recognised as one of the best rugby props in the world; captained his national team on several occasions. He played in all three tests on the British and Irish Lions tour of New Zealand in 1993. He played his club rugby for Greystones and professionally with Newcastle Falcons.

Power, Captain Con, Derrypatrick House, Summerhill, Co. Meath, born and reared in Templetown parish; was a member of the Irish Show jumping team that won the Aga Khan Trophy outright at the RDS Horse Show in Dublin, taking it three years in a row, 1977, '78 and '79. Remarkably, Con rode a different horse each year, Coolronan, Castlepark and the famous Rockbarton. He also gained many other international successes with Irish teams abroad. He was a member of the Army Equitation School. He later took up racehorse training in Co. Meath.

Power, Eamonn, Corse House, Templetown, farmer and board member of Glanbia Plc. Eamonn has served a number of years on the board and has overseen major growth and change in the multi-national during that time. A dairy farmer, he is also active in his local community in The Hook. Married to Eileen, née Gleeson, a nurse in Wexford General Hospital, the couple have three sons and one daughter.

Power, John, born 1933, at Forlorn Point, Ballyteigue Bay, Kilmore, author of *A Maritime History of County Wexford* in two volumes, the result of 15 years' research. John was a commercial fisherman for 37 years and is a former director of Bord Iascaigh Mhara. The books contain details of all the passenger and cargo ships that left County Wexford for Liverpool, the Bristol Channel and other ports from 1859. It profiles the lightship men who served around our coast along with Wexford merchant seamen involved in the First and Second World Wars, many of whom lost their lives. There is information on sailing vessels, ship owners, merchants and captains and nearly every shipwreck around the coast. He is a regular contributor to the Kilmore Parish Journal and is also author of *Above and Beyond the Call of Duty*, published in 1993.

St Peter's College Wexford, has won the All-Ireland colleges hurling title on four occasions – in 1962, 1967, 1968 and 1973. Remarkably, on each occasion the finals were drawn and they went on to win the replays. They also drew the 1982 final with St. Flannan's of Ennis, but this time lost the replay.

Power, Ned, Rhu Glen, Co. Kilkenny, spent many years teaching at St. Peter's College, Wexford, where he ended up as vice-principal; was a noted hurling trainer and coach before such titles were really well-known; helped St. Peter's teams to win four All-Ireland senior colleges titles, in 1962, 1967, 1968 and 1973; trained Wexford hurling county teams of the 1950s and 60s; well known also as producer of drama and musicals, in the college and with Wexford Light Opera Society, often in conjunction with his friend and colleague, Fr. John O'Brien (RIP). Power Park all-weather pitch at the college is named in his honour.

Power, Robbie, jockey, son of Irish show jumper Con Power, rode 33-1 outsider Silver Birch to victory in the 2007 Aintree Grand National. He was riding at Wexford races the night before he headed over to Aintree for his date with destiny. Robbie was a very promising show jumper before turning to racing, winning a silver medal at the European Young Rider Championships. He is one of the most accomplished and successful National Hunt riders in Ireland. His sister, Elizabeth, is one of Ireland's leading eventing riders.

Prendergast, Patrick J., BA, BAI, PhD, ScD, FTCD, MRIA, Provost Trinity College Dublin; from Raheenakeagh, Oulart, son of John, RIP, and Mary, née Goodall; he has two daughters and one son; past pupil of Oulart N.S. and St. Peter's College, Wexford; Honorary Principal Investigator, Trinity Centre for Bioengineering and, though Provost, still teaches engineering, mainly biomechanics and implant design but also mechanics of materials. His research field is mechanobiology – the science of how mechanical forces affect tissue growth and phenotype.

Purcell, Noel, Adamstown, received a scholarship from Adamstown hall committee c.1960 to attend St. Peter's College in Wexford. He spent all of his working life with the Ordnance Survey Department in Kilkenny. Now, in his mid-sixties, he retired a couple of years ago.

Quigley, Aidan, Carrig-on-Bannow, purchased landmark building, Loftus Hall, in 2011 and has opened the house to the public, it having been closed since 1994. Aidan is adamant that the Hook residents should receive all the plaudits concerning the revitalisation of Loftus Hall, its gardens and the surrounding area and their input in rebuilding stone walls and in providing the impetus to put this historic landmark back to its rightful elegance.

Quigley, Catherine, Boolabawn, Courtnacuddy, full-time carer, she has five sons Jason, Josh, Kevin, Conor and Dillon and one daughter, Louise. Catherine is a full-time carer for Louise, who has cerebral palsy and, after having four boys in a row, the birth of her little girl, was her happiest moment. The boys are a great help in taking care of their sister. Various fundraising events have been held, concerts and soccer match, to help meet some of the costs of the 24-hour-a-day care needed and the electronic equipment that is required for Louise.

Quigley, Gretta, Oylegate, since her arrival in Oylegate in 1983, the village has seen an upsurge in youth-based achievement. Along with her husband, Ray, retired Garda, they have made the local youth club a hub of activity which has amassed a record of national titles in fields as diverse as drama, unihoc, variety shows, debating and an All-Ireland camogie 7-a-side title. The latest and most significant achievement of the people of Oylegate, including the Quigleys, is the opening of a state-of-the-art Community Centre.

Quigley, Ryan, Davidstown, Irish General manager for ABBVie, a multinational pharmaceutical company based in Dublin and listed on the New York Stock Exchange. The company specializes in research and development with global revenues of €13 billion and employs four hundred in Sligo, Cork and Dublin. Ryan Quigley previously worked with Pfeizer and is son of the late, Pat Quigley and Eilish, née Ryan. He is a former Wexford senior county hurler and a member of the Rapparees/Starlights club in Enniscorthy. He is married to Sarah, née Crean, and the couple have three sons.

Quigley, Dan, born 1944, farmer. He was captain of the 1968 All-Ireland hurling winning team, when he was selected as the Texaco National Hurler of the Year; winner of three Leinster medals and one National League (1967); was full back on Wexford's only All-Ireland U21 winning team in 1965; with Rathnure he won 8 County senior medals, and three Leinster club titles.

Quigley, Martin, born 1951. Wexford town-based accountant has been involved in hurling and football all his life and is Wexford's most decorated All-Star, winning four successive awards from 1973. He has played senior for Wexford more often than any other man with 231 appearances - 181 in hurling and 50 in football - 40 more than George O'Connor in second place. He never did win an All-Ireland senior medal, with Cork being the big stumbling block in finals. He was selected at left half forward on the 1984 Special Centenary Year Team of the Century for non-All-Ireland winners. He won four Railway Cup hurling medals, an All-Ireland minor medal in 1968, and National League medal with win over Limerick in 1973. He won Leinster medals in minor, 1967, three U21s in succession from 1969, senior in 1970, '76 and '77, and five Leinster club medals with Rathnure, but he was on the losing side in all twelve of those All-Ireland finals, Cork doing the damage in ten of them. He won 10 county hurling titles with Rathnure. After his playing days, he managed the Wexford senior hurling team from 1989-92. His firm is the accountant to Wexford County Board, and he has been very involved with the St. Martin's club in his adopted Piercestown parish.

Quigley, John, born 1949. All-Ireland senior medal winner in 1968; won four Leinster senior medals, 1968, '70, '76 and '77; Leinster minors in 1966 and '67, U21s in 1966, and '69, won National League in 1973, and three Leinsters with his Rathnure club. John was selected at right corner forward on the 1974 All-Stars team, with his brother, Martin, picked at centre forward. John played 116 times for Wexford hurlers and 29 times with the footballers. Pat and Jim also lined out for Wexford at underage and senior level. Eoin, current Wexford hurler, is son of John.

Quill, Liz, née Redmond, native of Tomnalossett, Enniscorthy; married to Pat, they had four children, Noel, RIP, Maeve, Paudie and Lisa; played in ladies' Gaelic football from 1972, seven years before first County Board was formed; served as county chairperson from 1994 to 1997 as well as being vice chairperson, treasurer, and fixtures' chairperson; has also served as assistant secretary of Leinster Council and on Appeals committee at Central Council Level; played with Forth Celtic and Shelmaliers and was on the first ladies' football team to officially play for Wexford, against Offaly in 1979. She played camogie with the St. Mary's, Enniscorthy, and St. Ibar's Shelmalier. Daughters Maeve and Lisa have represented their club and county at all grades of football.

Quill, Pat, Johnstown, Castlebridge, National President of the Ladies' Gaelic Football Association 1985-1988 and 2009 up to 2015. From Castletownbere, Co. Cork, he came to Wexford town in 1976 to work in the Social Welfare Office. He played football with St. Joseph's and Shelmaliers in Wexford, and has been involved with ladies' Gaelic football in Wexford since its foundation in 1979; has served as both chairperson and secretary of the Wexford County Board; was instrumental in getting ladies' football played in Croke Park for the first time in 1986; has managed Shelmaliers and Wexford teams to All-Ireland success as well as the Leinster team to inter-provincial success.

Quinlivan, Tim, Glenville Road, Wexford, chartered accountant, partner at the firm of Sheil Kinnear, Sinnottstown Business Park, Drinagh. He qualified in 1978. A native of Rosslare married to Carmel, they have one daughter, Cathy, and three sons, Stephen, Brendan and Rory, who is a current member of the Wexford county senior football team. Tim is a lifelong member of Rosslare Golf Club, captain in 2007, and current chairman of the Greens' Committee.

Quinn, Mary, née Kehoe, Oylegate, born Wexford 1943, hotel kitchen assistant and part-time florist, Ballyharron, Crossabeg; married to James (RIP) with two daughters and four sons; faithful Fianna Fáil supporter; organiser senior citizens' Christmas party and local weekly 55+ Club; secretary Crossabeg Pastoral Centre Committee which recently received planning permission for the building of a new Personal Development and Pastoral Centre at Ardtramon.

Quirke, Madeline, Rosslare, Chief Executive Officer of Wexford Chamber of Commerce, with overall responsibility for the management and operational activities of the organization. Madeleine was Public Relations/ Administration Manager of Irish Ferries from 1996 to 2008 when she was appointed CEO of Wexford Chamber. She studied business and professional management at the Open University, and she is an influential figure on a number of committees, including Rosslare Harbour Development Board, the Water, Environmental and Emergency Committee of Wexford County Council and Wexford Tidy Towns' Committee. She also acts as volunteer press officer for Rosslare Lifeboat service, and has served as a leader with Rosslare Harbour Sea Scouts.

Rackard, Billy, Killanne, 1930-2009. He played for Wexford 132 times between 1949 and 1964, winning All-Ireland medals in 1955, 56 and 60, six Leinster titles, two National League titles and four Railway Cup medals with Leinster. He was captain of the Wexford team beaten by Tipperary in a great All-Ireland final in 1962. He won five county senior hurling medals with his club, Rathnure, and also one in football in 1952. Billy ran a shop in Wexford for many years, and developed a very fine par 3 golf course at St. Helen's near Rosslare, which has now become a championship class 18 hole golf course. He was interested in all sports and a great raconteur.

Rackard, Bobby, Killanne 1927-1996. Regarded as one of the best hurlers of all time, he played for Wexford from 1945, retiring after a farm accident before the 1957 championship began, having lined out 91 times. He won two All-Irelands, 1955, 56, four Leinster titles, a National League medal, a Railway Cup medal with Leinster and four senior hurling titles with Rathnure. His status in the game was clearly indicated when he was selected at corner back on both the Hurling Team of the Century in 1984, and on the Team of the Millennium in 1999. Billy and Bobby were jointly awarded a GAA All-Time All Star Award in 1992.

Rackard, Nickey, see Sport

Reck, Paul, born 1954 in Wexford town; son of Jimmy and Kathleen, the Faythe; award-winning international tax expert. Began his career at the Revenue office in Wexford; became an Inspector of Taxes with the Revenue Commissioners; served as secretary of the Commission on Taxation chaired by Miriam Hedderman O'Brien; joined major tax consulting company, Deloitte, in Dublin in 1988 and later became an international Tax Partner. He has served many global clients in the banking, insurance and capital markets sectors and was a member of the Banking and Treasury Group set up by the Irish Government to advise on the development of the financial services' sector in Ireland. In 2007, he relocated to the US for 18 months where he set up an Irish desk in Deloitte's New York office. He is co-author of the annual publication *Taxation Summary*. Living in Dublin, he is married to Moira, née Bridges, Davitt Road, Wexford, and they have three children, Linda, Simon and Darren.

Reddy, Mick, Tomanine, Rathnure, born 1952, painter and decorator; married to Elizabeth, née Murphy, Enniscorthy, they have two daughters; son of Mick Reddy, a gifted entertainer-actor-comedian, and Rita, née Codd. Mick is on the parish committee, the water board committee and is a member of the National Federation of Group Water Schemes. His greatest memory is of Rathnure beating a strong Fenians, Co. Kilkenny hurling outfit in a Leinster final in the 1970s with 13 men and also the great All-Ireland hurling final win of 1996 by the men of Wexford.

Redmond, David, Knocknaveigh, Oulart, current Wexford senior hurler and Oulart-The Ballagh player who was on winning team that defeated Ferns in 2013. Currently promoting new Lely revolutionary milking system in his work at Donohoe Agri in Enniscorthy.

Redmond, Paddy, Monaseed, Gorey, born Wexford 1964; married to Fiona, née Fennell, Clonegal, they have one daughter and twin sons; co-owner of Redmond Construction, the Ashdown Park Hotel, Gorey and Amber Springs Hotel, Knockmullen, Gorey; owner of Big Zeb, highly successful recently retired racehorse and winner of the Queen Mother Cheltenham Chase 2010.

Reidy, Sean, New Ross, born 1949; Chief Executive JFK Trust for past twenty-two years; son of well-known Kilkenny hurler Liam, and Mary, née Doyle, Clonroche. Eldest of their eight children, Sean was educated St. Kieran's College Kilkenny and UCD and the Institute for Public Administration. He worked in Customs and Excise for twenty-one years. Sean was instrumental on bringing the Dunbrody replica Famine Ship from concept to reality and now has a management role in the Kennedy Homestead Visitor Centre and is a Director of the Kennedy Summer School. Sean is married with five children has a great interest in music and was a member of folk group, Barrowside for more than twenty years.

Rice, Mary, Mayglass, ladies' Gaelic footballer; married to Peter; played her football with Forth Celtic, before setting up a club in her own parish; served as Secretary of Wexford County Board for most of the 1980s, a period of great growth; went on to be national treasurer for one year when she administered the Association's Injury Fund. Husband Peter a native of Portlaoise is a ladies' Gaelic football official for which he received the GAA President's Award for his service to the Ladies' Football Association

Ringwood, Harry, 1923-2013, Rectory Road, Enniscorthy, barber, married to Theresa, they have three sons and one daughter, he was predeceased by his second daughter, Noelle, in 2012; he was an award-winning producer and director of plays and musicals over at least 60 years; he and his wife, Theresa received the Bene Merenti papal medal in recognition of a lifetime of work for the Church and the parish of St. Senan's.

Roche, Aidan and John, Barntown, are a father and son team who have built up a powerful kennel of coursing dogs in recent years and they achieved the ultimate with Kingsmill Dynamo when winning the Coursing Derby at Clonmel. Dynamo is now a top sire. Aidan has trained dogs for many years and has had great success on the track also.

Roche, Ben, Cork, formerly Assagart, Foulksmills, is the National Collaborative Farming Specialist with Teagasc based at Moorepark, Cork. He is son of John, Rockview, Little Cullenstown, and Mary Kate, née McCabe, Ballyvergin. He was for many years a Regional Training Advisor with the Farm Apprenticeship Board in Cork. He is of the Roches of Levitstown dynasty whose Fr. James Roche was founder of the twin churches in Bride Street and Rowe Street, Wexford. He is married to Julia, née Fitzpatrick. They have two daughters, Kathy and Margo.

Roche, Billy, Wexford town, born Wexford 1949; playwright and author who has achieved international fame. Formerly a member of the local Roach Band, he turned to writing in the 1980s. His best known works include the Wexford trilogy, *A handful of Stars, Poor Beast in the Rain* and *Belfry* which won numerous awards. He has written eight plays in total many of which premiered in London. He has also written a novel *Tumbling Down* and a collection of short stories entitled *Tales from Rainwater Pond*. Billy Roche is also an actor of note and appeared in films including *The Cavalcaders* the screenplay which he wrote himself. He is married to Patti and they have three sons. Billy is also a member of Aosdána, a body of artists set up by the Arts Council to acknowledge the outstanding work in the field of arts given by its members.

Roche, Declan, Sycamore House, Killurin, married to Mary, née Carroll, Taghmon, publicans well known for their hospitality for more than fifty years. Declan's sister, Sandra, is mother of *Evening Herald* crime reporter, Ken Foy.

Roche, Jimmy, RIP, Coolcotts, Wexford town; played football with Sarsfields and for many years on Wexford county senior team; Wexford County Board chairman from 1970-1972 and Leinster chairman from 1975-77; was narrowly beaten in bid for presidency of the Association; served on many influential Croke Park Committees and had much to do with development of modern Wexford Park. He ran a well-known painting and decorating business in Wexford.

Roche, John, Davitt Road South, Wexford and Leixlip; 1936-2006, Garda Technical Bureau, Garda HQ, Dublin, popular singer with wife Maureen neé Fallon, of songs with a Percy French theme on RTÉ Television Late Late Show and RTÉ Radio Donncha O'Dulaing Highways and By-ways programme. Toured UK and USA with Garda Band. Siblings are Lar of Wexford Festival Singers; Elsie Dempsey, Piercestown; Nick former Garda Sergeant, Lucan; Pat, former Garda Sergeant, Dunleer; Tom, Dublin and Phyllis, London. A Garda photographic expert, he worked on Ireland's high profile criminal cases for more than 30 years from the 60s. Sons Simon, a designer and Jonah, also a Garda.

Roche, John, Assagart, Foulksmills, horse breeder; married to Catherine, née Winters, they have two sons, Cathal and Jamie; winner reserve champion brood mare Assagart Saviour and reserve champion three-year-old Assagart Master at this year's Dublin Horse Show 2013; Assagart Master has shown since at the Horse of the Year Show in London; John is also a boxer of note, GAA player and manager, actor and dancer.

Roche, Johnny, Fisher's Row Wexford Town, was an exceptional contributor to soccer development in the county. He served as Oscar Traynor team manager, and as soccer correspondent for the *People newspapers*, where his vibrant coverage and "snippets" section was a must-read for all sports fans. Outside football, Johnny served his local community with distinction as a councillor on Wexford Corporation for a time.

Roche, Kieran S., born John Street, Wexford, has written a biography of Richard Corish, who came to prominence during the 1911 lock-out in Wexford and who became a TD and Mayor of Wexford for twenty-five years. The book, entitled *Richard Corish – A Biography*, was published in 2012.

Roche, Niall, Duncannon, born 1979; married to Christina, née, Sheehan, Maynooth, they have one son; established the county's kite-surfing school and shop on Duncannon beach in 2010, now also teaching paddle-boarding.

Roche, Paddy, Rosslare Harbour, was GAA County Secretary from 1961 to 1979, and stayed involved at Bord nÓg level for many years after, being secretary 1981-1990.

Roche, Richard, Scar, Duncormick, born 1926; deputy editor of the *Irish Independent* and editor of the *Enniscorthy Echo* for a short time; author of a large number of books, including: *Here's Their Memory, The Norman Invasion of Ireland, Saltees – Islands of Birds and Legends,* with Oscar Merne, *The Texas Connection* and *Tales of the Wexford Coast.* A play pageant entitled *Selskar Tales* was performed at Selskar Abbey during the Wexford Festival Opera of 1994.

Roche, Fr Thomas, Wexford, wrote under the pen-name of Sahida. His poetry appeared regularly in *The People* Newspaper and a book of his poetry was also published.

Ronan, Andy, New Ross, competed in the marathon in Barcelona in 1992 and had to retire when brought down by a runner who fell in front of him at the nine-mile mark water station. His preparations had already been interrupted by injury. This was a bitter disappointment as he had posted some spectacular results in the previous two years. He was third in the world famous Boston marathon in 1991, just 20 seconds behind the winner after being in contention all the way. His 2.11.27 time is still the third fastest by an Irish runner, behind John Treacy and Mark Carroll. The same year he finished 7th in Berlin from over 14,000 runners and he was sixteenth in London in 1990. He twice ran for Ireland in the World Cross Country Championships. Ronan graduated from Providence University, Rhodes Island, USA, in 1986, a place attended by many Irish athletes. Having done six years in Providence, he has spent the last 14 years as head coach at Stonybrook University, Long Island, where he is credited with bringing about massive improvements.

8

Sport

County Wexford's sports heroes include local, national and international champions and Olympians.

SPORT STARS AND HEROES

Sport is a vital ingredient in the DNA of County Wexford life, not just for the thousands of participants in dozens of different disciplines, but for all the rest us as well – we all revel in the successes of our sports people, sharing a sense of identity and pride in their achievements.

We have produced stars and heroes in so many different sports, from various Gaelic games, to Olympic boxers, swimmers and athletes. We have renowned soccer and rugby players, world leading trainers and riders in equestrian pursuits, top exponents in ploughing, golf, snooker, darts, tug o' war, kick boxing and more, who have represented their country and county with distinction.

We give them due credit and honour; they are wonderful role models and a source of inspiration.

It is right to remember that these gifted people would not have achieved their lofty heights without a solid foundation having been laid by the thousands of volunteers who give their time in good and bad conditions, week in, week out, to mentor aspiring young stars of the future in fields, courts and halls in every corner of the county.

WEXFORD'S GAA AWARD WINNERS

The Texaco Irish Hurlers of the Year were first selected in 1958 and there have been four Wexford winners:
1960 – Nick O'Donnell, St. Aidan's, Enniscorthy.
1968 – Dan Quigley, Rathnure.
1976 – Tony Doran, Buffers Alley.
1996 – Larry O'Gorman, Faythe Harriers.

Camogie Champion Ursula Jacob lifts the O'Duffy Cup at Croke Park.

1954 All-Ireland Hurling Final programme.

The GAA All-Star Awards scheme began in 1971, but from the early 1960s up to 1967, an unofficial scheme was operated by the *Gaelic Weekly* magazine called the Cúchulainn Awards and were regarded as quite credible. Wexford's Cúchulainn Award winners:

Tom Neville, Geraldine O'Hanrahan's, New Ross – 1963, 1964, 1965

Billy Rackard, Rathnure – 1963

Phil Wilson, Ballyhogue – 1965

Tony Doran, Buffers Alley - 1967

HURLING ALL STAR AWARD WINNERS

Mick Jacob, Oulart/The Ballagh – 1972, '76, '77
Colm Doran, Buffers Alley – 1973
Martin Quigley, Rathnure – 1973, '74, '75, '76
John Quigley, Rathnure – 1974
Willie Murphy, Faythe Harriers – 1976
Tony Doran, Buffers Alley – 1976
Christy Keogh, Rapparees – 1977
Ned Buggy, Faythe Harriers – 1979
George O'Connor, St. Martin's, Piercestown – 1981, 1988
John Conran, Rathnure - 1987
Eamonn Cleary, Rathgarogue/Cushinstown – 1989
Liam Dunne, Oulart/The Ballagh – 1990, 1993, 1996
Larry O'Gorman, Faythe Harriers – 1996
Adrian Fenlon, Rapparees – 1996
Rory McCarthy, St. Martin's – 1996
Martin Storey, Oulart/The Ballagh – 1996, 1998
Larry Murphy, Cloughbawn – 1996
Tom Dempsey, Buffers Alley – 1996
Damien Fitzhenry, Duffry Rovers – 1997, 2004
Darragh Ryan, St. Anne's, Rathangan – 2001
All Time All Star Winners – Bobby and Billy Rackard, Rathnure – 1992.

FOOTBALL ALL STAR AWARD

Matty Forde, Kilanerin; was selected as Gaelic Players Association Player of the Year in 2004.
Opel Gaelic Players' Assoc. Football Team of the year Anthony Masterson, Castletown, goalkeeper – 2008.

ATHLETICS

Wexford Amateur Athletics Ireland was founded in 2002 when BLE and NACA amalgamated as AAI. Athletics in Wexford is administered by a Board of elected volunteer members who work in tandem with the affiliated clubs in the county. The Board has responsibility for the promotion of athletics at juvenile, junior, senior and masters levels.

There are 16 clubs in the county, with over 1000 active members in a very vibrant sport, which is serviced by a dedicated group of volunteer coaches and mentors all over the county. The Wexford clubs are Adamstown, Bree, Craanford Harriers, Croaghan AC, DMP, Enniscorthy AC, Kilmore, Macamores, Menapians, St. Anne's (Rathangan), St. Killians (Crossabeg, Ballymurn, Oylegate); St. Paul's (Kilrane); Slaney Olympic, Sliabh Buidh Rovers (Ferns); Taghmon, United Striders (New Ross).

Athletics in the county has a long and distinguished history over many years, much of it recorded by Jim Parle, Drinagh, Wexford in his book *Our Sporting Past*. Jim received a special award from Wexford County Board in recognition of his contribution from County Board chairman, Paddy Morgan.

Jimmy McDonald (race walking) and Andy Ronan (marathon), both from New Ross, have represented Wexford in athletics at the Olympic Games, and over the years people like Bill Esmonde, Toddy Moore, Denny Kehoe, Noel Hendrick, Kevin Cogley, Antoinette Furlong, Brendan O'Shea, Bronagh Furlong, Paul Crowe, Niall Shiel, Malachy Sheridan, Marie Walshe, Brenda Thompson, Norman Stephenson, Jim Stafford David Barron and Tommie McElwaine have performed with distinction. In past times John Mangan and Michael Crean were internationally recognised for their ability in field events.

David Hynes from Menapians was the only senior track and field winner in 2013, winning the 100 metres, but there was quite a lot of success at the various under-age levels.

2013 was a good year for the ladies' section in the National League. The team made up of seniors and juveniles all over the age of 16 won Division 1 of National league and will now compete in Premier League. They came from behind to take the title in the last race of the day, the 4x400 relay. The team performed well with Bronagh Furlong outstanding. She must be regarded as a top candidate for the Olympics in Rio in 2016

Only one Wexford man has been National President. Mick McKeown though born in Dublin was a member of DMP and based in Wexford town when he became president. Three Wexford men have held the position of Leinster chairman. The first was Bill Esmonde and then Toddy Moore served for three years. Recently Nicky Cowman also held that position and Nicky in 2013 is the only Wexford man serving on a national committee.

Athletics in Wexford have been hampered by the lack of good training facilities. Until recently most clubs depended on the local GAA club none of whom were in a postion to offer throwing circles, safety cages and an accurately marked 400m track. The good news is that an international standard 400m tartan track is being built in Enniscorthy.

The Athletes of the Year were presented with their awards in February 2013. The overall athlete of the year and winner of the Wexford Creamery Cup was Orla Furney of Menapians (and formerly of Gorey AC) who had a string of successes to her name, with her speciality being over hurdles.

Other Awards: U17 - The Harry Keyes Perpetual Cup for boys was won by Ciaran Joyce of Enniscorthy AC; the Ann O'Keeffe Cup for girls went to Saoirse Burke from Kilmore AC.

The senior track and field club of the year was DMP, and the Bro. Egan Cup was accepted by chairman, Michael Farrell; the Jim Redmond Memorial Cup for cross country club of the year was won by Sliabh Buidhe Rovers, Ferns, and was accepted by Tommy McElwaine and Paul Gibbons, from long-serving athletics legend, Toddy Moore.

The Kehoe Food Award for outstanding service to athletics in Wexford went to Jane (chairperson) and Graham (secretary) Porter of Slaney Olympic. They received their award from County chairman, Paddy Morgan, and County secretary, Nora Muldoon.

The Athletics Wexford County Board for 2013: chairman, Paddy Morgan, Kilmore; vice chairman, Emmett Malone, United Striders; secretary, Nora Muldoon, Adamstown; track and field secretary, Helena Hore, Taghmon; cross country/ road secretary, John Moore, Kilmore; treasurer, Eamonn Owens, St. Paul's; PRO, Marie Louise Byrne, Adamstown; assistant PRO, Jenny Higgins, St. Paul's; development officer, John Joe Doyle, DMP; County delegates to Leinster, Pat O'Leary (Bree) and Jim Corcoran (Bree).

Development Committee : Paddy Morgan, Kilmore; John Joe Doyle, DMP; Jim Corcoran, Bree; Marie Mooney, Adamstown; Eamonn Owens, St. Paul's; Nicky Cowman, St. Killians; Helena Hore, Taghmon; Emmett Malone, United Striders.

County Child Protection Officer, Eilish Culleton.

A Development Squad has been selected to keep the name of Wexford athletics to the fore – these 32 young athletes each had to achieve specified high performance levels to qualify for the squad; they are the hope of the future and will be given every possible assistance to progress. Members of the squad picked on 2013 performances in a variety of disciplines are:

BOYS - U15: Ryan Carthy Walsh, Adamstown; Sam O'Neill, David McDonald and David Murray, all Menapians. **U 17:** Ryan Murray, Bree; Mark O'Connor and Tim Bowler, James Fortune, all Enniscorthy AC; Peter O'Shea, DMP; Chris Vickery, Kevin MacRedmond, Ian Bennett, Mikey Cullen, all Menapians. **U19:** Colin Nolan, Ciaran Joyce, both EAC; Shaun Donohoe , Menapians.

GIRLS - U15: Aoife Rochford, Bree; Kathlyn Furlong, DMP; Shannon Wall, Adamstown. **U17:** Chloe Whelan, Aoife Fanning, Aideen Kane and Sophie McCabe, Bree; Mairead Fortune, Enniscorthy AC; Annie Stafford and Jane Shovlin, Menapians; Eimear O'Doherty and Eimear Gilhooley, DMP. **U19:** Niamh Cloke Rochford, Bree; Saoirse Burke, Kilmore; Hannah Mahon, EAC; Orla Furney, Menapians.

GAELIC GAMES

Officers of Wexford County GAA Board for 2013 are: chairman, Diarmuid Devereux (St. Patrick's, Ballyoughter); vice-chairman, Micheal Martin (St. John's Volunteers, Wexford); secretary, Margaret Doyle (St. Mary's Rosslare); assistant secretary, Mary Foley (Buffers Alley); treasurer, Andrew Nolan (Sarsfields); PRO, Rory Murphy (HWH-Bunclody); development officer, Ger Carthy (Our Lady's Island); Central Council Rep, Paddy Wickham (Davidstown-Courtnacuddy); Leinster Council

Reps, Joe O'Shaughnessy (Castletown-Liam Mellowes) and Derek Kent (Taghmon Camross); Childrens' officer, Dermot Howlin; Oifigeach na Gaeilge (Irish officer), Breda Jacob (Oulart-The Ballagh); coaching officer, Des O'Neill; management committee, Brian Foley; Coiste na nÓg (Juvenile Board) chairman, Bobby Goff; secretary, Marion Doyle; and PRO, P.J. Howlin.

Wexford GAA Supporters Club Committee: chairman, Arthur Quinn; secretary, Tom Boland; assistant secretary, Una Bird; treasurer, Larry Ryan; P.R.O., Maria Nolan; Bill Mernagh, Racing Committee; Denis Nolan, membership; Breda Curran, Ladies' Football; Rose Breen, camogie; Des Croke, golf committee; Ben Bernie, Club Wexford.

New Ross District Committee officers: president, John Hearn, Horeswood; chairman, Michael Bowe, Geraldine O'Hanrahans; vice-chairman, John McCormack, Gusserane; secretary, John Hanton, St. Mogues, Fethard; treasurer, Michael Wallace, Bannow-Ballymitty; assistant treasurer, Pat Walsh, St. James; P.R.O., Jimmy McDonald, Adamstown.

Enniscorthy District officers: president: John Curtis (Ballyhogue); vice presidents-Willie Kelly, Jim Bolger, Peter Sutton, Johnny Ryan; chairman, Seamus Whelan; vice-chairman, Tom Boland; secretary, Paddy Sullivan; treasurer, John Alcock; Irish officer, Tomás O Shea; PRO, Paddy Wickham.

Wexford District officers: president, Sean Pettit (Our Lady's Island); chairperson, Mary Whelan (St Brigid's, Blackwater); vice-chairman, Dave Ormonde (Clonard); secretary, Joe Sheehan (Clonard); treasurer, James Flood (St. Mary's Maudlintown); PRO, Tony Furlong (Kilmore); Oifigeach na Gaeilge, Michil O'Máirtín.

Gorey District Committee officers: presidents, Mons. Lory Kehoe, Dominic Murphy, Michael Murray; chairman, Jack O'Brien (Buffers Alley); secretary, Michael Maguire.

SOCCER

Soccer is one of the most widely played sports in Wexford. It is true to say it is a participation sport rather than a spectator one, but over 7,000 players line out every weekend all over the county in over 500 teams from the start of September until May. Currently there are one hundred men's teams competing in the league as well as 38 youths (U18) teams. The schoolboys' league has over 230 teams, while the ladies'/schoolgirls' league has another 144 teams this season.

How the Wexford League came into being:

At a meeting in early October 1959 in the Railway Hotel in Enniscorthy, plans were discussed for the running of a Wexford and District Junior Soccer League. Representatives from the five clubs present at the meeting were appointed as organisers - Raymond Spencer, Ballymoney; Aidan Grannell, PJ Kenny, John Doran and Seamus Kirwan.

The League was formally formed at a meeting held on October 19th, again in the Railway Hotel, Enniscorthy. The first committee elected was: chairman, P J Kenny (Enniscorthy); vice chairman, Aidan Grannell (Gorey); Hon. Secretary, Seamus Kirwan (St. Cormac's, Boolavogue); Hon. Treasurer, James Holden (St. Cormac's). Committee; Nickey Delaney, John Doran (both St. John's, Wexford), Pat McCann (Enniscorthy), Albert Spencer (Ballymoney), Pat Treacy and Ned Ellis (both Ferns). Affiliation fees of ten shillings were agreed.

There many difficulties in getting the league established as Wexford was still very much a GAA county, and very much in awe of the performances of the great hurling team of the 1950s which was still going strong and would win the All-Ireland again in 1960.

Like most fledgling organisations, there were some teething problems, but the League has steadily grown and the number of divisions inceased to cater for the additional teams. The current Premier Division was introduced in the season 1983/84.

The first Oscar Traynor (inter-league) team was entered in the 1971/72 season, with the late P. J. Leacy (Enniscorthy Town) as team manager, and Liam Brennan (Nawrik Rangers) assistant manager, and Wexford have pitted their teams against the best in the land ever since.

John Godkin of North End in Wexford Town was the manager of the Oscar Traynor team in 2010, when Wexford finally broke their duck in the premier competition in Irish Junior football with a comprehensive 6-0 win over Clare in the final played at Ennis. The Wexford team that day was: Lee Walker, Lee Chin, Thomas "Ducker" Hawkins, Gareth Larkin, Graham "Dax" Howlin,

Eugene O Brien, Sean "Eggy" Culleton, Leighton Gleeson, Kyle Dempsey, Mikey Grangel, Paul Murphy.

Subs used: Ricky Fox, Tom Elmes, and David Purcell.

Wexford team captain Leighton Gleeson of Courtown Hibs hit a fantastic hat trick in that game, and has represented Ireland at Amateur International level on several occasions, being a member of the Irish squad that lost out 2-1 to the Portuguese team in the UEFA Regions Cup Final in 2011, played in Braga, Portugal.

Mikey Grangel and John Paul Phelan of New Ross Celtic, brothers Jason and Paul Murphy of North End, Eugene O Brien of Courtown Hibs and Chris Kenny of Shamrock Rovers have also won International "caps" for their country which is a reflection of the level of talent within the Wexford League.

New Ross Celtic made history in 1983 by being the first team from Wexford to lift the Leinster Junior cup beating Dingle Utd 1-0 in the final played in Tolka Park, Dublin. Pat Ronan was the unassuming manager of that Celtic side, which was very dominant locally at the time, and he led a different set of players to the final of the FAI Junior in Cup in 1994 but they lost out this time to Clonmel Town.

THE PEOPLE CURRENTLY ADMINISTRATING SOCCER IN WEXFORD ARE:

WEXFORD AND DISTRICT JUNIOR FOOTBALL LEAGUE: chairman. Tom Connor, Garden City, Gorey; vice- chairman: Michael Larkin, Beech Park, Enniscorthy; secretary: Gertrude Rowlands, Mill Road, Bunclody; treasurer: Sean Parker, Abbey View, Campile; Administration: Pat Whitty, Heath Park, Newbawn; registrar: Willie Dempsey, St Itas Terrace, Wexford; Divisional Secretaries - Premier Division and Division 2:

Denis Hennessy, Ballyorrill, Enniscorthy; Division 1 and 2A: Pat Fortune,Mount Alexander, Courtown; Division 3 and 3A: Danny Kearney, 6 Hospital Lane, Enniscorthy; Division 4: John O Rourke, Ross Road, Enniscorthy; Division 4A: Gertrude Rowlands, Mill Road, Bunclody; Division 5: Pat Loftus,Ford of Lyng, Rosslare Strand; Youths: Michael Larkin, 15 Beechpark, Enniscorthy.

WEXFORD AND DISTRICT SCHOOLBOYS LEAGUE COMMITTEE:

Chairman: P.J. Murphy, Ballysekin, Kilmore; V. chairman: Ger Feeney, Willow Park, New Ross; secretary: Thomas Cowman, Askinvillar, Kiltealy, Enniscorthy; Hon. treasurer: Michael Carthy, King Street, Wexford; registrar: Willie Cottrell, Abbey View, Campile; PRO: Ian Lawlor, Mullinagower, Castlebridge;

Fxtures secretaries: U9, U11, U13 and U15 - Brendan Corish, Clonard Park, Wexford; U10, U12, U14 and U16 - Anthony Redmond, Prospect Green, Mount Prospect, Wexford. Committee - Anne Marie O'Neill, Clonhaston, Enniscorthy; Richard Busher, Ard Uisce, Wexford; Tricia Casey, Coolamaine, Oylegate; Robbie Moore, Prospect, Ballymoney, Gorey.

WEXFORD AND DISTRICT WOMENS AND SCHOOLGIRLS LEAGUES:

chairman, Daire Doyle; vice-chairman, Barry Dempsey; Hon. secretary, Martin Cahill; Hon treasurer, Ashling Kavanagh; administrator, Peter Doyle; committee – Áine Murphy, Adrian Kehoe, Tom 'Flash' Dunne, Sarah Merrigan, Elayne Grant, who is in charge of the League Training Centre; Wexford Youth Women AFC, Adrian Kehoe.

Wexford Youths' Football Club competes in the Airtricity League First Division. The club joined the league after being awarded a First Division licence for the 2007 season. The club alternate their colours between plain black and pink and black. Wexford Youths were founded by developer and TD Mick Wallace, who funded the construction of Ferrycarrig Park, a state-of-the-art complex for the new team at Crossabeg, near Wexford Town. Wallace managed the senior side for the first three seasons, as well as the U21s, U18s and U16s. Before the start of the 2010 season former Limerick FC manager and Wexford Youths assistant manager Noel O'Connor took the reins as manager of the senior squad. Current manager is Shane Keegan and club chairman is Dave Dempsey. They finished 4th in the First Division in the 2012-2013 season. Danny Furlong is the leading goalscorer for Youths, with 52 from 117 appearances.

The club also fields a team in the National Womens League and has made a good impact. Their National League squads successful season was recognised when the team of the season was announced last week with three players named on the eleven. Goalkeeper Mary Rose Kelly rounded off a great season by being named as the leagues best keeper; Lauren Dwyer was honoured at centre back and Rianna Jarrett was named as a forward, as well as being selected as the Young Player of the year. Mary Rose had won a GAA ladies' football All Star in the past. All three were presented with their awards at a dinner in the Aviva Stadium

CLUB OFFICIALS:

Chairman, Dave Dempsey; vice chairman, Ray Noonan; club secretary, Peter Crimmings; general manager, Seanie O'Shea; technical staff - Des Clarke, Paddy Carey, Peter Blanchfield; medical officer, James Phelan; club doctor, Ravi Kumar; Club Physio, Nigel Fitzharris.

RUGBY

There are four rugby clubs in Co. Wexford, situated in the main towns and they provide excellent facilities, games, training and coaching for their many members, from very young to adult. A popular new addition in the past decade has been the introduction of rugby for girls and women's teams.

Wexford Wanderers, located at Park Lane, on the Enniscorthy side of Wexford town, was founded in 1924. Officers 2013: president, Debbie Carty; chairman, Declan Rossiter; sec., Eamonn McCarthy; treasurer, John Fagan; director of rugby, John Hickey; PRO, Dermot Graham; youth co-ordinator, Ciaran Kavanagh; child welfare officer, Helen White; groundsman, Billy Morris.

Enniscorthy Rugby Club, based at Ross Road, was founded in 1912. Officers 2013: president, James McCauley; captain, Sean Wall; chairman, Rory Fanning; secretary, Annette Wall; treasurer, Rob Ryan; fixtures secretary, Liam Walsh; PRO, Liam Spratt; club coach, Damien McCabe; child welfare, Evelyn Owens; grounds, Peter Perkins.

New Ross Rugby Club is based at Southknock, was estsblished in 1970. Officers 2013: president, Des Moloney; chairman, Peter O'Brien; club captain, Paddy Delaney; ladies captain, Becky Ryan; director of rugby, Nicky Haberlin; club coach, Jared Dunbar; your co-ordinator, Maurice Quirke; membership secretary, David Burke; fixtures secretary, Bob Doyle.

Gorey Rugby Football Club, located at Clonattin, first formed in 1945. Officers secretary/past president, David French; president elect/media and marketing, Dave O'Neill; treasurer, Martin Savage; club captain, Matt Bater; Finance, Tommy Kidd; PRO, Robert Tubritt; grounds, Ben Furney; bar, John O'Loughlin; house, Denise Walsh.

HANDBALL

Handball is one of the most ancient of all Irish games, and there has always been a strong tradition in the sport in Co. Wexford. It has changed dramatically in more recent times, with roofed alleys and the introduction of the smaller 40x20 American style court. The proliferation of juvenile and veteran grades over the years has dramatically increased the number of participants.

The game in Ireland as a whole reached a whole new level in 2013 with the staging of the World Championships in a specially built 21-court complex at the Citywest hotel in Dublin. The figures from this event make the case for handball most eloquently.

2084 players from a total of 27 countries around the world took part; 3,286 matches in total were played – over 100 players from Wexford took part and four titles came back to the county, thanks to Ned Buggy, his son Gavin, Tommy Hynes and Daniel Kavanagh, all Wexford town. (see separate piece on the Buggy family).

Hynes joined with the legendary Michael Ducksie Walsh of Kilkenny to win the Masters A Doubles while Daniel Kavanagh (St.Joseph's, Wexford) who was introduced to the game of handball by Seamus Buggy when the new courts in St.Joseph's were opened in 2007, won the boys 13 and under World doubles title, partnered by Tadhg O'Neill (Cork). Daniel also reached the singles final and only lost out after a brilliant game to Cashel's Colin Ryan, in a field where close on 100 players started out.

The County Board officers looking after the growth and development of handball in Wexford are: president, Ger McWilliams; chairman, Alan O'Neill; vice chairman, JR Finn; secretary, Tony Breen; treasurer, Virginia Hanrahan; PRO, Noel Holohan; coaching, Gavin Buggy; development, Fergal McWilliams; facilities, John Roche.

Wexford can lay claim to having produced one of the all-time greats of the game in John 'Bull' Ryan of Bridgetown, ably assisted by his doubles' partner, John Doyle of Trinity. John Ryan was considered a genius in the handball court, able to display the full range of intuitive, brilliant shots. At that time the big finals were contested over the best of 5, or even 7, games and were major feats of endurance. Ryan could be volatile at times, and great credit is given to John Doyle for the role he played – perhaps less flamboyant but the epitome of quiet steadiness. Doyle's first big impact was when he won the Irish junior hard doubles with his brother, Peter, in 1949 and he was still playing in 1969 when he won a Masters' (veterans') doubles title with John Quigley Snr. of Taghmon.

Ryan won a total of 18 Irish senior titles in the 1950s, his greatest achievement coming in 1957 when he completed a very rare clean sweep of all four major titles – singles in softball and hardball, and both doubles with Doyle. In the 1950s Ryan won five senior softball and four hardball titles. The doubles' victories with John Doyle were hardball in '52, and then five in a row from 1954, and just that one softball in 1957. He also won three Gael Linn senior singles. Ryan suffered a serious leg injury in 1958 that impaired his mobility and practically ended his career. He did attempt a comeback some years later and reached a softball doubles final with Dick Lyng in 1964, but they were beaten.

Dick Lyng of New Ross, playing out of the Ballyanne Club, also had a brilliant career, winning three senior softball singles, in 1965, '71 and '78; he won Ireland's first world senior title with Seamus Buggy in the doubles' in 1970; he also won five senior doubles titles with three different partners – Seamus Buggy of Wexford in 1970, '77 and '79; he won with Pat Murphy of Taghmon in 1975, and with Jimmy Goggins of Wexford in 1982. He also won four Gael Linn singles title in the 1970s.

Murphy became only the third Wexford player to win a senior singles' title when he took the softball in 1972, and apart from his win with Lyng, he took doubles titles with his clubmate, John Quigley of Taghmon in 1972 and '74. Murphy and Quigley, along with George Mullins and Michael Furlong, took the Irish senior club team title to Taghmon in 1970.

When the smaller 40x20 American court was introduced in 1975, the first impact was made for Wexford by John Fleming and Pat Cleary of Cloughbawn who took the senior doubles in 1982 and '83.

Other significant people in Wexford handball in those days included Jimmy King, Joe Howlin (Wexford), Sean O'Leary (Enniscorthy), Jim Sydney, Seamus McLoughlin (Taghmon). When ladies' handball was introduced in 1970, the game was embraced by the Coolgreany club in particular, with the Mythen girls, Majella, Anne, Mary and Bertilla all claiming Irish titles.

In more recent times, the likes of Tommy Hynes, Barry Goff, Colin Keeling and others have kept the Wexford handball flag flying high. Hynes and Keeling won the Irish senior doubles in 2000, and then Barry Goff crowned a comeback after a few years out of the game to combine with Keeling again to lift the title in 2011. The pairing were winners of the Team of the Year accolade at the GAA

Handball annual awards ceremony in Croke Park.

The likes of Tom Rossiter, Brian Murphy, Tony Breen, Noel Holohan and other tireless workers have contributed not just on the court but and also in the nurturing of the game.

THE BUGGYS: THREE WORLD CHAMPIONS IN ONE FAMILY

Not many Wexford families can claim to have produced three world champions, but that has been achieved by the Buggys from Wexford town. Seamus and Ned Buggy are sons of James Buggy of Jenkinstown, Kilkenny, and Bridget Hurley of Roanmore, Waterford, who came to Wexford and settled in The Faythe, and Gavin is Ned's son.

Seamus was first to take on the world when the championships were staged in Ireland for the first time in 1970, at the specially designed Croke Park alley. He joined with the brilliant Dick Lyng of Ballyanne, New Ross, to claim the doubles' title, beating Simie Féin and Ray Naveau from America.

And there could have been a fourth world champion in the Buggy family – Seamus and his brother Martin reached the Golden Masters' A world final in Broadford, Co Clare, in 1994 but they were beaten after a brave effort.

Ned lost the World Mens B singles final in Phoenix, Arizona, in 1991 to Paul Walsh (Clare) and lost Masters A doubles final at the same championships when playing with John Kirby (Clare). Ned concentrated more on his hurling for a while, but he re-engaged after his break and in 2012 he joined with Eugene Kennedy of Dublin to win the Diamond A Masters final.

Ned's son, Gavin, has two world titles to his name; he won the Waterford Crystal World Mens Over 35 A singles' title 2009 in Portland, Oregon, with a 21-3, 21-2 victory over local lad, Robert Herrera. In 2012, in City West, Dublin, he won the World Over 35 A Doubles' championship with Dominick Lynch (Kerry).

Ned Buggy (born 1948 in Wexford town) had made his name as a hurler in a previous career; he was a prolific scorer for Wexford, and was selected as an All-Star Award winner in 1979 at left full forward. A deadly accurate free-taker from any range, Buggy became the first Wexfordman since Nickey Rackard to top the national scoring charts in 1978 when he nabbed 10 goals-103 points (total of 133 points) in 18 games. He became the only man other than Eddie Keher of Kilkenny to score more than 100 points in a season and he was more than 60 points clear of Limerick's Joe McKenna in second place. Buggy retained first place in 1979 with 5-100 (115 points). He still retains 5th place in the overall Wexford scoring charts, with a total of 42-361 (487 points) in 104 appearances between 1967 and 1982. He is headed only by Nickey Rackard, Tony Doran, Jimmy Holohan and Padge Kehoe.

Buggy won an All-Ireland minor medal with Wexford in 1966; he was a sub on the senior winning side of 1968 and was on the side beaten by Cork in the 1969 U21 final. He has three Leinster senior medals and was on the teams beaten by Cork in the 1976 and 77 senior All-Ireland finals. He won Railway Cup medals with Leinster in 1977 and '79.

CAMOGIE

Camogie in Wexford has enjoyed two distinct golden eras, in the late 1960s and 1970s and from 2007 to the current time. There was always a small but loyal following for the game in the county but they lived in the shadow of Dublin for decades and employment took some of Wexford's best players to the capital where they lined out with Dublin clubs. The breakthrough was finally made with a first All-Ireland win in 1968, and the title was retained the following year. They knocked on the door for a few years and it opened again with a third All-Ireland senior win in 1975.

It was to be 32 years before success came again- the exploits of Buffers Alley and Rathnure on the club scene being the only major highlights in between. Then in the early 2000s, a powerful team was built up in Coláiste Bríde in Enniscorthy, with three All-Ireland colleges' titles being won. This group of girls was the engine-room of Wexford's second coming. Stellah Sinnott steered the county to an All-Ireland in 2007, and then JJ Doyle guided them to three in a row in 2010, 2011 and 2012, with an intermediate crown also being won by the second string in 2011.

The club scene in the county is dominated by Oulart-The Ballagh and they supply many players to the county panels, but clubs like St. Ibars/Shelmaliers, Rathnure and St. Martin's are certainly keeping the flag flying also. Despite some setbacks in 2013, camogie in Wexford is now in a good place with the women having been the main purple and gold flagbearers for the past decade.

The County Board officers guiding the game in the county are: president, Eileen O'Brien, Blackwater; chairperson, Rachel Hogan, Rathnure; vice-chair, Noel Ryan, Bunclody; secretary, Mary O'Reilly, Glynn; vice sec., Ailish Whitty, Rathgarogue-Cushinstown; treasurer, Rose Breen, Monageer/Boolavogue; registrar, Majella Doran, Oylegate-Glenbrien; child officer, Bridget Moran, Oulart/The Ballagh; PRO, Barbara Ryan, St. Martin's.

A CAMOGIE DYNASTY

Wexford have won just 7 All-Ireland senior camogie titles and one family has been involved with them all. We have a mother who was one of only two Wexford players to be picked on the Team of the Century in 2004, and her daughters who have both captained Wexford to All-Ireland senior success. Between them they have won 11 All-Ireland county senior medals and six senior club medals.

Margaret O'Leary-Leacy, Buffers Alley and Oulart, was selected on the camogie team of the century in 2004, and winner of All Ireland medals with Wexford in 1968, 1969 and 1975. She played for Buffers Alley Club with whom she won four All Ireland Club titles in the early 1980s championships, and she had already won one with Eoghan Ruadh in Dublin 15 years earlier in 1967. She was selected as the Gaelic Weekly All Star Camogie Player of the Year in 1968 and was twice voted Wexford Powers

"Sport Star of the Year" in 1966 and 1968. She later became Chair of the Oulart-The Ballagh club where she trained five Féile na nGael teams to All Ireland success. Her team of the century citation read "a player of remarkable all round ability ... she was capable of turning defence into attack with one puck of the sliotar. Highly motivated, determined and full of energy she inspired her teammates." Her daughters, Mary and Una, have played with great distinction for Wexford in recent years.

Mary Leacy, born 1987; won camogie All Star awards in 2004, 2007 and 2010. She plays with Oulart-The Ballagh and has been a member of the Wexford senior inter-county team since 2001. Leacy captained Wexford to the All-Ireland title in 2007 and won further All Irelands in 2010, '11 and '12. Won two national Feile titles and was captain in 1999; won Leinster and All-Ireland senior club with Oulart in 2011-12.

Leacy Una, born May 17, 1988: winner of camogie All-Star awards in 2007, '10 and '11; her two early goals in 2007 helped Wexford win their first All-Ireland senior camogie title in 32 years. She won further All Ireland medals in 2010 when she was captain, 2011 and 2012; five All-Ireland Féile na nGael in 1998-2002 (a national record); and winner of All-Ireland senior medals in Colleges with Coláiste Bríde in 2003, 2004, 2005; Won Leinster and All-Ireland senior club with Oulart in 2011-'12.

THE JACOBS - A FAMILY OF SPORTS STARS

The Jacob family from Oulart have a remarkable sporting pedigree in both hurling and camogie.

Mick Jacob born Oulart 1946, was Wexford's first hurling All Star in 1972, and he also won All Stars in 1976 and '77, all at centre back. He was an outstanding player for Wexford and Oulart for many years; played in goal in the county's only All-Ireland U21 win in 1965 and won three Leinster U21 titles, but did not win the senior medals his skill deserved. Played for Wexford from 1969 to 1984, won three Leinster and a National league title but no All-Ireland, and had also retired before Oulart began their title-winning ways. Has an insatiable interest in hurling and Oulart, and has managed and coached teams at all levels in the club.

Christy Jacob, brother of Mick, born Oulart 1944. Played for Wexford and Oulart. Was on the U21 winning side of 1965 with his brother, Mick. Played senior on and off from 1966 to 1973 and and won a senior All-Ireland medal when Wexford beat Tipperary in 1968. Also has a National League medal.

Robbie Jacob, oldest of the brothers, was a very accomplished hurler who had retired from the game before Oulart made their championship breakthrough. Was on the losing Oulart side in three County senior finals, to Rathnure (1974), Buffers Alley (1975 and 1982).

Michael Jacob, born Oulart 1980, son of Mick and Breda; educated locally, at Enniscorthy CBS and Waterford IT, where he won two Fitzgibbon Cup medals. Played senior for Wexford 2001 to 2012 when he retired from countylevel. Won Leinster senior medal in 2004 and U21 Leinster medal in 2001. Has been a key player on the Oulart team that has been the dominant force in Wexford club hurling for the past decade.

Rory Jacob, born Oulart, 1983, brother of Michael: has been a regular on Wexford senior teams since 2002; has won three Leinster medals, (one senior, two at U21), and is a key player on the |Oulart club teams that have dominated Wexford senior hurling in recent years.

Breda Jacob (née McClean), played with Wexford

in the All Ireland junior camogie final of 1972 against Galway and has been a tireless club and County Board officer for many years.

Ursula Jacob, born May 21st, 1985, in Oulart: winner of camogie All Star awards in 2010, 2011 and 2012, All-Ireland Senior medals in those years and in 2007. She was captain in 2011 and scored a dramatic 52nd minute goal which changed the course of the 2012 All Ireland final and secured victory for Wexford, rated by many as one of the best goals scored in Croke Park. With a total of 3-54 she was the highest scoring player in the 2011 senior championship. In the 2012 final, in which Wexford beat Cork, she scored an amazing 2-7. Won All-Ireland Senior Colleges with Coláiste Bríde 2003, 2004 (captain); Won Leinster and All-Ireland senior club with Oulart in 2011 -12.

Helena Jacob, sister of Ursula, was on the senior panels that won All-Ireland camogie titles of 2007 and 2010, won three successive National League medals from 2009; was in goal for the County interemdiate team that beat Antrim in the All-Ireland final, 2012, and has won Leinster medals at senior, U18 and U14. Has been a regular club player for Oulart in most of their successes.

Bridie Doran (nee Jacob), who married Bill Doran of the famous Buffers Alley family, won an All-Ireland senior camogie medal with Wexford in 1975 and was on the team beaten by Cork in the 1971 decider. She was on all the Buffers Alley teams that won seven successive Leinster club titles from 1978, and five All-Ireland senior club titles in the same period.

THE KEHOES OF CLONLEIGH, Palace, were a formidable sporting family. Seven sisters were camogie achievers – Kit, Brigid, Annie, Josie, Gretta, Eileen and Bernie – and in the 1970s they played a number of fund-raising seven-a-side games against other families. Kit (now Codd from Piercestown) set the ball rolling when winning two All-Irelands with Dublin in 1965 and 66. Brigid (now Doyle) was winner of the B+I Camogie Star of the Year award in its first year in 1975 and an All Ireland senior winner in 1968, 1969 (when she was captain) and 1975. Sister Josie (now Gahan, Monageer) was on the '68 and '69 teams, and Annie played in 1969 also.

When Wexford next won the title in 1975, Brigid and Kit were on board and the team was captained by another sister. Gretta, who played in the final the day after her wedding to Ray Quigley of Oylegate. The Kehoe girls naturally backboned the Cloughbawn teams of the time and the 1976 senior team fielded six of the sisters and a niece, Josephine, in a county final. Kit's daughter, Aine of St. Martin's, was an All-Star in 2004 and won an All-Ireland with Wexford in 2007, while Bernie's son is Irish soccer international, Kevin Doyle; another son, Padraig, has played with St. Fintan's in their successive Wexford junior and intermediate county football championship successes in 2012 and '13.

There were even more boys in the Kehoe family from Clonleigh and they hurled with Wexford and Cloughbawn.

THE FATHER MURPHY'S GAA CLUB IN LONDON

The headquarters of The Father Murphy's GAA Club is the Emerald grounds, former Queens Park Rangers training ground, in Ruislip in North London.

The members come mainly from the Harlesden, Willesden, Kingsbury and Kilburn areas of London and they meet in Maggies in Kensal Rise, NW10, near Willesden.

Officers 2013

President - Tommy Harrell. Life Presidents -Sean Diviney, Tom Ryan and Mick Butler; vice-Presidents- Phil Roche, Josie O'Leary , Jim Howlin, Tommy Harrell, Tom Ryan and Don Deasy ; chairman- Jim Howlin; vice-chairman- Tony Grace; secretary- David O'Donoghue; treasurer- Paddy Doyle; Public Relations Officer – Lucia Butler.

Officers and committee members of the club are from Wexford and London home-places as follows: Tommy Harrell, Horeswood; Lucia Butler, Clongeen; Sean Diviney, Carrickbyrne; Tom Ryan, Rathnure; Mick Butler, Rathnure; Dick Butler, Adamstown; Phil Roche, Whitechurch, Glynn; Sean Holohan, Kilkenny; Paul Slattery, Co Clare; Josie O'Leary, Castlebridge; Johnnie Furlong, Taghmon; P.J.Fortune, Enniscorthy; Paddy Doyle, Ballybawn, Rathnure; Jim Dunne, Kilkenny; Jim Howlin Snr., Rathnure; Tony Grace, Rathangan, David Donohoe, Curracloe; Breda Weller, London born; Mick Meegan, Co Monaghan; Ger Redmond, Enniscorthy; Tom Moore, Castlebridge, Sean Howlin, London-born and Jim Howlin Jnr., London-born.

Joan Kirwan , nee Canny of Wexford town whose husband was Martin Kirwan (RIP), Ballinclay, former treasurer of Father Murphy's, youth team for over 20 years. Joan washed the kit for the youth team for many years. Don Deasy's wife Joan, is sister of the late and popular Seamus Keevans of Wexford.

THE INCREDIBLE FITZHENRY FAMILY

The Fitzhenry Family of Curraduff, Kiltealy, has made a remarkable contribution to the GAA in Wexford, and especially to their local Duffry Rovers Club and this was recognised in 2012 when they were presented with the Dermot Earley Family Award by GAA President Christy Cooney at a special ceremony in Croke Park.

Mark and Nancy Fitzhenry produced a family of 15, ten boys and five girls. The ten sons are MJ, Tom, Seamus, John, Martin, Ger, Noel, Paddy, Fran and Damien and all have played for the Rovers. The five girls are Bride, Kathy, Ann, Tina and Mary.

Damien lined out in the county's hurling goal for nearly 20 years, from 1993 to 2010 and his 56 championship appearances for Wexford is a record that may never be beaten, with Padge Kehoe of the 1950s and 60s team in second place on 44. He won an All-Ireland medal in the win over Limerick in the 1996 hurling final and was selected as an All Star in 1997 and 2004 and in 2007 he received a Players Association All-Star, voted on by the county players from all over the country. He has three Leinster senior medals He was one of the first goalkeepers to move up the field to take the close in frees, which he did with great success.

Seamus is recognised as one of the best dual players Wexford has seen, and he played 88 times for the county senior footballers, and 33 times for the hurlers. He is a regular analyst of football games on South East Radio. Martin has also played for both county sides. John, Noel and Paddy have all played senior championship football for Wexford. The boys have also represented their county at various other levels.

Tina has played camogie for Wexford at the very highest level, being on the losing team in two All-Ireland finals. She and her sisters, Mary and Ann, have lined out for Duffry Rovers in Wexford competitions.

It is with Duffry Rovers that the Fitzhenry's have carved out a special niche – the club won seven Wexford senior football titles in succession from 1986, a unique achievement; they lost out in 1993 but were back to capture their 8th title in 1994. Between them, the Fitzhenry's have over 50 Wexford senior football medals.

Seamus and Noel were on the starting 15 for all eight finals, while Ger (7), John (6), Paddy, Fran, Martin and Damien all played big roles too. Eight of the brothers lined up in the 1989 victory over Glynn-Barntown.

Nearly all the family members have been involved with the Duffry Rovers Club in various capacities, as officers and team mentors.

WEXFORD LADIES' GAELIC FOOTBALL

Ladies' Gaelic football was first set up in Wexford on an organised basis in 1979 with the first County Board was formed in May at a meeting presided over by Seamus Keevans. The first County Board elected was: Chairman, John Hanton (Fethard); Vice-Chairman, Larry Fitzharris (Gusserane); Secretary, Bridget O'Dwyer (Old Ross); Assistant Secretary, Mena Murphy (Old Ross); Treasurer, Statia O'Dwyer (Gusserane). There were eight clubs affiliated in that first year - Gusserane, Wexford Town, Forth Celtic, Old Ross, Ballyhogue, Fethard , Cloughbawn / Adamstown and Horeswood.

The game has grown steadily and in 2013 there are 36 clubs affiliated fielding 168 teams between them. There was also healthy competitions in Post Primary schools (junior and senior) and a Rackard league competition in the National Schools. There are almost 5,000 girls and ladies playing football in Wexford.

All Irelands won: in ladies' Gaelic football Wexford have won four All Ireland minor titles, three U16, and one U14. They were beaten in All Ireland senior finals in 1983, 1986 and 1989. They also contested junior finals in 1986 and 1987 and intermediate finals in 1999 and 2007. They were bearten by Offaly in the 2013 All-Ireland junior final at Croke Park. There have been three victories in the senior All Ireland Club Championship, Adamstown in 1988 and Shelmaliers in 1996 and 1999.

Wexford Ladies Football Board officers for 2013:

President, John Hanton, Fethard club; Gurtins, Saltmills, New Ross.

Chairperson and PRO: Peadar O'Connor, Crossabeg Ballymurn club; Oaklawn, Kyle, Crossabeg Co. Wexford.

Vice chairperson: Tony Cardiff, Kilmore club, Mulrankin Castle, Bridgetown, Co.Wexford.

Secretary: Andrea Cooney, Horeswood club; Grange, Campile, New Ross.

Assist. Secretary: Nicola Rochford, Ballyhogue club; Carrigunane, Clonroche.

Treasurer: Billy Stafford, St. Anne's club; Upper House, Baldwinstown, Bridgetown.

Assistant Treasurer: Michael Power, Clonard club; St George Guesthouse, Upper Georges St. Wexford.

Registrar: Karen Scallan, Adamstown club; Scullabogue, Foulksmills Co. Wexford.

Fixtures Chairperson: Sharon Drennan, Shelmalier club; Ballyhoe Lower, Screen, Co. Wexford.

Adult Fixtures Secretary: Ann Doyle, Crossabeg Ballymurn club; Development Officer: Thomas Whelan, Fethard club; Newtown, Fethard-on-Sea.

Ladies' Football All Stars

Wexford winners of Ladies' Gaelic Football All Star Awards are:

Siobhan Dunne (Shelmaliers)1987, 1989.

Christine Byrne (Clongeen) 1984.

Assumpta Cullen (Shelmaliers) 1999.

Edel Cullen (Shelmaliers) 1985.

Teresa Furlong (Shelmaliers) 1989.

Christine Harding (Shelmaliers), 1986.

Angie Hearne (Shelmaliers) 1986, 1989.
Jacinta Kehoe (Cloughbawn) 1983.
Mary Rose Kelly (St. Fintan's) 2007
Mary Moore (Adamstown) 1986, 1987, 1988, 1989.
Kathleen Moore (Adamstown) 1987, 1989.
Catherine Murphy (Cloughbawn) 1986.
Mary O'Gorman (Taghmon) 1993.
Mary Rice (Shelmaliers) 1985.
Leona Tector (Shelmaliers) 2005.
Anne Whelan Clongeen 1984.
Marie Thorpe (Shelmaliers) 1986.
Ann White (Kilmore) 1986.

HORSES

There is an enormous interest in all aspects of horse sports and breeding in Co. Wexford. The county boasts two of the world's leading racing trainers in Aidan O'Brien and Jim Bolger, there are over forty other trainers located in the county and many people from Wexford have done well as breeders, trainers and riders in Britain as well as here at home.

If you add in the thriving showjumping, pony club and gymkhana scene, which is served by a number of top class arenas in the county, hunts, riding schools, livery facilities, the horse industry has a very significant role in the economy and employment in the county.

List of Registered Wexford Racehorse Trainers:

Berry, John A, racehorse trainer, Ballyroe, Blackwater, Co. Wexford, flat and jumps.
Black, Anthony John, racehorse trainer, Ballinapark, Bunclody, Co. Wexford, Nat. Hunt.
Bowe, Colin, racehorse trainer, Kiltealy, Enniscorthy; Nat. Hunt;
Brennan, John Paul, racehorse trainer, Monasootha, Camolin, Co. Wexford; jumps, mainly point to point;
Byrne, Liam, racehorse trainer, Rathturtin, Clonroche, Enniscorthy, Co. Wexford.
Codd, John A, racehorse trainer, Clearystown House, Clearistown, Co. Wexford.; Nat. Hunt.
Codd, William F, racehorse trainer, Churchlands, Mayglass, Co. Wexford; Nat. Hunt.
Colfer, M J, racehorse trainer, The Leap, Adamstown, Co. Wexford.
Cousins, James, racehorse trainer, Ballyharty, Kilmore, Co. Wexford, jumps permit holder.
Cullen, Michael, racehorse trainer, Whitemoor, New Ross, Co. Wexford, jumps.
Day, Dermot, racehorse trainer, Moortown, Ballycogley, Co. Wexford, jumps.
Day, Patrick, racehorse trainer, Randlestown, Bridgetown, Co. Wexford, jumps.
Deacon, D, racehorse trainer, Belmont, Clonroche, Enniscorthy, jumps.

Bree Hunt at The Reisk, Killurin.

Devereux, James, racehorse trainer, Rostoonstown, Broadway, Co. Wexford; jumps.

Doran, Martina Anne, racehorse trainer, Ballyfrory, Duncormick, Co. Wexford; flat and jumps; gallops facilities.

Farrell, C W J, racehorse trainer, Ballypreacus, Bunclody, Co. Wexford- flat, jumps; gallops and schooling facilities.

Hickey, Denis, racehorse trainer, Garryrichard Stud, Foulksmills, Co. Wexford; jumps permit holder.

James, Thomas, racehorse trainer, Norrismount, Camolin, Co. Wexford; jumps.

Jordan, Brian, racehorse trainer, Rathangan, Duncormick, Co. Wexford; permit holder.

Kavanagh, F., racehorse trainer, Ballindaggin, Enniscorthy, Co. Wexford, Ireland; jumps.

Kenny, Liam, racehorse trainer, Ballydarragh, Craanford, Gorey; permit holder.

Lambert, Miss A. M., racehorse trainer, Grange, Killinick, Co. Wexford; jumps, permit holder.

Larkin, Seamus, racehorse trainer, The Kyle, Gusserane, New Ross; jumps, permit holder.

Martin, W J, racehorse trainer, Greenmount, Clonhaston, Enniscorthy; flat.

McCabe, Moses, racehorse trainer, Rathsilla, Adamstown, Co. Wexford; married to Queenie; jumps.

Murphy, Denis Paul, racehorse trainer, Ballyboy Stables, The Ballagh, Enniscorthy; jumps.

Murphy, Miss Bernadette A K , racehorse trainer, Ballinagore, Blackwater, Co. Wexford; jumps, permit holder.

Neville, Seamus, racehorse trainer, Brideswell, Bridgetown, Co. Wexford; flat, jumps.

O'Keeffe, R. P., racehorse trainer, Newtown, Taghmon, Co. Wexford; jumps.

Osborne, Sean, racehorse trainer, Park Lodge, Clonegal, Enniscorthy; jumps.

Pierce, Paul Martin, racehorse trainer, Blackhall, Killurin, Enniscorthy; jumps, permit holder.

Redmond, Philip, racehorse trainer, Torduff House, Ballygarrett, Gorey; jumps, permit holder.

Sheehy, Mrs Helen, racehorse trainer, Barnland Stables, Gorey; jumps, permit holder.

Sinnott, Patrick, racehorse trainer, Aughnaclappa, Caim, Enniscorthy; jumps.

Slevin, S., racehorse trainer, Kiltrea, Enniscorthy; jumps.

Sunderland, M. P., Kilcorral House, Castlebridge, Co. Wexford; flat and jumps.

Whitmore, Leonard, racehorse trainer, Inch, Blackwater, Co. Wexford; jumps.

GOLF

Golf is an important sport in Co. Wexford, with a number of top class clubs and courses dotted around the county, some of them very long established.

Teams from the Wexford clubs compete with some success in the various All-Ireland inter-club competitions. The county has produced some outstanding golfers, with Martin O'Brien and Mary Dowling from New Ross, and Elaine Dowdall and Ashling O'Leary from Wexford making a national impact.

WEXFORD GOLF CLUBS

Bunclody Golf Club, Carrigduff, Bunclody

Courtown Golf Club, Kiltennel, Gorey. Officers for 2013: captain, Karl Caulfield; President, Brendan Sheehan; lady captain, Barbara Long; lady president, Anne Targett; Junior Captain, Shannon Quinlan.

Enniscorthy Golf Club, Knockmarshall, Enniscorthy. Club officers 2013: captains -Martin Dempsey and Joan Dunbar; Junior captain, Michael O'Toole; Presidents – Jim Delaney and Stella Byrne.

New Ross Golf Club, Tinneranny. Officers for 2013: Presidents , Brian Dolan / Ann Conway; Captains, Seamus McGuinness / Ger Donohoe.

Rosslare Golf Club, Rosslare. Officers for 2013: Gents - president, Terry Fortune; captain, Len Fowler; ladies: president, Mary A. Doyle; captain, Moira Fortune; gents junior captain - Matthew Homan; Ladies Jun. Captain - Anna Gouldson.

Seafield Golf and Country Club, Ballymoney, Gorey.

St. Helen's Bay Golf Resort, Kilrane, Rosslare Harbour. Officers for 2013: captain, Maurice Cooper, ladies' captain, Peigi O Ruairc.

Tara Glen Golf and Country Club Ballymoney, Gorey.

Tuskar Rock Golf Club, Kilrane, Rosslare Harbour.

Wexford Golf Club, Mulgannon, Wexford town.

Officers for 2013: gents, president: Pat Geoghegan; captain, Paul Lauhoff; ladies' president elected was late Eleanor Conway; captain: Martina Dempsey.

COMMUNITY GAMES

Community Games has been one of the phenomenal success stories of Irish sport in past 50 years. Based on the parish or community principle rather than clubs, and covering almost every sporting discipline as well as entertainment, choirs, art, chess, draughts, etc, the Games became Ireland's Mini Olympics and provided an outlet for thousands of young people and their adult mentors who might not otherwise have become involved..

Wexford Community Games was founded in late 1969/70 by Bill Esmonde of Piercestown with the assistance of Toddy Moore, Kilmore, Peter Byrne, Bree and Jim French, Wexford. In 1970 four Areas competed in the athletics finals in the Billy Morton Stadium. Within 10 years, Community Games had grown to 27 Areas in the county.

NICKEY RACKARD, ICONIC LEADER OF WEXFORD'S GOLDEN HURLING ERA

By Phil Murphy

Nickey Rackard, born April 28, 1922; died April 10, 1976; married to Ailish; they had three children Marion, Berna and Bobby.

Nickey Rackard was a hurling colossus and inspirational motivator who is credited with doing most to lift Wexford hurling from one of its leanest periods to become the most powerful and charismatic team in the land during the 1950s.

Commentator Micheál Ó Muircheartaigh in his autobiography selected that Wexford team as the best of all time. This team gave a new sense of pride, confidence, achievement and joy to the people of Wexford during tough economic and social times.

Nickey Rackard practised as a veterinary surgeon in the Bunclody area; horses and horse sports were a major interest for the Rackard family. He had a tough battle with alcoholism for many years until he eventually conquered those demons, finally giving up drinking in 1970. Sister Consilio of Cuan Mhuire Rehabilitation Centre wrote of him: 'He showed great determination and courage in arresting his disease and God alone knows the good that he did in the short span of life left to him afterwards'.

After the All-Ireland final defeat by Limerick in 1918, Wexford were to win just one senior championship match in the twenty years up to 1939; it is against this background that the role of Nickey Rackard must be considered.

He is accepted as the leader of the hurling revival in the county that only began to make serious progress in the 1940s. They reached their first All-Ireland final since 1918 in 1951 but suffered a disappointing defeat to Tipperary. Wexford lost to Cork in a great final in 1954, but in the next two years the breakthrough was finally made. They beat Galway in the 1955 final and Cork in a classic game in 1956.

Nickey was son of Bob Rackard of Killanne, Rathnure, ironically enough a cricket lover, and Anastasia Doran of Davidstown, whose brother John won an All-Ireland senior football medal with Wexford in 1918. Nickey was one of a family of nine – preceded by sisters Sally and Essie, followed by Jim, Bobby, John, Billy, Molly and Rita. He was educated at his local school and then went to St. Kieran's College, Kilkenny, a hurling nursery.

Rackard made his senior inter-county debut for Wexford in both hurling and football in 1942. He was also an ever-present on the Leinster Railway cup team from 1943 to 1957 and in 1946 and 1950 he was picked on both the provincial teams. Rackard was a very accomplished footballer and he was on the side that won the county's last Leinster senior title in 1945. His final game for Wexford was the Leinster hurling final in August, 1957, the team shipping a heavy defeat by Kilkenny.

His first senior title was in the Dublin hurling championship in 1943, with Young Ireland's. He won County senior hurling medals with Rathnure in 1948, 1950 and 1955 and senior football in 1952.

In hurling, Nickey won All-Ireland medals with Wexford in 1955 and 56, and Leinsters in those years and in 1951 and 54. One of the team's most famous wins was in the 1956 National league final when they came from fifteen points behind Tipperary at half time to snatch victory, partly as the result of a strong breeze, but mostly because of a hurling hurricane generated by Rackard in a rousing half time speech.

Nickey Rackard broke all scoring records from his full forward position during the 1950s, many of his scores coming from play but he was also known as 'The King of the Close-In Free'. In the 1954 championship he scored

7-7 against Antrim – still a record - and 5-4 against Dublin; in 1956 he scored 5-4 against Galway and 4-3 against Laois. He hurled for Wexford 101 times, scoring 152 goals, 213 points and is still the county's top marksman; in football he played 53 times for Wexford, scoring 14 goals, 26 points. He was selected at full forward on the 1984 Hurling Team of the Century and there was controversy when he was omitted from the team of the Millennium.

A life-size statue of Nickey Rackard was unveiled in Selskar Square, Wexford, in 2012. It was executed by Mark Richards and inscribed on the plinth are some words from the ballad Cúchulainn's Son, written by the late Tom Williams.

Nickey's brothers Bobby and Billy, were also an integral part of the Wexford hurling team of the 1950s and early 60s, while a fourth brother, Jim, lined out in goal with the three of them in the 1951 Leinster final victory over Laois.

Recommended further reading: *Cúchulainn's Son, The Story of Nickey Rackard*, by Tom Williams.

Nickey Rackard in Selskar.

Ronan, Frank, born New Ross 1963. His first novel, *The Man Who Loved Evelyn Cotton* received the *Irish Times*/Aer Lingus Irish Literature Prize. His subsequent novels include: *A Picnic in Eden, The Better Angel, Lovely* and *Home*. His stories are collected as *Dixie Chicken* and *Handsome Men are Slightly Sunburnt*. He has lived in France and England.

Rossiter, Nicky, Wexford, is a writer and historian. His published books include: *My Wexford, The Streets of Wexford, Remembering Wexford and The Little Book of Wexford*

Rothwell, Keith, Moneytucker, Clonroche, established Beechdale Garden Centre in 1990 on a former mushroom farm site. They specialise in roses and in unusual and exotic plants. The Centre was completely refurbished in 2008, it now has a large covered area, with shop and the Wildflower Café, run by William Kinsella and Eamonn Doran.

Rothwell, Georgina, Ballyeaton, Glynn, Diocesan Secretary and Treasurer for the Diocese of Ferns; former president of County Wexford ICA; community activist; with Fr. Jim Fegan, Adm. Wexford, raised over €43,000 through their 2012 Christmas fast outside St. Iberius' Church in Wexford town.

Rowe, David, Wexford, born 1920. He was President of An Taisce, the National Trust for Ireland, and has co-edited the centenary volume of the Institute of Chartered Accountants in Ireland as well as a book of essays on auditing and accounting. With Christopher Wilson, he co-edited *High Skies – Low Lands*, which was published in 1996. With Eithne Scallan, he published *Houses of Wexford* and *You Can't Be Serious*.

Rowe, Edward, New Ross, wrote a number of plays, some of which were performed in the Abbey Theatre in 1972. He also had a number of plays produced in America.

Rowe, Joe, Old Boley, Barntown, Chief Executive of The Solutions Group, Old Dublin Road, Enniscorthy. Since 1987, has brought this local co-operative based company from providing farm relief services in Co. Wexford to now a major farm services provider in Ireland and the UK. Educated at Murrintown NS, St. Peter's College and Waterford and Tralee Institutes of Technology, Joe is married to Lily and has four children ranging in age from eight to eighteen.

Rowe, Pádraig, Bridgetown, Executive, Head Chef at Mount Juliet Resort in Thomastown, Co. Kilkenny. In 2013, Padraig was awarded a Michelin Star for his culinary expertise at the Lady Helen restaurant in Mount Juliet. His work had been monitored over a two-year period to get this award and says he possibly is the first Wexford man to get a Michelin Star. Padraig is son of Peter and Bernie, Bridgetown.

Ryan, Alan, Garrycullen, Saltmills, New Ross, born Laois 1972; Project Manager of the Colclough Tintern Abbey Walled Garden Restoration. Married to Ann, née Jordan, they have one son and one daughter.

Ryan, Bridget 'Bid', born 1955, Rosbercon, married to Matt, they have one daughter and one son; Bid is an active volunteer with New Ross Tidy Towns' committee, and attended a meeting with President Michael D. Higgins in Áras an Uachtaráin in October 2013 in recognition of her work. Husband Matt is a piper with New Ross and District Pipe Band.

Ryan, Con, New Ross town, RIP, was a great man to look after the local greyhound gallop that owners and trainers use every Sunday and Wednesdays. Con also won the coursing Oaks on several occasions.

Ryan, Jason, from Waterford, Wexford senior football manager for five years and is credited with raising the team to a new level, reaching an All-Ireland semi-final where they lost to Tyrone in 2008; Wexford also came close to toppling Dublin in Leinster on several occasions. Jason has recently been appointed manager of the Kildare senior football team.

Ryan, John, Bridgetown, RIP, one of Ireland's greatest ambidextrous handballers having won eighteen All-Ireland titles. He was known to have taken on a challenger playing with his feet only and won in his local handball alley in Bridgetown. He, with John Doyle, won the four senior titles in one season, singles and doubles in both softball and hardball.

Ryan, Liam, Templetown, born 1963, photographer and editor of *On the Hook* magazine, son of William and Mary Ann, née Tubritt. He is one of eight siblings. Liam developed his skill as a photographer through his work with Irish Lights as tern warden and a four-year term as senior warden at Rockabill lighthouse off the coast of Skerries, Co. Dublin. He was involved with the publishing of the story of the 'Helen Blake' shipwreck.

Ryan, Mary, New Ross, founder of Compassionate Friends, a charity for bereaved parents; married to Nick, they have two daughters and one son, their third daughter, Nicola, died suddenly in 2002 and Mary and Nick founded Compassionate Friends in her memory. They subsequently opened a centre for parents of children who have died, in Hoods Grove, New Ross. The centre is called Teach Beag. It has a Garden of Remembrance where people bring their own plants to sow. Parents can stay overnight, and the charity holds monthly meetings, and celebrates the lives of passed children. Mary's mother was Annie Moran from New Ross and her father and grandfather worked in the forge in Ballyneale. Husband Nick's parents were Nancy and Jimmy of Ryan's pub and coal yard on the Quay.

Morgan Byrne, Edward Roche, George Sparks and Father John Murphy of Boolavogue leaders of the United Irish Army achieved victory over the North Cork Militia on Oulart Hill, in County Wexford, on Whit Sunday, May 27th, 1798.

Ryan, Michael, Killowen, New Ross, born 1944; broadcaster and journalist; best known for his tri-weekly appearances in *Nationwide*, a programme he designed to increase RTÉ regional coverage. He has two sons and one daughter by his first wife, Anne Christine, née Kearney, who died in 1995. He married Liz in 2010. Michael spent two years as a seminarian before becoming a journalist with the *Evening Herald*. He joined RTÉ in 1966, reporting on *Newsbeat* for Frank Hall. He worked on two Jacob's award-winning programmes, the business show *Enterprise*, and the photographically-illustrated social history television series *The Day Before Yesterday*, which drew on the Father Browne collection. He retired from RTÉ in 2011.

Ryan, Simon, Newbawn Farm, Newbawn, born 1967, tillage farmer and bird seed provider; married to Anne, née Leech; one of chief organisers of The Gathering barn dance in aid Newbawn pitch committee walking-track fund.

Ryan, Tom, Monroe, Glenbrien. In 1915, at the age of 23, Tom went to Dublin and started work with the Dublin Gas Company, and became an active member of the IRA. On 21st Nov 1920, he attended the Tipperary-Dublin football match in Croke Park, an occasion that became infamous after the Auxiliaries and Black-and-Tans indiscriminately opened fire on the players and spectators. This was Domhnach na Fola, Bloody Sunday. As the Tipperary goalie, Michael Hogan, lay dying, it was reported that a "young Wexford man", who rendered him spiritual assistance, was wounded, and died later in Jervis Street Hospital. He was buried in Glasnevin. That young man was Tom Ryan.

Ryan, William, Clonmines, Wellingtonbridge, born 1972; carpenter; married to Elaine, née Power, they have two daughters and one son; established staircase manufacturing company in 1999 and 'GameBall' handcrafted Trophies and Gifts in 2010; presented Jean Kennedy Smith with a customised book by 'GameBall', made from Irish Maple surrounded by American Walnut symbolizing the strong Irish-American bond on the occasion of the 50th anniversary of JFK's visit to New Ross.

The Ryans of Tomcoole were a well-known and distinguished family who gave active support to the foundation of the State continuing right up to 1970. There were twelve in the family of John Ryan and Eliza

Sutton who farmed 150 acres at Tomcoole. John and Eliza were married on 16th November 1875. Eleven of their twelve children got secondary and third level education, something most unusual for their time

Joanna 'Jo' Ryan, 1877-1947, became a nun and joined the Loreto order taking the name Sister Stanislaus. She was a tutor at UCD and later became Mother Stanislaus in charge of Loreto Hall at 77, St. Stephen's Green, Dublin 2, which accommodated girls attending UCD. She adopted a neutral attitude on the Treaty.

Mary Kate, Kit or Cáit, Ryan, 1878-1934, graduated with first class honours in Modern Languages in 1902 and then went on to get a teaching qualification in Cambridge. From 1913 to 1918, she was temporary professor of French at UCD. During this period, her residence at 19, Ranelagh Road, was frequented by amongst others 1916 signatory Sean Mac Diarmada and Sean T O'Kelly. Following the 1916 Rising, Kit was arrested but was released on June 5th without charge. She married Sean T O'Kelly in 1918 but she continued her teaching in Dublin while he was away, as for a number of years he was envoy to Paris and to Washington. Kit Ryan was initially in favour of the Treaty but soon turned against it and advised her sister to leave her husband, Risteard Mulcahy, because he supported it. She continued lecturing in French until ill health forced her to give up. She died at 55 in 1934 and didn't have any family.

Eliza Mary, Lizzie, Ryan, born 1880, was the only Ryan not to receive third level education. She lived at home in Tomcoole and later in life was housekeeper for her sister, Nell and brother, Jack.

Ellen Mary, Nell, Ryan, 1881-1959. During the early years of the last century Nell Ryan taught in both Spain and Germany. On her return to Ireland, she became actively involved in the revolutionary movement. She was jailed in England for her activities in the 1916 Easter Rising. She also got involved in the Civil War and was imprisoned again and went on hunger strike for her activities supporting the Irregulars. Following the establishment of Fianna Fáil in 1926 she became actively involved and was a party member on Wexford County Council for a long number of years. She remained single and lived in Tomcoole for most of her life.

Martin Ryan, 1883-1929, was ordained a priest for the Diocese of Ferns. He became Professor of Theology at St. Peter's College and Seminary in Wexford. However, the Bishop of Ferns relieved him of his duty and dispatched him to the curacy of Poulfur possibly because of his nationalist views. He died at the young age of 46 from blood poisoning.

Josephine Mary, Min, Ryan, 1884-1977, lived the longest of the Ryan family. After graduating in Dublin she went to London where she also got a teaching qualification. After the outbreak of the First World War she returned to Dublin and taught German. She was also friendly with Sean Mac Diarmada and may have married him going on what he wrote before his execution. Min was active in Cumann na mBan. She married Risteard Mulcahy in 1919 and they had six children. Mulcahy and Min took the pro-treaty side in the Civil War and he became Commander in Chief of the army following Michael Collins' death 1922. This led to a bitter divide in the Ryan family which lasted for a number of years up until the 1930s. Min died at the age of 92 having been predeceased by her husband six years earlier.

Michael, Mike, Ryan, 1886-1949, remained in Wexford and farmed at Old Boley beside Tomcoole, he married Molly Shortall and they also had twelve children many of whom are well known, including John Ryan, undertaker, Wellingtonbridge; Martin Ryan, former member of Wexford County Council; Mike was a well-known publican in Taghmon.

John Joseph, Jack, Ryan, born 1887, entered the seminary at Maynooth but left it due to blindness. He took over the management of the farm in Tomcoole with the help of his sisters, Nell and Liz. He farmed beside his brother, Mike, and both have been described as quiet men whose attitude to the Treaty was less extreme than their sisters.

Agnes Ryan, 1888-1967, taught in the Domincan Convent in Belfast where she met her future husband, Denis McCullough. He was president of the Irish Republican Brotherhood and played a major role in the nationalist movement in the North. After the Rising, he spent time interned in Wales. Released in early August, Agnes Ryan married him in a double wedding with her sister Chris on the 16th of August 1916 in Taghmon. The ceremony was in Irish and was followed by a large gathering in Tomcoole. In memory of their dead and jailed friends, there was no dancing. Agnes and Denis settled in Belfast and they had six children

> Carnsore Point, Ireland's most south-easterly point, the closest point to England and France, a headland jutting out into the Irish Sea, was the scene of protests by thousands of people from here and abroad in 1978 and in the early 1980s against the Government and Electricity Supply Board's (ESB) plan of 1974 to build four small nuclear power plants at Carnsore to solve Ireland's energy needs. Today, a number of wind generating turbines are established there.

Christine Mary Ryan, 1890-1876, was also a qualified teacher and taught in Ireland and abroad. After marrying, Michael O'Malley in a double ceremony in Taghmon they settled in Galway. He was from a farming family of fourteen in Connemara and went on to become senior surgeon in Galway Regional hospital and subsequently Professor of Surgery at University College Galway. Chris Ryan took a more neutral role in the Treaty and acted as bridge between the warring factions of the family. Herself and Michael had a family of seven.

Saint Senan's Psychiatric Hospital at Brownswood Enniscorthy closed its doors for the last time in June 2013. It had operated for 145 years after the first patients were placed there in 1868. The landmark red-brick building housed more than five hundred patients at its peak.

Ryan, James, Jim 1891-1970, was involved in politics all his life and served in a number of government Ministries in Fianna Fáil-led governments. At the outbreak of the Easter Rising he was a medical student in Dublin and was appointed Chief Medical officer to assist the wounded at the GPO. After qualifying in 1917 he went into medical practice in Wexford. His work during the 'flu epidemic in 1918/19 ensured victory in South Wexford in the 1918 General Election. He was to remain in politics until 1969. Jim Ryan married Mairin Cregan, a writer of children's books, in 1919 and they had three children. In 1920 he was interned by the British on Spike Island. On the day the Four Courts in Dublin were shelled, he provided medical aid. He was arrested and went on hunger strike while interned in the Curragh. While there he was elected Sinn Féin TD for Wexford in 1923. With his health irreparably damaged, in 1925 he gave up medicine and bought a farm in County Wicklow. He helped set up Fianna Fáil the following year. He would go on to hold the posts of Minister for Agriculture, Health, Social Welfare and finally Finance. He retired from the Dáil in 1965 but went on to serve in the Seanad with his son, Eoin Ryan Senior, for another four years. He died on September 2nd 1970. His grandson, also Eoin Ryan, is a former TD and Senator and was a Member of the European Parliament.

Sabre, Maverick, Rap and soul singer real name Michael Stafford born in Hackney, London, in 1990; moved to New Ross at the age of four; educated at Good Counsel College but returned to London after Leaving Certificate age 17. Son of Victor and Maureen Stafford of Castlemoyle, the young Michael got his first break playing the lead role in *Oliver!* in a production by New Ross Musical Society at the age of eleven. At twenty three, he is now a leading singer and was the star performer at the Glastonbury Music Festival in the UK in 2013. He was also part of the Urban Proms at the Royal Albert Hall in London in 2013 where he performed with BBC Symphony Orchestra. His second album is to be released in 2014. The name Maverick Sabre came from using his initials MS but he thought the word Maverick and Sabre described him better.

Scallan, Eithne, is a Wexford historian and writer. She has published a number of books, including, *The Boat Club*, the story of Wexford Harbour Boat and Tennis Club, *The Celtic Story*, the history of Celtic Linen, and *The Twin Churches*. With David Rowe, she has also published *Houses of Wexford* and *You Can't Be Serious*.

Scallan, Karen, Scullabogue, Newbawn, born 1967; married to Thomas they have one son and two daughters; member of the Parents' Council, Parish Council, Ladies' football team and the local Gathering 2013 organising committee.

Seaver, Matt; Wexford town, is a management consultant specialising in the area of quality and food safety management systems. He also carries out inspections and audits for various government and private certification bodies. He is the author of several books on implementing quality management systems including *Implementing ISO 9000 2000, Gower Handbook of Quality Management 2003*and co-author of *ISA 2000: Mandatory Elements v. 1: The System for Occupational Health and Safety Management* by Matt Seaver and Liam O'Mahony, 1999. He is married to Una and is a member of the Wexford Sinfonia Orchestra.

Shapland Carew, Lord Robert was born on the 9th of March 1787 and died at his residence at Castleboro in late May 1856. He was passionately committed to civil and religious liberty and had campaigned for Catholic Emancipation. His Whig or Liberal principles anticipated modern democracy.

Shannon, James, who died on 17th October, 1933, was the shortest serving member of Dáil Éireann for the Wexford constituency. He was a Labour Party politician and trade union official, and he was elected to the Dáil as a Labour Party candidate in the June 1927, General Election. However, he lost his seat in the September 1927, General Election, and was an unsuccessful candidate in the 1932 General Election. He represented the Wexford constituency as a TD for only three months.

Shannon, Tom, Newbawn, born 1951; extensive dairy farmer; married to Eileen, née Bradley, Courthoyle, they have three daughters and two sons; previous chairman of Wexford IFA; staunch advocate of Macra na Feirme involved in stock judging, drama, public speaking, debating and quizzes during the 1970s.

Sharkey, Liam, Dranagh, Borovale, Enniscorthy, born Wexford 1979, secondary school teacher; entertainer; has written nine original pantos and four original musicals in collaboration with John O'Reilly. Pantomimes include: *Shrek: The Quest for Cinderella, Shrek and the Secret of the North Pole, The Fairest of them All, Pinocchio: Return to Oz, A Winter's Tale, Sulkyella and the Highland Adventure, Dorothy Rocks, Merlin and the Legend of the Golden Key* and *Goldilocks and* the *3 Sisters.* Musicals: *Torn Dreams, Fallen Angel, When I Grow Up and Eternal Flame.* Liam ran the Hope and Dream 10-mile run in Enniscorthy and wrote a diary for *The Echo* Newspaper over a number of weeks plotting his progress.

Sheehan, David, born Gurrawn, Rathnure, Chief Superintendent of the Limerick Garda Division. Eldest of a family of seven, he has three brothers in the police force, Laurence Ciaran and Gavin. David also served in the force in Wexford Waterford and Chief Superintendent in Thurles and Portlaoise before being posted to Limerick.

Sheeran, Ed, Suffolk, England, singer, songwriter, pop star. Edward Christopher Sheeran was born in Framington Suffolk in 1991, son of John and Imogen Sheeran, John's mother and Ed's grandmother hailed from Co. Wexford. He is one of the most popular international entertainers currently in 2013. In 2012 Ed won two Brit awards Best

British Male and Best Breakthrough, while his song "The A Team" was nominated in 2013 for a Grammy Award as the Song Of The Year. He has had a major tour of the US for six months in 2013 and lives in Nashville. Plans to buy a farm and return to Suffolk. Ed's father John is an art lecturer and along with his wife, Imogen, runs the Art Consultancy business Sheeran Lock. They have one other son, Matthew, who is a classical composer.

Sidney, Yvonne, native of New Ross, Yvonne spent many years as treasurer of Wexford Ladies' Gaelic Football County Board. She was also a sponsor and a tireless worker. Yvonne has also been a delegate for Wexford to Annual Congress.

Sills, Michael, a native of Murrintown, near Johnstown Castle; past pupil of the local national school and the Christian Brothers in Wexford town; former line manager with the multinational Chesebrough Ponds in London, now Unilever; president of the London Wexford Association. He attended CBS Wexford up to Inter Cert then went to work as a dental technician at Tommy Roche's in the Bullring, Wexford, before going to London. He joined the London-Wexford Association in 1969 and became known throughout London and south-east Ireland for his work for emigrants and for organising many events involving Wexford people back home. He received a Rehab County Wexford People for the Year Award in 2009 for Leadership.

Sinnott, Declan, St. Peter's Square, Wexford, is one of the most talented musicians produced by the Model County. He has been a prominent and influential figure on the Irish music scene since the early seventies. A guitarist of exceptional ability, he was one of the original members of the Horslips and wrote some of their best-remembered material. Declan later teamed up with Christy Moore and Donal Lunny to form Moving Hearts. During a lengthy collaboration with Mary Black, he played a crucial role in the huge success she achieved. He has been heard recently to much acclaim with the legendary Christy Moore in a number of sell-out concerts.

Sinnott, Francis David, known as 'Frank', born in Rosslare Strand in November 1951 to Marie, a cost accountant and Frank, jeweller and optician. At aged ten he was reading *Irish Times* editorials. At twelve, he won the letter of the week in an English magazine. At fourteen he had poetry published nationally. At fifteen he started the first ever school newspaper in Wexford. At sixteen he made a record with his brother Declan now one of Ireland's foremost musicians. At seventeen he started the Festival of Living Music and became the youngest festival director in the county. He wrote freelance for the *Irish Times, The Sunday Tribune, the Irish Press, Magill, Hot Press* and *The Phoenix*. In 1984, he started the first ever free newspaper in Wexford, 'The Boker'. He has published two books: *20 Years of View from a Bridge- Frank Sinnott's First Book* and *View from a Bridge, Volume 2*. He has co-published the book *Love from Zambia* by Fr. Fritz O'Kelly. He, his mother, Marie, and his brother Maurice, an English literature expert, live in Wexford town.

Sinnott, Richard, was born in Wexford and has written extensively about voting patterns in Irish elections. He wrote *Irish Voters Decide: Voting Behaviour in Elections and Referendums since 1918*, which was published in 1995. He co-edited *Public Opinion and International Governance.*

Sinnott, Michael, RIP, Garrywilliam, Crossabeg, was a member of Wexford County Council for many years. He was a keen GAA fan and played the game for many years. He was a staunch Fianna Fáil supporter and was regarded in many quarters as the un-elected leader of Fianna Fáil in County Wexford. He was tragically killed in a farm accident in 1995. Michael was married to Philomena, née Somers, and they had six children.

Sinnott, John, Duncormick, born 1929, publican, son of James and Frances, née Berry, from Scar. John's thatched pub in Duncormick predates 1795, the year his great grandmother first crossed the threshold to partake in a 'made match'. She came from the pub in Cullenstown which still survives. James Sinnott's grandfather was a first cousin to Fr. John Sinnott who founded St. Peter's College. Interesting visitors to Sinnott's include Chesley Millican, former manager of The Rolling Stones, The Grateful Dead and Stevie Ray Vaughan, whom John befriended over 35 years ago, while he was holidaying in Duncormick. Through Chesley, John met Charlie Watts, drummer of The Rolling Stones and Jerry Gaecia, guitarist with The Grateful Dead. He met Bruce Springsteen, Bob Dylan and Neil Young in 1989 in the Olympia stadium in Los Angeles with his good friend Timmy Corbett from Wellington Bridge. He also hosted Widgeon Holland in his pub for a month – Widgeon's father played music in Willie Nelson's band.

Sinnott, Thomas D., was Wexford's first County Manager, born in Ballyelland, Davidstown, in 1893; gifted poet and writer. His work entitled *Ninety-Eight – A Dramatic Symposium,* was published privately and was first performed in the Theatre Royal, Wexford, in December, 1937.

Skrine, Molly, 1904-1996, Ballyrankin, Clohamon, author, married to Bobby Keane; daughter of Walter and Agnes Skrine, an Irish-Canadian poet of note, who wrote under the pseudonym Moira O'Neill,. She lived at Ballyrankin until the late 1940s when she moved to Ardmore, Co. Waterford. She published eleven novels and four plays under the pseudonym MJ Farrell. The best known of these were *Devoted Ladies,* 1934, *Full House,* 1935 and *Rising Tide*, 1937. Her acclaimed comedy *Good Behaviour* was short-listed for the Booker Prize.

Somers, Ann, née Lennane, Irishtown, New Ross, born 1949, former hairdresser and volunteer, married to Bill, they have four children; she is the daughter of Paddy, Cappoquin, Co. Waterford and Mary Kate Fardy, New Ross. Ann has been a volunteer with hospice homecare for 24 years. She also helps with Sue Ryder, Daffodil Day, Happy Heart Day and The Irish Kidney Association. She loves reading, knitting and embroidery. Ann's father, Paddy, was the last stationmaster in Wellingtonbridge before it was closed down.

Somers, John, Oylegate farmer and a relative latecomer to competitive ploughing, qualifying for his first tilt at a national title in 1978. He won the ESSO Supreme trophy in both '79 and '84. He represented Ireland at four world championships, and his greatest achievement was in New Zealand in 1980, where he won two silver medals and a bronze overall in the World Ploughing Championships. John retired from competitive ploughing in 1985, due to ill health.

Spratt, Liam, Ballyboro, Clonroche, formerly Bree, owner of The Logo Centre which stitches logos and emblems onto clothing; married to Jane, née Flood, Castleboro, they have a daughter, Aoife and a son, Cathal; best known as South East Radio sports commentator but also widely acclaimed actor, comedian and star of pantomime and musicals . He spent much of his working life on the road as pharmaceutical sales rep. He is a brother of Ann Coppen, pharmacist, Enniscorthy.

Stafford, Betty, Clongeen, née Breen, Duncormick, married to Anthony; they have three children and three grandchildren; chairperson of Bannow-Rathangan show one of biggest agricultural shows in country which has grown hugely in recent years and under Betty's stewardship has continued to prosper. A primary school teacher by profession in Horeswood NS, Betty brings the communities of Bannow, Rathangan and surrounding parishes together. In 2013 the show was regarded as one of the best ever in almost tropical conditions on the site in Killag.

Stafford, Bill, born 1975, Director of New Ross Musical Society having been involved since 2000. He is the son of Matt and Bridie, née Cahill, Glenmore. Bill won best director at A.I.M.S. awards in 2009.

Stafford, Mairéad , Castlebridge Pottery Craftswoman and owner of Ballyelland Pottery, The Old Mill, Castlebridge; Mairéad completed the Crafts Council of Ireland Pottery Course in 1993. She honed her craft in both Ireland and U.K. before starting Ballyelland Pottery in Cambridge in 1997. She then returned to Ireland in 1999 to set up her studio in the 200-year-old mill in Castlebridge. The name Ballyelland comes from her home place in Davidstown where she grew up on the family farm daughter of Tom and Josie Stafford

Stafford, Michael, Ballyhurst, Taghmon, drama producer, actor, farmer, motor cycling enthusiast, a man of many talents; married to Pauline, they are parents to a large family; produced the highly-acclaimed Camross Passion Play in 2012 which also had a once-off performance in Wexford Opera House in conjunction with the Ferns Diocese. The Camross production is based on the Oberammergau play which is held every ten years in Germany.

Stafford, Victor J, is a member of one of Co. Wexford's most prominent and successful business families. In *The Sunday Times* Rich List, the Wexford-born entrepreneur is in 43rd place. He and his wife and family are reported to be worth €191 million. Through a company called Taghmon Investments, the couple own 28 per cent of the €153 million Stafford Holdings. The Stafford Group has been in existence for more than a hundred years and the tradition continues with the fourth generation family members now actively involved. At the helm is Chief Executive Mark Stafford, who oversees the running of the business with his father, Victor J. The group is involved in fuel distribution and shipping and is also behind the Lifestyle chain.

Storey, Martin, The Ballagh, born 1964, a psychiatric nurse; played hurling for Wexford from 1986-2001; was captain of Wexford team that won the All-Ireland in 1996, won 3 All Star Awards, 1993, right wing forward, 1996 and 1998, both centre forward; trained County camogie team and All-Ireland winning Coláiste Bríde colleges' teams, Enniscorthy; managed County minor hurling team; won five senior medals with his Oulart-the Ballagh club. His daughter Ciara has played camogie for Wexford; married to Rosaleen, from Donegal, they have three children – Anthony, Ciara and Martin Óg. In Sept. 2013 Martin was co-opted as Labour Party member of Wexford County Council, replacing his friend, the late Pat Cody, Enniscorthy.

Staples, Rev Leo, born 1925, went to school in Piercestown ordained in 1952; missionary priest with Kiltegan Fathers in Kenya for sixty one years. He comes home regularly to Wexford and is brother of the late Rev Frank and Rev Bob Staples of Ferns diocese.

Stephenson, Bill, Woodville, Bridgetown, has a cure for skin cancers, a cure which has been handed down through the family, from the late Willie Deacon of Old Ross to Leslie Deacon of Bridgetown.

Sutton, Josie, née Cowman, Fethard on Sea, formerly Ballindaggin, married to Kevin, they have three sons, Seán, Joe and James; secretary of Coiste na nÓg for four years and secretary of St. Mogue's for two years, her sons won U14 Féile final medals representing Wexford in Derry in 2010; Sean was captain. Josie's father was the founding member of the Ballindaggin Pipe Band. Josie herself played drums.

Swan, Rev Billy, Blackhall, Killurin, born 1969, son of the late Billy and Eileen, née Pierce; educated in Glynn N.S., St Peter's College, Wexford and University College Dublin from where he graduated with a degree in chemistry in 1991. Having worked as an industrial chemist for two years; entered St Peter's College seminary in 1993 and was ordained to the priesthood in 1998. Curate in New Ross for four years, he was sent for further studies in Rome in 2002. He graduated with a Licentiate in 2005 and a doctorate in Systematic Theology in 2012. In 2007 he was appointed as Director of Formation at the Irish College seminary, Rome until his return to the diocese of Ferns in 2012. He is author of two religious books and in 2013 is based in St Aidan's Cathedral, Enniscorthy.

Sweetman, Roger, who was born on 18th August, 1874, was a barrister and Sinn Féin politician. He was elected as a Sinn Féin MP for the North Wexford constituency in the 1918 General Election. When the Sinn Féin MPs refused to recognise the Parliament of the United Kingdom, they held a meeting in the Mansion House in Dublin and set up Dáil Éireann. He did not contest the 1921 elections. His cousin, John Sweetman, was an Irish Parliamentary MP and second president of Sinn Féin, and his son, Edmund Sweetman, was a Senator from 1948 to 1951.

Tantrum, Connie, Director of Piano Festival and Ros Tapestry; married to David, they have two daughters and one son; board member of Music Network; conducts the New Ross Singers community choir who perform concerts annually and donate all profits to charity, last year's production being Handel's *Messiah.*

Tector, Bill, born 1929 at Clonroche; died 1986 in Dublin; played three times for Ireland in full back in the then Five Nations' rugby championship in 1955, lining out against France and England at Lansdowne Road, and against Scotland at Murrayfield. He played his early rugby with the Enniscorthy club. The game against Scotland actually featured two Wexford men because Seamus Kelly from Wexford town lined out at out half.

Tector, Leona, Castlebridge, formerly Abbeyview, Campile, daughter of Willie and Mary, née Furlong from Foulksmills; long-standing member of the Wexford Ladies' Football team. All-Ireland finalist 2013, she has played for her county on several other occasions. Leona was a member of the winning Shelmaliers camogie team who won the Senior County Camogie Championship beating Oulart-the Ballagh in 2013. Leona has been a Central Council delegate from 1996 to date and received an All Star award in 2005.

Tobin, Bridie, Kilrush Club and Wexford County camogie player, won All-Ireland medals in 1969 and 1975 and ended her county career in 1976 when Wexford were beaten by Kilkenny in the AII-Ireland in Croke Park. Bridie married Pat Fox who also hurled with Kilrush.

Tobin, Pat, Marshalstown, came to live with his aunt in Edermine Mills as a young man; married Chris O'Brien, a local farmer's daughter, and went into business as a building contractor. Totally untrained, but with a natural skill for draughtsmanship and structural design, he left many fine buildings throughout the county as a testament to his ability. His real talents came to the fore when he changed to light engineering. In addition to fitting out most of Ireland's cattle marts, he designed and manufactured the Tobin Hammer Mill, which, with the advent of rural electrification, became an instant success, and thousands were installed all over Ireland. He was later given the RDS supreme award of a Silver medal at the Spring Show for his design of a vegetable harvester. He died in 1964 at the age of 57.

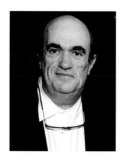

Tóibín, Colm, was born in Enniscorthy in 1955. He was educated at Enniscorthy CBS, where his father, Micheál was a teacher, then at St. Peter's College in Wexford. His novels are: *The South, The Heather Blazing, The Story of the Night, The Blackwater Lightship, The Master, Brooklyn,* and *The Testament of Mary.* His works have been shortlisted for the Booker Prize on three occasions. His stories are collected as *Mothers and Sons,* for which won the Edge Hill Prize, and *The Empty Family.* His non-fiction includes: *Homage to Barcelona, Bad Blood, The Sign of the Cross – Travels in Catholic Europe, Lady Gregory's Toothbrush, Love in a Dark Time: Gay Lives from Wilde to Almodovar* and *All a Novelist Needs: Essays on Henry James.* He has received honorary doctorates from the University of Ulster and from University College Dublin, from where he had graduated in the 1970s, and is a regular contributor to the Dublin Review, the New York Review of Books and the London Review of Books

Tuomey, John C., Taghmon, national school teacher; leased wretched cabins to impoverished people. He was a graphic writer of novelistic power: he published long erudite letters in the local newspapers. The Journal of the Kilkenny Archaeological Society published his extensive work called *The Bay and Town of Bannow,* 1851. He was also a gifted polemicist.

Turner, Nick, a Wexford man now based in Barntown, took over his operation from his late father, Reggie, a well-known figure in greyhound circles in Wexford for many years. He has had great success along with his late brother, Pat, recording many important winners, including the

Oaks at Shelbourne Park with Life's Beauty in 2002 and the Laurels in Cork when Tiger's Eye dead-heated in 1999. The Turner family business, Practical Printers, printed the race cards for many years for Enniscorthy and Waterford tracks.

Turner, Pierce, Wexford town-born musician, singer-songwriter, who began his career as choir boy and a member of a tin whistle band. His mother ran a record shop and saw that Pierce, like his siblings, was classically trained. He moved to New York in the 1970s where he and fellow Wexford musician, Larry Kirwan, formed "The Major Thinkers". Pierce has released several albums by himself and with others and regularly commutes between Wexford and New York where he lives. The world premiere of a Mass composed by Pierce Turner was celebrated as part of the Gathering in May 2013 in Bride Street Church in Wexford.

Turner, Sean, Strand Road, Rosslare, born 1933; retired; married to Maureen, née Cronin, Wexford, they have three sons and one daughter; Sean worked in research in Johnstown Castle for 34 years; played football with Our Lady's Island and trained St. Mary's Rosslare U14-U16 teams.

Twomey, Liam, Rosslare, born 1967; native of Clonakilty, Co. Cork; worked as general medical practitioner before entering public life; elected as an independent TD for Wexford in the General Election of 2002. He campaigned on a platform highlighting the deficiencies in the health service. In September, 2004, he joined the Fine Gael Party and became their spokesperson for health in the Dáil. He lost his seat in the 2007 General Election, but was subsequently elected to the Seanad on the Cultural and Educational Panel. He regained his seat in Dáil Éireann at the 2011 election.

Wall, Eamonn, was born in Enniscorthy in 1955. His poetry is collected as *Dyckman – 200th Street, Iron Mountain Road, The Crosses, Refuge at DeSoto Bend, A Tour of Your Country and Sailing Lake Mareotis.* His prose includes *From the Sin-é to the Black Hills, Notes on the New Irish,* which was co-winner of the Durkan Prize from the American Conference for Irish Studies for the best scholarly book on Language and Literature published in 2000, and *Writing the Irish West, Ecologies and Traditions.* He serves on the editorial board of the Journal of Franco-Irish Studies and An Sionnach: A Journal of Irish Studies. He is currently the Jefferson Smurfit Professor of Irish Studies at the University of Missouri-St Louis in the US. His father, MJ, was Editor of *Ireland's Own* magazine and proprietor of Murphy Floods Hotel.

Wallace, Mick, born in Wellingtonbridge on 9th November, 1955, is a property developer, former football manager and politician. He was elected to Dáil Éireann in the 2011 General Election as an Independent TD for the Wexford constituency. While he was a guest on the political programme 'Tonight with Vincent Browne' on 5th February, 2011, with only weeks to go before polling day, he made the announcement that he intended to contest the forthcoming General Election. It was a political bombshell when he topped the poll in the Wexford constituency with 13,329 votes. A few months after being elected, he revealed that he faced personal financial ruin and possibly the loss of his Dáil seat, following the appointment of receivers to his assets. On 10th October, 2011, the Commercial Court ordered him to repay more than €19 million owed to ACC Bank. He was appointed manager of the Youth Inter League team in 1991 and worked in raising the interest level in youth football to the point where Wexford now has the biggest youth League in Ireland. In the year 2000, Wexford beat Sligo-Leitrim 1-0 in Arklow to win their first ever National title with a team which included Leighton Gleeson and Kevin Doyle, who were to go on to greater things in their later careers. In 2005, Wexford managed to win the title again by beating the Eircom League in a final played at New Ross Celtic's ground in Butlersland. In 2007, Wexford took their third National title by beating Galway in the final, played on the fantastic new facilities at Ferrycarrig Park and a year later, Wexford retained their title by beating Waterford 1-0 in Ozier Park, Waterford. It was a level of success that was the envy of every League in Ireland, particularly at youth level where, because of the age limit, there has to be a constant changing of personnel each season. For good measure, his club, Wexford Youth, a newly formed youth team won the FAI Youth cup, for club teams, in 2008 by defeating Dundalk 4-0 in the final, with Danny Furlong bagging all four goals. In 2012 Wexford Youths managed to win that trophy again by beating Mount Merrion 2-1 in the final, with Mick's son, Joseph Barry Wallace, being a member of the team. An ardent fan of all things Italian, especially football, wine and food, he built the Italian quarter in Dublin, Mick has been bringing an U16 team out to Piedmont during the Easter school break for very many years now, so that these young lads can have a memorable sporting and cultural exchange with their Italian peers. He provided a state-of-the-art facility for football at Ferrycarrig Park and Wexford Youths FC began competing in the League of Ireland first division in 2007. A Wexford Youths women's team competed quite successfully in the fledgling Women's National League since that League's inception two years ago.

Walshe, Bob, formerly New Ross, married to Aileen, née Hamilton, they have two sons, Robbie and Neil; owner Meadow Lane Equestrian Centre in Ballynunnery, The Rower; one of eight children of Robert and Biddy, née Prendergast, The Quay, New Ross. His father died at a young age and Bob's sister, Yvonne, helped his mother to carry on the business; Bob himself was a hairdresser for 26 years. Yvonne, and Clare, another sister, carry on the business to this day, still going strong after 81 years. Bob is a talented musician and he gigs most weekends.

Walsh, Billy, born 1964, is one of Wexford's most distinguished sportsmen. Son of Liam and Kathleen, he is a native of Wolfe Tone Villas, Wexford town; married to Christine, they have a daughter, Sarah Jane, and two sons, Mark and Ryan. He is head coach of the Irish Amateur Boxing Association's (IABA) High Performance Unit and his charges have won seven medals at the last two Olympic Games in Beijing and London, and they have collected numerous World and European championship awards. He was made a Freeman of Wexford Town in Nov. 2012 to mark his achievements, only the sixth townsman and the first sports person, to be so honoured. He was also voted the Irish Sports Manager of the Year for 2012. Billy played underage Inter-county hurling and football and won a Leinster hurling medal; he also played at senior level with Faythe Harriers (hurling)

and Sarsfields (football), and played soccer with Wexford Albion. He was one of Ireland's most outstanding boxers in the 80s, winning seven out of ten National senior finals. He competed in the 1982 European Juniors and then graduated to the European Seniors the following year in Bulgaria. At the height of his career, Billy represented his country at the 1988 Olympic Games in Seoul, Korea, and admits he was marked by his first round defeat by a boxer he had previously beaten; he felt he had not done himself justice. He was only beaten in a box-off by his friend Michael Carruth in 1992 for a place on the Olympic team at Barcelona; Carruth won that and went on to win a gold medal at the Games. While all this was going on he worked as a fitter/welder in John Jackman's Engineering, Smiths and Pierces before taking over a Snowcream milk round in Wexford in 1992. He coached boys at the St. Ibar's/St. Joseph's club before the Irish coach, Nicholas Cruz Hernandez, offered him the position as his assistant in the year 2000, and the rest is history.

Walsh, Dan, Enniscorthy, born 1952; a native of Bree; author, journalist, ambulance driver; author of a number of books and has a regular weekly programme broadcast on South East Radio. His first book, *Bree – The Story of a County Wexford* Parish, was published in 1980. Amongst his other books is *Family History in Enniscorthy,* which was published in 1983. Dan is married to Margo and they have a grown up family.

Walsh, Dave: Ballydicken, Crossabeg. photographer, journalist, writer and polar communicator; son of Jimmy and Monica , a native of Galway. His brother, Michael, is a ships' officer in the US. He makes images that question humanity's relationship with planet Earth, and our profligate use of energy and resources. He sailed on Greenpeace expeditions in the Arctic and Antarctic.

He is a member of the Advisory Board of The Arctic Institute, an interdisciplinary, independent think tank focused on Arctic policy issues based in Washington DC. His photographs have been published in *National Geographic, GEO* (France), *The Guardian, The Financial Times, The Straits Times* (Singapore), Nature, Greenpeace International, *New Scientist, The Smithsonian, Sierra* magazine, *BBC Wildlife* magazine, *Conde Naste Traveller,* Forbes, and Fortean Times. He has written for several newspapers and magazines, including The Irish Times and is the author of *Haunted Dublin, A Load of Blather,* and *The Cold Edge,* a book of polar photography.

Walsh, Jim, Senator, New Ross, farmer, company director and politician. First elected to Seanad Éireann in 1997and has been a member ever since. A member of the Fianna Fáil party he also spent a number of years on Wexford County Council. He is Fianna Fáil Seanad Spokesperson on Foreign Affairs and Trade. Married to Marie, the couple have three children. Jim actively opposed the government's abortion legislation in 2013.

Walsh, Nellie, born Wexford 1913, a noted singer, she was the first soloist to be heard in Wexford Opera Festival in *The Rose of Castile.* Her autobiography *Tuppences were for Sundays* was published in 1996. She was sister of Dr. Tom Walsh, founder of Wexford Festival Opera.

Katie Nolan of Camross is 105 and her godson and cousin Denny Nolan, also from Camross is in his 90th year. Katie was born on 29th September 1908 and celebrated her 105th birthday in Oakfield Nursing Home, Gorey, last year. Denny, living in Camross, was born on 18th February 1924. Are they the oldest godmother and godson in the world?

Walshe, Oliver, Inch, Blackwater, born 1975, Fine Gael member of Wexford County Council since 2001. His late father, John, was also a member of the council. Oliver was co-opted on to council to fill Ivan Yates' seat and was subsequently elected in 2004 and in 2009; he became chairman of Wexford County Council in 2011. A farmer, Oliver is married to Elaine and they have two children, Isabelle and Jack.

Walsh Doctor Tom , born Wexford 1911, will always be remembered as co-founder of Wexford Opera Festival and the driving force behind the festival during its formative years. He was the festival's inspirational first artistic director and laid the foundations which enabled the festival to achieve an international reputation. In his medical career, Dr. Walsh was an anesthetist in Wexford County Hospital. He also wrote a number of books on opera including *Opera in Dublin 1707-1797, Monte Carlo Opera 1879-1909 and Second Empire Opera, The Theatre Lyrique Paris 1851-1870*. Many honours were conferred on him. He was made a Freeman of the Borough of Wexford in 1978. He died in 1988.

Walsh, Doctor Tom, Piercestown, was appointed by the Government as first director of An Foras Talúntais in 1958. Dr. Walsh was educated at Piercestown National School and Christian Brothers School, Wexford. He graduated from University College Dublin in 1937 with a B. Agr. Sc. Honours degree. He was awarded the M.Agr.;won the Reading Association of Ireland Award 2003.

Warren, Michael, Gorey, sculptor; designed Tulach an tSolais on Oulart Hill.

Whelan, Gerard, Enniscorthy; author; *The Guns of Easter* won Bisto Merit Award and Eilis Dillon Award; *Dream Invader* was the overall winner of the Bisto Book of the Year Award 1998, and *War Children*, won the Reading Association of Ireland Award 2003. Other books include *A Winter of Spies, Out of Nowhere* and *Spiked: Church-State Intrigue and the Rose Tattoo*.

Whelan, Rev Joe, Loughnageer, Clongeen, missionary priest with the Mill Hill Fathers, worked in Pakistan for many years; son of Kevin and Maureen, brother of Seamus retired Garda Oylegate. He is related to the late Fr. Peter Whelan also from Clongeen who was a missionary priest who served in the American Civil War. In 2013 a plaque in his honour was unveiled at his ancestral home, now owned by Jimmy and Agnes Curtis.

Whelan, John, Ballygarvan, Gusserane, born Wexford 1970, Dairy farmer; married to Margaret, née Redmond, they have three sons and one daughter. John is World Ploughing Champion 2013 having competed in Canada. He also holds four National Ploughing Championship titles and two European titles. He is also a board member of the National Ploughing Association

Whelan, Josie, Tullabards, Bridgetown, née Nolan, Tottenhamgreen, Taghmon; actress and producer of the Kilmore Variety Group which won the South East Tops competition; married to Noel, they have a grown-up family of four. Josie was very involved in Macra na Feirme during the 1970s.

Whelan, Professor Kevin native of Clonegal and has written extensively on historical subjects. Between 1995 and 1998, he was historical advisor to the Irish government on the Famine and the 1798 Rebellion. He was named the inaugural Michael Smurfit Director of the Keough Notre Dame Centre in Ireland in 1998. He has been a visiting professor at New York University, Boston College and Concordia University, Montreal. He has lectured in over a dozen countries, and at the Sorbonne, Cambridge, Oxford, Torino, Berkeley, Yale, Dartmouth and Louvain. He has written or edited fifteen books and over a hundred articles on Ireland's history, geography, literature and culture. One of a family of twelve he is married to Anne Kearney and they have four children, Beibhinn, Fionn, Ruaidhrí and Eamonn

Whelan, Malachy, Askasilla, Blackwater, from well-known sporting family, brother of Fr Brian Whelan and son of well-known GAA figure PJ now deceased and Mary. Malachy is the holder of at least ten All-Ireland handball medals and one World Championship runners-up medal.

Whelan, Noel, formerly Ballycullane, now Dublin, barrister, writer and political pundit. He has a degree and masters from UCD in History and Politics and also a Masters in International Relations. Once politically active, he stood unsuccessfully in the 1997 election for Fianna Fáil in the Dublin South East. Noel Whelan was called to the bar in 1998 and serves on the Dublin and South East circuit specialising in criminal law. He writes a weekly column in the *Irish Times* and has written a biography of Fianna Fáil. He is married and has one son.

Whelan, Paddy, 1926-2013, Lower Shannon Hill, Enniscorthy; retired Psychiatric Nurse, married to Maureen, née Terry, RIP 2009; they have two sons Gerard and Des, both involved with Slaney Search and Rescue; long-time make-up artist in the Athenaeum and for all Enniscorthy dramatic and musical productions for more than 40 years; one of the chief organisers of the Boys' Club Penny Bank savings scheme; lifelong pioneer; winner of papal Bene Merenti Medal, with Maureen, for services to Church and community.

Whelan, Pat, Castlebridge, accountant, actor/director of Bridge Drama Group for a number of years, won Best Director at the RTÉ Amateur All-Ireland Drama Festival in Athlone 2013 for his production of *Out Of Order*, this was his first qualification for an All-Ireland Drama Festival. Like his father Jimmy from Campile, who has been through accidents and injuries throughout his life and is still going strong in 2013, Pat is determined to achieve All-Ireland success in their production of *Big Maggie* in 2014.

Whelan, Seán, born 1947, formerly St. Aidan's Villas, now Bellefield; journalist; son of John J 'Jackie' Whelan and Lil, née O'Brien, Duffry Gate; staff reporter with *The Echo* newspaper 1968-2012; writer of two books, *Just a memory - GAA memories 1884-1984* and *Ghosts of Bygone Days*; brother of Gerard, award-winning children's writer; grandson of MJ Whelan, Island Road. Seán was superannuated in February 2012 and has been revelling in retirement ever since. He is a committed Manchester United supporter, a music fan and a man who loves to leaf through books on Charing cross Road in London whenever he can. He is a familiar and welcome sight on his daily walks around his native Enniscorthy.

Whelan, Seamus 'Shanks', Piercestown, greyhound trainer: a member of the All-Ireland winning Wexford hurling team of 1968, has been involved with greyhounds for over forty years and has enjoyed great success, notably winning the Prestigious SIS Gold Trophy at Shelbourne Park and the Waterford Masters, both group 1 stakes; reached the semi-finals of the Irish Derby with Piercestown Sand. Shanks has formed a great partnership with son-in-law, Ronnie Shenkwin in recent years.

White, Brian, Cushinstown, GAA referee, was in charge of three All-Ireland senior football finals, 1997 in which Kerry beat Mayo, 2000 replay in which Kerry beat Galway and 2003 in which Tyrone beat Armagh in the first all-Ulster final. He has also handled four football and three hurling senior finals in Wexford.

White, John, The Farmhouse, Bannow, racehorse trainer, had an accomplished riding career before turning to training. He will always be remembered as the 'winner' of the Grand National that never was, on Esha Ness in 1993. Chaos at the start saw a false start being declared, but lack of communication between course officials meant that seven horses ran the course in its entirety and first past the post was Esha Ness in the second-fastest time ever, ridden by John White and trained by Jenny Pitman. The race was declared void for the only time in its history.

> In 1798 in the Battle of Vinegar Hill overlooking Enniscorthy 20,000 men women and children faced 10,000 members of the Crown forces in a battle that lasted just four hours but left 1,500 dead.

White, Nicky, was chairman of the Ladies' Gaelic Football County Board for four years, the longest-serving chairman; has worked for the Association nationally and has also been a delegate to Central Council; has refereed two senior All-Ireland finals in Croke Park.

Whitty, Billy, Duncannon, born 1978; Chef, partner of Joanne Harding, they have one daughter; Seafood Chef of the Year 2013; owner of multi-award-winning restaurant and guest house, Aldridge Lodge, holder of the Michelin Bib Gourmand since 2007.

Whitty, Michael James, born in Duncormick in 1795. Intended for the priesthood, he went instead to London to become a writer. His *Tales of Irish Life* became an enormous success and was translated into French and German. He became Editor of the *Liverpool Journal* and then Chief Constable of Liverpool and organiser of the first English police force outside of London in 1836. Finally, he became owner-editor of the *Liverpool Daily Post,* one of the forerunners of the popular press.

Whitty, Pat, Old Ross, has been the Schoolboys and District League's fixtures secretary since 1977/78 season. He enjoyed moderate success as a player with Old Ross, Crystal Palace, Park Hotspur, Adamstown and Corach Ramblers. He represents Wexford on the Leinster Senior Council, and is also a member of the FAI's Senior Council. He also served a few years as Chairman of the FAI Junior Council. Among his FAI highlights is being on the official party to the United Arab Emirates in November/December 2003 for the U20 World Cup Finals.

Whitty, Thomas, Coolateggart, Taghmon, born 1994; student of Business and Computers at Bridgetown Vocational College; son of Martin and Christine; Student of Year at Bridgetown VC 2013; member of 2014 Special Olympics Team competing in pitch and putt, tennis and basketball

Wilde, Jane Francesca, born in Wexford in 1826, daughter of Archdeacon Elgee, she married Sir William Wilde, a distinguished surgeon, in 1851; as Lady Jane Wilde, published a number of works on folklore, including *Driftwood from Scandinavia, Ancient Legends of Ireland, Ancient Cures and Men, Women and Books* and under the pen name of 'Speranza', she contributed to *The Nation*. She was the mother of Oscar Wilde.

Williams, Aisling, Enniscorthy, soprano; daughter of Noeleen and James; studied classical singing and music theatre in the Royal Irish Academy of Music; launched 2013 Wexford Festival Opera Fringe Programme.

Williams, Dominic, Parkview, Wexford and formerly of Taghmon, a member of the bakery and supermarket family. A very keen Gaelic Games and all round sports fan and collector of memorabilia, he has penned the ultimate book on the facts and figures of the GAA in Wexford, *The Wexford Hurling and Football Bible 1887-2008*, a complete statistical history of Wexford GAA. He is brother of Tom, profiled elsewhere.

Yates, Ivan, born 1959, in Enniscorthy, businessman, broadcaster and former politician. He was elected as a Fine Gael TD for the Wexford constituency in the 1981 General Election and was re-elected at each election until his retirement from politics in 2002. He was aged 21 years and eight months when he was first elected and was the youngest member of the 22nd Dáil. He is also the fifth youngest ever member of Dáil Éireann. He joined the Fine Gael Front Bench in 1988, and was appointed Minister for Agriculture, Food and Forestry from 1994 to 1997. Following the resignation of John Bruton as leader of Fine Gael in 2001, there was much speculation that Ivan Yates would be a contender for the leadership. However, he announced that he was leaving full-time politics to concentrate on his business interests. His effort to save his company, Celtic bookmakers, ended in receivership. He is co-presenter of 'The Breakfast Show' on Newstalk radio and a national newspaper columnist.

"Zorro", William de Lamport, 1611-1659, was a hero of the Mexican Inquisition. He was born in Wexford town the youngest child of Richard Lamport and Anastatia Sutton. The Lamports were an old Wexford Catholic family who arrived here with Strongbow in the twelfth century. He was educated by the Augustinians and Franciscans in Wexford before heading for London in 1628. He joined a gang of pirates and fled to Spain. In 1632, as a well-educated and sharp twenty-one-year-old swordsman he was summoned to the court of King Philip the IV. He became a captain in the Spanish army. He was small but handsome with red hair and an eye for the ladies. In 1640 he was sent to Mexico as a spy and had now changed his name to Guillen Lombardo. Lamport moved in society circles, led a double life and became engaged to a rich heiress despite leaving a mistress and daughter behind in Spain. The governor of Mexico City issued a warrant for his arrest and he was found with the governor's wife in her bedroom. The governor sent him for execution but de Lamport managed to hang himself first. He had not reached the age of fifty. He became a folk hero for the Mexican independence movement. He was the inspiration for 'Zorro'.

9

Anthems

County Wexford songwriters and poets are noted everywhere for their celebration of love, the range of human emotions and battles, wars and sporting achievements. Their creations provide a context to the County's defining moments in history and in happiness.

CÚCHULAINN'S SON- THE STORY OF NICKEY RACKARD

Tom Williams, who wrote this song, is author of *With Heart and Hand – The Inside Story of Wexford's Hurling Resurgence* and the book

The challenge of an ancient game
Brought glory, glory to your name
Though March winds blew the crowds still came
To watch you gentle hero.
In life's long march you made us proud
And many a voice from out the crowd
Called out your name aloud, aloud
An echo still resounding.
And Blackstairs men who saw you then
Still speak of you in awe,

On Carman's green where you had been
They tell of what they saw,
We watched you on September fields
And lightning was the drive
You were the one Cúchulainn's son in 1955.
The hand that held the stick of ash,
And the man who led with style and dash,
Oh! Carrigtwohill once felt the crash
And Bennettsbridge and Thurles.
And when in later life you beat
The devil on that lonely street
You showed us how to take defeat
With dignity and courage.
The last parade was sad and slow
The last oration spoken low
And as, on green fields long ago

Nick Bailey leads Extreme Rhythm in Primal Scream at Wexford Opera House.

The Diamond stood beside you
Old friends they flanked you side by side
And the tears they shed were tears of pride
An ash tree toppled when you died
And scattered seeds at random.

DANCING AT THE CROSSROADS

Paul Bell and Brendan Wade, The Wild Swans. This
song is all about Wexford winning the All-Ireland hurling
final of 1996.

Well I remember as a young boy
The beginning of September
We were standing at the station
Waiting for a train.

There was priests and Christian Brothers
There was nuns and reverend mothers
There was guards and drunks and others
But everyone was just the same.

Well they came from Enniscorthy
From New Ross and Ferns and Gorey
There was buses from Bunclody
There was horses, carts and all.

And when they stepped out on the platform
They were shouting and screaming
And as they carried Larry Murphy
He looked twenty-five feet tall.

So what's the story Martin Storey
Now Wexford's really bound for glory
And when at last the cup was lifted
They said we brought it home for you.

Chorus
We were dancing at the crossroads,
In the shadow of a bonfire
Underneath the silver moon light
We were singing until dawn,
We were dancing at the crossroads,
With the poteen and the porter,
Dancing jigs and reels and polkas
Until the early morn.

In every bar down on the main street
They were hanging from the rafters
And they sang the boys of Wexford
Like it was going out of style

All the bingo halls were empty
And all the Masses finished early
Sure no one ever saw the likes of
Since the time of JFK

And when we look at young O'Gorman
And through the mid field he was stormin
And then the Cusack Stand erupted
When he scored from 60 yards
Chorus

And I think of George O'Connor
So many said he was a gonner
But when he stood up in the Hogan
I even saw an old man cry.
Chorus

Damien Fitzhenry, Ger Cush, Sean Flood,
Rod Guiney , Liam Dunne
Colm Kehoe, Billy Byrne
Martin Storey John OConnor,
Tom Dempsey, George O'Connor
Adrian Fenlon and
Larry O'Gorman,

Rory McCarthy, Larry Murphy, Garry Laffan
Eamon Scallan, Dave Guiney
Declan Ruth, Jim Byrne
Sean Carley, Paul Finn
Tom Kehoe, are the team
and the man that dared to dream his
name was Liam Griffin

Seamus Kavanagh, Joe Kerns,MJ Reck
and all the rest the brave young men of 96
will be remembered with the best
Rackard, Quigley, Wheeler, Doran,
Buggy, Murphy, Nolan, Flood
And the names I can't recall
Wexford heroes one and all.

BOOLAVOGUE

Patrick J McCall, 1861–1919

The Wexford insurgents were defeated at Vinegar Hill
on 21 June 1798. An estimated 30,000 people died in the
three months leading up to and including the battle.

At Boolavogue, as the sun was setting
O'er the bright May meadows of Shelmalier,
A rebel hand set the heather blazing
And brought the neighbours from far and near.
Then Father Murphy, from old Kilcormack,

Spurred up the rocks with a warning cry;
"Arm! Arm!" he cried, "for I've come to lead you,
For Ireland's freedom we fight or die."
He led us on 'gainst the coming soldiers,
And the cowardly Yeomen we put to flight;
'Twas at the Harrow the boys of Wexford
Showed Bookey's Regiment how men could fight
Look out for hirelings, King George of England,
Search ev'ry kingdom where breathes a slave,
For Father Murphy of the County Wexford
Sweeps o'er the land like a mighty wave.

We took Camolin and Enniscorthy,
And Wexford storming drove out our foes;
'Twas at Sliabh Coillte our pikes were reeking
With the crimson stream of the beaten Yeos.
At Tubberneering and Ballyellis
Full many a Hessian lay in his gore;
Ah, Father Murphy, had aid come over
The green flag floated from shore to shore!

At Vinegar Hill, o'er the pleasant Slaney,
Our heroes vainly stood back to back,
And the Yeos at Tullow took Father Murphy
And burned his body upon the rack.
God grant you glory, brave Father Murphy
And open heaven to all your men;
The cause that called you may call tomorrow
In another fight for the Green again

KELLY THE BOY FROM KILLANE

Patrick J McCall

What's the news, what's the news, O me bold Shelmalier
With your long barrel guns from the sea?
Say, what wind from the south brings a messenger here
With this hymn of the dawn for the free?
Goodly news, goodly news do I bring youth of Forth
Goodly news shall I hear Bargy man.
For the boys march at morn from the south to the north
Led by Kelly, the boy from Killane.

Tell me who is the giant with the gold curling hair
He who rides at the head of your band.
Seven feet is his height with some inches to spare
And he looks like a king in command.
O me boys that's the pride of the bold Shelmalier
'Mongst our greatest of heroes a man
Fling your beavers aloft and give three ringing cheers
For John Kelly, the boy from Killane.

Enniscorthy is in flames and old Wexford is won
And tomorrow the Barrow we'll cross
On the hill o'er the town we have planted a gun
That will batter the gateway to Ross.
All the Forth men and Bargy men will march o'er the heath
With brave Harvey to lead in the van
But the foremost of all in the grim gap of death
Will be Kelly, the boy from Killane.

But the gold sun of freedom grew darkened at Ross
And it set by the Slaney's red wave...
And poor Wexford stripped naked hung high on a cross
With her heart pierced by traitors and knaves.

Glory-o, Glory-o to her brave men who died
For the cause of long down-trodden man.
Glory-o to Mount Leinster's own darling and pride
Dauntless Kelly, the boy from Killane.

THE BOYS OF WEXFORD

Patrick J McCall

Chorus:
We are the boys of Wexford,
Who fought with heart and hand
To burst in twain the galling chain
And free our native land.

In comes the captain's daughter,
The captain of the Yeos,
Saying "Brave United Irishmen,
We'll ne'er again be foes.
A thousand pounds I'll bring
If you will fly from home with me,
And dress myself in man's attire
And fight for liberty."
Chorus

I want no gold, my maiden fair,
To fly from home with thee.
You shining eyes will be my prize,
More dear than gold to me.
I want no gold to nerve my arm
To do a true man's part -
To free my land I'd gladly give
The red drops of my heart."
Chorus

And when we left our cabins, boys,
We left with right good will
To see our friends and neighbours
That were at Vinegar Hill!
A young man from our Irish ranks
A cannon he let go;
He slapt it into Lord Mountjoy
A tyrant he laid low!
Chorus

We bravely fought and conquered
At Ross and Wexford town;
And if we failed to keep them,
'Twas drink that brought us down.
We had no drink beside us
On Tubberneering's day,
Depending on the long, bright pike,
And well it worked that way.
Chorus

And Oulart's name shall be their shame,
Whose steel we ne'er did fear.
For every man could do his part
Like Forth and Shelmalier!
And if for want of leaders,
We lost at Vinegar Hill,
We're ready for another fight,
And love our country still!
Chorus

SLANEY VALLEY

Paddy Kehoe

Astoreen Bawn, when first we met,
I can see the roses yet,
And the light that
lit your little eyes of blue.
I can hear your sweet voice say
Welcome as the flowers in May
In a dream, and when I whispered back to you

Chorus:
Will you come with me astór
When the summer day is o'er
And the rooks are winging homeward in the sky?
When the mountains fade away
On a field of gold and grey,
We'll go home to Slaney Valley, you and I.

Astoreen Bawn, when you said yes,
Brim full was my happiness.
Summer sped as ne'er before on flying feet
Never shone the moon so bright
In a starry cape of night.
Never sang the thrushes so divinely sweet.
Chorus

Astoreen Bawn for years you've been
In my heart, its rightful queen,
Ever loving, ever tender, ever true.
Like the sun your smile has shone,
gladdening all it glowed upon,
As it did when first I whispered back to you.
Chorus

Tree of Life, Rossdroit, by Denis O'Connor
and the children of St. Aidan's NS, Clonroche.

THE ENNISCORTHY CAROL

The Enniscorthy Christmas Carol is believed to be a traditional carol dating from 17th century. It had appeared in print in Co. Wexford broadsides and had been sung for a long number of years to several different tunes. The lyrics and air that we know today were brought to prominence by Dr William Henry Grattan Flood who transcribed and revised them a little and had the carol published in The Oxford Book of Carols in 1828, under the name 'The Wexford Carol'. This brought the unique carol across the world. Dr Grattan Flood was the organist and musical director at St. Aidan's Cathedral in Enniscorthy. He was a writer, composer and music teacher and editor of the Ireland's Own Songbook 1912.

I

Good people all, this Christmastime,
Consider well and bear in mind,
What our good God for us has done
In sending His beloved Son.
With Mary holy we should pray
To God with love this Christmas day;
In Bethlehem up on that morn
There was a blessed Messiah born.

II

The night before that happy tide
The noble Virgin and her guide
Were long time seeking up and down
To find a lodging in the town
But mark right well what came to pass
From every door repelled, alas
As was foretold, their refuge all
Was but a humble ox's stall

III

Near Bethlehem did shepherds keep
Their flocks of lambs and feeding sheep
To whom God's angel did appear
Which put the shepherds in great fear
Arise and go, the angels said
To Bethlehem, be not afraid
For there you'll find, this happy morn
A princely babe, sweet Jesus, born

IV

With thankful heart and joyful mind
The shepherds went the babe to find
And as God's angel had foretold
They did our Saviour Christ behold
Within a manger he was laid
And by his side a virgin maid
Attending on the Lord of Life
Who came on earth to end all strife

V

There were three wise men from afar
Directed by a glorious star
And on they wandered night and day
Until they came where Jesus lay
And when they came unto that place
Where our beloved Messiah lay
They humbly cast them at his feet
With gifts of gold and incense sweet.

ABIDE WITH ME

Henry Francis Lyte, who was an Anglican curate in Taghmon, written while he lay dying from tuberculosis

Abide with me; fast falls the eventide;
The darkness deepens; Lord with me abide.
When other helpers fail and comforts flee,
Help of the helpless, O abide with me.

Swift to its close ebbs out life's little day;
Earth's joys grow dim; its glories pass away;
Change and decay in all around I see;
O Thou who changest not, abide with me.

Not a brief glance I beg, a passing word,
But as Thou dwell'st with Thy disciples, Lord,
Familiar, condescending, patient, free.
Come not to sojourn, but abide with me.

Come not in terrors, as the King of kings,
But kind and good, with healing in Thy wings;
Tears for all woes, a heart for every plea.
Come, Friend of sinners, thus abide with me.

Thou on my head in early youth didst smile,
And though rebellious and perverse meanwhile,
Thou hast not left me, oft as I left Thee.
On to the close, O Lord, abide with me.

I need Thy presence every passing hour.
What but Thy grace can foil the tempter's power?
Who, like Thyself, my guide and stay can be?
Through cloud and sunshine, Lord, abide with me.

I fear no foe, with Thee at hand to bless;
Ills have no weight, and tears no bitterness.
Where is death's sting? Where, grave, thy victory?
I triumph still, if Thou abide with me.

Hold Thou Thy cross before my closing eyes;
Shine through the gloom and point me to the skies.
Heaven's morning breaks, and earth's vain shadows flee;
In life, in death, O Lord, abide with me.

POETRY

WRITERS OF THE RANGE

Joe Neal

Joe Neal is an author, journalist and poet from Castlebridge, Co. Wexford

You see our Billy Roche
coming down Main Street,
boxer-walking bard,
playwright laureate
lassoing leaping
spires and life-trapped
characters with his
lariat of chat.

Then, with bonhomie
of bounce, Eoin Colfer
chuckles in, all laughter
on the loose, uplifting
us to a manic, fairy
world of pure imagination.

On loan from Enniscorthy,
Colm Two-Town Toibin
canters in to corral
his creativity with
prescience of thought
and perfect drawl
of sentence on the page.

And John Banville,
prolific novelist on
everybody's Wanted list
- Johnny Big Guns,
firing prose like
bullets from the hip.
 Wexford Town, First Chance
Saloon, where from out
of Cat Malogen bursts
forth the witty,
wisely-spoken word.

CALLING MOTHER

Patrick Kehoe

From *Its Words You Want* by Patrick Kehoe is a former
teacher and is now an editor/producer with RTÉ
Television

On an offshore island in the West
In a yellow telephone box,
Your voice, intimate in the black shell
Both of us pecking away at small talk.
Mother murmur, dove soft;
Once heard
And I can see for miles
Down a prospect of blue-lapped sunlight.

On the Quays during Wexford Festival Opera.

The Producers

The Wexford Book – Who's What and Where's Where was produced in 2013 by an editorial team comprising some of County Wexford's experienced journalists, broadcasters, editors, researchers, photographers and designers. From top left to right are Helen Ashdown, editor, Michael Doyle, broadcast journalist, Michael Freeman, publisher, Phil Murphy, family magazine editor, Gerard Hore, photographer, Paddy Whelan, general researcher, Emily Rafter, photographic researcher, Noel Murphy, photographer and Sinéad McKenna, designer.

The editorial team was complemented by Clara Phelan, proof reader, David Mahon, illustration researcher, Peter O'Connell, media adviser and Valerie Byrne, photographer.

Acknowledgements

This book contains more than 800 profiles, more than 2,500 names and hundreds of place names associated with County Wexford.

The profiles were compiled through a combination of interviews and recommendations made by hundreds of people. The final selection was made by an editorial committee, advised by people from across the county

We thank in particular the following for their help in the production: Larry Banville, Phyllis Bolger, Gerry Breen, Joe Byrne, Paddy Byrne, Denis Cadogan, Ger Carthy, Mick Casey, Sean Condren, John Conran, Nicky Cowman, Paul Cullen, Michael Doran, Billy Downes, Eddie Doyle, Jim Doyle, Tom Doyle, Peter Earle, Billy Fox, Elaine Furlong, Jimmy Gahan, John Howlin, Teresa Hughes, Susan Kelly, Simon Kennedy, Fintan Lambe, Ger Lyons, Jimmy McDonald, Tom McDonald, Declan MacPartlin, Fintan Murphy, John Murphy, Derek Nally, Seamus O'Keeffe Michael O'Leary Paddy O'Reilly, Eamonn Power, Robert Rackard, Aidan Ryan and Michael Sinnott, and many others who were of assistance.

We thank the management and staff of the Stanville Lodge Hotel, Barntown, Wexford, the Whitford House Hotel, Wexford, The Horse and Hound, Ballinaboola, the Wildflower Café, Beechdale, Moneytucker, Clonroche, and the Carnegie Court Hotel, Swords, for their courtesy and helpfulness.

We thank our respective family members for their patience for the past nine months during the production of this work.

This book is a celebration of County Wexford people and a promotion of the county everywhere it is read.

It is a representation of all that is great about the county. We have made every effort to fulfil copyright and Data Protection Act requirements. We will be glad to rectify any omissions at the earliest opportunity.

Photographs:
Gerard Hore, South Main Street, Wexford
Noel Murphy, Clonleigh, Palace
Emily Rafter, Marley House, Killurin
Tommy Donohoe, Raheenahoon
Valerie Byrne, Rush, Co. Dublin
Michael Freeman, Galbally

Photography supplied
Paddy Darrigan
Jacqui Hynes, manager of the National 1798 Rebellion Centre

Fionnuala Hanrahan, County Librarian
JFK Dunbrody Trust
GAA 1954 programme from Tony Wickham collection and from the Dominic Williams collection
Enniscorthy brooch image from Trustees of the British Museum
Maps of County Wexford Ordnance Survey Ireland
iStock images.

Loch Garman Abú!

First published in 2013 by County Books Ltd.

Camross, Foulksmills, Co. Wexford.

© 2013 Michael Doyle, Michael Freeman, Phil Murphy

British Library Cataloguing in Publication Data

An entry can be found on request

978-0-9927149-0-1 (Cloth)

978-0-9927149-1-8 (Paper)

Library of Congress Cataloging in Publication Data

Typeset by www.sinedesign.net

Printed in Ireland by Naas Printing, Naas, Co. Kildare.

www.countybooks.ie

COUNTY
BOOKS